The
MUSHROOMS
and **TOADSTOOLS**
of Britain and
North-western Europe

Text by
Marcel Bon

Illustrated by
John Wilkinson . Denys Ovenden . Marcel Bon

Hodder & Stoughton
LONDON SYDNEY AUCKLAND TORONTO

First published in 1987

© in the text Marcel Bon, 1987
© in the paintings Domino Books Ltd., 1987

All rights reserved. No part of this publication may be reproduced, stored in a
retrieval system, or transmitted, in any form or by any means – electronic,
mechanical, by photocopying, recording or otherwise – without permission from
Domino Books Ltd., 7 Bond Street, St. Helier, Jersey

Paperback edition 0 340 39935 X
Hardback edition 0 340 39953 8

A **Domino Books** production

Colour reproduction by Adroit Photo-Litho, Birmingham
Filmset by Wordsmiths, London
Printed and bound in Spain by Heraclio Fournier, Vitoria

Introduction

This book is a guide to the more conspicuous larger fungi of north-western Europe: an area roughly north of the Alps and the Mediterranean zone, and west of a line from Finland to Venice. Thousands of species have been described from this region, the majority very small in size and impossible to distinguish outside a laboratory. The book has had to be selective, to be useful in the field or even portable.

We have therefore chosen the 1200-odd species (and many forms or varieties) which you are most likely to find – or in the case of rare species, to notice if you come across them. We have generally omitted diminutive species and those impossible to identify with any certainty without microscopic examination, including moulds and the carriers of cryptogamic disease. The book further concentrates on the "ordinary" mushrooms and toadstools with gills or pores under their caps – mainly Basidiomycetes, which also include all the best edible species. The numerous and difficult Ascomycetes are surveyed much more cursorily.

Within these adopted limits, all the commonest conspicuous species are included, and many more that are uncommon or rare. With a little practice, even the beginner should be able to place any mushroom he finds at least within its correct family, and often to be sure of the species; and he should rapidly become more confident as to their edibility.

Even the commoner fungi, however, differ from flowers or birds in their *unpredictability*. Some reappear regularly in the same places year after year, for decades or perhaps even centuries. Others do not, but appear here and there at random. And dates of appearance can vary from one year to the next by many weeks, sometimes from lack of rain. As most fungi decay in a matter of days it is all too easy to miss them unless one is visits the site at least once a week, even twice. For enthusiasts this uncertainty, and the profusion in good years, only adds to the excitement of looking for fungi.

The distinction between "mushroom" and "toadstool" in English (one not reflected in other languages) has little meaning and no scientific basis at all. "Mushroom" is often used for species of *Agaricus* (pp. 274-9), including the cultivated *A. bisporus*, while "toadstool" suggests something folkloric or vaguely sinister. Here we will use the general terms fungus or "mushroom" for all – like the French *champignon* and the German *Pilz*.

Text

Necessarily concise, the texts complement the illustrations: they must be considered together. The fungi are described in their scientific order and groups – though these and their names are generally far less firmly fixed than those of birds, mammals and higher plants. The most important **synonyms** for species names are therefore given, always in [square brackets]. To save the need for repetition, characteristics common to members of a group – whether an Order, a Family or some smaller division – are given in the introduction to the group. These should therefore be borne in mind when considering the description of a species.

Within the main text, some species have been given a subsidiary treatment. These are distinguished by having no spore drawing alongside, and by the first part of their scientific name being abbreviated. Their texts only indicate how they differ from the "main" species they follow. Thus on p. 34 the notes on *B. carpinaceus* must be read in connection with that for *Boletus edulis* immediately preceding it. They are sometimes also illustrated on the facing page when the differences are striking.

For brevity, scientific **authorities** – the often abbreviated names of botanists who gave the fungi their scientific names – are included only for the species themselves: not for higher groupings (Family, Subfamily etc), nor lower divisions such as variety or form; nor for synonyms.

English names are included – on the right of the heading – only where they are well-established. Unlike the rest of Europe, the English, Scots, Welsh and Irish never developed names for most of them – probably reflecting their relative unimportance as food for country people here.

The descriptions use the minimum of **technical terms**, but some – particularly in describing microscopic structures – are necessary for precision. These are explained below or in the glossary, pp. 14-17. **Measurements** given for caps indicate the range of widths usually found. Otherwise – for height and width of stem, and for spore dimensions – they are averages. This because cap width tends to increase with growth more than does the stem. Thus "Cap 8-12cm...stem 5x2cm..." indicates a species commonly 5cm high on a stem 2cm across, and whose cap will usually be from 8 to 12cm across. But fungi continue growing, and extra-large specimens frequently occur.

Taste and **smell** are often important, but can be difficult to communicate. Sometimes the nearest comparisons are with the smell of things unfamiliar to many people – the smoke of steam railway engines, the once universal stiff white office paste, certain wild flowers.

Spores are illustrated in line-drawings for all "principal" species, with their average measurements in microns (μm, $1/1000$th of a millimetre, pronounced "mu") given in the text together with notes on any important microscopic features.

Habitat is given for the British Isles, though this will generally be the same within Continental Europe. Notes on *frequency* also refer to the species' incidence in Britain and Ireland. A rough indication of their commonness or rarity beyond the Channel is given in symbols as follows: E1 is distinctly rare, E2 infrequent, E3 fairly common, E4 very common. These may be qualified by n, s, e, w, c (central), or m (mountainous). Thus Em3 indicates a quite common species in mountains, and sE3 (n1) one common in the south and rare in the north.

Edibility is indicated in the text for all species which are worth either eating or avoiding. The majority of fungi are neither: no indication of edibility or otherwise means that the species is simply without any culinary interest or value.

Illustrations

The colour paintings show a typical mature representative of the species. The scale is generally *half natural size* unless otherwise indicated – either beside an illustration or for a whole plate. Remember, however, that outlines as well as sizes may change markedly as the fungi develop. The colouring in some species can also vary widely with age, locality and weather, or can be partly washed away by rain. Where useful, a reminder of habitat is sometimes included, as in a leaf, or a cross-section or the colour of a chemical reaction as given in the text.

Collecting

Solitary collecting is quite feasible, but the beginner will learn far more with an experienced companion or by joining an organized 'foray', as fungus-collecting expeditions are called. These are organized throughout the country, both by the British Mycological Society and by local fungus or natural history societies. Addresses are usually available from one's nearest Museum.

The equipment needed is primarily a suitable container for one's finds. Of these, plastic bags are the very worst. In them, fungi get knocked together and broken, while the condensation inside plastic can start fermentation and rot. Best of all is a wide, shallow basket, where the specimens can lie in a single layer, upside down: their stems in the air. The serious collector may wrap up specimens in individual twists of paper (news or grease-proof) with notes of their habitat – or a leaf as a reminder. Some carry a little arsenal of small boxes for minute or fragile species.

Always collect the whole fungus, down to the base of the stem, which is often important for identification, but brush away any loose earth or vegetation. Discard old, rotting or maggot-infested specimens. When collecting for eating, take two baskets, one for edible species only. Poisonous or unidentified fungi should *never* be transported in the same container as those you will be eating: even spores contain the toxins.

The best periods for collecting differ with localities, and whether open or wooded. It is worth looking particularly a week or so after heavy rain, particularly if this follows a hot dry period or if the weather continues warm. Frost removes nearly all fungi except for brackets and other tough specimens. There is no truth in notions of mushrooms springing up overnight, though the slanting light of early morning and evening makes spotting them in other vegetation easier than when the sun is directly overhead. It is also worth moving through a wood far slower than one might think necessary; one covers more ground in a hurry, but finds less. As for 'expert' finders of edible fungi, their secret is largely knowing the spots to visit: getting them to divulge these is another matter.

Field observations. Place and manner of growth can sometimes be as helpful as colour, smell or spore size in naming a species. In particular:

Habit of growth, singly or in troops, in tufts or overlapping or in fairy rings.

Date, important for some spring or winter fruiting species. Most fungi fruit in autumn or earlier, during the course of the summer.

Geographical distribution. Some fungi are typically nordic or Mediterranean, maritime or alpine, atlantic or continental in distribution.

Relationship with higher plants. Some fungi, called *mycorrhizal*, can only develop with one or a few kinds of trees; they are in complete symbiosis with their hosts. This is not parasitism: the mycelium becomes closely attached to the roots of the tree and the exchanges of nutrients are beneficial to both parties. *Saprophytic* fungi live on dead and dying organic debris – from dead wood down to quite peculiar substrates (supports) like a horse's hoof or the body of a dead wasp. Such species may seem to be soil-dwellers if the substrate is buried in the soil. Thirdly, *parasitic* fungi are those which attack a living plant or animal and causes disease.

Habitat. Fungi of all kinds tend to have their particular habitats. Someprefer to grow in copses of hornbeam, others among *Vaccinium* in spruce plantations, in beech woods on chalk and limestone or oak woods; on light or heavy soils, on mossy ground, lawns or pastures and peat moors.

Edible species and cooking

Britain is a good country for collecting for the pot, since so few people do. Every year the woods are full of excellent fungi which rot to the ground unpicked, which beyond the Channel are hunted down by hordes of amateurs, and sell in local markets for £8 or more a kilo.

The first rule is to pick only those you know for sure to be edible; the second, to pick only healthy young specimens and to eat them within 24 hours, particularly in warm weather. An old specimen of even a good species may become toxic. The third is not to eat too many at a time, fungi being in general rather indigestible, nor to press them on other people who may not share your passion for free wild food. (See the excellent *Food For Free* by Richard Mabey, and *Wild Food* by Roger Phillips). And though you should never let an emergency arise at all, keep aside one of the fungi you are cooking. In a case of poisoning, this could be vital for identification: failing it, even the patient's vomit should be kept and taken with him to the hospital.

This is a field guide, not a cook-book, of which there are many. (See *The Mushroom Feast*, by Jane Grigson). In fact for the kitchen there is a limited number of distinct mushroom types and tastes, or basic ways of cooking them – at least by themselves. Nearly all good edible species are good when fried in a oil or butter with a little garlic and parsley or basil. The delicious Chantarelles are very good with eggs, scrambled or in omelettes, as are Morels. Lawyer's Wigs are better fried in batter, again with garlic or onions. Some people prefer to discard the tubes – easily removed – of ceps and other edible Boleti, as they can otherwise become disagreeably oil-sodden. Ceps and other more solid species, like the nutty-flavoured *Hydnum repandum*, naturally take more time to cook, but all these, and Field Mushrooms and most of the best edible species can also be eaten raw, sliced up in salads.

Certain fungi are toxic, even dangerous, in the raw state but supposedly safe once thoroughly cooked, with the first cooking water thrown away. The most notable example is *Gyromitra esculenta*, collected in the forests by many Northern European fungophiles and elaborately treated for eating. We suggest you leave these well alone.

For a brief survey of the toxins of poisonous fungi, see pp. 12-13.

Studying fungi

One is apt to think of a fungus as a sort of flowerless plant with some strange shape, with or without a cap and stalk. In fact, its true body, the permanent part, consists simply of a network of fine threads, called the *mycelium*, often hidden from sight in the ground or inside wood or visible as a growth of mould.

An individual thread is called a *hypha*, plural *hyphae*, and the fungus we collect – the *carpophore* or 'fruiting body' – results from the varied growth and interweaving of hyphae, coupled with their rapid expansion by absorption of water. The carpophore carries the fertile organs necessary for reproduction and dispersal of the species, and has sufficient distinctive macroscopic, microscopic and chemical features for it to be identified and classified. So in the study of fungi one has always to wait for appearance of the fruiting-body. There may be under one's feet a number of species present under the shape of commonplace moulds with nothing to betray their identity. It is like owning an orchard with numerous apple trees so much alike that one has to wait for the ripe fruit to be able to name them.

Reproduction. The reproductive mechanism of fungi is too strange and complex (sometimes involving *four* sexes!) to concern us here. The spores are produced by a thin layer of fertile cells, the *hymenium*. This is easily seen, though the actual reproductive organs, the individual cells in or on which the spores are produced, can only be seen under a microscope. The spores too are also microscopic, though one can see their collective colour when accumulated in a spore print. They have nothing structurally in common with seeds of the higher plants, but given the appropriate conditions, sometimes quite difficult to provide, they germinate to produce a mycelium and start a fresh cycle of growth.

The shape of a carpophore usually reflects the situation of the hymenium, and this gives us three main categories, as a start towards classifying fungi: whether the hymenium is *internal*, *external* or sited *beneath a cap*:

* Hymenium **internal** and remaining there until maturity; these are spherical or more or less stalked club-shaped fungi, in which what appears to be their flesh is in fact the hymenium which will ripen to a creamy, gelatinous or powdery mass. The spores will be liberated at maturity in various ways, such as through an apical pore (ostiole), or by opening up in a star-shape, or by general breakdown of the wall.

* Hymenium **external** and not protected by a cap. This includes fungi of very diverse shapes, from a simple membrane over a substrate (the surface on which that species grows) to more complex bodies – cup-like, saddle-like, sponge- or honeycomb-like, club-shaped or much-branched and bushy.

* Hymenium **external** but protected by a cap, on the under surface of which it is produced. In an early stage of the carpophore's development the hymenium may be internal, but it is exposed before the spores are mature through the fungus opening up in the course of growth.

In identification, the outline of the fungus is important, but so too are: the consistency of the flesh; the presence or absence of a stipe and its position, central or lateral; the habit of growth, whether solitary, gregarious, in tufts or with caps *imbricate* (overlapping like tiles on a roof); and examining the hymenial layer, which may be smooth, ribbed or veined, lobed, shallow-pitted, in pores, tubular, or covering pointed spines or gills radiating from a centre. The following aspects need to be noted:

Texture, especially a distinction between granular and the ordinary or fibrous texture of most species. The first case, where the stipe especially can be broken up into small fragments like bread crumbs, is a character of the family Russulaceae. In the second case one can lift whole fibres which strip away down the length of the stipe which does not crumble, unless totally dried up.

The shape of the **gills** or **tubes** and their method of attachment ("insertion"). See the two following pages for a survey of these and the terms used to describe them.

Rings and volvas arise as follows. The young toadstool or "primordium" (from the size of a pin-head to that of a small pea) may or may not have one or two primordial veils:

a   Here, the universal veil surrounds the entire carpophore and is torn apart during growth, so as to leave a volva round the stipe base and scale-like remains – bits of veil – on the surface of the cap. These are readily peeled off the underlying layer, like the shell of a hardboiled egg, and not to be confused with true scales which form part of the epidermis of cap or stipe.

b   The partial veil may merely connect the top of the stipe with the edge of the cap, temporarily concealing the hymenium. This is ruptured as the cap grows and leaves traces on the stipe in the shape of a small collar or ring, often also on the cap margin as flecks hainging from it (appendiculate). When the remnants of the partial veil are so fragile as to suggest a spider's web they are called a *cortina*.

c   The universal veil may adhere both to the cap and the stipe and be broken at the level of the hymenium like a simple ring. There is then an sheathing of the lower part of the stipe, often similar to that on the cap; this is a sheathing ring. If the stipe colour is different or its ornamentation smoother one may call it a simple ascending ring.

The forming of rings
and veils (see text)

Separability of cap from stipe is linked with the character of free gills, i.e. gills not touching the stipe. The hymenium is then an integral part of the cap which can be neatly separated from the stipe, or there may be a separating zone with colour difference or a sharp change in texture of the flesh, sometimes only visible under a hand lens or even microscope. Conversely, adnate or decurrent gills automatically imply a non-separable cap: the stipe and cap are *confluent*.

The flesh. Its consistency is important, e.g. in separating *Russulaceae* for example. So may be its colour and any change in colour when cut; whether there is milk present; and its taste and smell. Descripions of these last are often subjective and personal and may appear irrational. But they are valuable clues for those who have learned how to use them.

Surface characters are of great importance, especially those of the cap. The more or less ornamented cuticles are shown on page 17, but in the smooth category the degree of dryness, viscidity or matt-ness may be difficult to assess and may depend on the weather: obviously many cuticles may seem viscid in wet weather while after a dry spell genuine viscosity may only become apparent after the surface has been wetted, the best test is by "kissing", touching the cap with moist lips when a tendency to stick indicates viscosity. With a little experience you will find that it becomes easy to interpret macroscopically the microscopic texture of a cuticle, by noting its fibrillose, tomentose, micaceous, wrinkled or cracking surface.

Spore colour (and that of the mature gill) is given less importance today in classification than it used to be, but it is still useful in defining major groups. To get a spore-print, leave the cap to shed spores for several hours on to a sheet of white paper or a glass slide shut up in a moist atmosphere. You can cut the cap off, and leave it face down covered by a wet cloth, or the stipe can be dipped in a glass of water as shown. Where the spore colour is highly critical or the print is thin, you can scrape the shed spores into a heap to get a dense enough mass.

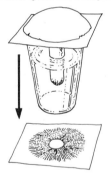

Making a spore print

There are other ways in which the observant student can get a rough idea of spore colour even in the field. Fungi which grow in tufts often leave a spore print shed on the caps of younger ones growing up beneath them; or you may find a spore print deposited on a stray plant leaf below the cap, or on the stipe of the fungus itself when this is bent or not vertical; or a ring or cortina may catch some spores. Finally one can note the colour of the mature gills, when this is changes from their colour when young. After some experience it is often possible with a hand lens to distinguish the spores on the gill as little white or coloured specks on a different coloured ground.

Chemical characters. We are not concerned here with analysis of chemical composition, which requires complex laboratory equipment. But the empirical tests of earlier mycologists have left us some very striking colour reactions which are often useful for identification:

Ferrous sulphate (FeSO$_4$ – "Fe reaction"), 10% solution in water. Rubbing with a crystal give a more variable reaction according to the degree of humidity on the flesh tested. Used with *Russula*, Boletes etc.

Phenol (2% phenolic acid in water) is used on *Russula* and *Cortinarius*. Phenolaniline gives similar or stronger reactions.

Ammonia (aqueous solution of ammonia gas NH$_3$) gives red or yellow, sometimes violet, reaction.

Soda or **Potash** (5 to 10%) is much used on *Cortinarius*.

Tincture of **gaiac** gives a positive blue reaction (sometimes violaceous), quick or slow according to the degree of freshness of the reagent which should be checked against species known to have a positive (*Russula vesca*) or almost negative (*R. fragilis*) reaction.

Formalin (standard solution of formic aldehyde) gives rather quick or slow pinkish reaction.

Iodine used either as tincture of iodine or better with chloral hydrate as Melzer's reagent gives somewhat blue or violet reactions on the flesh of boletes and can be used macroscopically to determine amyloidity of spores, directly on the gill if enough spores are present. Reaction blue-black.

Sulphoformol (Formalin + H$_2$SO$_4$) and TL4 (a Thallium base) are reagents giving bright blue, yellow or violet colours, used mainly on *Tricholoma*, *Lactarius* and *Cortinarius*.

Sulphovanillin used in microscopy also gives red or bluish reactions to the naked eye.

Microscopic characters.

This is a fundamental part of mycology. What follows is a mere outline of a fascinating but necessarily technical subject, for which he serious student will need textbooks (and a microscope of some 1000x magnification, equipped with a micrometre for measuring spores). Observations are made on material mounted on a glass slide, covered wtih a cover slip. A minute fragment of the tissue to be examined is stained by an appropriate reagent, and broken up by tapping enough to separate the elements it contains. The structure of fungi is suited to this treatment since their flesh consists of interwoven filamentous cells. These hyphae are like tiny, more or less branching septate (divided) tubes which usually easily separate under pressure. In some cases it is necessary to make a thin section to see the mutual relationship of the elements which is destroyed by squashing.

Spores of Ascomycetes and Basidiomycetes are distinguished by the way they are formed. *Ascospores* are produced inside asci, usually 8 to an ascus, less often 4 or a multiple of 8. *Basidiospores* are produced on the end of a basidium, usually 4, less often 2 or 6-8. As a rule one can recognise an ascomycete in the field by its hymenium being directed upwards. Ascospores are shot violently from the asci whereas in basidiomycetes the spores once detached from the basidium fall by gravity: the hymenium is accordingly directed downwards and generally situated on the under surface of a carpophore. Exceptions are found in the Phragmobasidiomycetes, with septate basidia, in which the hymenium is often on an upper surface. Ambiguous cases are those of narrowly club-shaped fruit-bodies in which the hymenium is roughly vertical; such occur in each class of fungi, *Geoglossaceae* among Ascomycetes, *Clavariaceae* among Basidiomycetes.

Since ascospores are produced within the protoplasm of an ascus they show no point of attachment or apiculus. Basidiospores, on the contrary, were attached to a basidium through the intermediary of a sterigma. Spore shape varies enormously, especially in ascomycetes, though it is quite constant for an individual species. Size ranges from 3 to 25μm for basidiospores and up to 100 (200)μm for ascospores.

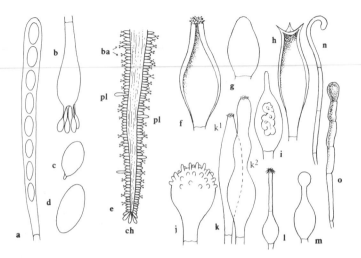

a, ascus; **b**, basidium; **c**, basidiospore; **d**, ascospore; **e**, cross-section of a gill showing the disposition of: **ba**, basidia; **pl**, pleurocystidia; **ch**, cheilocystidia; **f**, metuloid cystidium of *Incybe*; **g**,ventricose (*Agrocybe, Psathyrella*); **h**,spined (*Pluteus*); **i**, chrysocystidium (*Strophariaceae*); **j**, brush-like (*Mycena*); **k**, encrusted (*Melanoleuca*) – fusiform (k[1]) or bottle-shaped (k[2]); **l**, like a nettle-hair (*Melanoleuca, Grammopodiae*); **m**, capitate or skittle-shaped (*Conocybe*); **n**, crozier-like (*Otidia*); **o**, septate and pigmented (*Geoglossum*).

Spore walls may be smooth or ornamented, hyaline (translucent) or coloured. The membrane may be stained by specific reagents, of which the most important is Melzer's, in which the active agent is iodine, giving a blue-grey to blackish reaction in spore walls said to be amyloid or reddish brown in those that are pseudoamyloid or dextrinoid. A metachromatic reaction is one differing from that normal to the dye, e.g. pinkish mauve with cresyl blue instead of the normal bright blue.

Cystidia. These are sterile elements in the hymenium of a Basidiomycete, whether on the gill edge (cheilocystidia or marginal hairs) or on the gill face (pleurocystidia). They are of various shapes and also differ in their reaction with dyes and chemical reagents like ammonia and the sulpho-aldehydes as well as in thickness of wall and presence of crystals on the apex (metulocystidia).

Sterile elements in the hymenium of an Ascomycete are called paraphyses. These are usually long and slender, often clavate at the tip but they may have distinctive shapes, more or less recurved above, septate or branched.

Trama. The structure of the gill flesh or trama has considerable taxonomic significance and is best observed in thin sections, though with a little practice one can assess it from a squash preparation. The main types of structure are:

a Parallel or regular trama with almost unbranched hyphae lying parallel down the gill at right angles to the basidia.

b In an intermixed trama on the contrary the hyphae are branched, often at right angles and interwoven in all directions.

c A bilateral trama is similar to a parallel one in the centre but the hyphae diverge from this on each side to swing round almost in the same alignment as the basidia.

d In an inverse trama the hyphae are equally bilateral, without any central parallel strand, but curve upwards from the base of the basidia to converge at the centre of the gill flesh without anastomosing there.

The **cap trama** is generally filamentous and in the majority of Agaricales it consists of a single kind of hypha but in the brittle-fleshed Russulaceae it contains numerous spherical cells (sphaerocysts) not firmly attached to one another, hence the fragility of the flesh. In many polypores and their allies the hyphae are 2 or even 3 kinds and give the flesh of these fungi a leathery texture as tough as wood.

Cuticle. Over the apex of the cap the hyphae may be compacted or differentiated to form a sort of roof rather more impermeable to water than the rest of the carpophore. The arrangement or properties and shape of these terminal hyphae make it possible to distinguish several kinds of cap cuticle:

* Commonplace, filamentous, more or less interwoven hyphae, giving a smooth macroscopic appearance to the surface.
* Fastigiate, hyphae parallel or radially arranged, giving a fibrillose to streaky macroscopic appearance.
* Gelatinised, hyphae dispersed through a colourless gel not stained by dyes, macroscopically viscid or very greasy, sometimes silky.
* With distinct hairs, hyphal tips erect to form a "trichoderm"; sometimes some hairs may share the chemical ractions and shapes of the hymenial cystidia (and thus be Dermato- or Phileocystidia). Macroscopically the cap is then generally tomentose to velvety or fleecy but by supplementary gelatinisation it may be similar to **c**.
* Hymeniform or palisadic, shorter hairs packed closely side by side to resemble a palisade-like basidia in a hymenium, hence the name. Such caps are macroscopically often wrinkled or micaeous, sometimes finely cracked.
* Subcellular, hyphae broad or subglobose, sometimes with cells in short chains. In thin section the tissue simulates the parenchyma of higher plants but the cells are not firmly adherent to one another. Macroscopically similar to the last, or more micaeous or papery-matt.

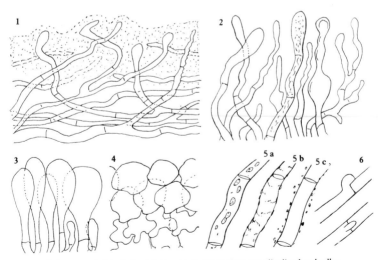

Cuticles : **1**, gelatinised; **2**, trichodermial; **3**, hymeniform or palisadic; **4**, subcellular. **Pigments**: **5a**, vacuolar; **5b**, membranal; **5c**, extracellular. **6 Clamp-connections.**

Pigmentation. Especially at the cap surface on immediately underlying layers of subcutis (mediopellis) and hypoderm (subpellis), pigment can be localised in 3 ways:

* Within the hyphae, then said to be *vacuolar* or intracellular.
* In or on the hyphal walls, then called *encrusting* and then sometimes striping the hyphae in a spectacular fashion.
* Outside the hyphae, epimembranal or *extracellular* with grains of pigment lying free in the spaces between the hyphae.

Clamp connections are today given considerable value in classification. There is no space here to explain their origin and function but they served for passage of a nucleus during the process of nuclear division in a multinucleate septate hypha. They are seen as swellings, bridges or clamps beside a septum.

Poisonous fungi

These are found in several groups, usually with good edible species in them: even the deadly Amanitas have the edible *Amanita rubescens* and *A. caesarea* as neighbours. To group the fungi according to the various toxic effects:

Minor digestive troubles. Many fungi can cause these, especially if inadequately cooked. Avoid all the following: *Russula* and *Lactarius* species with an acrid taste; *Boletus satanas* – which often causes nausea and prolonged and exhausting vomiting. *Agaricus xanthoderma* and *A. romagnesii*; *Macrolepiota venenata*; *Tricholoma josserandii* and some forms of *T. pessundatum* are the only objectionable Tricholomas, apart from *T. pardinum*, dealt with below.

Some ecological forms of the following may be barely tolerated: *Amanita rubescens* under conifers, *Clitocybe nebularis*, sometimes *Lepista nuda* and *Armillaria mellea* poorly preserved or old. *Russula olivacea* has caused illness in Italy. It is best to avoid all of the genera *Hebeloma*, *Hypholoma* and all but a few species of *Entoloma*. *Ramaria formosa* is merely purgative, but *R. mairei* seems to be more dangerous. Boletes (*Suillus*) of the *granulatus* group and sometimes even *S. luteus* are well known for purgative troubles.

Cardiovascular syndrome. Rare and a consequence of eating some species of *Coprinus* (*C. atramentarius*, *C. micaceus*) while drinking alcohol. It causes flushing and sweating, but passes. Treatment: avoid alcohol for a few days.

Hallucinogenic syndrome of the Psilocybes. In other parts of the world various fungi have been used as hallucinogens, sometimes in religious rites: e.g. species of *Stropharia*, *Psilocybe*, and sometimes *Lycoperdon*, in Mexico; *Russula* and Boletes in the Pacific. In Europe only *Psilocybe semilanceata* and a few species of *Panaeolus* seem to contain enough psilocybin but *Stropharia aeruginea* and *S. caerulea*, *Mycena pura* and a few *Hypholoma* and *Psathyrella* are also suspect.

Ergotic syndrome, caused by alcaloids contained in the ergot of grasses and cereals, which are the sclerotia of *Claviceps purpurea*. Usually accidental, this poisoning was frequent in parts of Europe in the Middle Ages, and called St Anthony's Fire. There can be intense vasoconstriction with gangrene of the extremities and sometimes loss of fingers or limbs.

Resinoid or **gastro-enteric syndrome**. A very distressing intestinal syndrome with intense abdominal pains developing rapidly, from a few minutes to one or two hours after ingestion. This from three fungi: *Tricholoma pardinum*, *Omphalotus* and *Entoloma lividum* (= *sinuatum*).

Muscarin syndrome. Slackening of the heart rate, lowered blood-pressure, diarrhoea, salivation and sometimes nausea and vomiting. The classic antidote is belladonna (atropine), used with caution. This from: numerous species of *Inocybe*, especially *I. patouillardii*, *I. fastigiate*, *I. asterospora*, *I. geophylla* etc. (it is best not to eat any of this genus); white species of *Clitocybe* in the groups *C. dealbata – C. rivulosa*, *C. candicans*, *C. cerussata* etc. *Amanita muscaria* itself contains only small quantities of muscarin with other toxins which have the opposite effects (see below).

Myco-atropinian or **Pantherinian syndrome**. The symptoms are the opposite of muscarin – increase in cardiac rhythm, vasoconstriction and hypertension, drying of mucous membranes etc. Some associated toxins have rather doping qualities – amphetaminic or adrenalinic more or less hallucinogenic or even aphrodisiac. The effects are felt quite quickly. The fungi involved are: races of *Amanita junquillea*, other forms of which are apparently harmless; *A. muscaria* which is not dangerous in small doses: fatalities are rare and occur from an overdose, taken as an excitant in the course of some peculiar orgy; *A. pantherina*, the most dangerous of the group, can be lethal. Treatment relies on sedatives.

Phalloidian syndrome. There are two consistent features: delayed onset of symptoms, from some hours up to 1 or 2 days after ingestion; and the gravity of the poisoning – which without quick treatment usually proves fatal. At first there is the delayed onset of a troublesome indefinable discomfort. Then acute gastroenteritis with vomiting, painful diarrhoea, foetid or bloody, sometimes for several days, with profuse sweating, dehydration and intense thirst. Periods of apparent recovery follow in which the patient feels much better – imagines himself cured. But this is illusory: the earlier symptoms reappear, with hypothermia, shivering, and a corpse-like pallor (the clinical picture of cholera), followed by prostration, coma and death.

It is crucial to get a sufferer to hospital quickly. His life depends on rapid diagnosis and special treatment: the destruction of liver cells is already advanced when the first symptoms appear. The main fungi concerned are the 'Phalloid' group of *Amanita*, responsable for 95% of deaths: *A. phalloides* and its var. *alba*, *A. verna* and *A. virosa* (p. 298). It usually happens through confusion of green and yellow-capped *Tricholoma* (*T. sejuncum*, *T. fucatum* and *T. equestre* groups) with the first species; and of *Agaricus*, *Lepiota* and white *Tricholoma* species in the case of the others. It is also important to take care when collecting the green *Russula virescens* and *R. cyanoxantha*.

However, the so-called **Paraphalloidian syndrome** is now regarded as identical with the above, has similar symptoms and may be almost as serious. It is caused by: species of *Lepiota* in the *helveola* group and its allies (*L. helveola*, *L. josserandii*, *L. kuehneri*, *L. brunneroincarnata*, *L. pseudohelveola* etc. No small *Lepiota* with cap less than 10 cm should be eaten, the few harmless members are too easily confused with the highly poisonous ones); *Galerina marginata* and its allies; and some *Conocybe* species.

The **Orellanian** syndrome. Here the effect on the liver may be less severe but it is often accompanied by acute nephritis which can lead to death through a crisis of uraemia. The species groups are: *Cortinarius orellanus*, *C. orellanoides*, *C. speciosissimus*, *C. gentilis* and their allies; (they are hard to confuse with any popular edible fungus but they are a menace to people who eat species of *Cortinarius* – which were formerly thought all to be edible); *Cortinarius splendens* and various members of the *Scauri* section of *Phlegmacium* with yellow or orange colouring, easily confused with the *equestre* group of *Tricholoma*. These species of *Cortinarius* do not always prove fatal but they do very serious damage to the kidneys, which is often irreversible.

Various species of *Dermocybe*, especially those with red pigment (*D. sanguinea*, *D. anthracina*, *D. phoenicea*, *D. cinnabarina* etc.), are now also suspect, and all those with russet, yellow or reddish colouring which normally contain the anthraquinone derivatives responsible for poisoning.

The **Gyromitrian** syndrome. The seriousness of this depends whether the fungi were eaten raw or inadequately cooked, in excessive quantity or at too frequent intervals. The species are: *Gyromitra esculenta* and allies; *Sarcosphaera crassa*. It is best to avoid this, even cooked. In the case of *Helvella crispa* and *H. lacunosa* thorough cooking should make them safe. *Paxillus involutus* should only be eaten in stews of after prolonged simmering. It is safer to avoid it entirely. As with other species (even sometimes Morels), an individual can become sensitised against it.

It is simple: you must be quite certain that a fungus you wish to eat *is* a good edible species and *is not* any of the above.

Glossary

aborted (gills), imperfectly developed
acute, pointed
adnate, see p. 16
alveolate, honeycombed
amyloid, see p. 10
anastomosing, connecting with others
annular, in a ring
annular zone, ring zone
apiculus, a little point
appendiculate, hanging from the margin
attenuated, narrowed
basidia, see p. 9

caespitose, clustered
capitate, with a head
ciliate, fringed with hairs
clamp connections, see p 16
clavate, club-shaped
clitocyboid, *Clitocybe*-like
collybioid, *Collybia*-like
concolorous, of the same colour
campanulate, bell- haped
coralloid, coral-like
cuticle, outer covering
cystidium, see p. 9

decurrent, see pp. 16
denticulate, with fine teeth
depressed, sunken
dermatocystidia, see p. 11

encrusted, see pp. 11-12
epicutis, outer layer of the cuticle
equal, straight-sided, see p. 16
excentric, not centred

excoriation, surface roughened
expanded, spread out, diffuse

fascicles, little bundles
fibril, a fine fibre
fibrillose, with fibrils
filiform, thread-like
floccose, woolly
fugaceous, fleeting
fusiform, spindle-shaped

glabrous, hairless, smooth
globose, roughly spherical
granulate, grainy

hyaline, translucent
hygrophanous, changing with humidity
hypha, see p. 6

imbricate, overlaping, like tiles
insertion, attachment (of gills to cap)
involute, with edges rolled inwards

lepiotoid, *Lepiota*-like
lignicolous, on wood

mycelium, see p. 6
mycenoid, *Mycena*-like

obtuse, blunt or rounded
obtuse (of margin), rounded
omphalinoid, *Omphalina*-like
operculum, a little lid, cover
orbicular, circular

palisadic, see p. 11
papillate, with nipples
pedicellate, with a stalk
pellicle, skin, membrane
peronate, woolly, mealy
pileus, cap

pleurotoid, *Pleurota*-like
plicate, folded in plaits
primordial, initial
pruina, bloom
pruinose, bloomed, frosted
pseudoamyloid, see p. 10
pubescent, downy
pulverulent, powdery
punctate, dotted with little points

radiately, around a centre
recurved, curved back
reflexed, bent back
refringent, reflecting
reticulate, netted
reticulum, network
rufescent, becoming reddish
rugose, wrinkled
rugulose, somewhat wrinkled

saprophytic, living on dead matter
sclerotioid, like a sclerotium
sclerotium, a dense mass of hyphae
sessile, without a stalk
sinuate, deeply wavy
spatulate, like a spatula
sphaerocysts, see p. 11
sphaeropedunculate, globose with a stalk

stellate, star-shaped
stipitate, stalked
striae, fine lines
striate, with striae
strigose, bristly
subcellular, see pp. 11-12
subcutis, inner layer of cuticle
sub-, denotes a lower degree
substrate, the host or support

tomentose, with a tomentum
tomentum, dense pubescence of short hairs
trama, see p. 10
trichoderm, see p. 11
tricholomoid, *Tricholoma*-like
tuberculate, with excrescences

umbilicate, with a navel or depression
umbo, a nipple or boss
umbonate, with an umbo

vacuolar, see p. 11-12
verrucose, warty
villose, shaggy
vinaceous, wine-coloured
viscid, sticky

Identification

The next 4 pages offer a general overview of the main forms of fungi with tubes or gills, to precede the formal Keys.

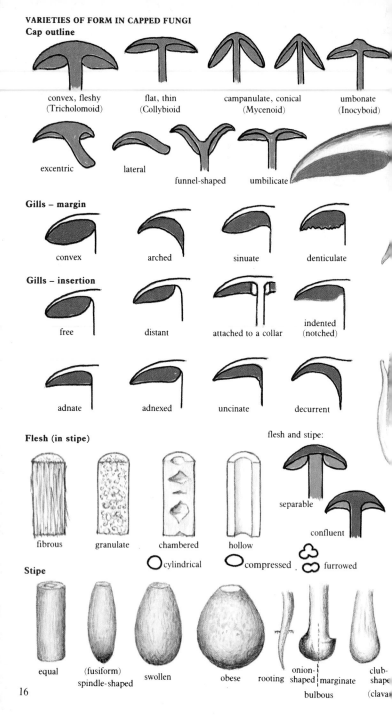

VARIETIES OF FORM IN CAPPED FUNGI
Cap outline

convex, fleshy (Tricholomoid)

flat, thin (Collybioid)

campanulate, conical (Mycenoid)

umbonate (Inocyboid)

excentric

lateral

funnel-shaped

umbilicate

Gills – margin

convex

arched

sinuate

denticulate

Gills – insertion

free

distant

attached to a collar

indented (notched)

adnate

adnexed

uncinate

decurrent

Flesh (in stipe)

flesh and stipe:

separable

confluent

fibrous

granulate

chambered

hollow

cylindrical

compressed

furrowed

Stipe

equal

(fusiform) spindle-shaped

swollen

obese

rooting

onion-shaped bulbous

marginate

club-shaped (clava

16

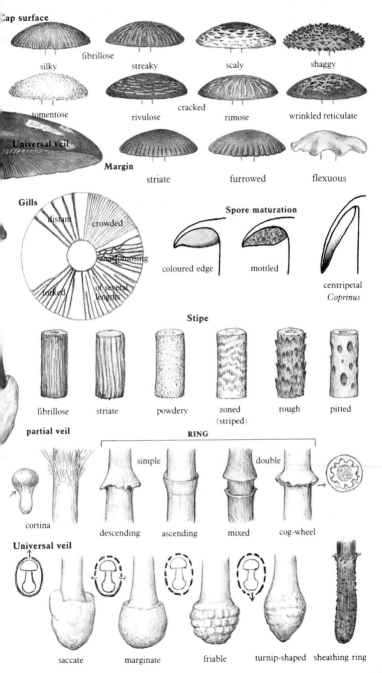

Cap surface

silky — fibrillose — streaky — scaly — shaggy

tomentose — rivulose — cracked — rimose — wrinkled reticulate

Universal veil

Margin

striate — furrowed — flexuous

Gills

distant — crowded — anastomosing — forked — of several lengths

Spore maturation

coloured edge — mottled — centripetal *Coprinus*

Stipe

fibrillose — striate — powdery — zoned (striped) — rough — pitted

partial veil

cortina

RING

simple — double

descending — ascending — mixed — cog-wheel

Universal veil

saccate — marginate — friable — turnip-shaped — sheathing ring

17

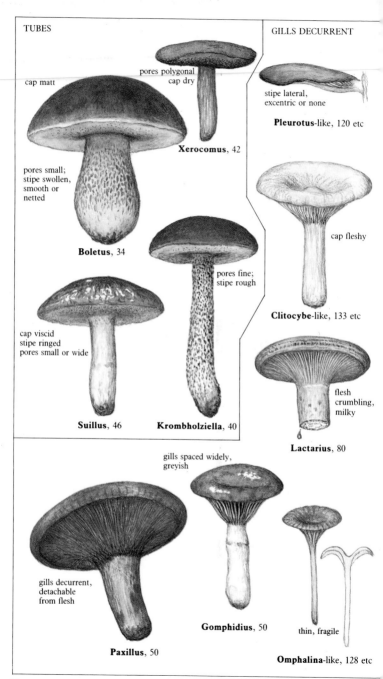

TUBES

GILLS DECURRENT

pores polygonal
cap dry

cap matt

stipe lateral,
excentric or none

Pleurotus-like, 120 etc

pores small;
stipe swollen,
smooth or
netted

Xerocomus, 42

cap fleshy

Boletus, 34

pores fine;
stipe rough

Clitocybe-like, 133 etc

cap viscid
stipe ringed
pores small or wide

flesh
crumbling,
milky

Suillus, 46   **Krombholziella**, 40

Lactarius, 80

gills spaced widely,
greyish

gills decurrent,
detachable
from flesh

Gomphidius, 50   thin, fragile

Paxillus, 50

Omphalina-like, 128 etc

18

3a With **g i l**ls. (Conventional gilled 'mushrooms and toadstools') ≫ **Key 1**
3b With **p o r**es or tubes (Boletes and polypores) ≫ **Key 4**, p. 28
3c Under **s**urface smooth, folded, ribbed or spiny (Aphyllophorales) ≫
              Key 5, p. 29

GILLS HORIZONTA**L**

GILLS FREE

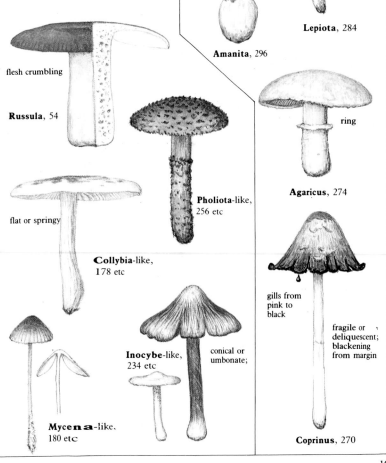

fleshy

gills indented

Tricholoma-like, 150 etc

ring and volva

Amanita, 296

concentric scales on cap

Lepiota, 284

flesh crumbling

Russula, 54

flat or springy

Collybia-like, 178 etc

ring

Agaricus, 274

Pholiota-like, 256 etc

Mycena-like, 180 etc

Inocybe-like, 234 etc

conical or umbonate;

gills from pink to black

fragile or deliquescent; blackening from margin

Coprinus, 270

19

11a Fleshy or somewhat funnel-shaped, with flesh neither elastic nor cartilaginous ⸴ truly *Clitocybe*-like outline: **12**
(If clustered or with a ring, see *Armillaria*, 162)
11b Slender fungi with ± umbilicate cap or flesh thin and ± cartilaginous (more

Subfamily *Boletoideae*. Pores small to medium, regular; cap surface glabrous to greasy, neither distinctly velvety nor truly viscid. Clamps absent, trama diverging and pigmented.

Genus *Boletus*. Robust species with stipe often very stout, swollen at the middle or spindle-shaped, with smooth, punctate or reticulate surface.

Section *Boletus* [*Edules*]. Pores white, ageing slightly yellowish to olivaceous but neither brightly coloured nor bruising blue.

Boletus edulis Bull.   CEP or PENNY-BUN FUNGUS
Cap 12-25cm, fleshy, surface greasy, date-brown with a slightly russet tint or fawn and often blotched reddish brown, sometimes tinged pink beneath the cuticle; margin persistently white. Pores slowly becoming yellowish to ± greenish, colour unchanged when bruised. Stipe 15×5cm, narrowed above and below, covered in the upper part only by a whitish reticulum on a pale ground, sometimes hard to make out or even absent, elsewhere slightly streaked reddish brown. Flesh white, tinged pink under the cuticle, taste mild, nutty. Spores 15×5μm. Under broadleaved trees or in mixed woods, glades or grassy copses. Common. Edible and excellent: the best Boletus. E4.

B. carpinaceus Vel., with paler greyish cap and pores rather yellower from the outset, seems to be known only under hornbeam in central Europe. A whitish variant under birch has been called *B. betulicola*. E1.

Boletus reticulatus Sch. [*B. aestivalis*]
Very like *B. edulis* in size or slightly less fleshy. Cap surface matt, sometimes granulate or wrinkled, uniformly pale brown without a whitish margin. Pores long persisting whitish. Stipe spindle-shaped, covered throughout by a whitish reticulum on a reddish brown ground. Flesh white, rather firm, seldom riddled by maggots, taste slightly sweet. Spores as in *B. edulis*, cap surface bearing rows of short cells. Under broadleaved trees, fruiting earlier than *B. edulis* and less abundant than it in England but almost as good to eat. E3.

Boletus aereus Bull.
Cap 15-30cm, very dark brown, tan or sepia; surface matt or slightly greasy. Pores remaining cream or slowly turning greenish. Stipe thickset to stout, 10×6cm, covered ± all over by a brown reticulum on a bright russet to almost concolorous ground. Flesh white, remaining firm and free from maggots. Spores 13×4.5μm. Under broadleaved trees in warm situations. Uncommon in England. May be confused with the darker forms of *B. edulis* such as f. *fuscoruber*, which is more reddish brown with a less reticulate stipe. Edible and good. sE3/nE1.

Boletus pinophilus Pil. & Derm. [*B. pinicola*]
Cap 15-30cm, often fleshy, thick, with a distinctive colour, a rather warm purplish brown; surface matt, minutely tomentose. Pores often slightly yellow, even bright enough to suggest species in the next section but not changing colour when bruised. Stipe thickset, cylindrical or slightly tapered above and below, 12×8cm, reticulate nearly all over, slightly reddish. Flesh white, firm. Spores 17×6μm. Under pines, with native Scots pine in Scotland and pine plantations in England. Edible and excellent. sE3.

B. clavipes (Peck) Pil. & Derm. is an American fungus which has been found also in central Europe; it resembles the above but with more ochraceous orange tint, especially towards the margin, and should be looked for in western Europe. cE1.

Boletus fragrans Vitt.
This resembles *B. pinicola* in its bright reddish brown to chestnut cap with almost greasy surface but has pores that soon turn bright yellow, as in members of the next section. Stipe 18×5cm, more markedly swollen and rooting, white, smooth above then increasingly dotted with ochre, sometimes pinkish near the base or slightly scaly. Flesh white, unchanging or bluing slightly, with strong fruity odour which changes to that of chicory as it dries. Spores 10×5.5μm. Grassy places or parks with broadleaved trees. Rare. Edibility doubtful. sE2.

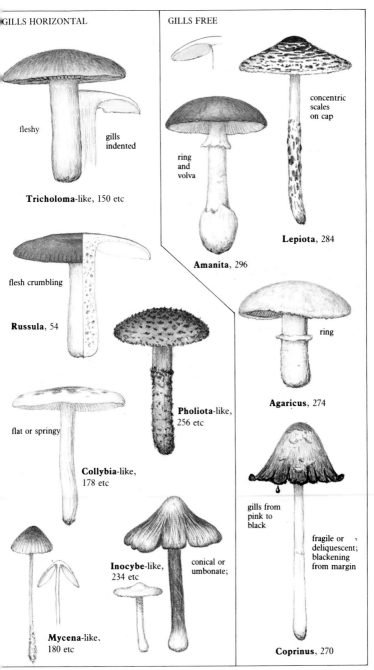

GILLS HORIZONTAL

GILLS FREE

fleshy

gills
indented

Tricholoma-like, 150 etc

concentric
scales
on cap

ring
and
volva

Lepiota, 284

Amanita, 296

flesh crumbling

Russula, 54

ring

Agaricus, 274

Pholiota-like,
256 etc

flat or springy

Collybia-like,
178 etc

gills from
pink to
black

fragile or
deliquescent;
blackening
from margin

Inocybe-like,
234 etc

conical or
umbonate;

Mycena-like,
180 etc

Coprinus, 270

19

The Keys

The keys which follow are designed to lead the reader to at least the correct group for the fungus he wishes to identify. They are deliberately simplified in places: keys that covered every possible species and variant would be extremely long and tedious.

These are 'dichotomous' keys, where the user is presented with a series of alternative (sometimes several) choices. He chooses the descriptions which best fit his specimen and follows the directions at the end of each 'answer' until he 'keys out' (indicated here by the symbol " >> ") to a name with a page reference. If you are not familiar with keys, it may help at first to work through them towards a fungus you already know or have identified in the main text.

Figures in **bold** type refer to alternative choices to be considered at each stage. Figures in normal type are page numbers for the species or start of the group.

More detailed keys precede the main text treatment of certain large or difficult groups:

Boletaceae, p. 30	*Tricholoma* and similar groups, p. 148
Russula, p. 52	*Cortinarius*, p. 200
Hygrophoraceae, p. 100	*Inocybe*, p. 232
Omphalina-like fungi, p. 126	*Lepiota* and allied genera, p. 280
Clitocybe and similar groups, p. 132	*Amanita*, p. 292

- and there are short keys to *Lactarius*, *Mycena* and *Agaricus* on pp. 337-9.

We start by considering the broadest divisions, by the location of the hymenium or spore-bearing surfaces:

1a HYMENIUM EXTERNAL on features which are originally smooth, eventually dusty. Flesh not changed in character with age though it may show colour changes when cut: **2**

1b HYMENIUM INTERNAL, right up to maturity. General shape of the fungus a ball or club when young, though this may split open like a starfish or a tub or to allow extrusion of a malodorous column. When ripe, the flesh which incorporates the hymenium (the gleba) may become gelatinous or a mass of powder. Spores set free through an ostiole (a little opening), by breakdown of the wall, or by being carried on rather turgid extruded structures. >> Gasteromycetes, **Key 2**, p. 25

2a Hymenium on the lower face of a cap. These are generally Basidiomycetes: **3**

2b Hymenium on upper surface or flanks of the fruit-body, generally smooth, sometimes lining the inner surface of pits but not protected by a cap; fungi of many shapes, from a simple membrane to a cup or sponge, sessile or stalked, sometimes slender clubs or much branched shrubby structures. Various groups, including all Ascomycetes and Phragmobasidiae. >> **Key 3**, p. 26

3a	With gills. (Conventional gilled 'mushrooms and toadstools') >>	**Key 1**
3b	With pores or tubes (Boletes and polypores) >>	**Key 4**, p. 28
3c	Under surface smooth, folded, ribbed or spiny (Aphyllophorales) >>	**Key 5**, p. 29

Key 1   Fungi with cap and gills: 'mushrooms and toadstools'

| 1a | Flesh fibrous, not easily crumbled (except when quite dry): **3** |
| 1b | Flesh granular, brittle or easily crumbled (*Russulaceae*): **2** |

| 2a | Yielding milk when broken; gills not forked, often sloping (*Clitocybe*-like outline) >> | *Lactarius*, 80 |
| 2b | No milk when broken; gills often forked, usually horizontal (*Tricholoma*-like outline) >> | *Russula*, 52 |

3a	Stipe excentric, lateral or absent (*Pleurotus*-like outline): **4**
	(If slightly excentric, in clusters, orange throughout, see *Omphalotus*, 50)
3b	Stipe central (may be curved when growing on a vertical host or when in tufts, but is not excentric): **8**

PLEUROTUS-LIKE OUTLINE

4a	Spore print white or slightly cream-lilaceous. Gills white to whitish or with whitish bloom when mature; *Pleurotaceae*: **5**
4b	Spore print or gills pink to brick-red: **6**
4c	Spore print ochraceous to brownish: **7**
4d	Spores violet or blackish. *Melanotus* or *Melanomphalia*. Rare and not considered further in this book.

5a	Putrescent fungi >>	*Pleuroteae* and allies, 120
	(If cap strongly umbonate and smell mealy, see *Lyophyllum ulmarium*, 166)
5b	Flesh leathery, elastic, drying without decay >>	*Lentineae*, 122, and *Panelleae*, 124

6a	Fleshy fungi, with a stipe, wholly bright salmon, slightly gelatinous surface becoming wrinkled or netted >>	*Rhodotus palmatus*, 172
6b	Slender or small fungi ± lacking a stipe >>	*Entoloma byssisedum* and *Clitopilus hobsonii*, 188
	(If whitish, hairy, leathery, with split double gills, see *Schizophyllum*, 320)

| 7a | Cap thin and white or ± gelatinous >> | *Crepidotus*, 244 |
| 7b | Cap more fleshy with ± orange gills (spore print pale) >> | *Paxillus panuoides*, 50 |

8a	Gills distant or thick, waxy to the touch; spore print white. >>	*Hygrophoraceae*, 100
	(If stipe with a ring on wood, or with a long root, see *Oudemansiella*, 170)
8b	Gills crowded or thin, or if distant they are ± rigid to the touch; spores white or variously coloured: **9**

| 9a | Gills sloping or decurrent (*Clitocybe*-like outline): **10** |
| 9b | Gills horizontal, notched, sinuate, or ascendant: **14** |

CLITOCYBE-LIKE OUTLINE

10a	Spores white or pale; gills whitish or if not then powdered with whitish bloom at maturity: **11**
10b	Spores pink to brick-red: **13**
10c	Spores ochre to brownish or rusty; gills forked or anastomosing >>	*Paxillus*, 50
	(If gills not forked, and a ± slender, whitish fungus, see *Ripartites*, 146)
10d	Spores blackish >>	Family *Gomphidiaceae*, 50

11a Fleshy or somewhat funnel-shaped, with flesh neither elastic nor cartilaginous; truly *Clitocybe*-like outline: **12**
(If clustered or with a ring, see *Armillaria*, 162)

11b Slender fungi with ± umbilicate cap or flesh thin and ± cartilaginous (more *Omphalina*-like outline) >> *Omphalina* and allies, 126

12a Gills not forked or scarcely so >> *Clitocybe*, 132
(If gills separable from flesh, and smell strongly aromatic, see *Leucopaxillus*, 162)

12b Gills ± strongly forked, bright orange >> *Hygrophoropsis*, 50
(If with shallow, blunt, false "gills", see *Cantharellus cibarius*, 306)

13a Fleshy fungi >> *Clitopilus* etc., 188
13b Thin fungi >> *Entoloma* subgenus *Eccilia*, 188

14a Gills free, not attached to the apex of the stipe; cap often easily separable from the stipe: **15**

14b Gills adnate, ± notched or ascendant but not free; cap and stipe confluent, not easily separable from each other: **18**

CAP AND STIPE SEPARABLE; GILLS FREE

15a Spores white to pale: **16**
15b Spores pink to reddish: **17**
(See also *Entoloma* subgenus *Nolanea*, with ascending gills which may seem to be free, 190)

15c Spores ochre to rusty: some *Galerina* species (248) have ascendant gills, which may seem to be free.

15d Spores blackish >> *Agaricus*, 274
(If fruit-bodies brittle or deliquescent when old, see *Coprinus*, 270)

16a Stipe ± ringed or sheathed, no volva at the base >> *Lepioteae*, 284
16b Stipe ringed or not, never sheathed but with a volva at the base, ± membranous but often powdery, and sometimes inconspicuous, with cap scales easily separable from the cuticle and never concentrically overlapping >> *Amanita*, 292

17a With no volva >> *Pluteus*, 196
17b With a membranous volva >> *Volvariella*, 198

CAP AND STIPE NOT SEPARABLE

18a Fleshy fungi with cap usually convex and often strongly umbonate (*Tricholoma*-like outline): **19**

18b Cap thin or flat (thickness not greater than ¼ the diameter), or with a low umbo; flesh often elastic (*Collybia*-like outline): **29**

18b   **18c**

18c Cap bell-shaped or hemispherical (*Mycena*-like), or only conical and sometimes flattened with age but keeping an acute umbo (*Inocybe*-like): **51**

TRICHOLOMA-LIKE OUTLINE

19a Spores white or pale >> *Tricholomateae*, 148
(If stipe cartilaginous and elastic, see *Collybia* section *Striipedes*, 178)

19b Spores pink to brick-red: **20**
19c Spores ochre to brown: **21**
19d Spores violaceous to black: **26**

20a Smell none or mealy >> *Entoloma* subgenus *Entoloma*, 192
20b Smell ± fruity or aromatic, or taste bitter >> *Rhodocybe*, 188
(If spores scarcely pinkish and gills ± separable from the flesh, see *Lepista* section *Rhodopaxillus*, 144)

21a Spore print and gills ± rusty at maturity: **22**

21b Spore print and gills brownish or dirty (cigar to chocolate colour): **24**

22a Terrestrial, occurring singly or nearly so. Stipe with cortina (when young, but often naked when old or handled) and sometimes a sheathing ring ≫
Cortinarius, 200

22b On wood, often in clusters: **23**

23a Stipe truly sheathed, concolorous with the cap which is usually concentrically scaly. Often in clusters ≫ *Pholiota*, 256

23b Stipe ringed or naked, sometimes with a cortina; taste bitter ≫ *Gymnopilus*, 244
(If slender and clustered species with a cortina, see *Pholiota* subgenus *Flammula*, 258)

24a Spore print and gills a peculiar dirty pinkish-ochre (milky coffee). Smell often of radish or cocoa ≫ *Hebeloma*, 228

24b Spore print and gills ± dirty (cigar) brown; ± terrestrial species: **25**
(If on wood, see *Hemipholiota*, 254)

25a Cuticle ± either velvety, woolly, fibrously splitting or scaly. Often in woods ≫
see fleshy species of *Inocybe*, 232

25b Cuticle smooth, matt, or sometimes cracked. Often in grass or on wood ≫
Agrocybe, 262

26a Terrestrial, occurring singly or nearly so: **27**

26b On wood, ± clustered or in tufts; stipe ± with a cortina or naked: **28**

27a Stipe with a ring; spores and gills ± violet ≫ *Stropharia*, 250

27b Stipe naked or with a cortina; spores and gills greyish to blackish ≫
some fleshy species of *Psathyrella*, e.g. *P. lacrymabunda*, 268

28a Stipe with a cortina; colours usually bright (yellow to reddish) ≫
Hypholoma section *Fascicularia*, 252

28b Stipe ± naked, or colours whitish or dull ≫
some *Psathyrella* species, e.g. *P. hydrophila, sarcocephala, cotonea*, 266

COLLYBIA-LIKE OUTLINE

29a Spores white or pale: **30**

29b Spores pink; cap ± umbilicate ≫ *Entoloma* subgenus *Leptonia*, 194

29c Spores ochre to brown: **42**

29d Spores violaceous to blackish: **48**

30a Stipe with a granulate, sheathing ring, concolorous with cap ≫ *Cystoderma*, 172
(If stipe shaggy at base, see *Collybia peronata*, 178)

30b Stipe naked or ringed: **31**

31a Flesh fibrous and putrescent like most fungi: **32**

31b Flesh leathery or elastic: **37**

32a Gills thick or distant: **33**

32b Gills normal, or habitat particular: **34**

33a On soil; colours rufous or violaceous; cuticle dry ≫ *Laccaria*, 146

33b On wood or roots; cuticle ± viscid, white or dull; stipe with a ring or a long root ≫ *Oudemansiella*, 170

34a On soil, wood etc: **35**

34b On decayed fungi; white and small or slender fungi ≫ *Collybia*, 180
(If greyish or ochre see *Asterophora*, 64)

35a Stipe brittle or hollow; often in clusters ≫ *Mycena* section *Rigidipedes*, 184

35b Stipe ± tough or solid: **36**

36a Terrestrial; smell ± mealy; colours dull or blackish ≫   *Dermoloma*, 170
(If bright colours, see *Calocybe*, 166)
36b On buried cones of conifers; smell not distinctive ≫
         Strobilurus and *Baeospora*, 176

37a Cap very thin or up to 1(2)cm: **38**
37b Cap more fleshy or 3-5(7)cm diameter: **40**

38a Cap with fluted margin (like a parachute); stipe thread-like, ± dark ≫
         Marasmius, 67
38b Cap with a smoother margin or shorter stipe: **39**

39a Cap shaggy, brownish; stipe rather thread-like; on old grass culms ≫
         Crinipellis, 174
(If malodorous when bruised, on conifer needles, *Micromphale perforans*, 176)
39b Cap smooth or wrinkled; on twigs, brambles etc. ≫   *Marasmiellus*, 176

40a Smell of garlic ≫   *Marasmius* group *alliaceus*, 174
40b Smell of cabbage, ± fruity or foetid ≫   *Micromphale*, 176
40c Smell otherwise or none; fungi ± clustered: **41**

41a Stipe tough, flexible without snapping when twisted; flesh not putrescent or
scarcely so ≫   *Marasmius* group *Wynnei-oreades*, 174
41b Stipe cartilaginous or elastic, but splitting when twisted; flesh putrescent ≫
         Collybia, 178
(If colours dull or greyish with greyish gills, see *Tephrocybe*, 168)

42a With a ring or sheathing ring (± garlanded); generally on wood: **43**
42b No sheathing ring; terrestrial ≫
         Cortinarius section *Tenuiores*, 220, or subgenus *Dermocybe*, 224
(If gills ± milky chocolate-coloured, see *Hebeloma* section *Indusiata*, 230)
42c Stipe naked, or at most ± fibrillous: **45**

43a Spores and gills ± rust-coloured; cap scaly, ± brightly coloured ≫
         Pholiota group *tuberculosa*, 256
(If cap and stipe very shaggy, brown, see *Phaeomarasmius erinaceus*, 246)
43b Spore print dark or dirty, cap smooth: **44**

44a In dense clusters, cap very hygrophanous ≫   *Kuehneromyces mutabilis*, 254
44b Singly, or not in dense clusters; cap less hygrophanous; ring not sheathing ≫
         Galerina marginata, 248
(In damp or sandy grassland, see also *Agrocybe sphaleromorpha*, 262)

45a Spore print ± rust-coloured: **46**
45b Spore print dull, brownish or milky chocolate: **47**
(See also *Agrocybe* species, 262)

46a Gills broadly adnate to somewhat decurrent ≫   *Tubaria* and allies, 246
46b Gills ± notched and colours ± bright or yellow ≫   *Gymnopilus*, 244

47a Cap surface dry or fleecy; often under alders or in damp woods ≫
         Naucoria, 230
47b Cap surface viscid ≫   small species of *Hebeloma* section *Denudata*, 228

48a Stipe with a cortina ≫   *Hypholoma* section *Psilocyboides*, 252
48b Stipe with a ring; gills violaceous ≫   *Stropharia*, 250
(If gills more greyish, see *Psathyrella leucotephra*, 268)
48c Stipe naked: **49**

49a Cap striate or grooved, ± deliquescent ≫   flattened species of *Coprinus*, 272
49b Cap smooth or slightly striate: **50**

50a Gills rather sinuate or notched; dull greyish ochraceous tints ≫
         flat species of *Psathyrella*, 268
(If colours somewhat vinaceous, on lawns, see *Panaeolus foenisecii*, 110)
50b Gills broadly adnate to slightly decurrent ≫   *Psilocybe* (group *montana*), 254

51a Spore print white or pale ≫ *Mycena* and allies, 180
(If flesh watery and gills distant, colours bright, see *Hygrocybe* subgenus *Hygrocybe*, 104)

51b Spore print pink to brick-red: **52**

51c Spore print ochre to brown: **53**

51d Spore print violaceous to blackish: **56**

52a Cap bell-shaped, ± fleshy, not striate; smell strong of fish or cucumber ≫ *Macrocystidia*, 196

52b cap ± conical, umbonate or hemispherical, rather thin (*Mycena*-like); smell fainter or none ≫ *Entoloma* subgenus *Nolanea*, 186

53a Cap thin fleshed, often striate; stipe sometimes with ring or cortina: **54**

53b Cap more fleshy or somewhat conical or acutely umbonate, stipe naked or cortinate, ± bloomed; *Inocybe*-like outline: **55**

54a Cap apex obtuse; cuticle glabrous or fibrillose ≫ *Galerina*, 248

54b Cap apex ± acute or conical; cuticle matt or micaceous ≫ *Conocybe*, 260

55a Stipe spindle-shaped or rooting; gills tinged orange or rusty; cuticle glabrous to viscid; smell ± of radish ≫ *Phaeocollybia*, 246

55b Stipe equal or sometimes bulbous, fibrillose, bloomed or with a cortina. Cuticle more fibrillose or often radially cracked. Smell peculiar, rather spermatic but never of radish ≫ *Inocybe*, 232

56a Ring or annular zone on stipe ≫ *Stropharia semiglobata*, 250
(If ring often near base of stipe and fruit-body soon deliquescent, see *Coprinus*, 270)

56b Neither ring nor annular zone present: **57**

57a Gills clouded or mottled grey and black; cap obtuse, not striate or deliquescent ≫ *Panaeolus*, 264

57b Gills blackening from margin upwards, cap fragile, striate or deliquescent ≫ *Coprinus*, 270

57c Gills maturing normally ≫ see *Psathyrella* subgenus *Psathyrella*, 266

Key 2   **Hymenium internal**: Gasteromycetes and Pyrenomycetes

1a Gleba gelatinous or brightly coloured, emerging at maturity from a volva like an *Amanita*. Smell often unpleasant: **2**

1b Gleba not gelatinous, at first fleshy, whitish to pale cream but often becoming coloured or reduced to a powdery mass at maturity or else enclosing hard bodies like seeds. Spores freed by splitting or flaking off of the outer membrane or through an opening. Smell usually not unpleasant: **3**

1c No gleba but a solid flesh beneath the rind of which are numerous tiny cavities containing the spores; Pyrenomycetes: **12**

2a Emergent body a simple column, with or without a pendant cap ≫ *Phallaceae*, 300

2b Emergent body an open-meshed sphere or a column with divergent arms ≫ *Clathraceae*, 300

3a Fruit-body opens to expose several seed-like bodies (peridioles), often looking like eggs in a tiny bird's nest ≫ *Nidulariaceae*, 300
(If much larger with gleba eventually powdery see *Pisolithus*, 302)

3b Fruit-body simple, not enclosing distinctive hard "seeds": **4**

4a Stipe well developed: **5**

4b Sessile or with a sterile base not sharply defined as a stipe: **6**

5a A small puffball on top of a slender stalk ≫ *Tulostomataceae*, 300

5b Stalk bears a solid head with tiny cavities beneath the skin ≫ see *Cordyceps*, 334

25

<table>
<tr><td>**6a**</td><td>Fruit-body subterranean or nearly so: **7**</td></tr>
<tr><td>**6b**</td><td>Fruit-body above ground or on wood, not subterranean: **9**</td></tr>
</table>

7a Ascomycetes, with strong aromatic smell and solid flesh ≫ *Tuberaceae*, 334
7b Basidiomycetes, smell faint or rubbery: **8**

8a Flesh hard, with tiny chambers, olivaceous ≫ *Rhizopogon*, 302
8b Flesh becoming purplish black and powdery ≫ *Scleroderma bovista*, 302

9a Fruit-body small to very small, envelope thin and papery ≫ *Myxomycetes*, 334
9b Fruit-body larger, envelope thicker and leathery or more than one layered: **10**

10a Envelope thick and leathery, a single layer, gleba grey to blackish ≫
    Scleroderma, 302
10b If the interior contains numerous small cells, yellowish then dark brown,
    powdery and crumbling away at the summit ≫ see *Pisolithus*, 302
10c Envelope 2 or 3-layered, surface layer distinctive scaly or mycelial: **11**

11a Surface layer warted or mealy, envelope not splitting stellately ≫
    Lycoperdaceae, 304
11b Surface layer matted, envelope splitting like a starfish ≫ *Geastraceae*, 302

11b

12a

12a Fruit-body hemispherical or irregularly encrusting wood, red-brown to black,
    flesh fibrous, purplish black ≫ *Hypoxylon*, 334
12b Fruit-body erect, clavate or strap-shaped, flesh white or bright coloured: **13**

13a

13a Fruit-body clavate or strap-shaped, black rind and white flesh ≫ *Xylaria*, 334
13b Fruit-body clavate, bright coloured ≫ *Cordyceps*, 334

Key 3   **Hymenium external** – not protected by a cap.

1a Flesh gelatinous, wobbly, or if cartilaginous then slippery: **2**
1b Consistency nongelatinous, fibrous, leathery or brittle: **8**

2a Sessile or nearly so: **3**
2b Stalked: **6**

3a

3a Brain-like or much lobed, yellow, orange to reddish brown, or unevenly effused
    and opalescent or dark coloured and shaped like a human ear ≫
    Phragmobasidiae, 324
3b Turbinate, flattened or slightly concave above: **4** **3b**

4a Dark brown to black: **5**
4b Pale pinkish, concave above ≫ *Neobulgaria pura*, 332
    (If bright violet see *Ascocoryne*, 332)

5a Upper surface dotted, not shedding black spore print ≫ *Exidia truncata*, 324
5b Upper surface smooth, surrounded by zone of black spores if left overnight while
    still fresh ≫ see *Bulgaria*, 332

6a Stalk emerging from a volva, with greenish or reddish, evil-smelling slime ≫
    Phallaceae, 300

7b

6b No volva: **7**

7a Stalk bears a lobed, viscid, yellow-brown head *Leotia lubrica*, 328
7b White stalk bears a clavate orange-yellow head *Mitrula paludosa*, 332
    (See also *Calocera*, 324, which feels slippery when fresh)

8b

8a Fruit-body club-shaped or branched and shrub-like, hymenium covering its
    flanks: **9**
8b Fruit-body cauliflower-like, a mass of branched strap-like lobes ≫ *Sparassis*, 308
    (For strap-like fruit-body covered with spines on under side see *Hericium*, 312)
8c Fruit-body cup-shaped, sponge or saddle-shaped, hymenium superior or lining
    pits: **15**

8d Fruit-body hemispherical or minute and ± spherical: **26**
8e Fruit-body membranous, broadly encrusting a substrate ≫ *Corticiaceae*, 316

9a More or less branched: **10**

9b Unbranched, simple clubs, or spatulate or capitate: **12**

10a Bright orange, feeling slippery, on wood of conifers ≫ *Calocera viscosa*, 324
10b Variously coloured but not slippery: **11**

11a Black and leathery with white powdery tips see *Xylaria hypoxylon*, 334
11b Not as above ≫ *Clavariaceae*, 308

12a Massive clubs 1-3(5)cm thick, sometimes truncated: **13**

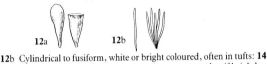

12b Cylindrical to fusiform, white or bright coloured, often in tufts: **14**
12c Dark brown to black, tongue-shaped or compressed or if brightly coloured with spatulate or lobed head ≫ *Geoglossaceae*, 332
(If brightly coloured, surface dotted with ostioles, see *Cordyceps*, 334)

13a Surface slightly ribbed, no internal cavities beneath it ≫ *Clavariadelphus*, 308
13b Surface dotted with ostioles of minute cavities beneath the rind ≫ see *Pyrenomycetes*, 334

14a On soil, usually over 1cm tall ≫ *Clavaria* and *Clavulinopsis*, 308
14b On wood, yellow, seldom over 1cm ≫ *Calocera cornea*, 324

15a Stipe distinct, clearly differentiated, often long: **16**
15b Stipe absent or ill-defined: **20**

16a Fruit-body with broadly pitted sponge-like head in spring ≫ *Morchella*, *Mitrophora*, 326
(Not to be confused with old dried up specimens of *Phallus*, 300)

16b Fruit-body like a finger or a glove, somewhat ribbed ≫ *Verpa conica*, 326

16c With brain-like lobed brown head, bigger than the stipe ≫ *Gyromitra*, 328
16d Cap with irregular reflexed lobes like a saddle ≫ *Helvellaceae*, 328
16e Cup-shaped to depressed disks: **17**

17a Stalk slender, not ribbed: **18**
17b Stipe stout, longitudinally ribbed ≫ *Paxina*, 328
(If there is a short stipe, not ribbed, often sunk in soil, see *Tarzetta*, 330)

18a Cup more than 1cm, hymenium red or grey: **19**
18b Cup up to 0.5(1)cm, often white, yellow or reddish brown ≫ *Heleotiaceae*, 332

19a 3-5cm, grey-brown ≫ *Macroscyphus macropus*, 328
19b 1-2cm, bright red hymenium, white outside ≫ *Sarcoscypha coccinea*, 330

20a Cup medium sized or expanded or deformed, (2)5-10cm, flesh thin or brittle: **21**
20b Very thick gelatinous flesh; top-shaped, flat to shallow concave above: **24**
20c Subsessile, cupulate to turbinate, usally well under 1cm diam.; on wood: **25**

21a Cup asymmetrical, slit down one side or vertically asymmetric or ear-shaped ≫ *Otidea*, 330
(If bright red-orange, see *Aleuria*, 330)

21b Cup more regular or broadly expanded and lobed horizontally: **22**

22a Neither surface veined: **23**
22b Upper surface radially veined, flesh thick, very brittle >>  *Disciotis venosa*, 326

22c Under surface veined from the base >>   **22b** *Paxina*, 328

23a Bright orange, thin-fleshed, no coloured ,uice >>   *Aleuria aurantia*, 330
23b Duller yellow or some shade of brown to nearly black >>   *Peziza*, 328

24a Black and shedding a halo of black spores >>   *Bulgaria inquinans*, 332
24b Pale pink, spores colourless >>   *Neobulgaria pura*, 332
24c Purplish violet >>   *Ascocoryne*, 332

24a   **25a**   **25b**

25a Bright yellow, ± sessile, in clusters on unchanged wood >> *Bisporella citrina*, 332
25b Bright blue-green slightly stiped cups on green-stained wood >>
   Chlorosplenium, 332

26a Hemispherical with perithecia sunk in a black-fleshed stroma, their ostioles
   appearing as dots or papillae on the surface, spores nearly black >>
   Hypoxylon, 334
26b Perithecia bright coloured, superficial, solitary or clustered on a stroma, spores
   white to pale brownish >>   *Nectria*, 334

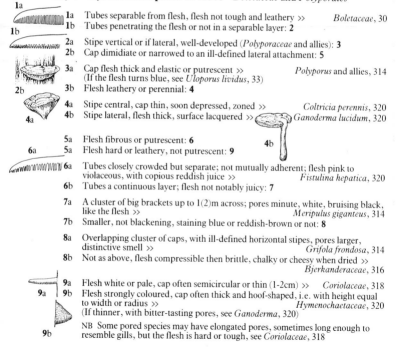

Key 4   **Hymenium in pores or tubes** – *Boletaceae* and *Polyporales*

1a
1b

1a Tubes separable from flesh, flesh not tough and leathery >>   *Boletaceae*, 30
1b Tubes penetrating the flesh or not in a separable layer: **2**

2a Stipe vertical or if lateral, well-developed (*Polyporaceae* and allies): **3**
2b Cap dimidiate or narrowed to an ill-defined lateral attachment: **5**

3a Cap flesh thick and elastic or putrescent >>   *Polyporus* and allies, 314
   (If the flesh turns blue, see *Uloporus lividus*, 33)
3b Flesh leathery or perennial: **4**

4a Stipe central, cap thin, soon depressed, zoned >>   *Coltricia perennis*, 320
4b Stipe lateral, flesh thick, surface lacquered >> *Ganoderma lucidum*, 320

5a Flesh fibrous or putrescent: **6**
5a Flesh hard or leathery, not putrescent: **9**

6a Tubes closely crowded but separate; not mutually adherent; flesh pink to
   violaceous, with copious reddish juice >>   *Fistulina hepatica*, 320
6b Tubes a continuous layer; flesh not notably juicy: **7**

7a A cluster of big brackets up to 1(2)m across; pores minute, white, bruising black,
   like the flesh >>   *Meripulus giganteus*, 314
7b Smaller, not blackening, staining blue or reddish-brown or not: **8**

8a Overlapping cluster of caps, with ill-defined horizontal stipes, pores larger,
   distinctive smell >>   *Grifola frondosa*, 314
8b Not as above, flesh compressible then brittle, chalky or cheesy when dried >>
   Bjerkanderaceae, 316

9a Flesh white or pale, cap often semicircular or thin (1-2cm) >>   *Coriolaceae*, 318
9b Flesh strongly coloured, cap often thick and hoof-shaped, i.e. with height equal
   to width or radius >>   *Hymenochaetaceae*, 320
   (If thinner, with bitter-tasting pores, see *Ganoderma*, 320)

NB Some pored species may have elongated pores, sometimes long enough to
resemble gills, but the flesh is hard or tough, see *Coriolaceae*, 318

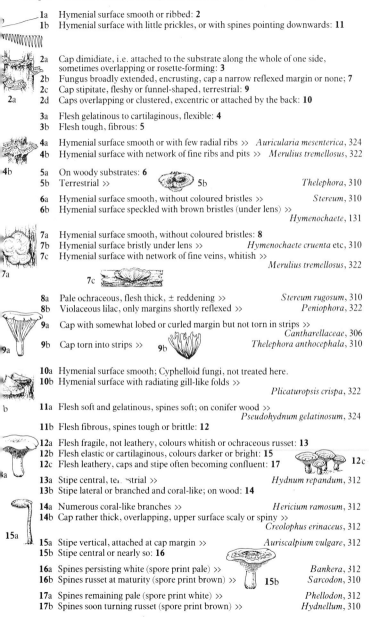

Key 5   Under surface of cap smooth, folded, ribbed or spiny.

1a Hymenial surface smooth or ribbed: **2**
1b Hymenial surface with little prickles, or with spines pointing downwards: **11**

2a Cap dimidiate, i.e. attached to the substrate along the whole of one side, sometimes overlapping or rosette-forming: **3**
2b Fungus broadly extended, encrusting, cap a narrow reflexed margin or none; **7**
2c Cap stipitate, fleshy or funnel-shaped, terrestrial: **9**
2d Caps overlapping or clustered, excentric or attached by the back: **10**

3a Flesh gelatinous to cartilaginous, flexible: **4**
3b Flesh tough, fibrous: **5**

4a Hymenial surface smooth or with few radial ribs » *Auricularia mesenterica*, 324
4b Hymenial surface with network of fine ribs and pits » *Merulius tremellosus*, 322

5a On woody substrates: **6**
5b Terrestrial »   *Thelephora*, 310

6a Hymenial surface smooth, without coloured bristles »   *Stereum*, 310
6b Hymenial surface speckled with brown bristles (under lens) »
Hymenochaete, 131

7a Hymenial surface smooth, without coloured bristles: **8**
7b Hymenial surface bristly under lens »   *Hymenochaete cruenta* etc, 310
7c Hymenial surface with network of fine veins, whitish »
Merulius tremellosus, 322

8a Pale ochraceous, flesh thick, ± reddening »   *Stereum rugosum*, 310
8b Violaceous lilac, only margins shortly reflexed »   *Peniophora*, 322

9a Cap with somewhat lobed or curled margin but not torn in strips »
Cantharellaceae, 306
9b Cap torn into strips »   *Thelephora anthocephala*, 310

10a Hymenial surface smooth; Cyphelloid fungi, not treated here.
10b Hymenial surface with radiating gill-like folds »
Plicaturopsis crispa, 322

11a Flesh soft and gelatinous, spines soft; on conifer wood »
Pseudohydnum gelatinosum, 324
11b Flesh fibrous, spines tough or brittle: **12**

12a Flesh fragile, not leathery, colours whitish or ochraceous russet: **13**
12b Flesh elastic or cartilaginous, colours darker or bright: **15**
12c Flesh leathery, caps and stipe often becoming confluent: **17**

13a Stipe central, terrestrial »   *Hydnum repandum*, 312
13b Stipe lateral or branched and coral-like; on wood: **14**

14a Numerous coral-like branches »   *Hericium ramosum*, 312
14b Cap rather thick, overlapping, upper surface scaly or spiny »
Creolophus erinaceus, 312

15a Stipe vertical, attached at cap margin »   *Auriscalpium vulgare*, 312
15b Stipe central or nearly so: **16**

16a Spines persisting white (spore print pale) »   *Bankera*, 312
16b Spines russet at maturity (spore print brown) »   *Sarcodon*, 310

17a Spines remaining pale (spore print white) »   *Phellodon*, 312
17b Spines soon turning russet (spore print brown) »   *Hydnellum*, 310

Class *Basidiomycetes*. Spores developed at the apex of cells called basidia, usually 4 (or 2) for a basidium.

Subclass *Agaricomycetes*. Fungi with caps, hymenium free before maturity, on gills or tubes, rarely veined or smooth.

Order *Boletales*. Hymenium tubular or on anastomosing veined or much forked gills, usually separable from the flesh.

Family *Boletaceae*. Hymenium tubular; pores simple or compound, minute, broad or hexagonal, sometimes radially elongated or nearly gill-like. Spores mostly fusiform or elongated. The following characters are useful to note:

* The **outline** – from very robust with ± hemispherical cap and swollen stem to small or slender with flatter cap and narrow or ± cylindrical stem.

* Size and shape of **spores**, from minute to enlarged, round to polygonal, and sometimes radially elongated as if imitating gills (e.g. *Boletinus*, 32). **Colour** of tubes and pores may be white (but rather ochraceous-greenish when old), yellow, pink, red, coppery or ± olivaceous to purplish bistre; and either unchanging or bluing when pressed.

* Ornamentation of the **stipe** – often smooth or fibrous but sometimes reticulated (netted), punctuate (dotted with little points), ± wrinkled-scaly, or rough like badly planed wood.

* Colour of the **flesh**, and whether changing when cut – especially bluing, from none to very strong and whether slow or rapid. Reaction with $FeSO_4$ (iron sulphate) is sometimes used/

* **Taste** – for edibility. Very bitter species like *Tylopilus felleus*, 46, are absolutely inedible. Peppery ones (*Chalciporus piperatus*, 44) may be cooked in small quantities for use like green peppers. The **smell** is occasionally useful for distinguishing species.

* **Cap colours** are mainly of four groups: whitish; pink to purple; ochraceous to yellow or orange; and brown to blackish.

Key to *Boletaceae* – genera and principal groups

1a	Pores minute (0.5-1mm), rounded or regular, not angular: **2**	
1b	Pores broad or angular, sometimes compound or radially elongated: **13**	
2a	Stipe containing cavities, brittle; pores very minute, whitish; spores whitish or very pale >>	*Gyroporus*, 32
2b	Stipe solid, flesh fibrous; pores somewhat coloured at maturity; spores cream, ochraceous, brown, olive etc: **3**	
3a	Cap surface smooth to rather greasy, neither velvety nor distinctly viscid; often robust fungi: **4**	
3b	Cap surface viscid; fungi medium size 5-10(15)cm, pores yellow or olivaceous, sometimes slightly coppery; *Suillus*: **9**	
3c	Cap surface matt or velvety: **11**	
4a	Stipe coarsely wrinkled-scaly, slender or a little spindle-shaped, lacking bright red or yellow tint; cap fairly fleshy, rather robust >>	*Krombholziella*, 40
4b	Stipe smooth or reticulate to finely punctate, often stocky, swollen or obese; often very fleshy fungi, some robust, massive, up to 30cm; *Boletus*: **5**	

5a Pores whitish then slightly yellowing or greening with age; stipe smooth or somewhat reticulate, not brightly coloured; flesh colour constant or only bluing slightly or casually ≫   section *Boletus*, 34
(If the reticulum is coarse and taste bitter see *Tylopilus felleus*, 46)
5b Pores yellow from the first; flesh ± bluing: **6**
5c Pores pink at maturity, taste bitter ≫   *Tylopilus felleus*, 48
5d Pores brownish to purplish bistre ≫   *Porphyrellus*, 48
5e Pores red to orange: **8**

6a Flesh bitter, cap white or very pale ≫   section *Calopodes*, 36
6b Flesh mild; cap ± coloured: **7**

7a Stipe reticulate or dotted ≫   section *Appendiculati*, 36
7b Stipe smooth or slightly veined; pores bruising blue ≫   *Xerocomus badius*, 44

8a Cap brown to ochraceous beige or dull orange; stipe nearly equal, rarely swollen, sometimes elongated ≫   section *Luridi*, 38
8b Cap white, pink or purple, stipe often obtuse, smell often strong ≫   section *Purpurei*, 38

9a Stipe with a ring: **10**
9b Stipe without a ring, surface granulate ≫   section *Granulati*, 46
(If pores are bright yellow and cap pink see *Aureoboletus gentilis*, 44)

10a Cap brown, ring membranous, pores yellow, not staining; under pine ≫   *Suillus luteus*, 46
10b Cap yellow to orange, pores bruising russet; ring floccose, typically under larch   *S. grevillei*, 46
(If there is no colour change on the pores and the fungus is from peaty soil see *S. flavidus*, 46)

11a Tubes decurrent, short, scarcely separable, cap finally somewhat depressed ≫   *Uloporus lividus*, 32
11b Tube layer adnate or sinuate, cap ± convex: **12**

12a Pores yellow ≫   yellow specimens of *Xerocomus*, 42
12b Pores rust to reddish ≫   *Chalciporus*, 44

13a Cap dry, velvety to rather scaly: **14**
13b Cap viscid: **17**

14a Pores radially elongated, compound or somewhat decurrent, yellow: **15**
14b Pores angular, medium sized: **16**
14c Pores regular, hexagonal, grey: cap covered with broad blackish grey scales, ring grey, floccose ≫   *Strobilomyces strobilaceus*, 48

15a Cap scaly, stipe with something of a ring ≫   *Boletinus*, 32
(If the pores are orange see *Suillus tridentinus*, 40)
15b Cap smooth, ring absent, tubes gill-like ≫   *Phylloporus*, 44

16a Yellow ≫   *Xerocomus*, 42
(If bluing is intense, even to blackening, see *Boletus pulverulentus*, 36)
16b Rusty or reddish ≫   *Chalciporus*, 44
16c Beige or olivaceous, cap fibrillosely scaly ≫   *Suillus variegatus*, 48

17a Pores bright yellow, not changing; cap pink, mottled ≫   *Aureoboletus gentilis*, 44
17b Pores pale yellow to orange, going russet or greyish; stipe with a ring; under larch ≫   *Suillus* section *Larigni*, 46
17c Pores beige russet, compound, ring absent, under pine ≫   *Suillus bovinus*, 46

Subfamily *Gyrodontoideae*. Tubes short, either scarcely separable and decurrent or with very minute pores and hollow flesh in the stipe. Clamps present.

Tribe *Gyrodonteae*. Spore print ± coloured, tubes decurrent or pores compound.

Genus *Uloporus* [*Gyrodon*]. Pores medium size, ring absent.

Uloporus lividus (Bull.) Quél.
Cap 5-20cm, not very fleshy, surface dry or slightly viscid, yellowish-grey, sometimes tinted pink or vinaceous towards the margin. Tubes distinctly decurrent with yellowish or greenish pores, bruising bluish. Stipe 5×0.8cm, attenuated towards the base, sometimes excentric, slightly fibrillose, concolorous then vinaceous brown from the base upwards. Flesh yellowish, bluing slightly, tinged reddish brown in the stipe. Spores short, 7×4.5µm. Under alders. Rare in Britain from Yorkshire southwards. E2.

Genus *Boletinus*. Pores broad or compound and radially elongated or angular; ring floccose.

Boletinus cavipes (Opat.) Kalchbr.
Cap 4-10cm, convex, fleshy or umbonate, tomentose to almost scaly, yellowish fawn to rusty tawny or even chestnut. Tubes short, pores compound, ± decurrent at first, yellow to olivaceous. Stipe 5×1cm, hollow, concolorous, with a whitish rather floccose ring. Flesh pale, not bluing. Spores 8×3.5µm. Under larch. Rare in England. E1 (m3).

var. *aureus* is golden yellow throughout. E1.

Boletinus landkammeri (Pil. & Svr.) Bon [*B. amabilis* s.s. Sing.]
Cap as in *B. cavipes*, umbonate, then convex, with greater contrast in scale colour, reddish brown to pinkish fawn, reminiscent of *Suillus tridentinus* (p. 40). Margin inrolled, persistently whitish-appendiculate. Pores and tubes as in *B. cavipes* or yellower and less decurrent. Stipe 8×2cm, slightly club-shaped, solid, with an annular zone slightly membranous or whitish at first. Flesh yellowish. Spores 9×4µm, clamps rare or almost none. Under conifers, especially Douglas Fir (*Pseudotsuga*). Not known in Britain. Apparently rare but liable to be overlooked because of its resemblance to *B. cavipes* and *S.tridentinus*. cE1 (Switzerland, Italy, Czechoslovakia).

Tribe *Leucosporelleae*. Spores colourless under the microscope, spore print pale; pores minute, not decurrent.

Genus *Gyroporus*. Stipe hollow or brittle.

Gyroporus castaneus (Bull.) Quél.
Cap 5-10cm, convex, fleshy, surface smooth or minutely velvety, rather uniformly rusty tawny to chestnut. Tubes and pores white to straw colour, very narrow, not changing colour when bruised. Stipe 7×2cm, tapered upwards, almost concolorous or paler, pruinose then smooth, slightly uneven, brittle. Flesh white, not changing. Spores 10×5µm. Under various broadleaved trees, sometimes in clusters. Rather common in England, especially under oak. Edibility suspect. E3.

Gyroporus cyanescens (Bull.) Quél.
Cap 6-15cm, convex, fleshy, surface almost smooth to velvety, becoming villose, then peeling rough or finally ± scaly, whitish to pale ochraceous, bruising blue. Pores whitish to pale ochraceous, bluing. Stipe 10×4cm, thickset or tapered above and below, whitish but browner from the base up to an indistinct or fléeting annular zone. Flesh white but turning instantly blue when broken. Spores 14×7µm. Under broadleaved trees and conifers on sandy soils. Uncommon in Britain, often with birch or spruce, especially in the north. Edible. E3.

var. *violaceotinctus*, a little more olivaceous tawny, with flesh turning somewhat lilac then indigo, has been described from North America. E1.

Uloporus
lividus

Boletinus
cavipes

Boletinus
andkammeri

Gyroporus
cyanescens

Gyroporus
castaneus

33

Subfamily *Boletoideae*. Pores small to medium, regular; cap surface glabrous to greasy, neither distinctly velvety nor truly viscid. Clamps absent, trama diverging and pigmented.

Genus *Boletus*. Robust species with stipe often very stout, swollen at the middle or spindle-shaped, with smooth, punctate or reticulate surface.

Section *Boletus* [*Edules*]. Pores white, ageing slightly yellowish to olivaceous but neither brightly coloured nor bruising blue.

Boletus edulis Bull. CEP or PENNY-BUN FUNGUS
Cap 12-25cm, fleshy, surface greasy, date-brown with a slightly russet tint or fawn and often blotched reddish brown, sometimes tinged pink beneath the cuticle; margin persistently white. Pores slowly becoming yellowish to ± greenish, colour unchanged when bruised. Stipe 15×5cm, narrowed above and below, covered in the upper part only by a whitish reticulum on a pale ground, sometimes hard to make out or even absent, elsewhere slightly streaked reddish brown. Flesh white, tinged pink under the cuticle, taste mild, nutty. Spores 15×5µm. Under broadleaved trees or in mixed woods, glades or grassy copses. Common. Edible and excellent: the best Boletus. E4.

B. carpinaceus Vel., with paler greyish cap and pores rather yellower from the outset, seems to be known only under hornbeam in central Europe. A whitish variant under birch has been called *B. betulicola*. E1.

Boletus reticulatus Sch. [*B. aestivalis*]
Very like *B. edulis* in size or slightly less fleshy. Cap surface matt, sometimes granulate or wrinkled, uniformly pale brown without a whitish margin. Pores long persisting whitish. Stipe spindle-shaped, covered throughout by a whitish reticulum on a reddish brown ground. Flesh white, rather firm, seldom riddled by maggots, taste slightly sweet. Spores as in *B. edulis*, cap surface bearing rows of short cells. Under broadleaved trees, fruiting earlier than *B. edulis* and less abundant than it in England but almost as good to eat. E3.

Boletus aereus Bull.
Cap 15-30cm, very dark brown, tan or sepia; surface matt or slightly greasy. Pores remaining cream or slowly turning greenish. Stipe thickset to stout, 10×6cm, covered ± all over by a brown reticulum on a bright russet to almost concolorous ground. Flesh white, remaining firm and free from maggots. Spores 13×4.5µm. Under broadleaved trees in warm situations. Uncommon in England. May be confused with the darker forms of *B. edulis* such as f. *fuscoruber*, which is more reddish brown with a less reticulate stipe. Edible and good. sE3/nE1.

Boletus pinophilus Pil. & Derm. [*B. pinicola*]
Cap 15-30cm, often fleshy, thick, with a distinctive colour, a rather warm purplish brown; surface matt, minutely tomentose. Pores often slightly yellow, even bright enough to suggest species in the next section but not changing colour when bruised. Stipe thickset, cylindrical or slightly tapered above and below, 12×8cm, reticulate nearly all over, slightly reddish. Flesh white, firm. Spores 17×6µm. Under pines, with native Scots pine in Scotland and pine plantations in England. Edible and excellent. sE3.

B. clavipes (Peck) Pil. & Derm. is an American fungus which has been found also in central Europe; it resembles the above but with more ochraceous orange tint, especially towards the margin, and should be looked for in western Europe. cE1.

Boletus fragrans Vitt.
This resembles *B. pinicola* in its bright reddish brown to chestnut cap with almost greasy surface but has pores that soon turn bright yellow, as in members of the next section. Stipe 18×5cm, more markedly swollen and rooting, white, smooth above then increasingly dotted with ochre, sometimes pinkish near the base or slightly scaly. Flesh white, unchanging or bluing slightly, with strong fruity odour which changes to that of chicory as it dries. Spores 10×5.5µm. Grassy places or parks with broadleaved trees. Rare. Edibility doubtful. sE2.

Boletus edulis

Boletus reticulatus

Boletus aereus

Boletus fragrans

Boletus pinophilus

All × ⅓

Section *Appendiculati*. Pores yellow, ± bluing. Cap ± coloured, or at least not whitish at first. Stipe spindle-shaped or rooting, with reticulate or punctate surface. Flesh ± bluing, taste mild.

Boletus appendiculatus Sch.
Cap fleshy 13-18cm, with slightly greasy surface, uniformly reddish brown to chestnut. Pores bright yellow. Stipe 13×4cm, spindle-shaped or slightly swollen, attenuated below or even rooting, with an often incomplete yellowish reticulum on a yellowish brown to reddish ground. Flesh yellow, tinged reddish near the surface of the stipe or towards the base, bluing slightly, especially in the upper part, with a faint but distinctive smell of nuts or fresh meat. Spores 11×5µm. Under broadleaved trees, mainly oak in England. Not common. Edible. E3.

Boletus regius Krombh.
Size as in *B. appendiculatus* but with cap pink to pale blood-red at first, then streaked vinaceous on a pink ground and finally reddish brown. Pores bright yellow. Stipe 12×3cm, not markedly swollen, bearing a yellow reticulum on a yellow to pale pinkish ground. Flesh yellow, ± bluing. Spores as in *B. appendiculatus*. Under broadleaved trees in SE England, rare. Edible. E2.

B. speciosus Frost is more fleshy, with swollen reddish brown stipe bearing an obscure or incomplete reticulum, more decurrent pores and hard flesh. sE2.

Boletus impolitus Fr.
Cap 10-15cm, dull grey ochraceous to yellowish, surface matt or hoary. Pores yellow to almost orange. Stipe 13×3cm, spindle-shaped or slightly rooting, without a reticulum but covered with yellow dots like a *Krombholziella*, occasionally flushed reddish above. Flesh pale yellow, scarcely bluing, with smell of iodine. Spores 14×5µm. Under broadleaved trees, especially oak on heavy soils in England. Edible but not very good. Uncommon. E3.

B. depilatus Redeuilh [*B. obsonium* p.p.] has more brown or pinkish tints; cuticle containing sphaerocysts and thus more apt to develop fine cracks with age; and stipe smoother or striate and more rooting. On calcareous soil. E2.

Boletus pulverulentus Opat.
Because of its moderate size, with cap 8-13cm on an almost cylindrical stipe this fungus might be looked for in *Xerocomus*, especially as its surface is initially matt or rather pruinose, only later becoming greasy, dingy brown mingled with yellow. Pores yellow, small. Stipe 8×1cm, yellow, pruinose above, dotted reddish brown below. The entire surface bruises blue, then blackish, the most intense reaction in the family. Flesh yellow, instantly turning dark blue when broken. Spores 14×4.5µm. Under broadleaved trees, especially oak in southern and western Britain. Edibility doubtful. Uncommon. E3.

Section *Calopodes*. Pores yellow, cap white at first; taste bitter.

Boletus calopus Pers.
Medium to large, cap 10-15cm on a slightly club-shaped or swollen stipe, 10×2cm, recognisable by the contrast between the whitish cap with bright yellow pores and the red stipe covered by a white reticulum. Flesh light yellow, bluing somewhat, taste rather bitter and disagreeable. Spores 16×5µm. Under broadleaved trees and conifers, widespread in Britain, especially under beech and oak on acid soils. Edible after blanching, but not very good. E4.

Boletus radicans Pers. [*B. albidus*]
Stout or fleshy with cap 15-25cm, long remaining hemispherical or very thick; dingy white, greying slightly with age or handling. Pores yellow, bruising blue. Stipe 15×5cm, stout, often globose at first, then swollen with a narrowed rooting base; reticulum obscure or concolorous, with a pinkish zone about the upper third in var. *pachypus*. Flesh pale, bluing, definitely bitter. Spores 12×4.5µm. Under broadleaved trees or in copses and parkland, not uncommon with beech and oak in southern England. Not edible. E3.

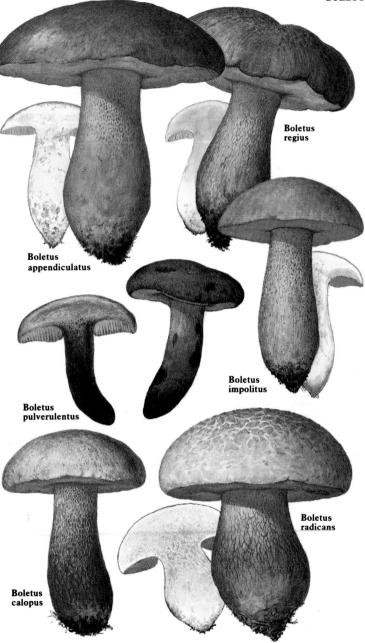

Boletus regius

Boletus appendiculatus

Boletus impolitus

Boletus pulverulentus

Boletus radicans

Boletus calopus

All × ⅓

37

Section *Luridi*. Pores red, cap ± brownish to orange-brown, neither white nor purplish pink; fungi of moderate size with stipe not markedly swollen.

Boletus luridus Sch.
Cap 10-13cm, surface slightly matt, dingy ochre sometimes tinged olivaceous umber, rarely tinted orange or reddish towards the margin. Pores carmine, tubes reddish or dull pink. Stipe 10×2cm, rather cylindrical, covered with a red reticulum on a yellowish ground, dull grey towards the base. Flesh yellowish sometimes slightly vinaceous in the base and typically with a red zone immediately above the tubes, turning blue when cut. Spores 14×6μm. Under broadleaved trees on calcareous soils, fairly common with beech and oak in England. Edible. E3.

Boletus erythropus Pers.
Often larger than *B. luridus*, cap 15-20cm, typically chestnut brown, sometimes more ochraceous towards the margin. Pores deep red. Stipe 15×4cm, slightly swollen then spindle-shaped, closely dotted with red on a yellow ground, without a reticulum, bruising blue. Flesh yellow, instantly bluing intensely when broken. Spores 18×6μm. Under broadleaved trees on acid soils, in forest clearings and glades, also under conifers in Britain. Common. Often regarded with suspicion because of the spectacular bluing but actually an excellent edible fungus; the blue colour disappears during cooking. E4.

B. dupainii Boud., with similarly punctate stipe but shining tomato-red cap, is much rarer; not good to eat. Not British. sE2.

Boletus queletii Schulz.
This resembles *B. erythropus* in its punctate, non-reticulate stipe but is easily distinguished by its slightly matt brick-orange cap, yellow to orange pores, outlined red under a lens and yellowish flesh, bluing when cut, and typically beetroot red in the lower part of the stipe. Spores 13×6μm. Under broadleaved trees, locally common with beech, lime and oak in southern England. Edible. E3 .

Section *Purpurei*. Pores red, often very large fruit-bodies with white, pink or purplish cap and stipe swollen from the outset; taste not bitter but often nauseating, or with a distinctive smell.

Boletus rhodopurpureus Smotl. [*B. purpureus* p.p.]
Cap 12-20cm, at first pinkish or orange becoming entirely purplish, bruising blue. Pores small, bright purplish red, tubes yellower. Stipe 16×8cm, stout, becoming swollen, with a small-meshed reticulum, red on a yellow ground. Flesh bright yellow, bluing strongly, with fruity, often alcoholic smell. Spores 14×6μm. Under broadleaved trees in warm places on calcareous soil. Rare in England. Probably edible but best avoided because of possible confusion with *B. satanas*. sE3/nE1.

var. *rhodoxanthus* may be distinguished by its cap being whitish at first, then pink, bluing moderately, with a weak odour. sE2.

Boletus legaliae Pil. [*B. satanoides*, *B. splendidus* p.p.]
Similar size. Cap pinkish rather than purplish. Stipe swollen then ± elongated, with an incomplete or apical bright red reticulum on a paler ground, lower part ± punctate. Flesh pale yellow, bluing feebly, with fruity smell changing to that of chicory with age. Spores 13×4.5μm. Under broadleaved trees in southern copses and margins of woods. Uncommon under oak in SE England. Edibility doubtful. E3.

B. lupinus Fr. has a more sour smell, like a *Scleroderma*, and a stipe almost wholly covered with red dots, without a reticulum. E2.

Boletus satanas Lenz
Cap large, 15-30cm, persistently hemispherical, entirely white with generally no trace of pink but greying a little when handled, eventually olive-grey. Stipe 13×8cm, long remaining rounded, with a bright red reticulum. Pores red. Flesh white, bluing slowly, soon softening and discolouring; smell unpleasant, eventually even nauseating. Spores 14×5μm. Under broadleaved trees in warm places, local under beech and oak on calcareous soils in southern England. Very indigestible and somewhat poisonous, giving acute gastric attacks. Not to be eaten. E2.

Boletus
luridus

Boletus
erythropus

Boletus
rhodopurpureus

Boletus queletii

Boletus satanas

Boletus legaliae

All × ⅓

Genus *Krombholziella* [*Leccinum*.] Stipe almost cylindrical or slightly spindle-shaped, finely scaly or rough. Cap dull coloured or reddish orange. Fe reaction grey to ± greenish blue.

Krombholziella aurantiaca (Bull.) R. Mre. [*K. rufa*]
A massive fungus, cap 12-20cm, very fleshy, often hemispherical at first, surface orange, slightly wrinkled. Cap with ± appendiculate margin. Pores pale at first. Stipe 18×4cm, slightly spindle-shaped, white, covered with small scales at first white, turning orange-brown. Flesh white, then discoloured, turning grey-violet when cut. Fe reaction blue-green. Spores 19×4μm. Under aspen and birch. Widespread but not common. Edible and good. E3.

K. quercina (Pil. ex Green & Watl.) Bon has a more reddish brown to chestnut brick cap with scales on the stipe less white at first, then bright reddish brown or darker. Under oak. Local in southern England. E3.

Krombholziella versipellis (Fr.) Bon [*Leccinum testaceoscabrum*]
Scarcely less massive than the above, cap duller orange or dingy yellow, sometimes finely scaly at first, margin strongly appendiculate. Pores drab to greyish. Scales on the stipe dark brown to black from the outset. Flesh greying or slate coloured, sometimes blue-green in stem-base; Fe reaction dark blue-green. Spores 16×4μm. Under birch and poplar. Common throughout Britain. Edible. E2.

Krombholziella duriuscula (Schulz.) Imler
Similar in size or less massive, cap 10-12cm, greyish with margin irregularly append-iculate. Pores dingy white then greyish. Stipe 12×4cm, slightly swollen below, with dark grey scales in a network or irregularly scattered. Flesh hard, turning grey-lilac and pinkish in the stipe; Fe reaction light greenish. Spores 18×6μm. Under poplar. Rare. Edible. E2.

K. rugosa (Fr.) Bon has a more wrinkled cap, club-shaped stipe more scaly and blackish; Fe reaction greyish. E2.

Krombholziella scabra (Bull.) R. Mre.
Cap 8-13cm, convex, brownish, slightly greasy, margin not appendiculate. Pores beige then greyish. Stipe slender, 15×2cm, cylindrical or club-shaped, with pale scales. Flesh white, unchanging; Fe reaction greyish. Spores 13×5μm. Under broad-leaved trees, especially birch, common throughout Britain. Edible. E4.

Several allied species or forms are difficult to differentiate. **K. roseofracta** (Watl.) Bon, has white flesh immediately turning coral colour, and a black, reticulate stem base. E2. **K. mollis** Bon, flesh soon becoming soft and greenish at top of stipe. E3. **K. melanea** (Smotl.) Sutara, a dark, almost black cap. E2.

With a *white* cap there occur albino forms of normally coloured species but also **K. holopus** (Rost.) Sutara, with a hint of green in the cap and white flesh, Fe reaction grey-green. Under birch, often among *Sphagnum*, not uncommon in the N. E1-2.

Krombholziella variicolor (Watl.) Sutara [*L. oxydabile* p.p.]
Cap 6-10cm, mouse-grey, mottled sepia or ochraceous, as though sooty, margin not appendiculate. Pores staying pale, bruising pink. Stipe 12×2cm, slightly spindle-shaped, with fine black scales in a network, base often blue-green. Flesh white, reddening, often blue in stipe base; Fe reaction pale yellowish. Spores 16×5μm; cap cuticle containing hyphae 12-15μm wide (cylindrocysts). Under birch, rather common. Edible. E3.

Krombholziella carpini (Schulz.) Bon [*Leccinum griseum* p.p.]
Cap 8-13cm, convex, surface dented, finely cracking, dingy ochraceous brown or with olivaceous tints. Pores yellowish buff. Stipe 10×1cm, slender, with small scales often arranged in vertical lines. Flesh reddening then blackening. Fe reaction green, with Formalin bright pink. Spores 18×5μm. Under hornbeam and especially hazel in Britain. Common. Edible. E4.

Krombholziella crocipodia (Let.) R. Mre. [*B. nigrescens*]
Cap 10-15cm, yellowish brown to orange fawn, at first rugose then soon with a network of cracks. Pores yellow. Stipe 15×3cm, spindle-shaped or attenuated and rooting slightly, with pale yellowish scales. Flesh reddening, then greying. Spores 18×7μm. Under broadleaved trees in warm places, with oak in southern England. Edible. E3.

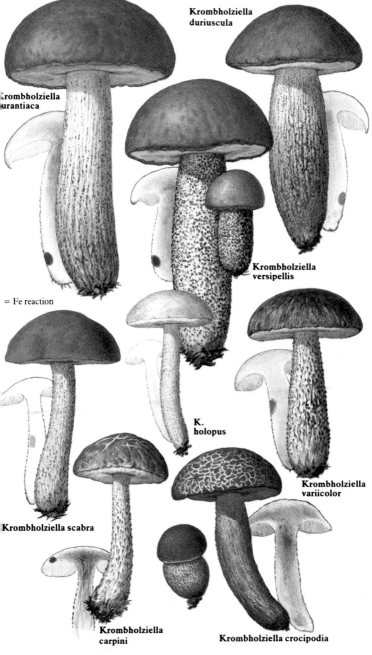

KROMBHOLZIELLA

Krombholziella
duriuscula

Krombholziella
aurantiaca

= Fe reaction

Krombholziella
versipellis

K.
holopus

Krombholziella
variicolor

Krombholziella scabra

Krombholziella
carpini

Krombholziella crocipodia

All × ⅓

41

Subfamily *Xerocomoideae*. Cap surface dry or velvety, often cracking; pores often broad or compound, yellow to rust colour. Trama parallel, colourless, without clamps.

Genus *Xerocomus*. Pores yellow, regular, not becoming gill-like.

Section *Xerocomus* [*Subtomentosi*]. Pores broad and compound, bright yellow. Cap ± velvety, bluing feeble or none.

Xerocomus subtomentosus (L.) Quél.
Cap 6-12cm, convex, tomentose, creamy ochraceous to pale yellowish or olive-brown. Pores golden yellow, broad. Stipe 8×1cm, slender, equal or attenuated downwards, smooth or furrowed, creamy yellow. Flesh pale, ammonia reaction negative or pale pink on cap surface. Spores 13×4μm. Under broadleaved trees. Common. Edible. E3.

X. lanatus (Rostk.) Sing. with cap a little more felted or woolly; ammonia reaction blue-green. E3.

Xerocomus spadiceus (Fr.) Quél.
Similar size. Cap dark, russet brown, matt. Pores and tubes as above. Flesh white, bluing slightly; ammonia reaction blue-green on cap surface. Under broadleaved trees and conifers. Uncommon. Edible. E2.

X. leguei (Boud.) Bon., sometimes regarded as a synonym, has the stipe more reticulate towards the apex; ammonia reaction as in *X. subtomentosus*. E2.

Xerocomus parasiticus (Bull.) Quél.
Cap 4-7cm, with surface like that of *X. subtomentosus* but cracking sooner. Pores less broad or more ochraceous, finally with a hint of orange. Stipe 4×1cm, smooth, dingy ochre, often curved at the base. Flesh lemon yellow, not bluing. Spores 18×4μm. Growing attached to the base of *Scleroderma*. Common in England, less so in Scotland. E1.

Section *Chrysenteri*. Cuticle soon cracking, distinctly bluing, flesh often bright yellow or reddish beneath the cuticle. Ammonia reaction nil or not characteristic.

Xerocomus chrysenteron (Bull.) Quél.
Cap 8-12cm, convex, cuticle soon cracked, dry, dingy ochre or olivaceous over a pink layer which is exposed in the cracks. Pores rather angular, dingy yellow then greenish. Stipe 6×1cm, equal or club-shaped, often bearing red granules. Flesh yellow, ± bluing or greening. Spores 14×4μm. Under broadleaved trees. Very common throughout Britain. Edible. E4.

X. pruinatus (Fr.) Quél. has a purplish bay cap covered by a distinctive hoary bloom; stipe a beautiful yellow to orange hue. Mainly under oak. Uncommon. E2.

Xerocomus rubellus (Krombh.) Quél. [*Boletus versicolor*]
Cap 5-7cm, entirely scarlet to vinaceous red, smooth. Pores small, pale yellow. Stipe 6×1cm, smooth, yellow, spotted red below. Flesh pale, only slowly tinged blue. Spores 13×5.5μm. Under broadleaved trees, especially oak in southern England. Edible. E3.

Xerocomus armeniacus (Quél.) Quél.
Cap similar to *X.rubellus* but more matt and cracking sooner, dull orange (apricot) turning rather brick colour. Pores broad, bright yellow, bluing slightly. Stipe 5×1cm, narrowed below or almost rooting, finely striate, yellowish, typically orange towards the point, outside and in. Flesh elsewhere pale, bluing slightly. Spores 13×6μm. Under broadleaved trees in meadows. Edible but dull. Fairly common. E2.

X. pascuus (Pers.) Gillet resembles *X. chrysenteron* often with orange tints in the cap and an orange or red stipe, beetroot colour at the base. In grass, often far from trees. E2.

Xerocomus porosporus Imler
Aspect of *X. chrysenteron* or smaller but with cap dingier, 5-8cm, more olivaceous, with a tendency to greenish grey in the flesh or the bruised stipe. Flesh pale, quickly browning. Distinguished microscopically by the occurrence in many spores of a truncate germ-pore. Spores 13×5μm. Under broadleaved trees, especially oak. Fairly common. E1.

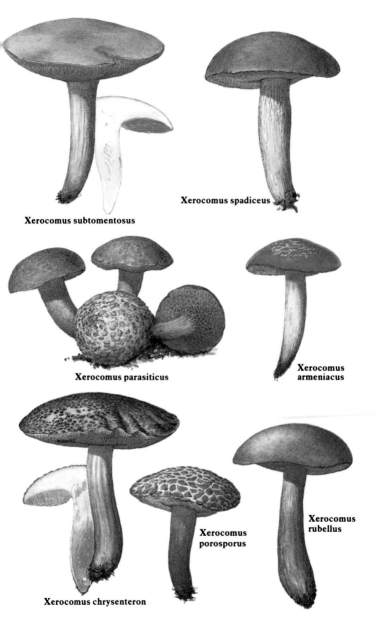

Xerocomus subtomentosus

Xerocomus spadiceus

Xerocomus parasiticus

Xerocomus armeniacus

Xerocomus chrysenteron

Xerocomus porosporus

Xerocomus rubellus

Section *Pseudoboleti*. Pores small, as in *Boletus*.

Xerocomus badius (Fr.) Kühn. & Gilb.
Resembles the section Boletus (p. 34) in size, cap 8-15cm, bay or chestnut, smooth, greasy when moist. Stipe 12×2cm, slightly tapered above and below, streaked or blotched russet. Pores cream to lemon, bluing at a touch. Flesh pale bluing only slightly in places. Spores 14×4μm. Under broadleaved trees and conifers, especially with Scots pine in Britain. Common. A good edible fungus. E4.

Xerocomus leonis (Reid) Bon [*Boletus leoninus*]
Medium size, thin fleshed, cap 5-9cm, convex, dry, yellowish brown. Pores medium, pale yellow. Stipe slender, up to 12×1cm, spindle-shaped, pale yellow, slightly floccose. Flesh pale ochre, not bluing. Spores 10×5.5μm. Under broadleaved trees, especially oak in southern England. Rare. E2.

X. moravicus (Vacek) Herink [*Boletus tumidus*] has shorter stipe, spindle-shaped or almost rooting and more russet coloured cap, often cracked. Under broadleaved trees. Rare. E2.

Genus *Chalciporus*. Pores copper, rust colour or reddish. Cap ± dry, smooth or velvety.

Chalciporus piperatus (Bull.) Bat.
Medium to small, cap 3-7cm, orange fawn or rust colour. Pores medium size, coppery orange. Stipe 6×8cm, yellowish, bright yellow inside and out at the base. Flesh ± yellow, base sometimes orange; taste peppery. Spores 10×4μm. Under broadleaved trees, in Britain especially with birch but also beech, oak etc. Common. Inedible because of the flavour. E3.

Ch. pierrhuguesii (Boud.) Bon [*Ch. amarellus* p.p.] is smaller with reddish pores and paler flesh, rather bitter instead of peppery. Under pines, often with *Rhizopogon*. Rare. sE1.

Chalciporus rubinus (W.G. Smith) Sing.
Cap 3-5cm, brownish fawn. Pores carmine red, somewhat decurrent. Stipe 3×0.5cm, reddish above, yellower below. Flesh pale; taste not peppery. Spores almost round, 7×5.5μm. Under oak in grassy places, especially in SE England. cE1.

Genus *Phylloporus*. Pores becoming gill-like, transitional to the Family *Paxillaceae* (p. 50).

Phylloporus rhodoxanthus (Schw.) Bres.
Cap 3-8cm, soon flat or depressed, dry, brown to reddish brown. Pores radially elongated to gill-like, anastomosing or labyrinthine, bright yellow. Stipe 4×1cm, concolorous with the cap or paler. Flesh pale. Ammonia reaction blue-green as in *X. spadiceus* (p. 42), which it may superficially resemble. Spores 11×4.5μm. Under broadleaved trees, especially beech on sandy soils. Uncommon in southern England, rarer northwards. E2.

Genus *Aureoboletus*. Cap viscid. Transitional to the next subfamily.

Aureoboletus gentilis (Quél.) Pouz. [*B. cramesinus*]
Cap 3-7cm, a distinctive pink colour, spotted or streaked vinaceous (crushed strawberry), very viscid. Pores medium size, angular, bright yellow, contrasting with the cap. Stipe equal, 6×0.8cm, pinkish, slightly viscid. Flesh pale, not bluing. Spores variable 16×6μm. Under broadleaved trees, mainly in southern England. Uncommon. E3.

Buchwaldoboletus is a similar genus of more robust fungi with a fugaceous mealy veil, like the wholly yellow **B. hemichrysus** (Bk. & Curt.) Pil. [*Boletus sulphureus*] found rarely on stumps, logs and sawdust of conifers.

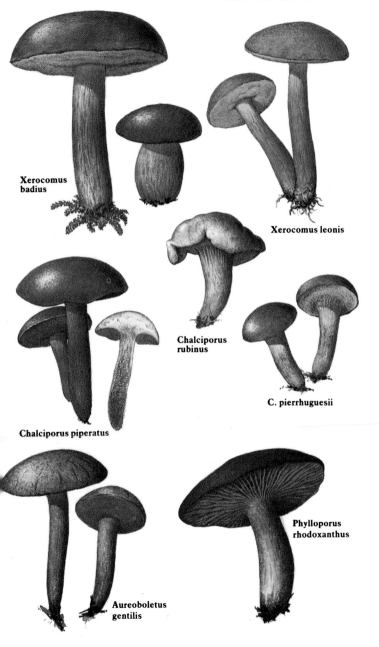

Xerocomus
badius

Xerocomus leonis

Chalciporus
rubinus

C. pierrhuguesii

Chalciporus piperatus

Phylloporus
rhodoxanthus

Aureoboletus
gentilis

45

Subfamily *Suilloideae*. Cap usually viscid, pores yellow to ochraceous or olivaceous. Stipe sometimes with a ring or a granulate surface. Trama parallel as in *Boletus*.

Genus *Suillus*. Fungi medium size or not fleshy, pores various.

Section *Suillus* [*Lutei*]. Pores small, ring membranous.

Suillus luteus (L.) S.F. Gray
Cap fleshy, convex, 8-13cm, dark brown to rust colour, often blotched by the gluten. Pores yellow, minute and regular. Stipe 6×1cm, yellowish, bearing reddish brown granules above a white ring, the under surface of which is tinged vinaceous. Flesh ± yellow. Spores 10×3.5µm. Under pines, especially Scots pine in Britain. Common. Edible but sometimes purgative. E4.

S. flavidus (Fr.) Sing., more slender, with yellow cap, broad angular pores and pale slightly viscid ring, occurs among *Sphagnum* under Scots Pine, especially in Scotland. E2.

Section *Larigni*. Pores broad or compound, rather decurrent; ring narrow or floccose, mainly with larch.

Suillus grevillei (Klot.) Sing. [*S. elegans*, *Boletus flavus* p.p.]
Cap 5-15cm, smooth, viscid, yellow orange, often umbonate or at first conical. Pores medium size, simple, yellow to orange, bruising rusty. Stipe 10×1cm, reticulate above the ring, pale yellow to yellowish brown, Flesh lemon yellow, bluing only in the extreme base when cut. Spores 11×4µm. Common under larch, less so under pines. Edible, but not very good. E3.

Suillus tridentinus (Bres.) Sing.
Outline similar to *S. grevillei* or slightly smaller, surface rather less viscid, rusty orange. Pores broad or compound, sometimes elongated near the stipe, slightly decurrent, orange to reddish brown, unchanged when bruised. Stipe 10×1cm, concolorous with slightly woolly ring. Flesh dingy yellow to rusty ochre. Spores 15×6µm. Rather uncommon, under larch and yew in southern England. Edible, but not very good. E2.

Suillus laricinus (Berk.) Kuntze [*Boletus viscidus*, *B. aeruginascens*]
Cap 5-10cm, convex, soon flattened but fleshy, viscid, a peculiar olive grey. Pores broad or compound, greyish then flushed vinaceous buff. Stipe 10×1cm, concolorous or paler. Flesh pale, greening slightly when cut. Spores 14×6µm. Under larch, uncommon in Britain. Harmless but not worth eating. E2.

var. *bresadolae* is more yellowish russet, like a transition to *S. tridentinus*. E1.

Section *Granulati*. Ring absent but stipe granulate or weeping milky droplets. Pores minute or not compound. .

Suillus granulatus (L.) Kuntze
Cap medium size or thin fleshed, 5-10cm, bright reddish brown, sometimes lighter or tinged orange, uniform or slightly blotched. Pores small, regular, light or bright yellow, ± weeping at first. Stipe 10×1cm, pale yellowish, with milky whitish granules which turn yellow then slightly orange. Flesh pale. Spores 10×4µm. Under pines but not uncommon in Britain. Edible but apt to be purgative. E4.

Suillus collinitus (Fr.) Kuntze [*S. fluryi*]
More fleshy than S. granulatus, cap 10-15cm, often slightly misshapen or lumpy, surface darker brown, ± blotched like *S. luteus*. Pores bright yellow, medium size, not or scarcely weeping. Stipe 8×2cm, rather thickset, dotted bright russet and typically tinted pink at the base by the mycelium. Flesh yellow, especially in the stipe, more orange to pink in the base. Spores 9×3.5µm. Habitat and edibility as in *S. granulatus*. E3.

Suillus bellini (Inz.) Watling, with cap whitish at first, becoming blotched sepia is one of a group of critical Mediterranean-Atlantic species. sE2.

S. placidus (Bonord.) Sing. and **S. plorans** (Roll.) Kuntze are strictly associated with 5-needled pines, the first with whitish cap and pores, the second with browner cap and olivaceous pores. Both E1.

Suillus
luteus

Suillus
grevillei

Suillus
tridentinus

Suillus
laricinus

S.
flavidus

Suillus granulatus

Suillus bellinii

Suillus collinitus

47

Section *Fungosi*. Pores rather large, beige to olivaceous, stipe without granules.

Suillus bovinus (L.) Kuntze
Cap 5-10cm, dull orange to brownish ochre, smooth, viscid with paler margin. Pores large and compound, often radially elongated near the stipe, slightly decurrent, beige russet to olivaceous. Stipe 5×1cm, ochraceous, smooth. Flesh brownish cream to slightly pink. Spores 10×4μm. Common under pines, especially Scots pine. Edible. E4.

Suillus variegatus (Swartz) Kuntze
Cap 8-15cm, convex, surface rather more scaly or punctate, not very viscid, dingy yellow to olivaceous. Pores ochraceous to olivaceous, rather small, simple. Stipe 10×1cm, pale to almost concolorous. Flesh yellowish, sometimes bluing; smell of chloride or perhaps like *Scleroderma*. Spores 10×3.5μm. Common under conifers. Edible. E3.

Subfamily *Strobilomycetoideae*. Spores greyish to pinkish.

Genus *Tylopilus*. Spores and pores pink.

Tylopilus felleus (Bull.) Karst.
A robust fungus, in size recalling the *Edules*. Cap 6-15cm, chamois or with olive grey tint, dry or matt. Pores white then salmon, small. Stipe 12×3cm, rather massive, sometimes swollen, almost concolorous, ornamented with a coarse dingy brown or olivaceous reticulum, finely velvety. Flesh white, odourless but very bitter. Spores 12×4μm. Under beech and oak on acid soils, especially in England. Inedible because of the taste; formerly used as a substitute for gentian bitters in drinks. E2.

Genus *Porphyrellus*. Pores small, spores greyish purple; ring absent.

Porphyrellus porphyrosporus (Fr.) Gilb.
Resembling a *Krombholziella* but with darker pores and smoother stipe. Cap 8-13cm, convex, dark brown or olive grey, sometimes mottled, smooth or matt. Stipe 10×2cm, fairly equal, olive grey to almost concolorous or tinged sooty grey. Flesh pale, then yellowish or greening. Spores variable, 10-20×5-10μm. Mainly under beech or oak, occasionally conifers, uncommon in Britain, mostly in the north. Edible but poor quality. E2.

P. pseudoscaber Sing., usually regarded as a synonym, may be separable by having a blacker cap and rather reddening flesh. Under conifers in the mountains. Rare. E1.

Genus *Strobilomyces*. Pores grey, large, polygonal; ring present.

Strobilomyces strobilaceus (Scop.) Berk. [*S. floccopus*]
Cap fleshy, hemispherical, 10-20cm, covered with very large, thick, fibrillose scales, grey-brown to blackish or slate colour on a barely paler base. Pores hexagonal, greyish. Stipe 12×2cm, a similar colour with a thick, sheathing shaggy ring, remnants of which may persist appendiculate to the cap margin. Flesh greyish, reddening then turning slate colour. Spores broad, 12×10μm, greyish, ornamented by a reticulum. Under broadleaved trees and conifers, often with old beech. Rare in Britain except for a few localities in the Severn and Thames basins. E3.

The edibility and toxicity of Boletes.

a. Intense bluing is not an indication of toxicity; quite the contrary, the poisonous species show only slight bluing (*B*. *satanas*, p.39) or none at all (*Gyroporus castaneus* p. 33) while *B*. *erythropus* (p. 39) and *Gyroporus cyanescens* (p. 33), which blue strongly, are very good edible fungi.

b. Species with white caps are all either indigestible, poisonous or bitter.

c. Species with viscid caps often have laxative properties.

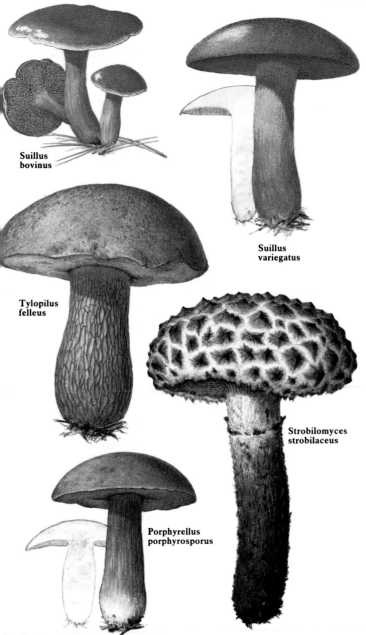

Suillus
bovinus

Suillus
variegatus

Tylopilus
felleus

Strobilomyces
strobilaceus

Porphyrellus
porphyrosporus

49

Family *Paxillaceae*. Gills decurrent and anastomosing, readily separable from the flesh, or forked, crowded. Spores ochraceous or whitish. Genus *Paxillus*. Gills soft, separable from the cap; spores ochre.

Paxillus involutus (Batsch) Fr.
Cap 10-15cm, at first umbonate then somewhat depressed with a grooved persistently inrolled margin; surface slightly viscid or greasy at first, becoming almost dry, yellowish brown with reddish or olivaceous tints. Gills crowded, pale ochre, bruising rusty, anastomosing, wrinkled towards the base. Stipe 4×1cm, often short or curved, enlarged at the apex, concolorous, fibrillose. Flesh soft, rather yellowish. Spores 9×5μm. Very common throughout the British Isles in broadleaved woods of all kinds, but especially birch and oak. **Poisonous** if eaten raw or inadequately cooked. E4.

Paxillus atrotomentosus (Batsch) Fr.
A large fungus, cap 12-20cm, with margin inrolled but little grooved, colour dingier than in *P. involutus*. Gills yellowish, anastomosing at the base. Stipe 5×2cm, often excentric, tomentose, blackish, especially below. Flesh pale, yellowish to pinkish, bitter. Spores 6×4μm. On dead wood of conifers, sometimes in clusters, common on Scots pine. Edibility suspect. E3.

Paxillus panuoides (Fr.) Fr.
Recognised by its pleurotoid aspect with stipe lateral or absent and bright orange-saffron gills. Cap 3-7cm, pale yellowish brown or olivaceous, sometimes tinged violaceous at the base (var. *ionipus*). Spores 5×3μm. Uncommon on stumps and coniferous debris, especially of Scots pine. Of no culinary value. E2.

Hygrophoropsis aurantiaca (Wulf.) R. Mre.
Aspect of a *Clitocybe*, cap 3-6cm, centre soon depressed, surface matt to downy, orange to orange-brown, whitish in var. *pallida*. Gills forked, bright orange, soft. Stipe 4×0.5cm, sometimes slightly excentric, narrowed below, almost concolorous or orange yellow. Flesh pale, soft. Smell and taste not distinctive. Spores 7×4μm, white. Under broadleaved trees and conifers, often on woody debris. Very common everywhere. Edible. E4.

Omphalotus illudens (Schw.) Sacc.
Cap 8-15cm, surface smooth or fibrillose, at first a beautiful bright orange but soon turning darker to a dingy reddish brown. Gills markedly decurrent, not soft and not separable, bright orange, becoming dingy, luminous. Stipe 8×1cm, distinctly excentric, concolorous, smooth. Flesh pale, fibrous. Spores 7×6μm. In clusters on wood, especially sweet chestnut. Very rare in Britain – a few stations in SE England. **Poisonous.** E2.

Family *Gomphidiaceae*. Gills distant, decurrent, blackish at maturity; spores fusiform as in *Boletus* but blackish. Cystidia ± cylindrical, conspicuous, 80-120×10-15μm.

Gomphidius glutinosus (Sch.) Fr.
Cap 7-12cm, relatively fleshy, slightly umbonate at first, viscid, greyish, sometimes with a pinkish tint. Gills greyish, at first pale. Stipe 8×1cm, slightly club-shaped, nearly concolorous or yellower towards the base, with a slightly glutinous annular zone. Flesh pale, distinctly yellow at the base of the stipe only. Smell and taste not distinctive. Spores 18×7μm. Under conifers, especially spruce, uncommon in Britain. Edible. E3.

G. roseus (Nees.) Gill., with pink or vinaceous cap, grows under pines, often with *Suillus bovinus*. E2.

Chroogomphus rutilus (Sch.) Miller [*Gomphidius viscidus*]
Cap 5-7cm, umbonate then flat, viscid, drying matt, dull orange to copper, paling to ochraceous brick, sometimes greyish. Gills concolorous at first. Stipe 8×0.8cm, slightly attenuated below, concolorous, slightly viscid with a floccose veil forming an annular zone. Flesh uniformly pale orange yellow, becoming slightly ochraceous. Odourless and tasteless. Spores 23×7μm. Common under pines, Edible. E4.

C. helveticus (Sing.) Moser. More robust, less viscid or even almost velvety, cap not umbonate, bright orange. Under conifers. British record doubtful. cE2.

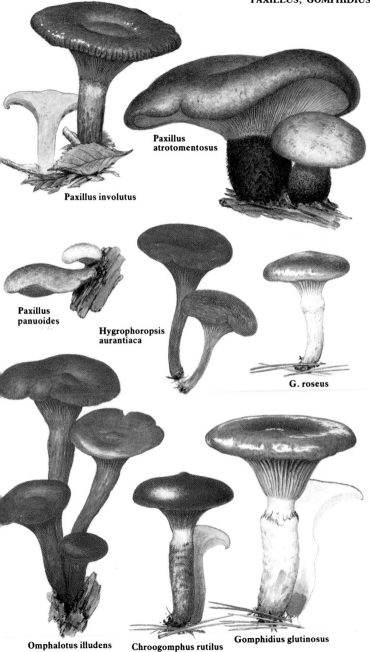

Paxillus
atrotomentosus

Paxillus involutus

Paxillus
panuoides

Hygrophoropsis
aurantiaca

G. roseus

Omphalotus illudens

Chroogomphus rutilus

Gomphidius glutinosus

51

Order *Russulales*. A single family: *Russulaceae*. Flesh granular and brittle; spore print white, cream, ochraceous or yellow, spores with an amyloid ornament.

Genus *Russula*. No exudation of milky fluid when the flesh is broken; fruit-body with commonplace outline, gills horizontal, rarely at an angle, often forked, stipe with length often equal to cap diameter.

With *Russula* the following characters have to be taken into consideration:

* The nature of the **flesh** when broken, its fragility or firmness: a firm flesh is usually juicy or changes colour through pink to black. Colour changes, also those following handling or rubbing, include blackening with or without previous reddening, browning, russeting and yellowing.

* **Taste**, whether mild or acrid. Though indispensable in identifying most species, this character must be used with discretion since some mild species have gills more or less acrid when young (*R. artesiana*, *R. grisea* and allies) while some slightly acrid species become virtually mild under certain conditions of humidity or drying (*R. atropurpurea*, *R. maculata* etc). The flesh of the stipe gives the most reliable reaction. Smell may also be important at specific level.

* **Spore colour**. Ideally the spore print should be heavy enough to allow comparison with a colour chart; here the main divisions I-II-III-IV of the Romagnesi colour chart are used, indicating respectively white, cream, ochraceous or yellow.

  One can try to estimate the colour of a spore print by that of the mature gills, but this needs experience and comes up against difficulties and makes such as yellowing gills which suggest too high a level of colour (*R. puellaris*) or a pale margin to the gill, which leads to underestimation of the colour (*R. integra*). These problems can be overcome to some extent by varying the incidence of the light on the gills, by tilting the cap held by the stipe. It may also be hard to be sure how mature the specimen is and thus fall into error.

* The appearance of the **cap cuticle**, in relation to its anatomy. A smooth or shining, almost greasy, aspect is usually that of a cuticle containing dermatocystidia. A matt or granular appearance generally indicates the presence of primordial hyphae with acid-resistant encrustation. Cuticles with ordinary hairs and no distinctive chemical reaction have an almost velvety appearance (*R. olivacea*, *R. violeipes*). But these general rules are subject to many exceptions and in doubtful cases microscopic observation is essential.

* **Chemical reactions**, often very important, especially those with ferrous sulphate, phenol, ammonia, tincture of gaiac and sulfovanillin.

Key to *Russula* – sections and groups of species

1a   Dull colours, greyish brown to dingy ochre or bistre, ± mingled with dull yellow, bright or distinctive warm colours lacking. Gills not forked or only occasionally so: **2**

1b   Bright colours, yellow, red, green, violaceous, or warm, fulvous, brick, sometimes particoloured. Gills often forked, at least near the stipe: **5**

2a   Flesh hard or firm, juicy or reddening; gills not forked; section *Compactae*: **3**

2b   Flesh more tender or friable. Gills ± forked. Taste acrid or smell unpleasant; section *Ingratae*: **4**

3a   Flesh ± reddening then blackening. Cap convex, gills horizontal or sloping »
           subsection *Nigricantinae*, 54

3b   Flesh unchanged ± juicy when cut. Cap often depressed, gill arched or decurrent, weeping; smell fruity then of crab or herring »
           subsection *Plorantinae*, 54

4a Cap margin acute, markedly grooved or tuberculate; smell distinctive, nauseating, rubbery or of bitter almonds >> subsection *Foetentinae*, 78

4b Cap margin obtuse, even or glabrous, smell weak or fruity >> subsection *Felleinae*, 78

5a Taste mild, sometimes slightly acrid in gills of young specimens or in species ± bruising russet: **6**

5b Taste acrid, at least in the stipe: **15**

6a Spore print and gills white or pale (I-II): **7**

6b Spore print and gills ochre or bright yellow at maturity (III-IV): **9**

7a ± robust species, some shade of green, violaceous or lilaceous to pinkish brown, bright fawn or purple, without a trace of bright red or pure pink; cuticle shining or almost greasy; dermatocystidia, rarely downy, with commonplace hairs: **8**

7b ± robust species coloured red or bright pink or small fragile species colour ± lilaceous or bluish; cuticle matt or punctate, granulate, with encrusted hyphae >> section *Lilaceae*, 60

(If browning or darkening, see section *Decolorantes*, 64)

8a Spore print and gills white (I), gills rather elastic when stroked >> section *Heterophyllae*, 56

8b Spore print and gills cream to pale ochraceous II(III); Fe reaction pink >> section *Griseinae*, 58

9a Tender or fragile species with a soft, compressible stipe: **10**

9b Rather robust or fleshy species; stipe stiff or corticate, not compressible except when old and effete: **11**

10a Cuticle shining, with dermatocystidia; species ± yellowing or greying slightly; spore print ochre to yellow; taste mild or becoming somewhat acrid in the gills >> section *Tenellae*, 62

10b Cuticle matt or granulate, sometimes viscid at the centre, encrusted hyphae present; species not changing colour or only yellowing on the stipe by deposition of spores; taste ± tart when chewed >> section *Lilaceae*, 60

11a Noticeably browning or blackening: **12**

11b No colour change or only slight yellowing: **14**

12a Predominantly blackening; Fe reaction unremarkable or pinkish >> section *Decolorantes*, 64

12b Turning brown or yellowish russet: **13**

13a Fe reaction unremarkable, smell weak or of honey >> see group of *R. melliolens*, 64

13b Fe reaction green, strong smell or crab or herring, especially when rubbed >> section *Viridantes*, 64

14a Colours pure red to brick orange >> section *Coccineae*, 68

14b Colours varied, never pure red, at most pinkish to reddish brown, rosewood or carmine >> section *Polychromae*, 66

15a Spore print white or pale cream (I-II); section *Russula*: **16**

15b Spore print cream ochraceous (III); section *Sanguineae*: **21**

15c Spore print yellow (IV) >> section *Insidiosae*, 76

16a Colour persistently bright red or fading to pinkish white without a trace of any other colour >> subsection *Emeticinae*, 70

16b Polychrome species or with a ± violaceous to carmine red: **17**

17a Spore print white (I) >> subsection *Atropurpurinae*, 72

17b Spore print cream (II), rather fragile species >> subsection *Violaceinae*, 72

Section *Compactae*. Gills sloping down to stipe, not forked, flesh compact, watery, unchanging or reddening then sometimes blackening.

Subsection *Nigricantinae*. Flesh reddening or blackening. Spore print white, spore ornament very low.

Russula nigricans Fr.
Gills widely spaced and thick. Cap 15-25cm, at first white and convex, then bistre and flat, strongly cracking with age. Flesh turning bright red throughout, then black. Stipe 7×3cm, white, then brownish. Taste mild, smell none or slightly fruity at first. Spores 8×7μm, with a delicate reticulum. Under broadleaved trees, less often conifers. Common throughout Britain. Edible when young. E4.

Russula albonigra (Krombh.) Fr.
Gills moderately spaced, creamy ivory. Cap 6-12cm, convex, then expanded and sometimes deformed, whitish then blotched blackish. Stipe 5×1cm, whitish, browning. Flesh blackening without a preliminary reddening phase, except in var. *pseudonigricans*. Taste a little bitter as in *R. lepida*, smell slight. Spores 9×6μm, ornament finely punctate to crested. Under broadleaved trees. Uncommon. Edible. E3.

R. anthracina Romagn. has more crowded regular gills, slightly pinkish, and more acrid flesh, except in var. *insipida*; blackening throughout. E3.

Russula adusta (Pers.) Fr.
Gills fairly crowded, sloping to somewhat decurrent eventually. Cap 13-20cm, soon depressed, pale beige to brownish. Stipe 9×3cm, stout, enlarged and irregular at the base, veined, whitish then beige throughout, scarcely greying. Flesh turning pink before greying; smell and taste weak. Spores 9×7μm, finely cristate. Under oak, sometimes conifers, often on sand, gravel or shale. Edible. Uncommon. E3.

Russula densifolia Gill.
Gills very crowded. Cap 5-10cm, convex or irregularly lobed, later somewhat depressed, surface matt, beige to pale bistre, sometimes becoming slightly yellowish brown. Stipe 4×1cm, white to beige or brownish. Flesh slowly reddening then greying; taste somewhat acrid, smell rather like old casks or dust. Spores 8×6μm, with low warts and connecting lines. Under broadleaved trees on acid soils, heaths or oak woods. Common. Edible. E4.

R. acrifolia Romagn. is more robust, 9-15cm, with a more depressed cap, reddish brown, shining or greasy, and with less crowded gills; taste very acrid, at least in the gills. E3.

Subsection *Plorantinae*. Flesh watery, colour unchanged, gills sloping or ± decurrent, weeping; cap depressed or with aspect of a *Lactarius*. Spore ornament more prominent.

Russula delica Fr. [*Lactarius exsuccus*]
Gills moderately spaced to fairly distant. Cap 12-20cm, much depressed with permanently inrolled margin, surface first glabrous and dingy white, then distinctly rugulose or pitted, dingy beige, often carrying patches of soil. Stipe 4×2cm, whitish. Flesh white, hard and brittle, smell fruity becoming slightly fishy with age. Spores 11×8.5μm, subreticulate, whitish-cream in the mass. Under broadleaved trees on calcareous soil, common throughout Britain. Edible but poor. E4.

R. pseudodelica Lange. Spore print cream to pale ochraceous, cap surface smoother and gills yellowish. E2.

Russula chloroides (Krombh.) Bres.
Gills more crowded than in *R. delica*, sometimes with a ± distinct greenish tint or a bluish band at their base. Cap only 8-12cm, whitish, not much pitted. Stipe 3×1cm. Smell feeble. Spores 9×7μm, with rather isolated warts. Under broadleaved trees on ± acid soil. Edible but poor. E3.

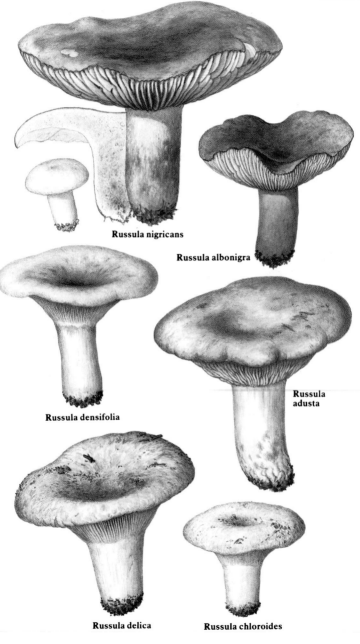

Russula nigricans

Russula albonigra

Russula densifolia

Russula adusta

Russula delica

Russula chloroides

55

Section *Heterophyllae*. Rather robust species, mild, colours various but never pure red, spore print white.

Russula cyanoxantha (Sch.) Fr.
Cap 5-12cm, variously coloured, from greenish or steely blue to violaceous or lilac, ± mingled with yellowish; cuticle shining or slightly radially streaked. For var. *peltereaui*, see under *R. cutefracta* below. Gills soft and elastic, white. Stipe 7×1cm, equal, pure white; flesh persistently white without a distinctive smell or taste. Fe reaction negative or slowly greenish. Spores 9×6μm, with isolated warts. Common throughout Britain under broadleaved trees of all kinds. A good edible fungus. E4.

R. langei Bon differs in its harder texture, cap distinctly slaty violet, cream gills, stipe ± tinged violaceous and Fe reaction more distinctly greenish grey. E2.

Russula cutefracta Cke.
Cap as in *R. cyanoxantha* but cuticle typically punctate and cracking apart from the margin inwards, as in *R. virescens*, but tinted darker green, dark bronze or tinged dingy blue-green, sometimes with a vinaceous tint beneath the cuticle. Gills as in *R. cyanoxantha* or creamier. Stipe sometimes short, 5×1cm, whitish. Fe reaction negative or slowly greenish. Spores like those of *R. cyanoxantha* or with pairs of warts linked by a line. Under various broadleaved trees. Edible like *R. cyanoxantha* though slightly acrid forms occur. E2.

R. cyanoxantha var. **peltereaui** has the same colours, or sometimes more lilac-bluish, but its cuticle is persistently smooth or at most streaked. E2.

Russula virescens (Sch.) Fr.
Cap fleshy, 10-15cm, soon depressed with margin broadly inrolled; cap cuticle extensively finely cracked or flecked from the margin inwards, bluish green or verdigris colour on a whitish ground, matt, as though mildewed. Gills fairly distant, creamy white, finally slightly sloping. Stipe 5×2cm, white, then stained with a few rusty spots. Flesh white, smell slight, becoming slightly cheesy with age or on drying; taste nutty. Fe reaction bright orange-pink. Spores 9×6μm, ornament variable; epicutis containing tapered hairs and a cellular base. Under broadleaved trees, especially beech and oak on light soils. Fairly common north to the Moray Firth but not in the Hebrides. A good edible fungus. E4.

Russula mustelina Fr.
Cap 10-15cm, convex and fleshy, surface smooth then matt, brownish chamois to reddish brown, sometimes slightly purplish or blotched with ochraceous cream, *Boletus edulis* colour. Gills creamy white to rusty ochraceous. Stipe 8×3cm, swollen or irregular, creamy white to brownish. Flesh pale or yellowish under the cuticle, browning slightly, smell and taste not distinctive, slightly cheesy on drying. Fe reaction pink. Spores 11×8μm, ornament subreticulate but not prominent. Under conifers in the mountains. Very rare in Britain. Edible. E1 (m4).

Russula heterophylla (Fr.) Fr.
Cap 8-15cm, cuticle smooth or shining, yellowish green to bronze, rarely with a tinge of reddish brown at the centre. Gills noticeably forked near the stipe, rather crowded, eventually rather decurrent, white, sometimes speckled with reddish brown. Stipe 8×1.5cm, persistently white or spotted rusty brown below. Flesh white or ochraceous, smell slight, taste sometimes a little bitter when chewed. Fe reaction bright pink. Spores small, 6.5×4μm, with isolated warts. Under various broadleaved trees, uncommon in Britain. A good edible fungus in spite of the colour resemblance to the lethal *Amanita phalloides*, which must be carefully distinguished from it. E3.

Russula vesca Fr.
Cap 5-9cm, colour pinky brown typically merging into dingy yellow at the centre; cuticle readily separable especially at the margin where it tends to retract enough to expose the gill ends, "showing its teeth" or "dressed in short clothes" as we say. Gills and stipe pure white or eventually ± spotted rust colour. Fe reaction very bright pink. Smell faint, taste nutty. Spores 8.5×5μm, finely warted with a few short lines. Common throughout Britain under various broadleaved trees on neutral to acid soils. Edible and good. E4.

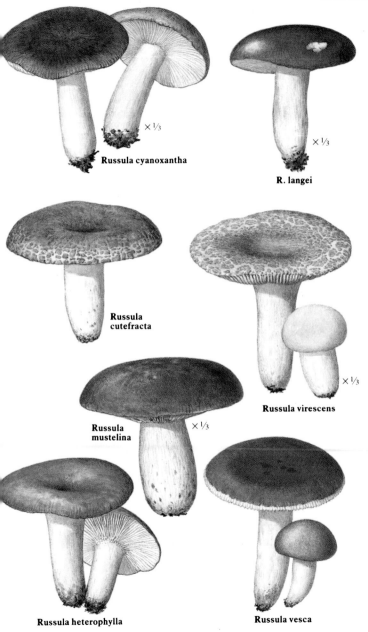

× ⅓

Russula cyanoxantha

× ⅓

R. langei

Russula cutefracta

× ⅓

Russula virescens

Russula mustelina

× ⅓

Russula heterophylla

Russula vesca

Section *Griseinae*. Like *Heterophyllae* with cream spore print and cream-ochraceous gills; Fe reaction ± pink, sometimes dingy. Taste often a little acrid in the gills when young. With dermatocystidia and ± septate hairs.

Russula grisea Fr. [*R. palumbina*]
Cap medium to fairly robust, 8-10cm, entirely violaceous grey or slate colour with traces of lilac especially where wounded, glabrous or pruinose towards the margin. Gills not crowded, cream ochraceous, sometimes with a lemon tint. Stipe 6×1cm, white. Flesh white, pink under the cuticle. Smell weak. Fe reaction bright pink. Spores 8×6μm, warted with a few crests; cuticular hairs rather elongated and septate. Under various broadleaved trees, uncommon in Britain but confused with *R. parazurea* in the past. Edible. E2.

Russula ionochlora Romagn. [*R. grisea* p.p.]
A little less robust or more fragile than *R. grisea* and with more diverse colours, typically zoned with green, violaceous or lilac, and with more shining cuticle. Gills crowded or thin, fragile, pale cream. Smell slightly fruity. Spores 7×6μm, with low rather isolated warts. Under beech. Widespread, although not common in Britain. E3.

Russula parazurea J. Schaef.
Cap 5-10cm, surface matt to ± pruinose towards the margin, a distinctive blue-grey mingled with glaucous green, sometimes lilaceous or pinkish brown at the centre or on drying. Gills pale cream, moderately spaced. Stipe 7×1cm, white, or tinged violaceous in var. *dibapha*. Flesh slightly creamy ochraceous, smell weak but rather cheesy on drying. Fe reaction weak or yellowish. Spores 8×6μm, reticulate; cuticular hairs closely septate below. Under broadleaved trees, along roadsides and in parks, common with lime in England. Edible. E3.

Russula anatina Romagn.
Cap somewhat resembling *R. parazurea* but more dark green, sometimes steel blue with cuticle finely cracking from the margin inwards, like *R. cutefracta*, centre ± ochraceous with age or tinged pinkish on drying. Gills pale. Stipe 4×1cm, whitish. Flesh white; Fe reaction dingy pink to grey-greenish. Spores 8×6μm, with rather coarse isolated warts; cuticular hairs mingled with chains of short cells. Under broadleaved trees especially in damp places. Uncommon. E2.

Russula aeruginea Lindbl. [*R. graminicolor*]
Cap 8-12cm, remaining convex, recalling *R. heterophylla* in its green colour but often duller, sometimes greyish. Gills somewhat forked, rather bright yellowish ochraceous at maturity. Stipe 5-8×1cm, white, yellowing slightly, often narrowed below. Almost odourless and tasteless. Fe reaction pinkish grey, moderate. Spores 9×6.5μm, with low warts and a few connecting lines; cuticular hairs narrow. Under birch, spruce and other conifers. Common. Edible. E3.

Russula amoena Quél.
Cap 3-7cm, fairly uniformly carmine colour with velvety cuticle. Gills ochraceous, often pink on the edge. Stipe 6-8cm, rather slender, a pretty pastel pink, at least in part. Flesh creamy white, with strong smell of cooking Jerusalem artichokes. Phenol reaction purple. Spores 8×6μm, subreticulate; cuticular hairs tapered, mingled with basal chains of cells. Under various broadleaved trees and conifers on sandy soils. Uncommon in England. E1 (m3).

R. amoenicolor Romagn. is more robust, 8-13cm, with more varied coloration, green and pink or vinaceous. Stipe velvety, pale or slightly lilaceous. Flesh (smell) and cuticle as in *R. amoena*. Phenol reaction not purple. Spores subglobose, 7-8μm with a coarse high reticulum. Rather common under broadleaved trees and conifers in lowland areas.

Russula violeipes Quél.
More robust or with a slender stipe 13×2cm, typically tinged a delicate violet but white in f. *citrina*. Cap soon depressed, yellow or tinged violet towards the margin, matt or downy. Smell less strong or mixed, eventually suggestive of crab. Spores subglobose 9×8μm, with an incomplete reticulum. Common under broadleaved trees. Edible but of poor quality. E3 (f.*citrina* E2).

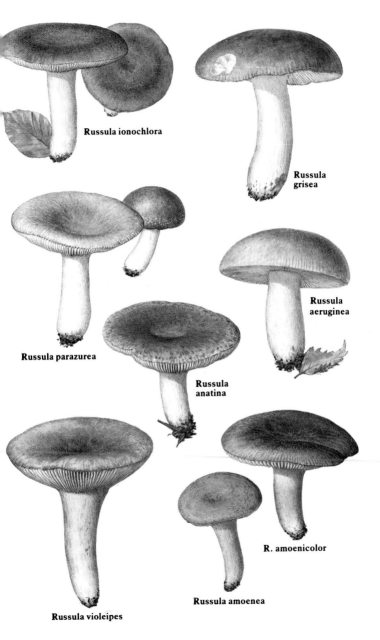

Russula ionochlora

Russula
grisea

Russula aeruginea

Russula parazurea

Russula
anatina

R. amoenicolor

Russula amoenea

Russula violeipes

59

Section *Lilaceae* [*Incrustatae*]. Mild Russulae with yellow or white spore print; downy surface, often granular towards the margin or matt (cuticle with encrusted primordial hyphae). Taste often slightly tart.

Russula lilacea Quél.
Slender or fragile fungus, cap 3-5cm, margin slightly furrowed, granulate, lilaceous mauve to reddish brown. Gills moderately spaced, white. Stipe 6×0.7cm, soft, compressible, white or flushed pink. Flesh white, smell and taste weak. Sulfovanillin reaction bluish. Spores white, 8×6μm, with almost isolated warts. Under broadleaved trees. Uncommon. E2.

Russula azurea Bres.
A little more robust or fleshy than *R. lilacea*, cap 6-8cm with pruinose surface somewhat zoned with bluish, violaceous or greyish tints, rarely with a trace of olivaceous. Gills white, rather crowded. Stipe 6×1cm, whitish pruinose. Flesh white, insipid. Sulfovanillin reaction bluish. Spores white, 10×7.5μm, subreticulate. Under spruce in mountain districts (not in Britain). Fairly common in Britain. Em2.

R. emeticicolor (J. Schaef.) Romagn. ex Bon is bright red like the next species (but more slender) from which it is mainly separated by the weak sulfovanillin reaction. E2.

Russula aurora Krombh. [*R. rosea*]
Cap 8-12cm, slightly depressed with margin incurved, cuticle matt, delicate pink round the margin, more ochraceous or faded towards the centre. Gills soft, moderately spaced, white. Stipe 12×3cm, often expanded below the gills or slightly club-shaped, pure white, mealy at the apex, smoother or veined below. Flesh white, soft, without distinctive smell or taste. Sulfovanillin reaction bright pink. Spores white, 8×6μm, with fine low warts linked by a few lines. Under broadleaved trees, especially beech, common throughout Britain. Edible. E3.

R. minutula Vel. with cap 2-4cm, brighter red, especially under hornbeam, resembles a miniature *R. emetica*. E2.

Russula lepida (Fr.) Fr. [*R. rosacea* p.p.]
Cap resembling *R. aurora* but more compact, scarcely depressed with a non-separable velvety cuticle, matt, finally finely cracking, more uniformly a warmer bright red, rarely faded in patches but entirely creamy white in var. *lactea*. Gills moderately spaced, with a trace of cream. Stipe 7×1cm, equal or club-shaped, hard, flushed red at least on one side or at the base. Flesh leathery, chalky, white, sometimes yellowing in var. *speciosa*. Smell and especially the taste rather of menthol or pencil wood. Sulfovanillin reaction bluish or dirty, not pink. Spores white, 8×7μm, reticulate; cuticular anatomy mixed, with dermatocystidia. Especially under beech. Common throughout Britain. Edible but poor quality. E4.

R. amarissima Romagn. & Gilb. has very bitter flesh and its cap is a warmer or carmine red which may also tinge the gill margins. E2.

Russula risigalina (Batsch) Sacc. [*R. lutea* p.p.]
Small fragile fungus, cap 3-7cm, cuticle matt, pure yellow in the typical form, margin pink in f. *luteorosella* and particoloured in f. *chamaeleontina*. Gills bright yellow, ± orange at maturity contrasting vividly with the white stipe. Stipe 5×0.7cm, brittle, unchanging white, except where tinged yellow by shed spores. Flesh soft, white with slight fruity smell as it decays. Spores yellow, 9×8μm, with short isolated spines; cuticular hairs capitate. Under broadleaved trees, common under oak in Britain. Edible. E4.

R. lutea (Huds.) S.F. Gray [*R. vitellina*] is also entirely yellow but more shining lemon to egg yellow. E2.

Russula turci Bres.
Cap 6-10cm, often with a low umbo, surface at first somewhat gelatinous, soon matt from the edge inwards as it dries, Typically with a ring of varying colour (violet, amethyst or lilac to pink) around a much darker centre which dries paler or discolours yellowish. Gills medium to bright yellow. Stipe 6×1cm, relatively robust, pure white. Flesh white with a distinctive odour of iodine, green soap etc., best detected at the stipe base. Spores 9×7μm, reticulate. Under pine, less often spruce. Edible but of poor quality. E4.

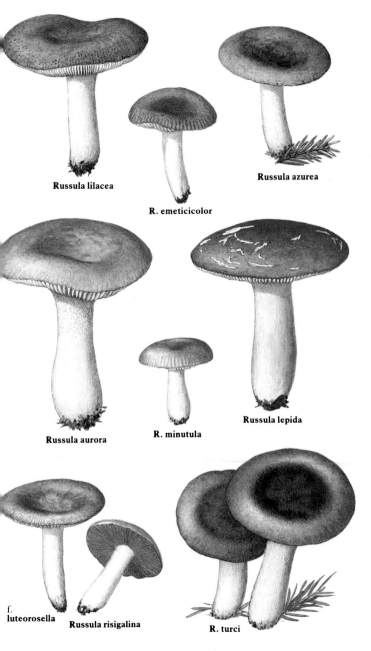

Russula lilacea

R. emeticicolor

Russula azurea

Russula aurora

R. minutula

Russula lepida

f.
luteorosella

Russula risigalina

R. turci

Section *Tenellae*. Rather fragile fungi, caps variously coloured, taste mild, cream to yellowish spore print. Cuticle shining, not matt (dermatocystidia present).

Russula puellaris Fr.
Cap 3-7cm, margin slightly furrowed, colour ranging from pinkish brown to chamois or purple at the centre, staining yellow to rust brown. Gills cream, bruising yellow though the spore print is pale. Stipe 7×1cm, club-shaped, white, veined then flushed saffron yellow from the base. Flesh yellowing to become entirely saffron; smell and taste weak. Spores cream, 9×7μm, rather strongly warted with a few short ridges. Under various broadleaved trees. Common throughout Britain. Edible. E4.

Russula puellula Ebb., Møll. & J.Schaef.
Resembles *R. puellaris* but cap more uniformly pink, yellowing only slightly or not at all. Gills remaining pale, spore print cream. Stipe 3×1cm, remaining white. Flesh white or cream to yellowish grey, remaining pale; smell and taste none. Spores cream, 8×6μm, warted with an incomplete reticulum and a few small ridges. Under beech. Edible but of poor quality. E3.

Russula versicolor J. Schaef.
Slightly fleshier than the two preceding species; cap 5-8cm, margin not striate, surface more pinkish to pale vinaceous mingled with a greenish tint. Stipe 7×1cm, white, distinctly yellowing in var. *intensior*, otherwise only slightly or less widely. Smell weak, taste slightly acrid in young gills. Spores cream-ochraceous,variable, often narrowly elongated for a *Russula*, 9×6μm, ± crested. Common throughout Britain under birch. E3. **R. pseudopuellaris** Bon, on sandy, gravelly or shaly soils, is almost inseparable from *R. puellaris* without microscopic examination. E2.

Russula brunneoviolacea Crawsh.
Cap 6-10cm, not very fleshy, cap soon flat, typically violet or dark purple with minute rusty specks visible under a lens. Gills and spore print cream. Stipe 5×1cm, white, rather firm and only slightly yellowing. Flesh cream to yellowish, odourless. Spores cream-ochraceous, about 8×7μm, with isolated rather long pointed warts. Under broadleaved trees, especially beech, hazel and oak, throughout Britain. Uncommon. Edible. E3. **R. unicolor** Romagn. is paler, otherwise like *R. versicolor*. E2.

Russula nitida (Pers.) Fr.
Cap 6-8cm, with furrowed margin, glossy reddish to vinaceous, finally colour of rosewood. Gills yellowish ochre at maturity. Stipe 8×1cm, slightly club-shaped, white or lightly tinged reddish near the base. Flesh white or with a few yellowish patches in the stipe, almost odourless. Spores ochraceous, 10×8μm, with numerous isolated pointed warts. Under birch, often in *Sphagnum*. Common. Edible. E3.

R. sphagnophila Kfm. has more diversely coloured cap and somewhat reticulated spores. In marshy ground under broadleaved trees, in *Sphagnum*. E2.

Russula nauseosa (Pers.) Fr.
Small or fragile, 3-5cm, margin furrowed, colour various, from violaceous pink to purple and greenish to yellowish or olivaceous. Gills not crowded, bright yellow. Stipe 4×0.6cm, fragile, whitish, greying with age. Flesh slightly acrid at first. Spores yellow, 10×8μm, with numerous isolated pointed warts. Under pines in Scotland, and in Europe mountain spruces. E1 (m3).

Russula cessans Pears.
A little more fleshy than *R. nauseosa*, cap 5-8cm, margin not striate but colouring just as variable. Gills orange at maturity. Stipe slightly club-shaped, 6×1cm, becoming ± grey. Flesh dingy white, smell none, taste unpleasant. Spores 10×8.5μm, incompletely reticulate. Under conifers, especially Scots pine in the Highlands. Edible. E3.

Russula odorata Romagn.
Small to medium, cap 3-8cm, reddish, purple or coppery lilac, rarely olivaceous bronze. Gills and spore print deep yellow. Stipe 5×1cm, white, fragile, yellowing slightly. Flesh white, almost unchanged, with strong smell, first of pelargonium, then of honey. Spores yellow, 8×6μm, subreticulate with rather coarse warts. Under oak and other broadleaved trees and in copses. Uncommon. E2.

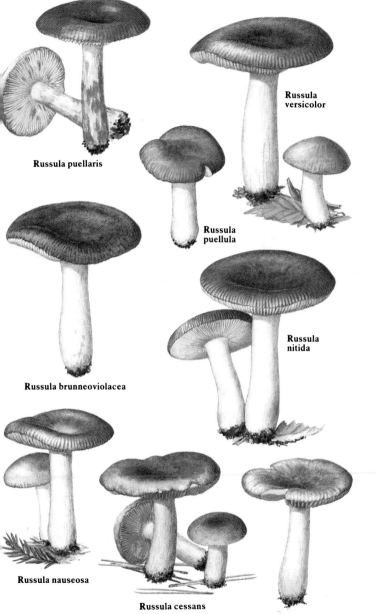

Russula puellaris

Russula
versicolor

Russula
puellula

Russula brunneoviolacea

Russula
nitida

Russula nauseosa

Russula cessans

Russula odorata

63

Section *Decolorantes*. Mild fleshy fungi, discolouring either through grey to blackish or reddish to brownish. Spore print cream.

Russula decolorans (Fr.) Fr.
Cap 8-12cm, hemispherical then truncate or expanded, orange to copper-coloured, soon turning brownish and blackening in places round the margin especially. Gills moderately spaced, pale cream, blackening on the edges. Stipe 7×1cm, dingy white to greyish, blackening at the base. Flesh greying, odourless, slightly acrid. Spores 13×10µm, with coarse warts and a few connecting lines; dermatocystidia present. Fe reaction pinkish. In wet places under conifers, in Europe especially in mountains. Uncommon, except remnant Scots Pine forest in Scotland. Edible. E1 (m3).

Russula vinosa Lindbl. (*R. obscura*)
Rather like *R. decolorans* but with cap more quickly expanded and even depressed, entirely dark purple. Gills and spores cream ochraceous. Gills and stipe discolouring greyish. Spores 10×9µm with isolated pointed warts; cuticle with encrusted primordial hyphae. Rare. Em2.

Russula claroflava Grove
Similar size but with first matt then shiny bright yellow cap and ochraceous gills. Stipe 6×1cm, white, bruising grey to blackish. Spores 9×7µm, with coarse warts connected by fine lines; cuticle and affinities as *R. vinosa*. Common under birch but also with alder and aspen, often in *Sphagnum*. E2.

Russula melliolens Quél.
Cap 9-12cm, bright red or carmine to orange tinged ± purple or brick colour, then spotted saffron russet like a big *R. puellaris*. Gills pale, looking more yellow when discoloured; print cream. Stipe 10×2cm, slightly swollen, with uneven profile, discolouring russet, sometimes pinkish. Flesh cream then yellowish, smell weak when gathered, becoming stronger as it dries, like honey; taste mild. Spores subglobose, 10×9µm, without warts but with a fine barely visible reticulum; cuticle with dermatocystidia. Under broadleaved trees. Uncommon. E3.

Russula artesiana Bon [*R. viscida* var. *occidentalis*]
Cap 10-25cm, soon depressed, greasy, at first vinaceous purple like *R. krombholtzii*, (p. 72), then almost entirely paling or turning russet from the centre outwards. Gills pale cream, often sloping or ± decurrent. Stipe 13×3cm, white, browning, dotted russet at the base. Flesh white, becoming reddish brown from the base upwards, smell weak, rather sour, taste rather sharp, the most acrid of the mild species. Spores a little less globose that in *R. melliolens* with more distinct reticulum; cuticle with dermatocystidia sometimes lightly encrusted. Under oak. Fairly common in Belgium and northern France, unknown in Britain. E2.

Section *Viridantes*. Similar in turning brown but smelling of crab and Fe reaction green. Spore print cream to ochraceous.

Russula xerampelina (Sch.) Fr. [*R. erythropoda*]
Cap 8-15cm, convex blackish purple or reddish to somewhat carmine at the margin, paling to rusty pink or ochraceous russet from the centre. Gills ochraceous, discolouring russet; spore print ochre. Stipe 7×2cm, ± entirely reddish, bright rusty towards the base. Flesh yellowing when cut; smell and reactions of the group. Spores 9×8µm, with rather isolated coarse obtuse warts. Common under pines, less often spruce. E4.

Russula graveolens Romell.
Cap 3-7cm, purplish brown or vinaceous, sometimes mingled with greenish or yellowish bronze. Gills tinged lemon then spotted russet; spore print cream ochraceous. Stipe 6×1cm, white, turning russet. Smell and reactions of the group. Spores 8×6µm, warted with some connecting lines. Under broadleaved trees mainly on acid soils. Common but usually included under *R. xerampelina* in British literature. E3.

R. faginea Romagn. is more robust, 12-15cm, reddish yellow, gills and spore print yellow ochre; smell at first weak, Fe reaction sometimes with pinkish zones. Under beech. E2.

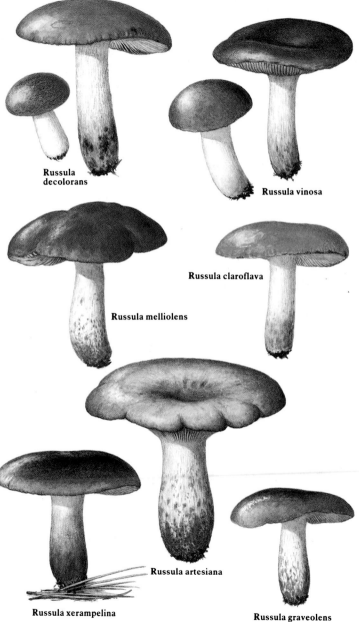

Russula
decolorans

Russula vinosa

Russula claroflava

Russula melliolens

Russula artesiana

Russula xerampelina

Russula graveolens

Section *Polychromae*. Robust, mild species, with yellow gills and cap various colours but not pure red. Spore print yellow.

Russula amara Kucera [*R. caerulea*]

Cap 8-10cm, conical then strongly umbonate, outline almost unique in the genus; cuticle smooth or shining, violaceous or slaty blue to vinaceous, sometimes spotted with russet. Gills medium yellow. Stipe 7×1cm, club- or spindle-shaped, sometimes almost rooting, white. Flesh white, smell weak, slightly fruity; taste ± bitter, especially in the cuticle. Spores 9×7μm, closely warted with an incomplete reticulum; cuticular hyphae encrusted. Sulfovanillin reaction red. Common throughout Britain under pines on acid soils. Edible. E3.

Russula integra (L.) Fr. [*R. polychroma*]

Cap fleshy, 6-15cm, yellowish brown mingled with shades of purplish brown or olive, dark purple without a brown tinge in f. *purpurella*, various greenish tints in f. *pseudoolivascens*. Gills medium yellow with paler edges. Stipe 10×2cm, white, then brownish ochre or greying slightly. Flesh creamy white with fruity smell; taste nutty, rather like paper after chewing. Spores 10×8μm with isolated pointed spines; cuticle with encrusted dermatocystidia and pointed hairs. Under conifers, especially fir and spruce, in the mountains, not uncommon under pines in the Highlands. Edible. Easily confused with *R. badia* (p. 76), which is acrid. E1 (m4).

Russula romellii R. Mre.

General outline like *R. integra* or with cap flattened sooner, brighter coloured, violaceous lilac ± mingled with red or green, rarely uniformly coloured (cf. *R. rubroalba*, (p. 68). Gills bright yellow to orange, brittle or splitting. Stipe 8×2cm, white. Flesh white, tinged lemon under the cuticle, not discolouring; smell and taste not distinctive. Spores 9×6.5μm, reticulate; dermatocystidia not encrusted. Under broadleaved trees, especially beech. Edible. E3. **R. carpini** Heinemann & Girard has much more varied cap colour with stipe yellowing like *R. puellaris* and less fragile gills; spores with long pointed warts. In copses under hornbeam. E2.

Russula curtipes Møll. & J. Schaef.

The same fleshy aspect as *R. integra*, but cap becoming depressed a little sooner, with pink or vinaceous tints round the margin but soon discoloured to cream ochraceous at the centre, sometimes a little olivaceous. Gills bright yellow, sometimes splitting. Stipe not always short but thickset 6×2cm, white. Flesh white, only slightly fruity. Spores 9×7μm, warted with an incomplete reticulum; dermatocystidia not encrusted. Under broadleaved trees especially beech. E2.

Russula curtipes Møll. & J. Schaef.

Russula carminipes Blum

Similar to the last but with cap a little more matt or pruinose round the margin, more persistently vinaceous purple, sometimes coppery or brick colour, seldom paling at the centre or only slowly so. Gills yellow. Stipe 8×2cm, often flushed pink up one side or near the base. Flesh white, firm with only a weakly fruity smell. Spores 9×7.5μm, with low warts and partial reticulum; dermatocystidia ± encrusted. Under broadleaved trees. Rare. E2.

Russula olivacea (Sch.) Pers.

Robust, cap 10-20cm, with distinctive, ± matt cuticle, often concentrically wrinkled towards the margin, variously coloured, greenish at first then ± carmine red. Gills bright yellow, edge sometimes pink. Stipe 13×3cm, white, pink at the apex, sometimes only in a narrow band beneath the gills. Flesh white, yellowing slightly, smell fruity when fresh. Phenol reaction bright purple. Cuticle with neither dermatocystidia nor encrusting primordial hyphae. Spores 11×9.5μm, with large isolated warts. Under beech and spruce. Edibility suspect. Not uncommon. E4.

Russula alutacea (Pers.) Fr.

Very similar to *R. olivacea*, but rather smaller, cap 8-15cm; cuticle smoother or shining, purplish red or vinaceous passing into yellow at the centre. Gills rather distant, bright yellow to orange, not very brittle. Stipe 10×2cm, ± red from the base or on one side. Flesh yellowing slightly; smell weak, sometimes like honey. Phenol reaction and cuticle as in *R. olivacea*. Spores 9×8μm, with reticulum and prominent ridges. Under broadleaved trees on calcareous soil. Uncommon. E2.

R. vinosobrunnea (Bres.) Romagn. is more diversely coloured, rather like *R. carpini*, but its stipe is seldom pure white and it does not discolour yellow. E3.

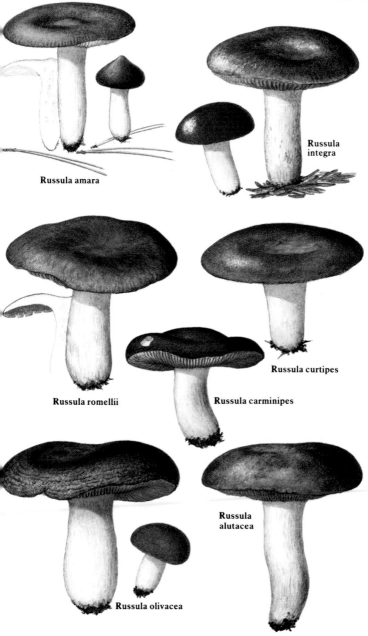

Russula amara

Russula integra

Russula romellii

Russula carminipes

Russula curtipes

Russula olivacea

Russula alutacea

Section *Coccineae*. Mild, ± robust species, coloured red, with ochre to yellow spore print.

Russula paludosa Britz.

A large fleshy fungus, cap 8-15cm, a distinctive fine bright red, pinkish or carmine to purple or ± orange, centre sometimes discoloured with age. Gills wide, obtuse, cream ochraceous yellow, sometimes with a pink edge. Stipe 13×3cm, slightly club-shaped, white or tinged pink, then greying slightly. Flesh white, soon soft and greying, odourless and tasteless. Spores ochraceous, 11×7.5μm, warted with an imperfect reticulum. Under conifers, especially pine and often in bogs, common in Scotland. E1-2.

Russula velenovskyi Mlz. & Zv.

Small or medium size, cap 5-12cm, not very fleshy, with a low central umbo in a depressed surface emphasising the diversity of shades of red present, more brick colour at the centre, sometimes coppery or rather orange in the median zone and more carmine round the margin. Gills rather narrow, with paler edges sometimes tinged pink towards the cap margin. Stipe equal, 7×1cm, often spotted pink at the base or on one side. Flesh white, smell weak or none. In var. *cruentata* the cap is more blood red and the gill edges distinctly pink. Spores ochraceous, 9×7μm, with mainly isolated warts; dermatocystidia ± attenuated or refringent. Under broadleaved trees, especially birch and oak, but also pine on acid soils, heaths. Not uncommon. Edible. E3.

Russula aurea Pers. [*R. aurata*]

Medium sized, cap 6-10cm, recognised by its colours, brick-red sometimes a little brownish or orange; underlying flesh bright yellow. Gills bright yellow from the first. Stipe 5×1cm, white or yellow. Flesh ± yellow near the surface, virtually odourless. Spores yellow, 9×7μm, subreticulate; cuticle with neither dermatocystidia nor encrusted hyphae. Under broadleaved trees in warm places. Uncommon in England. Edible. E3.

R. a. f. axantha lacks the yellow pigment and hence resembles the following two species. Difficult to recognise without microscopic examination. E2.

Russula laeta Møll. & J. Schaef.

Medium sized, resembling *R. aurea*, with shining cuticle, pinkish red, sometimes purplish or brick colour like *R. velenovskyi*, less often rusty or tinged olivaceous at the centre. Gills bright yellow. Stipe 6×1cm, white or greying slightly. Flesh white, with faint fruity smell, taste like *R. lepida*. Spores yellow, 9×8μm, with rather isolated warts; dermatocystidia scanty, not encrusted. Under broadleaved trees, especially beech. Uncommon. E2.

R. borealis Kfm. differs mainly in lacking the peculiar flavour and having encrusted dermatocystidia. E2.

Russula rubroalba (Sing.) Romagn.

Originally described as a red variety of *R. romellii* with which it shares all the other features, especially the fragile gills, orange yellow at maturity, the pure white stipe (8×2cm) and odourless flesh. Spores a little less reticulate; dermatocystidia as in *R. romellii* (p.66). E2.

Russula pseudointegra Arn. & Gor.

Cap 10-15cm, convex, fleshy, often hemispherical at first, uniformly fine cherry red with slightly rugose cuticle, often with a white bloom near the margin. Gills bright yellow or with salmon tint. Stipe 10×2cm, white, often veined, typically with a plaster white pith the consistency of bread crumbs. Flesh dull white with a strong fruity smell, like menthol or blackberry jam. Taste bitter. Spores yellow, 9×8μm, with low warts, partially connected by short lines; cuticle with encrusted primordial hyphae, of the *Chamaeleontinae* type. In copses of broadleaved trees especially in damp places. Not uncommon in southern England. E3.

R. aurantiaca (J. Schaef.) Romagn. ex Bon is smaller with the same smell but colour a little more brick red, approaching that of *R. velenovskyi*, and has ± encrusted dermatocystidia in the cuticle. E2.

Russula paludosa

R. borealis

Russula velenovskyi

Russula aurea

Russula laeta

Russula pseudointegra

Russula rubroalba

69

Section *Fragiles* [*Piperinae*]. Acrid species, not very fleshy, with white or pale cream spore print. Cuticle with dermatocystidia.

Subsection *Emeticinae*. Cap red, spore print white.

Russula emetica (Sch.) Pers.
Cap 3-10cm, a fine bright red, cherry or vermilion tint, discoloured to yellowish at the centre in var. *silvestris*, cuticle separable, subcuticular flesh white. Gills white, moderately spaced. Stipe 7×1cm, white, rather soft and compressible. Flesh persistently pure white with distinctive smell of coconut, taste very acrid. Spores 12×10μm, with coarse warts and a fairly complete reticulum. The typical form occurs on wet ground under conifers or in *Sphagnum*. E2. The var. *silvestris* comes under beech on dry acid soils. Common throughout Britain. E4.

R. nana Kill. [*R. alpina* p.p.], its homologue in alpine areas (Scotland), is less acrid. Em2.

Russula fageticola (Melz.) Lund.
Cap 3-8cm, relatively fleshy or hard, with slightly matt surface, bright vermilion to carmine, reminiscent of *R. lepida*, cuticle peeling readily to expose pink flesh. Gills rather crowded, white or tinged yellowish. Stipe 4×1cm, and flesh showing a slight tendency to yellowing. Taste acrid, smell fruity, sometimes a little like *R. emetica*. Spores 9×7μm, with smaller warts that in *R. emetica* and a ± complete reticulum. Under beech. Very common throughout Britain. Easily confused with *R. emetica* var. *silvestris* (above) from which it differs especially in having the cap cuticle less commonly discoloured and crowded, and sometimes glaucous gills. E4.

R. mairei Sing. is more compact with a slightly velvet cuticle and a smell of honey with age. Very common in Britain under beech. E2.

Russula griseascens (Bon & Gaugué) L. Marti
Cap bright red like *R. emetica*, to which it was first referred as a variety, margin slightly furrowed, eventually becoming dingy carmine pink and greying. Gills somewhat distant, greyish. Stipe 6×1cm, slightly spongy, veined, soon greying. Flesh dingy white to greyish with a weak coconut smell. Spores as in *R. fageticola*. In bogs with *Sphagnum*. E2.

Russula luteotacta Rea
A little like *R. mairei*, with more firmly adnate cuticle, separable near the margin only, with the colour soon washed out and yellowing strongly though slowly, especially at the level of the gills or the stipe. Gills sloping to subdecurrent, rather distant in var. *oligophylla*, which has a rather crenulate margin. Stipe rather short, 4×1cm, white, tinged pink and yellowing strongly where bruised or scratched but only slowly, sometimes only by the next day. Smell none, taste moderately acrid. Spores 9×7μm, warted with a few connecting lines. In damp copses, often under hornbeam, in ruts on clay soil or the edge of ponds, on more basic soils in England. E3.

Russula betularum Hora
A small, fragile fungus, cap 3-5cm, with readily separable cuticle, and slightly striate margin, pale pink or whitish turning to ochraceous or slightly bluish lilac at the centre. Gills, stipe (3×0.5cm) and flesh pure white, brittle; with a faint smell like *R. emetica*, fairly acrid. Spores as in *R. emetica* or smaller. Very common under birch throughout Britain. E3.

Russula knauthii Sing.
This is often regarded as only a red form of *R. fragilis* (p. 72), but is placed here because its cap is bright red, scarcely tinged with lilac. Cap 5-8cm with striate or slightly crenulate margin. Gills fairly distant, white. Stipe 6×1cm, rather firm, white. Flesh white with the sweet smell of the *R. fragilis* group. Spores 10×8μm, warted and reticulate rather like *R. emetica*. Under various broadleaved trees, often in damp places. Common. E2.

Russula emetica

R. e.
var. silvestris

R. mairei

Russula griseascens

Russula betularum

Russula fageticola

Russula luteotacta

var. oligophylla

Russula knauthii

71

Subsection *Atropurpurinae*. Acrid species with white spore print and cap various colours but not pure red.

Russula krombholzii Shaffer [*R. atropurpurea*]
Cap 8-15cm, convex, soon flattened, margin not striate. Reddish purple, blackish at the centre, or carmine-purple towards the margin, often quickly losing colour and becoming pale with age or spotted pinkish. Gills dull white or pale dingy cream. Stipe 5×1cm, white, turning grey when soaked, often with rusty spots towards the base. Flesh dull whitish, smelling of apples, not very acrid (the mildest of the acrid group). Spores 8×7cm, with small warts and a complete reticulum. Under broad-leaved trees, especially in grassy glades; common throughout Britain, especially under oak. E4.

Russula aquosa Leclair
More fragile and watery, cap 5-8cm with margin striate when moist, rather uniformly coloured a distinctive pinkish violet, sometimes rather carmine-lilac at the centre. Gills fairly distant, dull white. Stipe 8×1cm, white, soft or spongy, greyish when sodden. Flesh soft and fragile, hyaline. Smell weak, sometimes of radish or like that of *R. emetica*; taste fairly acrid. Spores 9×7µm, with low warts and fairly complete reticulum. Under spruce or pine in swamps or among *Sphagnum*; in Scotland. E2.

Russula atrorubens Quél.
Similar in outline but less fragile; cap 6-8cm, margin scarcely striate, darker coloured or banded with a purplish black centre and carmine pink margin. Gills not crowded, whitish. Stipe 5×1cm, slightly club-shaped, white, occasionally tinged pink, yellowing slightly at the base. Flesh white with a faintly fruity smell and quite acrid taste. Spores 8×6µm, with a fairly complete reticulum. Under conifers, often in wet places. E3.

Russula fragilis (Pers.) Fr.
Cap thin or fragile, 2-6cm, margin striate, colour varied from lilaceous violet to olivaceous or greenish, less often mingled with pinkish or yellowish tints. Gills white, margin typically denticulate. Stipe 3×0.5cm, soft, dingy white or yellowing on drying. Smell strong and sweet, rather like amyl acetate or boiled sweets; taste very acrid. Spores 9×7.5µm, with low warts and a complete fine-meshed reticulum. Very common throughout Britain under broadleaved trees. E4. Colour forms occur under conifers: f. **violascens** is entirely lilaceous violet; f. **fallax** banded like *R. turci*.

Subsection *Violaceinae*. Rather fragile, acrid species with a cream spore print and often a distinctive smell.

Russula violacea Quél.
Cap 4-6cm, not very fragile, with margin scarcely striate; coloured green or violaceous to lilac, sometimes in concentric zones with green predominant towards the centre. Gills cream, yellowing slightly, fairly distant. Stipe 4×1cm, soft, yellowing, as does the flesh. Smell fruity, rather like pelargonium. Spores 9×7µm, with isolated rather long pointed warts. Under various broadleaved trees. E3.

Russula cavipes Britz.
A variable species, cap 2-8cm, from fragile to rather fleshy, with the varied coloration of *R. fragilis* and often a striate margin. Gills white, rather distant, yellowing. Stipe 6×1cm, slightly club-shaped, soon becoming hollow, yellowing strongly to almost saffron from the base upwards. Flesh white, then yellow with a strong distinctive smell of saffron or laudanum. Ammonia reaction pink. Spores 9×8µm, with rather coarse crowded warts connected by a few lines. Under conifers. E2.

Russula pelargonia Niolle
Similar to the two preceding species, cap 4-6cm, margin striate, colour more lilac or darker to wine colour, rarely tinged greenish. Gills distant, dingy cream. Stipe (5×8cm) and flesh greying slightly. Smell strong, of pelargonium. Spores 9×8µm, with rather coarse warts and short ridges. Under broadleaved trees in damp places, especially poplar and willow. E2.

R. clariana Heim ex Kuyper is more fleshy, margin not striate, coloured violaceous and green like *R. violacea* but discolouring rather greyish and with strong smell of pelargonium. Under white or grey poplar. E2.

Russula krombholzii

Russula aquosa

Russula fragilis

f. **violascens**

Russula atrorubens

Russula violacea

Russula cavipes

Russula pelargonia

Section *Sanguineae*. More or less robust acrid fungi with ochraceous-cream gills and spore print; cap colour red or violaceous, sometimes mixed with green. Cuticle with dermatocystidia.

Russula gracillima J. Schaef.
Not fleshy but relatively slender, cap 3-7cm, with pastel shades of pink and leaf green, sometimes with lilac zones, margin slightly lobed, not striate. Gills pale; spore print cream. Stipe 7×0.6cm, rather soft, flushed pink at least on one side. Flesh remaining white, with faint rather fruity smell, taste slightly acrid. Spores 9×7μm, with isolated warts. Especially under birch and willow. Common throughout Britain. E3.

Russula exalbicans (Pers.) Mlz.-Zv.
More flrts. Especially under birch and willow. Common. E3.

Russula exalbicans (Pers.) Mlz.-Zv.
More fleshy, cap 10-15cm, soon flattened, at first entirely pink or vinaceous red but quickly discolouring, starting at the margin, rarely tinged greenish. Gills crowded, dingy pale ochre. Stipe rather stout, 9×1cm, white, rarely tinged pinkish but greying with age. Flesh dingy white, smell faint, taste fairly acrid. Spores 9×7.5μm, warts partially linked by an imperfect reticulum. Under birch especially on calcareous soils. Probably common in Britain but confused with *R. pulchella*. E3.

R. pulchella Borsz. has been confused with *R. exalbicans* which it resembles in colour but with the size of *R. gracillima*. cE2.

Russula persicina Krombh. [*R. rubicunda*]
Similar in outline to *R. emetica*, cap cherry red with smooth, shining, separable cuticle but distinguished by the gills which are ochre at maturity. Stipe 7×1cm, white, seldom tinged pinkish, flesh persistently white with a faint smell rather like that of *R. emetica*. Var. *intactior* becomes generally discoloured or tinged greyish so as somewhat to resemble *R. exalbicans*. Spores 8×7μm, with rather isolated warts linked by a few short ridges. Under hornbeam and lime. E2.

Russula sanguinea (Bull.) Fr. [*R. rosacea* p.p.]
Cap 8-12cm, rather fleshy with obtuse margin, not striate, cuticle not readily separable, slightly granular, shining, bright blood-red, not paling apart from eventually a few ochraceous patches towards the centre. Gills slightly arched to subdecurrent, ochraceous. Stipe thickset, 6×2cm, sometimes spindle-shaped, bright red like the cap or mottled red on an ochraceous ground, yellowing towards the base. Flesh firm, finally ochraceous, smell faint, taste pungent. Spores 9×7.5μm, with isolated warts. Common throughout Britain under conifers, especially pine. E3.

Russula queletii Fr.
A little more slender than *R. sanguinea*, cap 6-8cm, purplish pink or redcurrant colour, margin rather carmine, paling throughout with age or when soaked by rain. Gills cream to ochraceous, slightly greenish where damaged. Stipe 6×1cm, a distinctive carmine red, somewhat veined or subreticulate. Flesh pearly white with fruity smell like stewed apple; taste weakly acrid. Spores 9×7μm, with isolated warts. Under pines or planted spruce on calcareous soil; in mountains. E1 (m4).

R. fuscorubroides Bon has a darker cap, purplish black, scarcely paling, gills not greening, and slightly crested spores. E3.

Russula torulosa Bres.
Cap 10-15cm, convex, fleshy, cuticle shining, dark violaceous purple to carmine. Gills dull ochre. Stipe short, 5×2cm, violaceous with bluish tints, pruinose. Flesh pale, strong smell of fresh apples, taste weakly acrid. Spores 10×8μm, reticulate. Under pine on sandy or calcareous soils, often on hillsides of basalt or limestone in Europe. E3.

R. fuscorubra (Bres.) Sing., with the same smell and habitat, has a more slender stipe, a more blackish cap and barely reticulate spores. E2.

Russula drimeia Cke. [*R. sardonia* p.p.]
Characterised by the bright lemon tint of the gills, especially while still unripe. Cap similar to *R. torulosa* but stipe 10×2cm, more slender, a beautiful bright violaceous colour, slightly veined. Flesh lemon colour under the cuticle, smell faint, taste very pungent. Spores 9×7μm, with an incomplete reticulum. Very common in Britain under pine on sandy soils. E4.

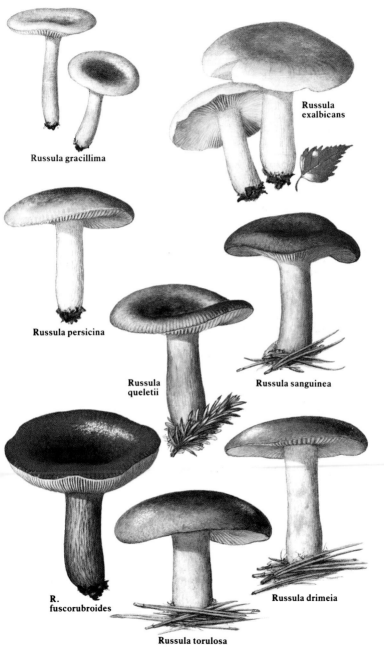

Russula gracillima

Russula
exalbicans

Russula persicina

Russula
queletii

Russula sanguinea

R.
fuscorubroides

Russula torulosa

Russula drimeia

75

Section *Insidiosae*. Acrid fungi with yellow to orange spore print. Dermatocystidia.

Russula firmula J. Schaef. [*R. transiens* s.s. Romagn.]
Medium sized cap, 6-8cm, surface glossy, vinaceous violet to bluish grey or slightly olive brown at the centre; margin not striate. Gills tinged orange. Stipe 7×1cm, firm, white, yellowing slightly or spotted with rust. Smell that of *R. pseudointegra* or recalling pelargonium. Spores 9×7.5μm, finely warted to ± conspicuously banded. Under conifers in the mountains, often among bilberry. Em4.

Russula urens Romell [*R. adulterina* p.p.]
Cap 9-12cm, convex becoming slightly depressed, margin striate, cuticle smooth or shining, green ± tinged with grey, olive or bronze-lilac. Gills rather distant, broad, obtuse, bright yellow then orange. Stipe 10×2cm, equal, white. Flesh whitish, almost odourless, slowly acrid. Spores 10×8μm, with coarse isolated spines; cuticle with dermatocystidia mixed with compact, nodulose, pointed hairs. Under broadleaved trees. E2.

This belongs to the **R. cuprea** Krombh. complex, not known in Britain, which comprises a series of varieties or forms with cap colours ranging from the typical coppery fawn to reddish brown, grey violet, yellow orange etc., all with striate margin and broad orange gills. E3.

Russula badia Quél.
Cap 8-13cm, blackish purple to reddish brown, sometimes rather carmine or rose-wood colour, with shining cuticle; margin not striate. Gills pale yellow, sometimes pink on the edges. Stipe 8×1cm, white, often with a pink patch on the side. Flesh white with smell of cedar oil or pencil wood, sometimes only faint; taste the most acrid in the genus though sometimes slow in developing in the mouth. Spores 9×7μm, with small warts and a ± developed reticulum. Under conifers, chiefly in Highland Scotland. El (m3).

Russula veternosa Fr.
Cap 6-10cm, soon depressed, margin finally slightly striate, cuticle reddish round the margin, sometimes a little vinaceous or discoloured towards the centre or with livid ochraceous tints. Gills rather crowded and brittle, bright yellow. Stipe 5×2cm, pure white at first, becoming ashy ochraceous, soon soft and spongy except in f. *duriuscula* which is more compact with washed out colouring. Smell rather like pelargonium then like honey. Spores 8×6.5μm, with isolated spinose warts. Under broadleaved trees. E2.

Russula maculata Quél.
Cap 8-12cm, persistently hemispherical, fleshy or with incurved margin, mottled red, orange and yellow, becoming ± spotted rusty as in *R. melliolens*. Gills somewhat distant, bright yellow. Stipe hard, thickset, 5×2cm, white, eventually slightly ochraceous, seldom flushed pinkish. Flesh pale ochraceous cream with rather fruity smell like the wood of a pencil; taste only slightly acrid, sometimes almost mild. Spores variable, 9-12×8-9μm, warted with very incomplete reticulum. Under broadleaved trees, especially beech, on calcareous soils. Uncommon. E3.

R. mesospora Sing. has much more beautiful colouring, bright orange-red, seldom or only slowly discoloured to coppery or ochraceous. Spores 8×6μm, warted with a few short ridges. Under birch. El.

Russula decipiens (Sing.) K.-R. ex Svr.
Cap 10-15cm, soon depressed, with incurved margin, cuticle smooth, shining, vinaceous red round the margin, discoloured to ochre or olivaceous at the centre. Gills broad, bright orange at maturity. Stipe 10×2cm, white, greying slightly. Flesh dull white, with faint fruity smell a little like *R. emetica*; taste rather acrid. Spores 10×8μm, with warts often in rows or fused to form ridges. Under broadleaved trees on rather acid soils. E3.

R. rubra (Lamk.) Fr. is brighter red than the above, or with a paler margin, more like *R. pseudointegra*, its smell is less distinct, more like honey and its taste is much more acrid. In microscopic characters it is akin to *R. lepida*. E2.

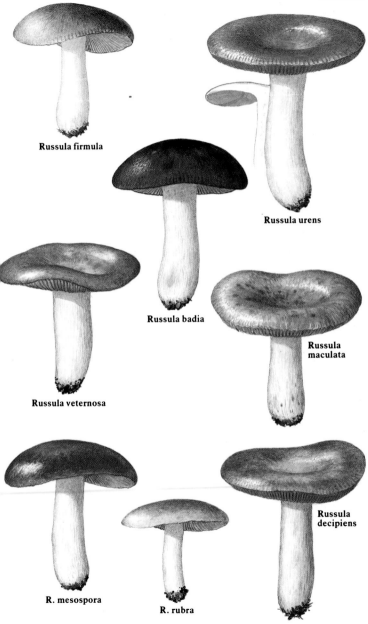

Russula firmula

Russula urens

Russula badia

Russula maculata

Russula veternosa

Russula decipiens

R. mesospora

R. rubra

Section *Ingratae*. Colours dull, taste or smell unpleasant. Spore print white or pale cream.

Subsection *Foetentinae*. Margin acute, striate or furrowed. Stipe hollow, smell strong. Dermatocystidia short or conical.

Russula foetens Pers.
A large fungus with cap 12-20cm, globular at first, then expanded and wavy, russet to bread crust colour, margin tuberculate, with long parallel furrows. Gills ± distant, dingy cream. Stipe 13×4cm, a similar colour or paler, often misshapen. Flesh pale, foetid, taste unpleasant. Spores 11×8.5μm, with coarse isolated spines. Very common in Britain under broadleaved trees and conifers, especially in damp woods. Sometimes not breaking much above the soil surface. Not edible. E4.

Russula laurocerasi Melzer [*R. fragrans*]
Rather less robust, cap 8-12cm, ± russet, rather like *R. foetens*. Gills whitish or speckled rusty brown. Stipe 10×2cm, almost equal, pale. Flesh white, with strong smell of cherry laurel or bitter almond, sometimes almost foetid with age and slightly recalling that of *R. foetens*. Taste unpleasant. Spores ± globose, 11×10μm, with a few very prominent long ridges. Under broadleaved trees, especially oak, fairly common in Britain. Edible but poor quality. E3.

This is a collective species within which have been distinguished: **R. fragrantissima** Romagn., with margin scarcely tuberculate and a strong, clean smell (E2); and **R. illota** Romagn., with a hint of violet in the cap mucus and black dots on stipe and gills (E3).

Russula amoenolens Romagn. [*R. sororia* p.p.]
Cap 7-10cm, coloured greyish or bistre, at least at the centre. Stipe 5×1cm, similar or pale. Gills pale. Strong smell of Jerusalem artichokes; taste acrid. Spores 8×6μm finely warted with only a few connecting lines. Under broadleaved trees and in grassy glades. E3.

R. pectinatoides Peck, often found with *amoenolens*, is paler and distinguished by a rubbery smell and a mild but unpleasant taste. E3.

Russula farinipes Romell
Cap not fleshy, 5-7cm, margin thin, rather elastic, undulating or furrowed, cuticle matt, rather bright pale yellow. Gills rather distant, remarkably flexible and elastic, white. Stipe white, 6×0.6cm, apex mealy. Flesh not very brittle, white, smelling of apples. Taste fairly acrid. Spores 7×6μm with small rather distant warts. Under broadleaved trees on clay soil, rather uncommon in southern England. E2.

R. pectinata Fr. may be similar in colour but has the normal *Russula* texture, a nauseous smell and more acrid taste. E1.

Subsection *Felleinae*. Cap margin obtuse, not striate, stipe solid; transitional to sections *Fragiles* or *Lilaceae*.

Russula fellea (Fr.) Fr.
Cap 6-10cm, convex, soon flattened, with rather uniform colouring, ochraceous russet in the cap and similar but paler tint in stipe and gills. Stipe 6×1cm. Flesh persistently creamy ochraceous with a smell of stewed apple, sometimes slightly of pelargonium, and acrid taste. Spores 9×7.5μm, warted with an incomplete reticulum. Under spruce but especially beech in Britain. Common. E4.

Russula consobrina (Fr.) Fr.
Cap similar in outline or larger, 8-12cm, surface rather dingy bistre brown. Gills whitish, darkening. Stipe 10×2cm, concolorous with cap or tinged grey brown about the middle. Flesh pale, greying or reddening. Smell weak, taste fairly acrid. Spores 10×8μm, reticulate. In willow beds or muddy spruce plantations. E1.

Russula ochroleuca Pers.
Cap 8-12cm, convex, soon flattened, a bright or dull shade of yellow ochre, sometimes olivaceous. Gills white, contrasting with the cap. Stipe 7×1cm, whitish, greying when wet or yellowing when dry. Flesh pale, odourless, taste more or less acrid. Spores 10×8μm, warted with a ± complete reticulum; cuticular hyphae often encrusted with yellow pigment. Ubiquitous under broadleaved trees and conifers, very common throughout Britain. E4.

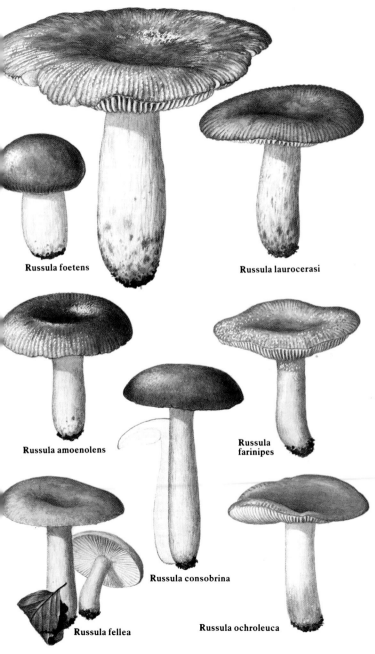

Russula foetens

Russula laurocerasi

Russula amoenolens

Russula
farinipes

Russula consobrina

Russula fellea

Russula ochroleuca

Genus *Lactarius*. Flesh yielding milky fluid when broken. Gills sloping to somewhat arched or decurrent. See key, p. 338.

Section *Dapetes*. Milk red or orange. Taste mild, sometimes unpleasant or bitter. Spore print white.

Lactarius deliciosus (L.) S.F. Gray

Robust, cap 10-20cm, margin often lobed, cuticle slightly viscid, with hoary zones or concentric bands of orange staining on a ground of ochraceous orange to pale brick colour. Gills bright orange. Stipe short or thickset, 5×2cm, expanded below the gills, almost concolorous, pitted. Milk and flesh orange or paler, then turning green, becoming vinaceous in f. *rubescens*; smell faint. Spores 8×6μm, reticulate with a few marked ridges. Under pine on neutral to calcareous soils. Widespread, though not common in Britain. Edible. E3.

L. quieticolor Romagn. has regular cap 7-12cm, a more reddish grey colour to dull brownish and occurs under pine on acid soils. E3.

Lactarius deterrimus Gröger [*L. deliciosus* var. *piceae*]

Less robust, cap 10-12cm, more regular or soon becoming depressed, margin acute, circular; zones crowded towards the margin, in radial streaks towards the centre, without distinctive stains, bright orange all over, scarcely hoary, greening with age. Gills orange, arched or almost decurrent. Stipe equal, 7×1cm, somewhat orange not pitted or slightly so, pruinose with a white belt below the gills. Flesh and milk orange, slowly reddening and finally green; smell fruity or of carrot, taste unpleasant. Spores 10×6.5μm, banded. Strictly associated with spruce. Edible, but less good than *L. deliciosus*. E4.

Lactarius salmonicolor Heim & Lecl.

Rather fleshy, cap convex, 10-15cm, sometimes lobed or wavy, not markedly zoned but marked with orange stains on a ground colour of ochraceous orange, pale pinkish or salmon. Gills more horizontal, pale orange, sometimes stained vinaceous brown where wounded. Stipe 8×2cm, equal, barely pitted, concolorous or paler. Milk and flesh orange, often turning reddish brown in a few minutes; smell weak, slightly soapy; taste bitter. Spores 11×7.5μm, reticulate with a few distinct bands. Under fir (*Abies*) only. Edible, best grilled. E3.

Lactarius semisanguifluus Heim & Lecl.

Medium size, 5-10cm, cap fleshy, only slightly depressed, surface only slightly hoary, dull or pale orange, sometimes a little vinaceous brown towards the margin, soon greening then paling again. Gills orange then with flesh coloured tints, vinaceous where wounded. Stipe 6×1cm, paler, not pitted. Flesh orange then vinaceous in a few minutes, turning green by the following day. Spores 10×8μm, with almost complete reticulum. Under pine, often on calcareous soil. Edible. E2.

Lactarius sanguifluus (Paul.) Fr.

Cap like the preceding but more hoary and often zoned with pinkish and orange, only slightly greening. Gills orange with distinctive pinkish tint, finally a little vinaceous. Stipe 5×1cm, ± pitted, reddish orange, sometimes with violaceous tints. Flesh whitish when cut, reddened by the milk which immediately turns vinaceous red like blood. Spores 9×7μm, ± reticulate. Under pine, perhaps only within the limits of vine cultivation. Not British. A good edible species. sE4.

There are also species with bluish green milk, either throughout as in **L. indigo** (Schw.) Fr. in North America and southern France, or only in the cap as in **L. hemicyaneus** Romagn., in France and the Netherlands. Both E1.

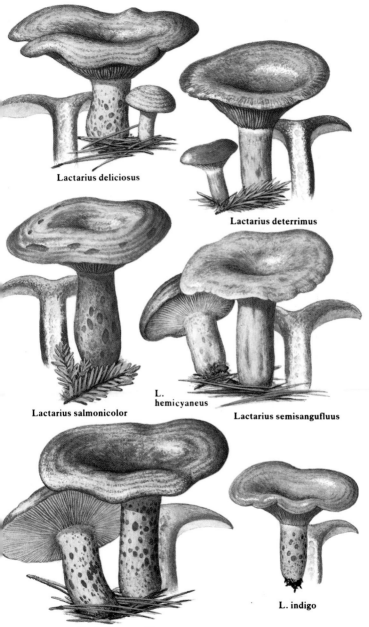

Lactarius deliciosus

Lactarius deterrimus

L. hemicyaneus

Lactarius salmonicolor

Lactarius semisangufluus

Lactarius sanguifluus

L. indigo

Section *Zonarii*. Cap glabrous, slightly viscid, ± zoned, colours yellowish to russet or orange, milk permanently white. Taste acrid. Spore print white.

Lactarius zonarius (Bull.) Fr.
Cap 8-12cm, of pale yellowish ground colour, zoned ochraceous. Gills white, arched. Stipe 5×1cm, whitish, smooth, pitted in var. *scrobipes*. Flesh white, slowly turning pinkish; smell faint. Spores 8×6μm, ± reticulate. Under broadleaved trees in copses on heavy calcareous soils. Edible after blanching but poor quality. E2.

L.evosmus K.-R. is said to differ in being paler, with no colour change in the flesh and with a stronger fruity smell, but is not recognised by some authors. E2.

Lactarius acerrimus Britz. [*L. insulsus* p.p.]
Often larger, cap 10-15cm, irregular or lobed to somewhat excentric, with ochraceous russet zones on a cream or ochraceous ground near the margin and a glabrous ochraceous russet centre. Gills pinkish, often contorted or anastomosing near the point of attachment to the stipe. Stipe short 5×2cm, pitted, whitish. Flesh white, smell pleasant or fruity. Spores variable, 12-15×8-10μm, ± reticulate, on 2-spored basidia. Under broadleaved trees in damp woods, on tracks and in cart ruts. Uncommon in Britain. E3.

Lactarius porninsis Roll.
Cap 5-10cm, scarcely depressed, quite orange, zoning vague, fleeting or formed by water-soaked stains of the milk. Gills cream, crowded. Stipe 6×1cm, concolorous, slightly pitted. Flesh pale with distinctive smell, rather aromatic or like that of *Russula emetica*. Spores 8.5×7μm, reticulate with a few stronger ridges. Exclusively under larch. E2.

Section *Tricholomoidei*. As *Zonarii* but margin bearded and fleecy.

Lactarius torminosus (Sch.) S.F. Gray
Medium size, cap 8-12cm, soon umbilicate, centre viscid, margin ± zoned, brick colour on a pinkish ground, cap edge very fleecy and bearded. Gills pinkish, nearly horizontal. Stipe 8×1cm, white with pinkish pits. Flesh white, smell of pelargonium or faintly fruity; taste very acrid. Milk staying white or only yellowing on a handkerchief. Spores 9×6μm, reticulate. Under birch. Very common throughout Britain. Not edible. E4. **L. pubescens** (Schrad.) Fr. [*L. blumii*] is whitish to pale pinkish cream throughout, not zoned, with spores 7×5μm, under birch on calcareous soil, or in gardens or parkland. E3. **L. favrei** Jahn [*L. pubescens* p.p.] is smaller, scarcely bearded and occurs in bogs. E2.

Lactarius mairei Malç.
Similar to *L. torminosus* but more reddish brown, not pink, somewhat zoned with orange in var. *zonatus*; margin heavily bearded, sometimes dishevelled. Gills rather sloping, white to cream. Stipe 5×1cm, almost smooth or a little furrowed, not pitted, dingy cream to ochraceous. Flesh pale, flushing slightly pink or grey, sometimes drying olivaceous; smell of pelargonium, taste acrid, especially the milk. Spores 8×6.5μm, ± reticulate to striped. Under broadleaved trees. Rare, under oak. sE2.

Lactarius scrobiculatus (Scop.) Fr.
Large fungus, cap 12-25cm with incurved margin slightly fleecy with only short beard, yellow to ochraceous russet, ± zoned. Gills rather distant, cream, yellowing. Stipe short or thickset, 6×3cm, with yellowish pits. Flesh white, quickly yellowed when cut by the white milk which goes yellow on exposure to the air; smell faint, taste acrid. Spores 9×7μm, with a few prominent bands. Under conifers in the mountains, and in Highland Scotland. Inedible though not toxic. Em4.

Lactarius citriolens Pouz. [*L. resimus* p.p.]
A large fungus similar to *L. scrobiculatus* but with cap surface more pale yellowish a heavily bearded margin and a few rather velvety inner zones. Gills sloping, cream, yellowing. Stipe 8×3cm, slightly enlarged or irregular and hairy at the base, whitish or cream ochraceous. Flesh yellowing when cut, smell distinctive, rather fruity, of pelargonium or lemon; taste acrid and bitter. Spores 8×6μm, reticulate. Under broadleaved trees on calcareous soil. Edible but of poor quality. E3. **L. resimus** (Fr.) Fr. is similar but entirely white at first and occurs on heaths or under various broadleaved trees on acid soils. E2.

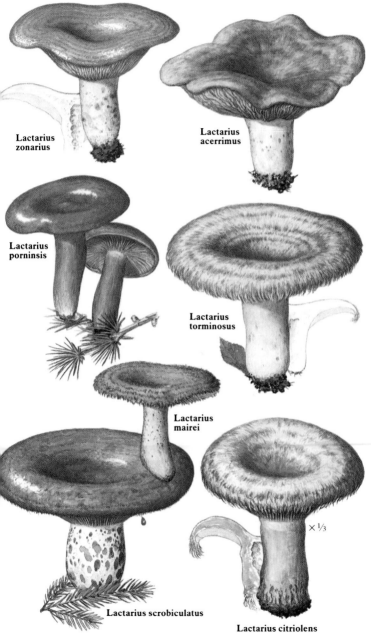

Lactarius
zonarius

Lactarius
acerrimus

Lactarius
porninsis

Lactarius
torminosus

Lactarius
mairei

Lactarius scrobiculatus

$\times 1/3$

Lactarius citriolens

83

Section *Pyrogali*. Viscid. Milk remaining white, not staining the gills on drying, there may be at most a slight yellowing or greening.

Lactarius pallidus (Pers.) Fr.
Medium size, cap 5-10cm, regularly convex, not zoned or rarely with a few bands of sodden spots, pale pinkish cream to whitish, ageing to almost beige. Gills nearly horizontal, white. Stipe equal, 7×1cm, white. Flesh white, odourless; taste acrid. Spores 9×7μm, ± reticulate. Under beech. Quite common in England and north to the Moray Firth. E3.

L. musteus Fr. is a rare fungus of damp conifer woods in the mountains, and in Highland Scotland, more ochraceous in colour, with a matt to downy cuticle and somewhat pitted stipe. Em1.

Lactarius curtus Britz. [*L. hysginus* p.p.]
Medium size, with cap 8-10cm, characterised by a ± pinkish or violaceous zoning on a yellowish ochraceous ground, by gills with a lemon tint and a strong aromatic odour like sealing wax. Stipe short, 4×1cm, pale, almost the colour of the gills, rarely pitted. Taste acrid. Spores 8×6μm, reticulate. Under broadleaved trees in damp places, acid soils or among *Sphagnum*. Rare in Britain, under conifers. E2.

Lactarius pyrogalus (Bull.) Fr.
Cap 5-8cm, soon depressed, not or rarely zoned, livid ochre, sometimes slightly olivaceous or with a hint of lilac. Gills distant, orange-ochre. Stipe 5×1cm, smooth or furrowed, whitish. Flesh white, almost unaltered, as is the milk; odourless, taste very acrid, especially the milk which burns the tongue (hence the name.) The milk usually turns yellow with KOH reaction but the reaction is not specific or constant. Spores variable, 6-9×5-7μm, banded. Especially under hornbeam and common under hazel throughout Britain. E3.

Lactarius circellatus Fr.
Usually but not invariably distinguished from *L. pyrogalus* by the cap being zoned with greyish bands on an ochre ground, becoming slightly violaceous with age, sometimes hoary or only slightly viscid. Gills more crowded than in *L. pyrogalus* but the same orange ochre. Stipe 5×1cm, often tinged pale violaceous bistre or greyish lilac. Flesh remaining white, KOH reaction none or doubtful. Spores 7.5×5μm, banded. Fairly common, often under hazel on the Continent, but in Britain almost invariably under hornbeam. E3.

Lactarius roseozonatus (V. Post.) Bat.
Remarkable for its relatively fleshy cap, 6-10cm, with margin sometimes lobed and wavy, surface with rather vague grey-pink zones on a pinkish cream to lilac ground. Gills distant as in *L. pyrogalus* but at most cream. Stipe rather short, 4×2cm, almost concolorous, striate above by decurrence of the gills. Flesh pale, milk acrid, unchanging. Spores 8×7μm, ± reticulate. Under broadleaved trees and pines. E2.

L. flexuosus (Pers.) S.F. Gray is typically less zoned, with whitish stipe and more crowded gills, sometimes spotted but the name has been interpreted in different ways. E2.

Lactarius trivialis (Fr.) Fr.
Robust fungus with cap 12-20cm, fleshy, scarcely depressed, viscid, at first a fine purplish violet, stained with darker zones, then paling to pinkish and beige pink throughout so as to be unrecognisable eventually as the same thing. Gills pale to cream ochraceous, or sometimes spotted very pale greenish yellow by the milk. Stipe elongated or club-shaped, 13×4cm, often hollow and sodden, whitish to cream. Flesh pale, smell rather like *Russula emetica*, taste quite acrid. Spores 10×8.5μm, reticulate. Under conifers in damp places, bogs and *Sphagnum* and also under birch. E3.

Lactarius pallidus

Lactarius curtus

Lactarius pyrogalus

Lactarius circellatus

Lactarius roseozonatus

× ¹/₃

Lactarius trivialis

Section *Vieti*. ± viscid. Milk greying or browning on drying and gills spotted with it.

Lactarius vietus (Fr.) Fr.
Small to medium, cap 4-10cm, often thin and wavy, surface only slightly viscid, soon dry, pale lilac grey or with brownish violet tints. Gills cream ochraceous with hint of orange, then spotted grey-brown. Stipe often slender, 8×1cm, sometimes club-shaped, soon hollow, white to greyish. Flesh white, nearly odourless, not very acrid. Spores 8×6.5μm, ± reticulate. Under birch, most luxuriant among *Sphagnum*. Common throughout Britain. Edible after blanching. E4.

Lactarius blennius (Fr.) Fr.
Medium stature, cap 6-10cm, first convex, then depressed, very viscid and slippery in wet weather, ± zoned brown-violaceous to grey-purple, or greenish in var. *viridis*, sometimes more plentiful than the type. Gills white, spotted olive-grey where rubbed. Stipe 5×1cm, pale pinkish grey or whitish. Flesh white, milk also remaining white if isolated; odourless, acrid. Spores 8×6μm, banded. Under beech and common wherever this tree is planted, throughout Britain. E4.

Lactarius fluens Boud.
Cap similar to *L. blennius* or more fleshy, rather more olivaceous brown, sometimes pinkish, distinctly zoned, less viscid. Gills cream, spotted reddish brown. Stipe 6×2cm, whitish. Flesh white and milk particularly plentiful, hence the name. Spores 9×6.5μm, banded or ridged; cuticular hairs ± capitate. Under beech. E3.

Lactarius plumbeus (Bull.) S.F. Gray [*L. necator, L. turpis*]
Cap 5-12cm, rather fleshy, finally depressed with incurved margin slightly velvety at first; surface not very viscid, soon matt, colour unusual, ochraceous olive-brown with bronze tints or yellowish sometimes blackening with age. Gills dull whitish or glaucous, spotted olive brown where rubbed, by the milk. Stipe 6×1cm, nearly the same colour as the cap, sometimes pitted. Flesh glaucous, browning slightly; smell faint, taste becoming bitter, like ivy or spinach. Ammonia reaction striking purplish violet. Spores 9×7μm, banded. Common throughout Britain especially under birch, sometimes with pine. Not a good edible fungus. E4.

Section *Uvidi*. Viscid. Milk turning violet on exposure to the air.

Lactarius uvidus (Fr.) Fr.
Small to medium size, cap 5-8cm, remaining convex, viscid, coloured pale lilac beige. Gills pale cream ochraceous, nearly horizontal or arched, discoloured violet when rubbed. Stipe 8×1cm, whitish like the flesh, then lilac-violet when cut; odourless, acrid. Spores 9×7.5μm, ± reticulate. In damp woodland throughout Britain, especially with birch, but more common in Scotland. E3.

L. violascens (Otto) Fr., with cap 7-12cm, is darker, violet brown to grey brown-ochre, zoned, and less viscid. Spores 11×8μm, with a coarse reticulum. E2.

L. cistophilus Bon & Trimbach, similar but smaller and paler, with spores 13×9μm, occurs under *Cistus* in the Mediterranean region. sE2.

Lactarius flavidus Boud.
Like *L. uvidus* but with more yellowish tints, often a little zoned or with ochraceous spots. Gills cream. Stipe 6×0.8cm, yellowish soon becoming hollow. Flesh pale, almost odourless and only slightly acrid, becoming violaceous. Spores like those of *L. uvidus* or less reticulate. Under broadleaved trees on heavy calcareous soils. E2.

L. aspideus (Fr.) Fr. is more slender and whitish, flesh flushed slightly lilac when cut. Under willow in muddy places. E2.

L. repraesentaneus Britz. is rather more robust, whitish cream with a fleecy bearded margin, and occurs under birch in the Highlands, often in *Sphagnum* bogs. E1 (m2).

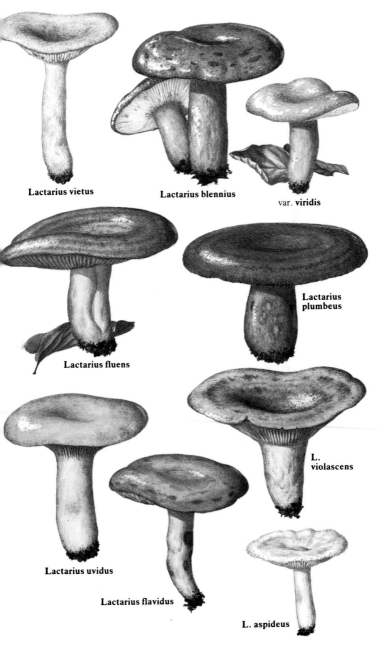

Lactarius vietus

Lactarius blennius

var. viridis

Lactarius fluens

Lactarius
plumbeus

L.
violascens

Lactarius uvidus

Lactarius flavidus

L. aspideus

Section *Colorati*. Cap not viscid, ± woolly. Milk scanty or watery.

Lactarius helvus (Fr.) Fr. [*L. aquifluus*]
Cap 5-15cm, fleshy then expanded and depressed, surface at first ± velvety then shaggy to almost scaly, ochraceous russet with pinkish tint at first, later yellowish fawn. Gills pale ochre, not crowded. Stipe 8×1cm, similar colour or paler. Flesh pale, smell faint at first but strong of chicory or celery when dried. Milk clear, sparkling, quickly dried up; taste mild. Spores 9×7μm, warted with a fine incomplete reticulum. Fairly common in Britain under pine and birch, especially on peat. E2.

Lactarius glyciosmus (Fr.) Fr.
Small fungus, cap 2-7cm, flat, soon depressed, downy to somewhat woolly or silky, pinkish grey to lilac, fading to dull pinkish beige. Gills tinged ochre. Stipe slender 4×0.5cm, whitish like the flesh. Smell distinctive, of dried coconut, taste slowly becoming slightly acrid. Spores 8×7μm, ± reticulate. Very common under birch throughout Britain. E3.

Lactarius fuscus Roll. [*L. mammosus* p.p.]
Hardly any fleshier than *L. glyciosmus* but darker coloured, pinkish bistre to greyish. Gills dingy cream orange. Stipe 6×1cm, tinged similarly. Flesh white or greyish, smell rather like *L. glyciosmus* but more aromatic, like cinnamon; taste bitter rather than acrid. Spores 8×6.5μm, striped. Under pine and birch on the Continent, but rare in Britain, and only with conifers. E2.

Lactarius lilacinus (Lasch) Fr.
Cap 3-8cm, not fleshy or soon depressed, surface downy, then woolly to almost scaly, bright lilac pink, discolouring to dull ochraceous. Gills ochraceous, not crowded. Stipe 5×0.5cm, soon becoming hollow, pale to pinkish ochre. Flesh pale or slightly grey-green on drying, smell sometimes of pelargonium taste, nearly mild. Spores 9×7.5μm, ± reticulate. Under alder throughout Britain, sometimes growing in tufts. E2.

L. spinosulus Quél. is similarly coloured but with more prominent pointed scales, especially towards the margin which may even be shaggy. Uncommon in Britain, under alder, birch, beech and hazel. E1.

Section *Rufi*. Cap surface hoary to downy. Milk white, ± plentiful. Smell faint or none.

Lactarius rufus (Scop.) Fr.
Cap 5-10cm, convex, usually with a low umbo, surface downy to hoary, brownish brick-red occasionally verging towards orange when under birch. Gills arched, cream. Stipe 7×1cm, pale or similar to cap. Flesh white, smell faintly resinous or none, taste very acrid though usually slow to react. Spores 8×6.5μm, ± reticulate. Very common throughout Britain under conifers, occasionally under birch. E4.

Lactarius alpinus Peck [*L. alpigenes*, *L. luteus*, *L. kuehneri*]
Cap 3-7cm, flat then depressed, surface downy, bright yellow to ochraceous or with orange to fawn zones in the end. Stipe 4×0.5cm, yellowish like the gills and flesh. Smell faint, slightly fruity, taste not very acrid. Spores 7×5μm, with rather sparse warts. Under green alder in the mountains of Europe. Em3.

L. lepidotus Hesl. & A.H. Smith is more grey, sometimes cracked, without any trace of yellow on stipe or gills and also occurs under alders. E1.

Lactarius glyciosmus

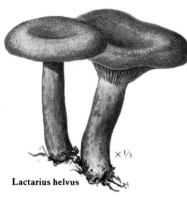

× ¹/₃

Lactarius helvus

Lactarius fuscus

Lactarius lilacinus

Lactarius alpinus

Lactarius rufus

Section *Subdulces*. Cap surface dry and glabrous. Colour dull or pale, milk staying white even on a handkerchief.

Lactarius subdulcis (Pers.) S.F. Gray
Cap 3-6cm, convex then flat, typically beige chamois with a hint of pinkish, margin similar colour, slightly scalloped, drying paler in small spots. Gills pale cream or tinged pinkish. Stipe 6×1cm, creamy yellowish or tinged orange at the apex, becoming progressively pinkish brown downwards. Flesh pale, smell rubbery or a little like a *Scleroderma*; taste almost mild. Spores 9×6.5μm, ± reticulate. Very common under broadleaved trees, especially beech, throughout Britain. Edible. E4.

Lactarius quietus (Fr.) Fr.
Cap 6-10cm, convex, dingy, reddish brown, typically zoned with hoary patches. Gills whitish or cream. Stipe 7×1cm, vinaceous brown, progressively darker towards the base. Flesh pale, with a vinaceous tint in the stipe, smell distinctive, described as "like bed-bugs" or "laundry or wet linen". Milk immediately tinged cream but not yellowing further. Taste slightly acrid. Spores 9×7μm, ± reticulate. Only under oak, very common throughout Britain. Too unpleasant to eat. E4.

Section *Mitissimi*. As *Subdulces* but colour orange to fawn.

Lactarius aurantiofulvus Blum ex Bon [*L. mitissimus* p.p.]
Cap 3-7cm, convex, regular, uniformly rather bright orange. Gills pale, almost horizontal. Stipe 6×1cm, cream to pale orange. Flesh almost odourless, occasionally approaching *L. subdulcis*; taste becoming a little acrid when chewed. Spores 8×6μm, reticulate. Under various broadleaved trees in the lowlands, common under conifers in the mountains. Edible but poor. E4.

Lactarius aurantiacus (Vahl) S.F. Gray
Similar to *L. aurantiofulvus* but cap more quickly depressed or wavy, surface more viscid, more orange at the centre with the margin often paling yellowish. Gills more sloping and redder. Stipe and flesh pale, taste rather bitter. Spores 9×7.5μm, with a confused reticulum. Often under conifers. E2.

Lactarius fulvissimus Romagn.
A little more fleshy, cap 7-10cm, soon depressed, orange fawn at the centre or sometimes russet, paler yellowish orange at the margin. Gills sloping, yellowish cream, slightly tinged reddish brown. Stipe 6×1cm, rather spindle-shaped, colour similar to the cap, veined or almost reticulate. Flesh pale, smelling like *Lepiota cristata*, taste mild but unpleasant; milk remaining white. Spores 8×6.5μm, ± reticulate. Under broadleaved trees on heavy or calcareous soils. Edible but poor. E3.

L. britannicus Reid, more bay brown in the centre, with a somewhat viscous cuticle and slowly yellowing milk, occurs under beech in Britain but seems to be unknown on the Continent.

L. subsericatus K.-R. ex Bon is more reddish, approaching *L. rufus*, with milk yellowing slightly on a handkerchief, and occurs typically under conifers (E2); but there is a f. **pseudofulvissimus** under broadleaved trees, resembling *L. fulvissimus*, with a more matt surface and the smell of *L. subdulcis*. (E3).

Lactarius rubrocinctus Fr.
Cap 7-12cm, slightly depressed and wrinkled (brain-like) at the centre, bright reddish orange with a paler margin. Gills pinkish, quickly spotted violet brown when rubbed. Stipe 7×1cm, paler or a similar tint, with a reddish band below the gills and often striate by their decurrence. Flesh pale with a faint smell recalling *L. quietus*, taste becoming bitter. Spores 9×6.5μm, ± reticulate; cap cuticle ± cellular over the disk. Under broadleaved trees especially beech. E2.

L. tithymalinus (Scop.) Fr. has a similar cuticular structure but is duller coloured, orange-brown to russet, unspotted gills and stipe without the reddish band. E2.

Lactarius subdulcis

Lactarius quietus

Lactarius aurantiofulvus

Lactarius aurantiacus

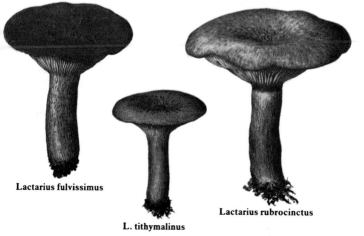

Lactarius fulvissimus

L. tithymalinus

Lactarius rubrocinctus

Section *Tabidi*. Cap glabrous. Milk yellowing in the air, best seen when deposited on a white handkerchief.

Lactarius chrysorrheus (Fr.) Fr.
Cap 5-10cm, convex, flattening, sometimes lobed, with vague reddish ochre zones on a paler yellowish ground. Stipe 6×0.8cm. Stipe and gills pale bruising yellow. Flesh whitish, almost odourless, taste mild then slowly slightly acrid, milk more acrid, turning bright golden yellow. Spores 9×7μm, ± reticulate. Common under broadleaved trees, restricted to oak in Britain. Edible. E4.

Lactarius decipiens Quél.
Cap convex, 5-7cm, pale pinkish ochre or sometimes slightly dingy brick colour. Gills pale, horizontal. Stipe 5×0.8cm, similar colour, flesh rather pink with smell of pelargonium, taste not very acrid. Milk yellowing in a few seconds on a handkerchief. Spores 7×5.5μm, reticulate. Under various broadleaved trees. E3.

Lactarius lacunarum Romagn. ex Hora
Cap similar to *L. decipiens* but quickly expanded or with thin margin; colour more brick reddish, discolouring in small spots from the margin inwards. Gills pale, sometimes yellowed by dried milk. Stipe short, 4×0.6cm, a fine reddish orange, then turning reddish brown from the base. Flesh cream, yellowing in drying. The milk does not stain a handkerchief much but may dry in bright yellow droplets. Spores like those of *L. decipiens*, or slightly broader, cuticle formed of short cells. Habitat distinctive, edges of drying out ponds or muddy ground on rotten leaves of willows, alders, ash etc. Not uncommon in Britain. E2.

Lactarius hepaticus Plowright ap. Boud.
Cap convex, soon flattened or depressed, 3-6cm, a distinctive dull reddish brown, liver colour, when tinged olivaceous, becoming much paler on drying. Gills ochraceous then spotted reddish brown. Stipe 5×0.8cm, colour similar or darker at the base. Flesh pale, yellowing slightly. Milk quickly yellowing on a handkerchief. Spores 9×6.5μm, ± reticulate; cuticle structure somewhat palisadic. Under conifers, especially pine and spruce. Common throughout Britain. E2.

Lactarius badiosanguineus K.-R.
Stature as in *L. hepaticus* or more fleshy, colour reddish bay, sometimes dark when fresh but discolouring to dingy orange on drying. Gills russet to pinkish. Stipe 5×1cm, similar, slightly wrinkled. Flesh pale, smell faint, rather like *L. quietus*. Milk rather watery, only slowly yellowing on a handkerchief, perhaps in 30 seconds. Spores 9×7μm, striped to ridges; cap cuticle as in *L. hepaticus*. In subalpine meadows, sometimes with conifers. Em2.

Lactarius sphagneti (Fr.) Nhf.
Rather like *L. badiosanguineus* in outline and colouring but with margin paler, rather pinkish, from the outset and the centre persisting darker, dark bay colour. Gills pale or pinkish. Stipe like the cap, darker at the base. Flesh pale, milk apt to be watery, yellowing slowly, sometimes taking more than a minute. Spores 9×7μm, ± reticulate; cuticle structure hyphal. Under conifers, especially fir (*Abies*), often among *Sphagnum* E2.

Lactarius tabidus Fr.
Cap 5-8cm, not fleshy, margin faintly striate when moist; colours pinkish ochraceous, paling in little spots leaving an ochraceous centre, slightly depressed and wrinkled around a small persistent umbo. Gills pale. Stipe 5×0.6cm, smooth, pale ochre to ± concolorous. Flesh ochraceous or pinkish, smell like that of *L. quietus* mixed with *Russula emetica*. Milk yellowing in a few seconds on a handkerchief. Spores 10×7.5μm, reticulate; cap cuticle somewhat palisadic. Under broadleaved trees in rather damp places, very common in Britain. E3.

L. theiogalus (Bull.) S.F. Gray is like a slender version of *L. tabidus* with thin striate margin, found with *Sphagnum* in peat bogs; spores with rather isolated warts. E2.

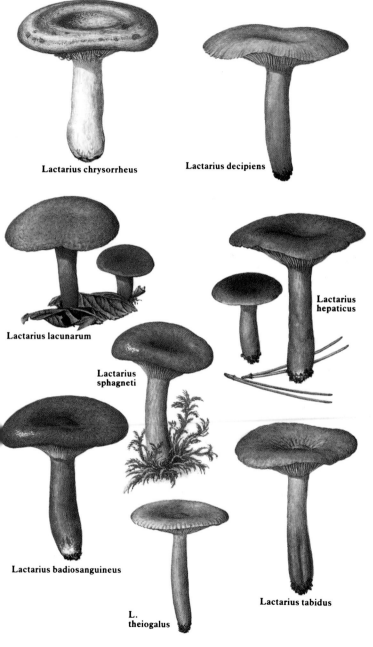

Lactarius chrysorrheus

Lactarius decipiens

Lactarius lacunarum

Lactarius hepaticus

Lactarius sphagneti

Lactarius badiosanguineus

L. theiogalus

Lactarius tabidus

Section *Fuliginosi*. Surface downy to wrinkled, with palisadic cuticle; flesh and/or milk somewhat reddening or turning russet. Spore print ochraceous.

Lactarius acris (Bolton) S.F. Gray
Cap 7-10cm, the only viscid member of the section, pale milky coffee or mottled sepia. Gills ochraceous, then bright pinkish where wounded. Stipe 6×1cm, pale to almost concolorous, then pinkish ochre. Flesh white, reddening, smell faint, taste acrid. Milk turning bright pink even when apart from the flesh. Spores 9×8μm, with prominent bands. Under broadleaved trees. Edibility doubtful. E2.

Lactarius fuliginosus (Fr.) Fr. [*L. azonites*]
Cap about 6-8cm, not fleshy, downy, greyish brown to milky coffee colour. Gills creamy ochraceous. Stipe 6×1cm, similar colour but white in var. *albipes*. Flesh slowly pink, smell faint, taste slightly acrid. Milk not reddening when separated from the flesh. Spores globose, strongly reticulate, 8-9μm. Under broadleaved trees, common in Britain under beech and oak. Edible but poor quality. E2.

Lactarius romagnesii Bon [*L. speciosus*]
Cap rather more fleshy, 10-15cm, dark coloured, slightly reddish sepia, sometimes with vinaceous tints. Gills not crowded, dark ochre. Stipe 7×1cm, pale or similar to the cap. Flesh ochraceous, reddening slowly to slightly orange russet. Milk unchanging. Spores 8-9μm, ± reticulate or with thick lines. Under broadleaved trees. E2.

Lactarius picinus Fr.
This is very like *L. romagnesii* except for its habitat. Cap convex and more blackish. Gills quite crowded, white or pale. Stipe coloured like the cap but whitish at the extremities. Flesh ochraceous to russet, very acrid. Spores 9-10μm, ± reticulate with thick lines. Under conifers in the mountains of Europe. Em3.

Lactarius lignyotus Fr. ap. Lindb.
Cap 6-10cm, distinctly umbonate, blackish, with a few wrinkles round the umbo. Gills distant, white, then pale ochre, decurrent by a thread causing the stipe apex to appear striate. Stipe slender, 8×1cm, nearly concolorous, often furrowed. Flesh remaining white or reddening only very slowly. Smell faint, taste slightly acrid. Spores 9-11μm, reticulate. Under conifers in damp places, especially spruce with bilberry. Edible but poor. Em3.

Lactarius pterosporus Romagn.
Superficially like *L. fuliginosus*, with cap 6-8cm but much more wrinkled or veined at the centre and often with a white edge. Gills cream, soon reddish, crowded. Stipe 5×1cm, similar in colour to the cap, bruising reddish. Flesh quickly becoming bright reddish, the colour of pink tooth powder as in *L. acris*, but the milk does not change colour when apart from the flesh. Smell reminiscent of *Russula emetica* or even *Lactarius glyciosmus*; taste slightly acrid. Spores 8×7μm, girdled by wing-like ridges up to 3-4μm high. Under broadleaved trees on heavy calcareous soil. Edible of poor quality. E3.

L. ruginosus Romagn. is more robust, with crenulate margin, distant gills and a rather russeting flesh; under beech and oak. E2.

Section *Pseudoalbati*. Flesh turning dark brown, sepia; spores cream, elongated.

Lactarius brunneoviolascens Bon
Medium stature, cap 4-7cm, white, slightly hairy or almost fleecy towards the margin, turning brown when rubbed. Gills cream with a pinkish tinge. Stipe 5×1cm, white. Flesh white, milk turning brownish violet in a few minutes on exposure to the air; smell like that of *L. volemus*. Fe reaction green. Spores 9×6.5μm, slightly striped with prominent ridges. Under broadleaved trees in warm situations. Rare. E1.

L. luteolus Peck is a similar North American species but there is a var. *kuehnerianus*, more yellow than *L. brunneoviolascens*, with flesh only slightly browning and smell faint, found under holm oak in the Mediterranean area. E1.

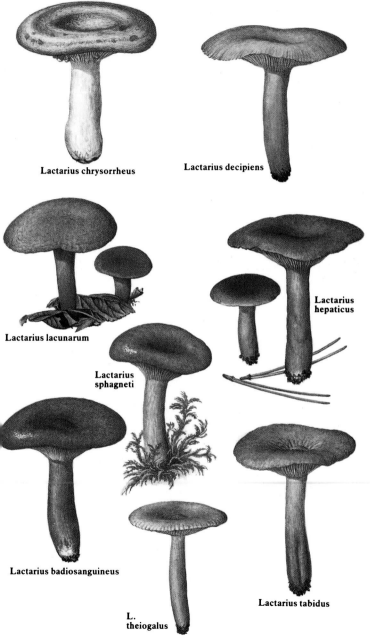

Lactarius chrysorrheus

Lactarius decipiens

Lactarius lacunarum

Lactarius hepaticus

Lactarius sphagneti

Lactarius badiosanguineus

L. theiogalus

Lactarius tabidus

93

Section *Volemi*. Cap surface matt to rugose. Smell strong.

Lactarius volemus (Fr.) Fr.
Cap 10-15cm, fleshy, convex, finally slightly depressed, surface matt to downy, like suede, characteristically wrinkled, pale orange to ± brownish, in var. *oedematopus* the cap is purplish red-brown. Gills ± crowded, slightly sloping, yellowish, bruising reddish. Stipe 6×2cm, a little swollen or club-shaped, coloured like the cap or paler. Flesh pale, a little ochraceous-brownish when broken, with very copious milk, Fe reaction green. Smell of Jerusalem artichokes, becoming fishy, taste mild. Spores ± globose, 10×9μm, reticulate; cuticle a palisade of hairs. Under broadleaved trees, especially oak in Britain, where it is now rare. Edible when young. E3.

Lactarius rugatus K.-R.
Very like *L. volemus*, with still more matt surface, cracking from the centre outwards and coloured rather reddish brown. Gills horizontal, thick, rather distant, whitish. Stipe as in *L. volemus* or more irregular. Flesh pale, only slightly browning, smell fainter, Fe reaction pink. Spores 10×7.5μm, reticulate; cuticular hairs forming a loose palisade. Under broadleaved trees in warm situations. E2.

Section *Albati*. White species, odourless or nearly so.

Lactarius piperatus (Scop.) S.F. Gray [*L. pergamenus* s.s. Romagn.]
Cap 6-12cm, soon becoming cup-shaped with persistently incurved margin, surface lumpy or brain-shaped at the centre, a little rugose elsewhere, persistently creamy white. Gills very crowded and decurrent, cream to slightly flesh coloured. Stipe elongated, 8×2cm, glabrous, persistently white like the flesh. Milk remaining white, even after treatment with KOH, other chemical reactions negative or doubtful, very acrid. Smell faint. Spores 8×6μm, with a slight reticulum; cuticle subcellular. In copses under broadleaved trees on neutral to calcareous soils, often fruiting early. Edible after being dried but not of high quality. E3.

Lactarius pergamenus (Swartz) Fr. [*L. piperatus* s.s. Romagn.]
Cap 12-18cm, expanded, soon depressed with acute margin, surface smooth or glabrous, not rugose, dull white, tinged glaucous with handling. Gills sloping or a little decurrent, fairly crowded, whitish with a glaucous tinge. Stipe 5×2cm, white, bruising greenish. Flesh white, drying glaucous green. Milk white, more acrid than the flesh, turning orange yellow with KOH. Reaction with sulfoformol and TL$_4$ blue or violaceous. Spores 7×6.5μm, ± warted with a slight reticulum. Cuticle with ± elongated hairs. More uncommon than *L. piperatus* or later. Edibility as for *piperatus*. E2.

L. glaucescens Crossl., also slightly tinged glaucous, has hardly decurrent gills with weaker chemical reactions. E1.

Lactarius vellereus (Fr.) Fr.
Cap 12-35cm, convex soon depressed, with an inrolled, ± lobed margin and creamy white, velvety surface. Gills arcuate, very distant, white. Stipe stout or short, 7×4cm, velvety and white. Flesh white with copious and unchanging milk (becoming pink in var. *hometii*); no reaction with KOH. Smell none or slightly like pelargonium in var. *odorans*, taste acrid. Spores 10×9μm ± globose, with little crests; cuticle filamentous or trichodermial. Very common under broadleaved trees. Edible but worthless. E4.

L. bertillonii (Nhf. ex Z. Sch.) Bon differs in its moderate size and yellow reaction with KOH; taste only slightly acrid. The milk turns slightly yellowish in var. *queletii*. E2.

Lactarius controversus (Pers.) Fr.
This whitish species, placed here for convenience and belonging actually with the section *Zonarii*, is recognised by the pinkish zones of the glabrous, viscid cap (10-20cm), sometimes with shortly bearded margin; gills reddish pink, stipe short, 4×1cm, white as for the flesh. Smell slightly fruity, taste not very acrid. Spores 7×6μm, almost reticulate. Under broadleaved trees, chiefly poplar and willows. Edible but poor. E3.

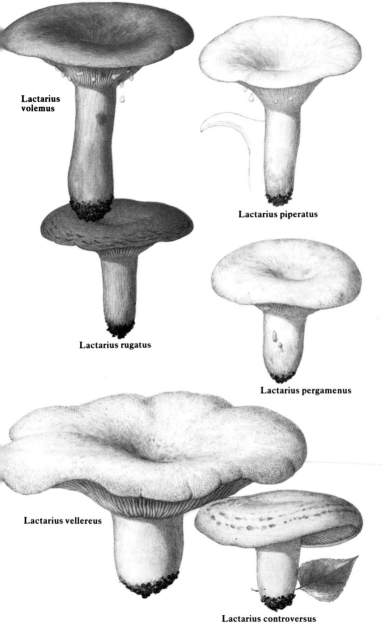

Lactarius
volemus

Lactarius piperatus

Lactarius rugatus

Lactarius pergamenus

Lactarius vellereus

Lactarius controversus

Section *Fuliginosi*. Surface downy to wrinkled, with palisadic cuticle; flesh and/or milk somewhat reddening or turning russet. Spore print ochraceous.

Lactarius acris (Bolton) S.F. Gray
Cap 7-10cm, the only viscid member of the section, pale milky coffee or mottled sepia. Gills ochraceous, then bright pinkish where wounded. Stipe 6×1cm, pale to almost concolorous, then pinkish ochre. Flesh white, reddening, smell faint, taste acrid. Milk turning bright pink even when apart from the flesh. Spores 9×8μm, with prominent bands. Under broadleaved trees. Edibility doubtful. E2.

Lactarius fuliginosus (Fr.) Fr. [*L. azonites*]
Cap about 6-8cm, not fleshy, downy, greyish brown to milky coffee colour. Gills creamy ochraceous. Stipe 6×1cm, similar colour but white in var. *albipes*. Flesh slowly pink, smell faint, taste slightly acrid. Milk not reddening when separated from the flesh. Spores globose, strongly reticulate, 8-9μm. Under broadleaved trees, common in Britain under beech and oak. Edible but poor quality. E2.

Lactarius romagnesii Bon [*L. speciosus*]
Cap rather more fleshy, 10-15cm, dark coloured, slightly reddish sepia, sometimes with vinaceous tints. Gills not crowded, dark ochre. Stipe 7×1cm, pale or similar to the cap. Flesh ochraceous, reddening slowly to slightly orange russet. Milk unchanging. Spores 8-9μm, ± reticulate or with thick lines. Under broadleaved trees. E2.

Lactarius picinus Fr.
This is very like *L. romagnesii* except for its habitat. Cap convex and more blackish. Gills quite crowded, white or pale. Stipe coloured like the cap but whitish at the extremities. Flesh ochraceous to russet, very acrid. Spores 9-10μm, ± reticulate with thick lines. Under conifers in the mountains of Europe. Em3.

Lactarius lignyotus Fr. ap. Lindb.
Cap 6-10cm, distinctly umbonate, blackish, with a few wrinkles round the umbo. Gills distant, white, then pale ochre, decurrent by a thread causing the stipe apex to appear striate. Stipe slender, 8×1cm, nearly concolorous, often furrowed. Flesh remaining white or reddening only very slowly. Smell faint, taste slightly acrid. Spores 9-11μm, reticulate. Under conifers in damp places, especially spruce with bilberry. Edible but poor. Em3.

Lactarius pterosporus Romagn.
Superficially like *L. fuliginosus*, with cap 6-8cm but much more wrinkled or veined at the centre and often with a white edge. Gills cream, soon reddish, crowded. Stipe 5×1cm, similar in colour to the cap, bruising reddish. Flesh quickly becoming bright reddish, the colour of pink tooth powder as in *L. acris*, but the milk does not change colour when apart from the flesh. Smell reminiscent of *Russula emetica* or even *Lactarius glyciosmus*; taste slightly acrid. Spores 8×7μm, girdled by wing-like ridges up to 3-4μm high. Under broadleaved trees on heavy calcareous soil. Edible of poor quality. E3.

L. ruginosus Romagn. is more robust, with crenulate margin, distant gills and a rather russeting flesh; under beech and oak. E2.

Section *Pseudoalbati*. Flesh turning dark brown, sepia; spores cream, elongated.

Lactarius brunneoviolascens Bon
Medium stature, cap 4-7cm, white, slightly hairy or almost fleecy towards the margin, turning brown when rubbed. Gills cream with a pinkish tinge. Stipe 5×1cm, white. Flesh white, milk turning brownish violet in a few minutes on exposure to the air; smell like that of *L. volemus*. Fe reaction green. Spores 9×6.5μm, slightly striped with prominent ridges. Under broadleaved trees in warm situations. Rare. E1.

L. luteolus Peck is a similar North American species but there is a var. *kuehnerianus*, more yellow than *L. brunneoviolascens*, with flesh only slightly browning and smell faint, found under holm oak in the Mediterranean area. E1.

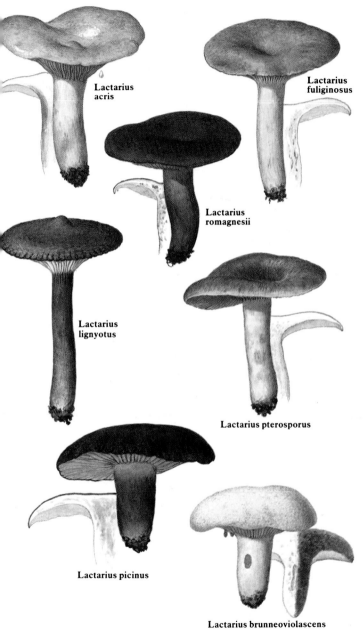

Lactarius
acris

Lactarius
fuliginosus

Lactarius
romagnesii

Lactarius
lignyotus

Lactarius pterosporus

Lactarius picinus

Lactarius brunneoviolascens

Section *Olentes*. Slightly fleshy, cap 3-10cm with matt, uneven surface, margin not striate; smell strong; milk watery. Spores ± globose. Spore print cream-ochraceous.

Lactarius camphoratus (Bull.) Fr.
Cap 5-7cm, russet brown to dark chestnut at first, margin fading to a more reddish tint. Gills pinkish ochre to slightly vinaceous when touched. Stipe about 5×0.6cm, similarly coloured, base darker, deep vinaceous brown. Flesh pale, smell like *L. quietus* when fresh, intensifying to that of chicory when dried. Milk whitish. Spores 8×6.5µm, warted with a few connecting lines; cystidia present on gill face. Under broadleaved trees or conifers, often on mossy bases of trunks, sometimes in clusters. Edible but not good because of the smell. E3.

Lactarius cremor Fr.
More slender, cap 3-5cm, soon depressed, margin slightly crenulate, colour fawnish orange or spotted rusty. Gills ochraceous flesh colour, sloping. Stipe short, about 2×0.5cm, often bent or rather excentric, similarly coloured to cap. Flesh pale, smelling first of ivy, then chicory. Milk whitish to watery. Spores 8×5µm, ± reticulate; facial cystidia present. Under broadleaved trees in copses on heavy calcareous soils. E2.

Lactarius subumbonatus Lindgr.
Cap 3-8cm, slightly convex, margin sometimes lobed, surface roughened and grained, dark sepia brown, paling on drying and eventually olivaceous ochre. Gills arched, bright ochraceous orange. Stipe rather short, 3×0.6cm, concolorous or yellower at the apex. Flesh pale, smell like *L. quietus*, then like chicory. Milk watery. Spores globose, 7-8µm, reticulate, often strongly ridged; cystidia absent. Common in damp woods of broad-leaved trees, often in cart ruts. This has often been called *L. cimicarius* or *L. serifluus*. E3.

L. cimicarius (Batsch) Gill. s.s. This has a smoother, more reddish cap surface, slightly pinkish gills and a smell like that of *L. cremor*. E1.

Lactarius atlanticus Bon
Cap like *L. subumbonatus* but smoother, a fine warm orange-red to reddish brown. Gills sloping slightly, yellow ochre. Stipe rather slender, 8×0.5cm, colour rather like the cap, very hairy at the base in var. *strigipes*. Flesh pale, smelling strongly like *L. quietus* at first, then of ivy or chicory on drying. Milk watery. Spores ± globose, 9×8µm, ± reticulate; cystidia absent. Under holm oak. sE3.

L. serifluus (DC.) Fr. is very similar, with duller colouring, more like *L. camphoratus*, and a fainter smell, found under broadleaved trees in more northern districts, under beech and oak in Britain. E1.

Section *Obscurati*. Small fungi, about 1-3cm with wrinkled surface and striate margin. Smell faint; milk scanty or soon dried up; spores white, rather elongated, spore print white.

Lactarius obscuratus (Lasch) Fr.
Cap 2-3cm, soon depressed with a small dark central umbo, often greenish or olive; surface elsewhere somewhat wrinkled, orange-brown towards the margin. Gills arched, dingy ochraceous orange, rather distant. Stipe 3×0.4cm, russet. Flesh ochraceous, no change in colour of milk. Spores 8×6µm, ± reticulate. Under alders, common throughout Britain. E3.

Lactarius omphaliformis Romagn.
Cap like an *Omphalina* with strongly striate margin, somewhat furrowed, pinkish orange, darker at the centre but not olivaceous, slightly roughened. Gills distant, pinkish, sloping. Stipe slender, 3×0.2cm, coloured like the cap or darker at the base. Flesh odourless, milk yellowing on a handkerchief. Spores 9×7µm, ± reticulate. Under birch with *Sphagnum* and also under alder. E2.

Lactarius cyathuliformis Bon
Cap like the preceding with rather furrowed or wavy margin, centre sometimes olivaceous, paling. Gills distant, pale orange. Stipe short, 2×0.3cm, reddish brown. Flesh pale, milk only slightly or slowly yellowing. Spores 11×8µm. striped. Under alder. E2.

Lactarius camphoratus

Lactarius subumbonatus

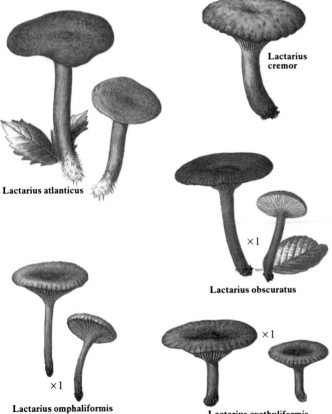

Lactarius atlanticus

Lactarius cremor

×1

Lactarius obscuratus

×1

Lactarius omphaliformis

×1

Lactarius cyathuliformis

Order *Tricholomatales*. Gilled species with fibrous flesh; cap and stem running together; white or pallid spores.

Family *Hygrophoraceae*. Gills distant, thick or with a waxy consistency (elongated basidia), inserted in various ways from decurrent or adnate to somewhat ascending and free. Cap surface also diverse, dry, ± scaly to smooth, greasy or very viscid. Stipe smooth, dry or viscid, rarely with a ring or sheathing ring.

Key to *Hygrophoraceae* – principal groups

1a   Gills definitely decurrent or arched: **2**

1b   Gills adnate or sinuate, cap flattened or convex and umbonate; *Hygrocybe* subgenus *Pseudohygrocybe*: **14**

1c   Gills ascending or somewhat free; cap campanulate or conical, umbonate or pointed; flesh brittle, watery ≫   *Hygrocybe* subgenus *Hygrocybe*: **30**

2a   Cap surface dry, matt or scaly; flesh not very thick: **3**

2b   Cap surface smooth, greasy or viscid: **4**

3a   Cap surface matt but smooth or at most ± velvety but not scaly; not brightly coloured, rarely pale orange ≫   Genus *Cuphophyllus*, 102
     (If there is a foetid smell or the stipe is dotted black see *Camarophyllopsis*, 170)

3b   Cap surface ± minutely scaly; colours yellow to red or bright orange ≫
     Hygrocybe section *Squamulosae*, 110
     (For ± vinaceous pink fleshy species see *Hygrophorus* section *Rubentes*, 116)

4a   Bright colours, yellow, pink or reddish: **5**

4b   White or whitish to pale creamy ochraceous: **7**

4c   Russet, fawn or vinaceous pinkish: **11**

4d   Blackish or greenish-olivaceous, dark coloured: **13**

5a   Cap very viscid, pink; stipe viscid with a greenish tinge ≫   *Hygrocybe laeta*, 112

5b   Not this peculiar colouring: **6**

6a   Cap yellow to orange or reddish, greasy to somewhat viscid; stipe concolorous only slightly viscid; gills yellow; in lawns ≫
     Hygrocybe ceracea var. *vitellinoides*, 108

6b   Cap yellow-orange, only slightly viscid; stipe somewhat viscid with a fleeting annular zone or slightly banded; under larch ≫
     group of *Hygrophorus lucorum*, 118

7a   Stipe viscid, ± slender woodland species ≫   *H*. section *Eburnei*, 114

7b   Stipe dry, cap less viscid: **8**

8a   Thin-fleshed fungi on lawns and pastures; genus *Cuphophyllus*: **9**

8b   Fleshy woodland fungi ≫   *Hygrophorous* section *Clitocyboides*, 114

9a   Pure white, margin striate, slightly hygrophanous ≫   *Cuphophyllus niveus*, 102

9b   Whitish or tinged greyish to ochraceous, margin scarcely striate: **10**

10a   Smell faint or none ≫   *Cuphophyllus berkeleyi*, 102

10b   Strong persistent smell of Russian leather ≫   *Cuphophyllus russocoriaceus*, 102

11a   Stipe viscid or glutinous, somewhat dotted orange, cap orange ≫
     Hygrophorus pudorinus, 114
     (Orange at disc only and stipe paler in *H*. *lindtneri*, 114)

11b   Stipe dry: **12**

12a   Gills pale to almost concolorous, not dotted; cap smooth or slightly radially streaky, scarcely viscid, fawn or russet tints dominant ≫
     Hygrophorus section *Fulventes*, 116

12b   Gills and sometimes cap also soon dotted vinaceous pink, sometimes darkening to purple ≫   *Hygrophorus* section *Rubentes*, 116

13a   Stipe dry, naked or dotted slightly in the upper part; cap only slightly viscid with greyish tints dominant ≫   *Hygrophorus* section *Camarophylli*, 118

13b   Stipe ± viscid, garlanded or with a sheathing ring; colours often olivaceous to dark greenish ≫   *Hygrophorus* section *Olivaceoumbrini*, 118

14a Cap surface matt to velvety or slightly scaly: **15**
14b Cap surface smooth, greasy to ± viscid: **20**

15a Small fungi with thin flesh and scaly surface: **16**
15b Rather fleshy fungi, orange yellow, cap surface matt but not scaly: **17**
15c Dull colours: **18**

16a Cap scales concolorous, scarcely perceptible without a hand lens, colour bright
red »   *Hygrocybe miniata*, 110
16b Scales of cap blackish on a red or pale orange ground »   *Hygrocybe turunda*, 110

17a Gills distant, sinuate; smell soapy or of washing »   *Hygrocybe quieta*, 108
17b Gills closer, broadly adnate; smell pleasant or of honey »   *Hygrocybe reidii*, 110
(Compare also *H. strangulata* 110, which is similar but odourless.)

18a Whitish beige, smell earthy or none »   *Hygrocybe fornicata*, 112
18b Brownish, with distinct odour: **19**

19a Smell nitrous or flesh dingy reddish »   *Hygrocybe* sect. *Olidae*, 112
19b Smell mealy »   *Porpoloma metapodium*, 162

20a Rather fleshy or robust fungi with red cap: **21**
20b More fragile or thinner-fleshed fungi, cap 1-4cm: **23**

21a Cap flat or scarcely umbonate, bright scarlet, fading to pink or orange in drying;
stipe and flesh rather orange »   *Hygrocybe coccinea*, 108
21b Cap more convex or umbonate: **22**

22a Robust fungus coloured pomegranate red, changing to brownish; flesh white »
Hygrocybe punicea, 106
22b Cap less fleshy or more umbonate, bright rather tomato red, fading little in
drying, gills rather ascending to almost free; stipe and flesh bright orange »
Hygrocybe splendidissima, 106

23a Cap lemon yellow, not viscid or only slightly so, flesh ± firm, not watery: **24**
23b Cap yellow but distinctly viscid or fragile and watery-fleshed; splitting: **25**
23c Cap not uniformly yellow, often red or dull coloured: **26**

24a Margin striate, gills whitish »   *Hygrocybe citrina*, 108
24b Margin scarcely striate, gills concolorous »   *Hygrocybe ceracea*, 108

25a Stipe very viscid »   *Hygrocybe chlorophana*, 106
25b Stipe and cap only slightly viscid »   *Hygrocybe euroflavescens*, 106

26a Cap bright red, ± viscid: **27**
26b Cap not predominantly red: **29**

27a Taste bitter »   *Hygrocybe reai*, 108
27b Taste mild: **28**

28a Cap barely viscid, red with a yellow edge »   *Hygrocybe insipida*, 108
28b Cap very viscid, bright red; stipe viscid, apex persisting red; gills white »
Hygrocybe subminutula, 108
28c Cap red, partly garnet colour, stipe apex and gills with an olivaceous tinge »
Hygrocybe sciophana, 112

29a Colour greenish mingled with yellow and reddish; cap and stipe both viscid »
Hygrocybe psittacina, 112
29b Colour blackish to grey-bistre; stipe rather furrowed, hollow and very brittle,
stipe and cap both very viscid »   *Hygrocybe unguinosa*, 112

30a Blackening species »   section *Conicae*, 104
30b Colour not changing or only slowly or very slightly greying: **31**

31a Cap surface dry or fibrillose, various colours »   section *Obrusseae*, 104
31b Cap surface smooth or viscid, colours yellow, red or orange, sometimes greying
slightly at the base of the stipe »   section *Macrosporae*, 106
(If the cap is bright red, dry with firmer, not watery flesh, see *H. splendidissima*,
106)

Genus *Cuphophyllus* [*Camarophyllus*]. Gills decurrent, cap dry to greasy but not viscid, colour dull; gill trama interwoven.

Cuphophyllus pratensis (Pers.) Bon
A medium to rather stout fungus, cap 5-10cm, broadly umbonate, eventually depressed, with acute margin, surface matt, dull orange, often cracking round the centre. Gills distant, broad, sometimes interveined, almost concolorous or paler. Stipe 5×1cm, often attenuated below, similar colour. Flesh pale, smell and taste merely fungal. Spores 7×4.5μm. Meadows, lawns and in copses of broadleaved trees, very common throughout Britain. Edible and very good. E3.

Cuphophyllus niveus (Fr.) Bon [*C. virgineus* p.p.]
Small or only slightly fleshy fungus, cap 1-5cm, surface smooth to greasy, hygrophanous, pure white, margin translucent when moist. Gills distant, decurrent, white. Stipe 2×0.5cm, white, sometimes pinkish in f. *roseipes*. Flesh white, odourless and insipid. Spores 11×6μm. Very common on lawns, pastures and moors throughout Britain. A good edible fungus but open to confusion with some poisonous white species of *Clitocybe*. E3.

C. borealis (Peck) Bon is more fleshy or umbonate, with matt, dry cuticle, like a white form of *H. pratensis*. E2.

Cuphophyllus berkeleyi (Orton & Watl.) Bon [*H. pratensis* var. *pallida*]
Like *H. nivea* but a little more fleshy, dingy white, tinged pale bistre towards the centre or ochraceous on drying. Gills similar colour to pale beige. Stipe concolorous, rather slender, 6×0.5cm. Flesh whitish, smell faintly aromatic. Spores 9×6μm. On lawns etc, often among the preceding species. Edible and very good. E2.

C. russocoriaceus (Bk. & Mill.) Bon is very like *H. nivea*, usually small and creamier white, easily recognised by the penetrating odour of Russian leather, even when dried. Very common in Britain, especially in the north, in roadside grass etc. E2.

Cuphophyllus colemannianus (Blox.) Bon
Resembling *C. pratensis* but uniformly slightly pinkish grey-brown beige, margin slightly striate. Gills thick, often interveined or crinkled, similar in colour. Stipe 4×0.6cm, concolorous, flesh pale. Spores 9×6.5μm. Pastures on limestone or chalk. Edible. E2.

C. subradiatus (Schum.) Bon. Smaller; has an almost translucent, striate and paler margin with whitish less distant gills, cap umbonate, or depressed, flesh colour to greyish brown. Quite common on pastures and heaths in Britain. E2.

Cuphophyllus flavipes (Britz.) Bon [*Hygrophorus lacmus* p.p.]
Cap 2-5cm, rather fleshy or umbonate, greyish or a little violaceous, matt to downy. Gills pale or similar to cap. Stipe 5×0.7cm, greyish with a yellow base. Flesh pale. Spores 7×6μm, ± globose. On lawns and mossy pastures and heather. Fairly common in Britain. E1.

C. lacmus (Schum.) Bon s.str. Shows a paler yellow base to the stipe and has elongated spores, 8×5μm. It offers a transition to the following species. E2.

Cuphophyllus subviolaceus (Peck) Bon
Like *H. flavipes* or slightly larger, cap about 6-7cm, a little more viscid, with dark brown to slaty umbo and slightly lilaceous striate margin. Gills grey violaceous. Stipe (5×0.7cm) and flesh pale lilac grey, whiter towards the base. Smell sometimes a little earthy. Spores 11×7μm; cap cuticle slightly gelatinous. Acid pastures and heaths. E1.

C. cinereus (Fr.) Bon is more slender, light grey, with spores not exceeding 9μm. Uncommon in similar situations. E1.

C. grossulus (Pers.) Bon [*Omphalina wynniae*], pallid greyish with yellow gills, occurs on wood. Spores 7-10×5-6μm, hyphae without clamps. E2.

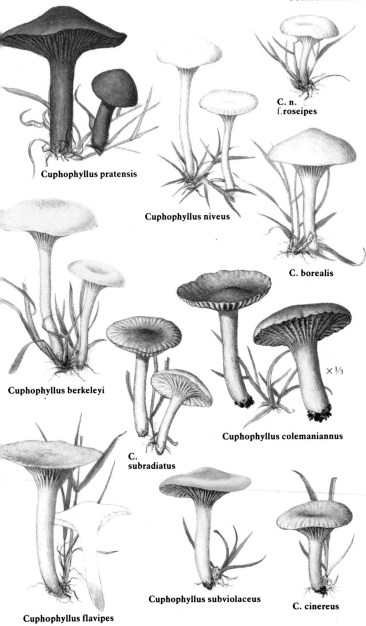

Cuphophyllus pratensis

C. n. f.roseipes

Cuphophyllus niveus

C. borealis

Cuphophyllus berkeleyi

C. subradiatus

× ⅓

Cuphophyllus colemaniannus

Cuphophyllus flavipes

Cuphophyllus subviolaceus

C. cinereus

Genus *Hygrocybe*. Generally vividly coloured fungi. Gills with variable insertion and regular trama.

Subgenus *Hygrocybe*. Fragile fungi or with a watery consistency, cap often conical, sometimes blackening. Gills ascending, often free or sinuate; with parallel trama of elongated broad hyphae; basidia stocky.

Section *Conicae*. [Godfrinia]. Blackening species, with conical cap and ascending or ± free gills.

Hygrocybe conica (Scop.) Kumm.
Cap 2-4cm, conical, bright orange to tomato red. Gills pale or yellowish, almost free. Stipe 4×0.5cm, orange or flushed reddish. Flesh pale, concolorous beneath the surface, quickly turning grey-green to black. Var. *chloroides* is a greenish version. Spores variable, 12-14×8-9μm on 2-spored basidia. In pastures and woodland glades. Edibility suspect. Common throughout Britain. E4.

H. nigrescens (Quél.) Kühn. is often larger, cap 5-7cm and stem more fibrillose, turning more slaty grey. Spores 11×7μm on 4-spored basidia. Equally common in similar places. E4.

Hygrocybe conicoides (Orton) Orton & Watl.
Cap 3-5cm, a little fleshier than in *H. conica* or rather obtuse and lobed, very bright tomato red, blackening more slowly or not all over. Gills salmon or reddish, at least towards the base. Stipe 6×0.8cm, ± orange with a whitish or greenish base. Flesh pale to almost concolorous, blackening slightly. Spores variable, 12-15×6-8μm, on 2- or 4-spored basidia. On ± grassed-over coastal dunes. Occasional in Britain. E3.

Hygrocybe tristis (Pers.) Møll.
Like *H. nigrescens* but with cap colour only a dull orange or sometimes greenish. Gills yellowish. Stipe 7×1cm, whitish to almost concolorous, blackening like the flesh. Spores and basidia as in *H. nigrescens*. On lawns or forest glades. E2.

Section *Obrusseae*. Species with conical cap but not blackening, surface ± dry.

Hygrocybe calyptraeformis (Bk. & Br.) Fayod
Cap 5-7cm tall, very pointed at first (pixie's cap), a beautiful pink, eventually discolouring to lilac-beige, unique in the genus. Gills pale, tinged pink. Stipe white, seldom pinkish, often tall, 10×0.8cm. Flesh whitish or pink near the surface. Spores 8×6.5μm. Lawns, pastures and woodland glades, throughout Britain but seldom abundant. E1.

Hygrocybe spadicea (Scop.) Karst.
Cap 5-7cm, rather fleshy or obtuse, rather warm brown to sepia, contrasting with bright yellow gills. Stipe 7×1cm, ± yellow. Flesh white to yellowish. Spores 10×7μm. Pastures on limestone or basalt. Edible. Uncommon in Britain. E2.

Hygrocybe intermedia (Pass.) Fayod
Rather robust, cap 5-8cm, fleshy or obtuse, surface fibrillose to rather scaly, yellowish orange ± flushed a fiery red. Gills yellowish to bright orange. Stipe 8×1cm, fibrillose, tinged red on a yellowish ground. Flesh pale. Spores 10×6μm. Among grass on calcareous slopes with junipers, throughout Britain in pastures but except in western Scotland nowhere common. E1.

H. cystidiata Arnolds [*H. obrussea* p.p.] is more yellow, with smooth surface, easily confused with species in the Section Macrosporae (p.106) unless the spore size is checked. Throughout Britain in grassy places but apparently not very common. Spores 9×5μm. E2.

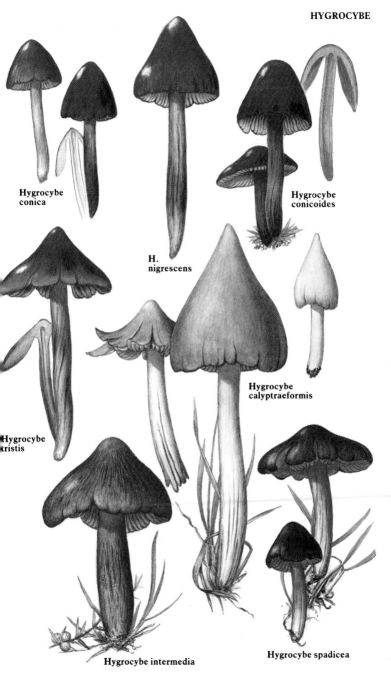

Hygrocybe conica

Hygrocybe conicoides

H. nigrescens

Hygrocybe calyptraeformis

Hygrocybe cristis

Hygrocybe intermedia

Hygrocybe spadicea

Section *Macrosporae*. Cap conical, smooth or viscid, not blackening or only greying slightly in the basal flesh. Spores cylindric or larger than in section Obrusseae (p. 104).

Hygrocybe persistens (Britz.) Sing. var. **langei** [*H. acutoconica* p.p.]
Cap medium size, 5-7cm, rather pointed and narrow or incurved at the base when young (pixie's cap), bright yellow to pale orange throughout (var. *persistens* is more orange-reddish); viscid. Gills pale. Stipe 6×0.8cm, nearly concolorous or paler, whitish at the base. Spores variable, 12-18×6-10μm on 2-spored basidia; cap cuticle gelatinised. Lawns and pastures, especially on limestone, common in Britain but less so than *H. conica*. Edibility uncertain. E2.

H. subglobispora (Orton) Moser differs in its pale yellow cap, white gills and ± globose spores 11×9μm. E2.

Hygrocybe konradii Haller
Cap more obtuse or at least blunt-tipped, surface drier, pale orange-yellow, seldom more orange, or flushed reddish in var. *pseudopersistens*. Gills and stipe (6×1cm) similar or bright yellow. Flesh concolorous at the surface, greying a little towards the base. Spores variable, 12-15×9-11μm, not really cylindrical, on 4-spored basidia. Pastures on limestone, often under juniper. E3.

H. aurantiolutescens Orton. Similar but on fixed coastal dunes. Smaller spores only 6-7μm wide. E3.

Section *Obtusae*. Cap not pointed but obtuse or flattened, resembling subgenus Pseudohygrocybe (below) but anatomically like section Obrusseae.

Hygrocybe chlorophana (Fr.) Wünsche
Cap 3-7cm, convex, very viscid, lemon to bright yellow with a hint of greenish; orange in var. *aurantiaca*. Gills similar colour, deeply notched at the stipe. Stipe 4×0.6cm, concolorous, very viscid. Flesh pale. Spores 8×4.5μm, hyphae of the cap cuticle very slender and branched in colourless mucus. Among grass on lawns, pastures, heaths and grassy open woodland with broadleaved trees. Throughout Britain. E4.

Hygrocybe euroflavescens Kühn. [*H. flavescens* p.p.]
Cap similar to *H. chlorophana* or rather bell-shaped and ± umbonate, less viscid and coloured bright yellow to orange. Gills pale. Stipe 5×0.8cm, dry, non-viscid. Flesh concolorous. Spores like those of *H. chlorophana* or somewhat almond-shaped, cuticular hyphae less gelatinised. Lawns and pastures, common throughout Britain. E3.

Subgenus *Pseudohygrocybe*. Cap rather obtuse or only slightly conical, less brittle than in subgenus Hygrocybe, flesh not watery, gill insertion various but not free. Trama of short hyphae, basidia elongated.

Section *Puniceae*. Outline somewhat conical and suggestive of section Macrosporae (above).

Hygrocybe punicea (Fr.) Kumm.
Cap fleshy, 8-12cm, conico-convex with smooth to slippery surface, pomegranate red, sometimes verging on brownish or eventually the colour of Brazilian rosewood. Gills ascending or almost free, ± yellow. Stipe 12×2cm, yellow, seldom tinged with orange, white at the base. Flesh white, at least in the pith. Spores 10×5.5μm; cap cuticle slightly gelatinised. Pastures or in open grassy woodland, sometimes with conifers, throughout Britain. Edible and good. E3.

Hygrocybe splendidissima (Orton) Svr.
A little more slender than *H. punicea*, cap 5-10cm, bright tomato red, scarcely verging to brick at the end. Gills nearly free, yellow to orange. Stipe 10×1cm, ± bright orange, as is flesh. Spores 9×6μm; cuticular hyphae not gelatinised. Acid pastures and heaths, fairly common especially in the north. E1.

Hygrocybe
konradii

H. k. var.
pseudopersistens

Hygrocybe
persistens var. langei

Hygrocybe
chlorophana

Hygrocybe
euroflavescens

. c.
r. aurantiaca

Hygrocybe punicea

Hygrocybe splendidissima

107

Section *Pseudohygrocybe* [*Coccineae*]. Cap obtuse, surface dry but glabrous, colour red or orange.

Hygrocybe coccinea (Sch.) Kumm.
Cap 3-6cm, obtuse, soon flattening, bright red, paling to orange and drying pinkish white. Gills adnate, yellow or reddish. Stipe 5×0.8cm, reddish or orange. Flesh yellow or orange. Spores 10×6μm; cuticular hyphae not gelatinised. Very common everywhere in pastures, lawns, moors and grassy open woodland. Edible. E3.

H. marchii (Bres.) Møll. has a more orange cap with margin often scalloped. E1.

Hygrocybe quieta (Kühn.) Sing. [*H. obrussea* auct.]
Cap 5-10cm, soon flattened, dry, even matt, yellow orange or sometimes reddish, but can have olivaceous tinge with age. Gills notched at the stipe, very distant, thick, often interveined, concolorous, remaining yellow. Stipe 8×1cm, slightly spindle-shaped, dry, yellow orange. Flesh similar colour with soapy smell or more like that of *Lactarius quietus*. Spores 9×5μm, constricted in the middle; cuticular hyphae 5-8μm wide in a trichoderm, not gelatinised. Pastures and grassy woodlands or copses. Throughout Britain. E2.

Section *Insipidae*. Small red ± viscid species.

Hygrocybe reae (R. Mre.) Lange
Cap 1-3cm, convex with slightly striate margin, viscid, reddish orange, paling. Gills almost decurrent or arched, orange. Stipe 5×0.3cm, similar colour, viscid. Flesh bitter. Spores 8×5μm, constricted or wider at the base. In pastures or grassy woodland. Rather uncommon, although throughout Britain. E3.

Hygrocybe insipida (Lange ex Lund.) Moser
Cap 2-4cm, convex, slippery or slightly viscid, red but typically with orange or yellow margin. Gills slightly arched, similar colour. Stipe 4×0.3cm, concolorous or paler with age, dry. Flesh yellow orange, taste milk. Spores 7.5×4μm elliptical, not constricted. Pastures, fairly common throughout Britain. E3.

Hygrocybe subminutula Murr.
Similar in stature to *H. insipida* but with cap entirely red and very viscid. Gills adnate, white, contrasting with the top of the stipe, which is as red as the cap except for a yellow or white base, viscid, 6×0.3cm. Flesh yellow or white. Spores narrow, 7×3μm, occasionally slightly constricted. Lawns, uncommon in Britain. E2.

Section *Subvitellinae*. Caps yellow, glabrous to somewhat viscid, gills adnate or decurrent.

Hygrocybe ceracea (Wulf.) Kumm.
Cap 1-4cm, slightly convex to somewhat depressed, greasy to slightly viscid, bright yellow to pale orange, sometimes reddish in f. *rubella*, margin striate, often paler. Gills ± adnate or sloping to somewhat decurrent (var. *vitellinoides*); yellow. Stipe slender, 3×0.3cm, not viscid, yellow or orange. Flesh somewhat yellow. Spores 8×4.5μm, cylindrical or constricted. Pastures. E2.

H. vitellina (Fr.) Karst. though similar in appearance to var. *vitellinoides* above, is more viscid, with pale gills and spores not constricted. E1.

Hygrocybe citrina (Rea) Lange
Cap convex, 1-3cm, lemon yellow with striate margin. Gills whitish, notched. Stipe 4×0.3cm, yellow, scarcely viscid. Flesh pale. Spores narrow, 8×3μm, not constricted. Pastures, uncommon. E2.

H. glutinipes (Lge.) Haller is more viscid, especially on the stipe, and occurs more under broadleaved trees. E2.

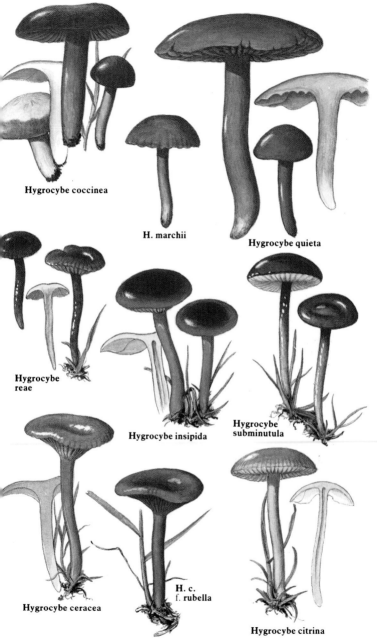

Hygrocybe coccinea

H. marchii

Hygrocybe quieta

Hygrocybe reae

Hygrocybe insipida

Hygrocybe subminutula

Hygrocybe ceracea

H. c. f. rubella

Hygrocybe citrina

Section *Squamulosae*. Cap surface dry, downy to rather scaly; cuticle a trichoderm of erect hyphae, strongly septate or forming chains of cells of various widths up to 10, 20 or sometimes 30μm.

Hygrocybe miniata (Fr.) Kumm.
Cap 2-5cm, convex, surface covered with tiny concolorous scales, bright red fading to orange. Gills adnate or notched, similar colour. Stipe 6×0.4cm, dry, concolorous or yellower. Flesh orange, odourless. Spores ovoid 9×5.5μm; cuticular hyphae 15-25μm wide. Pastures, moors and grassy woods, common especially in the north. E4.

Hygrocybe reidii Kühn. [*H. marchii* ss. Reid]
Cap 3-6cm, soon flat then depressed, margin somewhat undulating, surface downy-felted becoming distinctly scaly only when old or in dry weather, orange red. Gills adnate to ± decurrent, concolorous or paler. Stipe 4×0.5cm, pale orange, dry. Flesh similar colour, smelling of honey (or like *Clitocybe phaeophthalma* [*hydrogramma*]). Spores 8×4.5μm, rarely slightly constricted, cuticular hyphae 6-10μm wide. Lawns and pastures, from the alpine zone to coastal dunes, common throughout Britain. E2.

Hygrocybe strangulata (Orton) Svr.
Cap like *H. reidii* or more omphalinoid, a little redder, eventually scurfy-scaly over the centre. Gills somewhat decurrent, concolorous. Stipe reddish, rather short, 2×0.5cm. Flesh reddish, odourless. Spores 9×5μm, mostly constricted; cuticular hyphae narrow, 8-12μm wide. Pastures on acid soils and among heather: fairly common especially in the north. E2.

Hygrocybe lepida Arnolds [*H. cantharellus*]
Cap 4-7cm, soon depressed, surface finely concolorously scaly as in *H. miniata*, red or fading orange, margin crenulate. Gills often distant, deeply decurrent, paler or yellowish. Stipe 5×0.4cm, concolorous, dry. Flesh orange, odourless. Spores 11×8μm, elliptical or often a little uneven in outline; cuticular hyphae broad as in *H. miniata*. Lawns, shrubberies and moors, fairly common especially in the north. E1.

Hygrocybe moseri Bon [*H. miniata* var. *mollis* p.p.]
Aspect of *H. lepida* but more slender or with less decurrent gills; cap 2-4cm, convex, downy to ± scaly, yellow to orange, fading to yellowish. Gills rather crowded, somewhat decurrent, yellow. Stipe 4×0.3cm, yellow, dry. Flesh pale. Spores 9×5μm, cylindrical or slightly constricted; cuticular hyphae 10-12μm wide. Lawns and heaths, sometimes in damp copses and peat moors. E2.

H. helobia (Arnolds) Bon can be distinguished microscopically by having a gill trama of *Godfrinia* type, with elongated hyphae and stocky basidia. E1.

Hygrocybe turunda (Fr.) Karst.
Cap convex, 2-4cm, reddish orange, paling, with dark brown to blackish scales over the centre, on a ± yellowish ground. Gills adnate or sloping, yellowish. Stipe concolorous, 4×0.6cm. Flesh yellow to orange. Spores 10×5.5μm; cuticular hyphae 15-25μm wide, with brown intercellular pigment. On wet pastures and in Highland mossy woods, uncommon. E1.

var. **sphagnophila** is redder and more slender. It occurs on *Sphagnum* like *H. coccineocrenata* below, with which it may be confused. But its colours are paler and the margin is not crenate. E1.

Hygrocybe coccineocrenata (Orton) Moser
Similar to *H. turunda*, but with small blackish scales on a red ground and crenate margin to the cap. Gills more decurrent, white to orange. Stipe 10×0.3cm, elongated, red. Flesh pale. Spores 12×7μm, cylindrical; cuticular hyphae as in *H. turunda*. Among *Sphagnum* in peat bogs, especially in the Highlands. E2.

Hygrocybe miniata

Hygrocybe reidii

Hygrocybe strangulata

Hygrocybe lepida

Hygrocybe moseri

Hygrocybe turunda

Hygrocybe coccineocrenata

Section *Fornicatae*. Colours dull or pale, cap surface dry, glabrous or fibrous. Smell earthy or none.

Hygrocybe fornicata (Fr.) Sing.
Cap 4-8cm, convex or conical, then flat to depressed, margin splitting, surface glabrous or fibrous, whitish, pale, or somewhat grey brown at the centre. Gills notched, whitish. Stipe 7×1cm, pallid or white. Flesh whitish, smell ± earthy. Spores 9×6μm; cuticle scarcely differentiated, like those in the genus *Cuphophyllus*. In grassland and copses, chiefly in Scotland. E2.

H. streptopus (Fr.) Bon. Somewhat darker, more conical and deformed or with bent stipe, in grassland. E2.

Section *Olidae*. Reddening and/or with a nitrous smell.

Hygrocybe ingrata Jensen & Møll. [*H. nitiosa* p.p.]
Cap medium size, 5-8cm, pale brownish grey, fibrous to finally almost scaly. Gills pallid, reddening. Stipe 6×1cm, pallid or nearer cap colour, reddening like the flesh. Smell nitrous. Spores 10×7.5μm; cuticle slightly trichodermic. Among grass in wet places. E2.

Hygrocybe ovina (Bull.) Kühn.
Cap 8-12cm, convex or fleshy, olive-brown to reddish black, fibrous then cracked. Gills distant, thick, greyish-brown, reddening to browning or blackening like *Russula nigricans*. Stipe fibrous, 8×2cm, sometimes furrowed, brownish or reddening, like the flesh; nitrous smell faint or inconstant. Spores 9×5.5μm. Damp copses. Uncommon in Britain, mostly in the North. E2.

H. nitrata (Pers.) Wünsche [*H. murinacea*] does not redden but has a strong nitrous odour. E1.

Section *Psittacinae* [Subgenus *Gliophorus*]. Very viscid, caps particoloured or grey. Clamps scanty.

Hygrocybe psittacina (Sch.) Kumm.
Rather slender, margin striate, cap (2-5cm) particoloured green, yellow and reddish, sometimes wholly salmon orange or rosé wine colour with age, when frosted or dried. Gills yellow or greenish, adnate or notched. Stipe 5×0.4cm, very viscid, coloured like the cap or persistently green at the apex. Flesh concolorous. Spores 9×5.5μm; cuticular hyphae slender in a mass of mucus. Common on lawns, pastures, in open grassy woodland and copses throughout Britain; var. *abietina* under conifers. E4.

Hygrocybe laeta (Pers.) Kumm.
Cap 2-5cm, flat, then omphalinoid, pinkish to saffron ochre or pinkish beige. Gills decurrent, pink, with gelatinised margin. Stipe slender, 7×0.5cm, pale pinkish to saffron, olivaceous at the apex. Flesh pale. Spores 7×4.5μm; cuticular hyphae without clamps. Very common in pastures, heaths, moors and grassy damp woods. Throughout Britain, but in heathy areas often under bracken. E3.

H. perplexa Arnolds [*H. sciophana* p.p.] appears rather intermediate between the above two species, with cap colour a beautiful red mingled with olive, especially at the apex of the stipe. E2.

Hygrocybe unguinosa (Fr.) Karst.
Cap rather fleshy, 3-6cm, convex, surface gelatinised and slimy, coloured brown to blackish bistre. Gills horizontal or adnate, pale. Stipe 6×0.5cm, typically undulating, brittle, slimy, light grey. Spores 7×5.5μm, ovoid. Lawns, pastures and moors, often in swarms and clustered. Throughout Britain. E4.

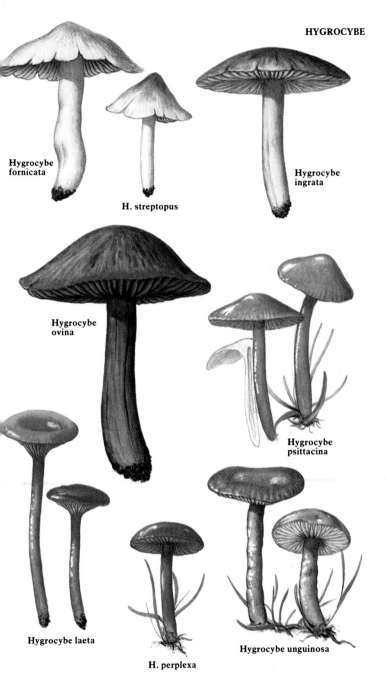

Hygrocybe
fornicata

H. streptopus

Hygrocybe
ingrata

Hygrocybe
ovina

Hygrocybe
psittacina

Hygrocybe laeta

H. perplexa

Hygrocybe unguinosa

Genus *Hygrophorus*. Rather fleshy to robust fungi with adnate or often decurrent gills, many rather viscid, variously coloured but seldom brightly so. Trama bilateral or diverging.

Section *Clitocyboides*. Cap scarcely viscid, stipe dry, colour white or pale.

Hygrophorus penarius Fr.
A large fleshy fungus, cap 10-15cm, surface matt or slightly downy, creamy white. Gills distant or thick, arched, concolorous. Stipe thickset, 6×2cm, often expanded above or almost rooting, fibrous, creamy white. Flesh white, firm. Spores 8×5µm, elliptical. Under broadleaved trees in warm situations, rare in Britain. Edible and good. E3.

H. fagi Becker & Bon, a little more slender, more creamy or pinkish with slightly mottled stipe, occurs under beech. E2.

Hygrophorus karstenii Sacc. & Cub.
Similar to *H. penarius* but smaller. Cap 5-6cm, with deep yellow gills contrasting with the white cap and stipe (5×1cm). Spores 10×6µm. Under conifers, especially spruce, among bilberry. Rare in Britain. E1.

Section *Eburnei*. Cap and stipe ± viscid, colours whitish to cream, pinkish ochre or pale orange.

Hygrophorus cossus (Sow.) Fr.
Cap not very fleshy, 5-7cm, moderately viscid, dull white. Gills arched, cream, rather distant. Stipe 6×1cm, white. Flesh white, smelling strongly of cooked Jerusalem artichokes or goat moth larvae. Spores 8×5µm. Under beech or holm oak. Common in Britain. E4.

H. piceae Kühn. is more slender, not very viscid, odourless, under conifers in the mountains. Em2.

Hygrophorus eburneus (Bull.) Fr.
A little more slender than *H. cossus*, creamy white, very slimy. Stipe tall, up to 8×0.5cm, attenuated to the base. Gills cream to slightly ochraceous, tinged pinkish like the stipe in var. *carneipes*. Smell strong and fruity, like mandarin peel. Not browning with age. Spores 9×6µm. Common under beech. E4.

H. discoxanthus (Fr.) Rea [*H. chrysaspis*] looks very like *H. eburneus* but readily bruises brown when handled and the smell is fainter. KOH reaction yellow, then rusty. Common under beech in Britain. E4.

Hygrophorus chrysodon (Batsch) Fr.
Cap not very fleshy, 4-7cm, coloured like *H. cossus* but elegantly speckled golden yellow round the margin and over the stipe apex. Stipe 6×0.8cm, white elsewhere. Smell faint, slightly of Jerusalem artichokes. Spores 9×7µm. Under broadleaved trees in warm places, with beech and oak in Britain, not common. E2.

Hygrophorus lindtneri Moser [including *H. carpini*]
Cap 5-7cm, not fleshy apart from below umbo, viscid, orange at the centre then pale fawn with a cream to whitish margin. Gills arched, tinged pinkish cream. Stipe 7×1cm, attenuated at the base, cream to pale pinkish, viscid. Smell faint. Spores 9×5µm. In copses under broadleaved trees. E2.

Hygrophorus pudorinus (Fr.) Fr.
Cap 8-12cm, very viscid and glutinous, pale orange to fawn, more cream or pink at the margin. Gills arched, pallid or similarly coloured. Stipe 10×2cm, slightly swollen in the middle, pallid to concolorous, with glutinous dots and orange fibrils, browning ± from the base upwards. Flesh pale with a resinous smell; taste acrid or like the smell of turpentine. Spores 9×6µm; epicutis of nodular gelatinised hyphae. Under conifers, rare in Britain. E1(m3).

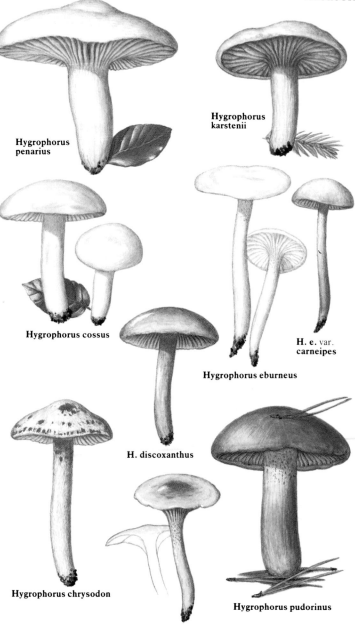

Hygrophorus
penarius

Hygrophorus
karstenii

Hygrophorus cossus

H. e. var.
carneipes

Hygrophorus eburneus

H. discoxanthus

Hygrophorus chrysodon

Hygrophorus lindtneri

Hygrophorus pudorinus

Section *Fulventes*. Colours yellowish-fawn to russet brown or pinkish. Stipe dry, cap not very viscid.

Hygrophorus nemoreus (Pers.) Fr.
Cap 8-12cm, margin incurved, surface greasy, rather fibrillose, streaky or pruinose towards the centre, fawn orange, paler towards the margin. Gills whitish or tinted pinkish, sinuate to slightly decurrent. Stipe 7×2cm, pale to almost concolorous, apex granular. Flesh white, coloured beneath the surface. Spores 8×5µm. Under various broadleaved trees, rare in Britain. Edible and good. E3.

Hygrophorus arbustivus (Fr.) Fr.
Cap smaller or less fleshy, 6-8cm, surface fibrillose to streaky, fawnish orange to pale pinkish bistre, margin thin and whiter. Stipe 6×0.8cm. Gills and stipe white, scurfy below the gills. Flesh pale, yellowing slightly. Spores 8×5µm. Under broadleaved trees, especially beech, often late in the season, rare in Britain. Edible. E3.

H. leporinus Fr.,with somewhat brick-orange or vinaceous colours and rather paler gills and stipe, may be transitional to section *Rubentes* below. In grassy woodlands. E2.

Hygrophorus poetarum Heim
Cap 10-18cm, fleshy, pale flesh colour to salmon, margin creamy yellowish or pinkish, somewhat lobed and incurved, scarcely viscid. Gills pallid with pinkish tint. Stipe 12×3cm, similarly coloured, apex punctate, pale. Flesh pale with a pleasant smell of cinnamon or *Inocybe bongardii* (p.234) etc. Spores 9×6µm. Copses on calcareous soil in warm places, not common. E1.

Hygrophorus discoideus (Pers.) Fr.
Cap 5-6cm, convex, viscid, beige ochraceous to russet, distinctly reddish brown over the centre. Gills whitish. Stipe 4×0.8cm, whitish, with a viscid annular zone. Flesh white, mild and odourless. Spores 8×5µm; hyphae with coloured walls. Grassy pine woods on calcareous soils. Edible. E2.

H. unicolor Gröger [*H. leucophaeus* p.p.] has similar but duller colouring with drier stipe lacking the viscid ring. E1.

Section *Rubentes*. Colours rather pink to purplish, gills and stipe often speckled purple, not particularly viscid.

Hygrophorus russula (Sch.) Quél.
A fairly robust, fleshy fungus, cap 12-20cm, fleshy, often with irregular humps, finely spotted vinaceous brown on a pale pinkish ground. Gills very crowded for this genus, broad, adnate, pinkish, speckled vinaceous with age. Stipe 10×3cm, similarly coloured, apex granulate. Flesh pale with vinaceous tints, smell pleasant, grassy, taste rather bitter. Spores 9×6µm; hyphal walls speckled with pigment. Under beech and holm oak on calcareous soils, very rare in Britain. Edible. E3.

Hygrophorus erubescens (Fr.) Fr.
Rather less fleshy than *H. russula*, cap 8-10cm, pinkish, ± spotted, or yellowing. Gills normally spaced, scarcely pinkish or speckled. Stipe 7×1cm, swollen at the middle or almost rooting, sparsely speckled pinkish. Flesh yellowing, taste becoming bitter. Spores 10×6µm. In beech and fir woods in the mountains, rare in Britain. Edible after blanching. Em3.

var. **persicolor** is a little more robust with mild flesh, not yellowing. E2.

Hygrophorus capreolarius (Kalchbr.) Sacc.
Cap 5-7cm, convex with incurved margin, surface somewhat fibrillose, dark vinaceous purple, ± spotted. Gills dark coloured, finally dingy vinaceous brown. Stipe 6×1cm, fibrous, similar colour or paler. Flesh vinaceous, darker at the base. Spores 9×5µm; hyphae heavily pigmented, in zones. In damp coniferous woods or *Sphagnum* bogs. Not likely in Britain. Em2.

H. purpurascens (A.-S.) Fr. is somewhat similar but with paler gills and a fleecy ring zone on the stipe. Not likely in Britain. E2.

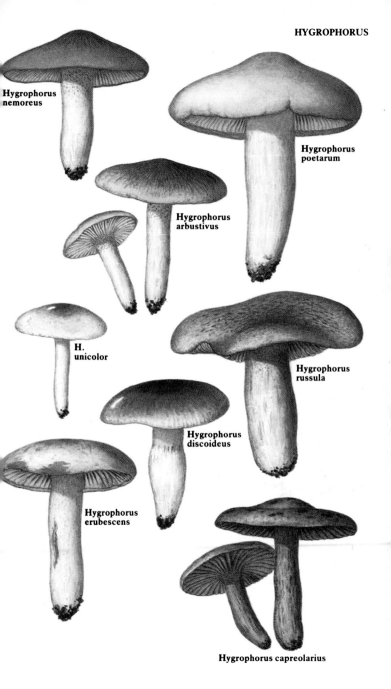

Hygrophorus nemoreus

Hygrophorus poetarum

Hygrophorus arbustivus

H. unicolor

Hygrophorus russula

Hygrophorus discoideus

Hygrophorus erubescens

Hygrophorus capreolarius

Section *Camarophylli*. Dry or slightly viscid fungi with grey or blackish tints. Stipe dry, punctate or not.

Hygrophorus camarophyllus (A.-S.) Dum., Grandj. & R. Mre. [*H. caprinus*]
Cap 7-12cm, convex, silky-fibrillose, slightly viscid, bistre to soot-colour. Gills arched, slightly decurrent, white to yellowish. Stipe 9×1cm, whitish to soot-colour, striate-fibrillose. Flesh pallid to greyish, odourless. Spores 9×5.5μm. Under conifers on acid soil. Very rare in Britain. E3.

H. atramentosus (A.-S.) Haas & Haller is more blackish, fibrillosely streaked, in mixed woods on calcareous soil. Not likely in Britain. cE2.

Hygrophorus calophyllus Karst.
Like *H. camarophyllus* but cap rather more viscid, yellow-brown to olivaceous. Gills arched, a fine pink to salmon colour, distant. Stipe and flesh as in *H. camarophyllus*. Spores 9×5μm; cuticle rather palisadic, gelatinised. In pine woods on limestone or basalt. Not likely in Britain. E1.

Hygrophorus marzuolus (Fr.) Bres.
Cap fleshy, 10-15cm, often deformed, whitish then mottled greyish, sometimes slaty blue. Gills becoming glaucous. Stipe thickset, 4×1cm, pallid to almost concolorous. Flesh white, smell pleasant. Spores 8×5μm. Fruiting in early spring under pines or mixed open woodland in the mountains, often in clusters. Not likely in Britain. Em2.

Hygrophorus agathosmus (Fr.) Fr.
Cap 6-10cm, convex, surface granular over the centre, greyish to brownish grey, sometimes violaceous pink. Gills arched, white. Stipe 8×1cm, pallid with white granules at the apex, base sometimes eventually yellowish. Flesh white, smell of cherry laurel. Spores 10×6μm. Under conifers, in Britain mainly in the Highlands. E3.

H. pustulatus (Pers.) Fr. is like a miniature *H. agathosmus* but odourless. E2.

H. hyacinthinus Quél. is paler, sometimes pinkish, with a strong smell of hyacinths or amyl acetate. E2.

Section *Olivaceoumbrini*. Viscid all over, colours grey or olivaceous to orange. Stipe garlanded or obscurely ringed.

Hygrophorus olivaceoalbus (Fr.) Fr.
Cap 5-8cm, umbonate, slimy, fawn brown to olivaceous, paler or marbled and streaky towards the margin. Gills whitish. Stipe slender 12×0.8cm, elegantly striped with olive-brown up to an indistinct ring zone, white above that. Flesh whitish. Spores variable: 12-16×6-8.5μm; cuticular hyphae strongly coloured or spangled. Mossy woods of conifers with bilberry, sometimes in *Sphagnum*, rare in Britain outside the Highlands. E1 (m3).

H. persoonii Arnolds [*H. dichrous*] is a similar but rather darker coloured fungus under broadleaved trees, distinguished by a green reaction with ammonia. Not uncommon in Britain. E2.

Hygrophorus latitabundus Britz. [*H. limacinus*]
More robust with cap 10-15cm, pale or blotched brownish to olivaceous with a white margin. Gills white. Stipe stout, 13×3cm, white at first, flecked with gluten, finally almost concolorous. Flesh pale. Spores 12×7μm; hyphae bearing lumps of oily exudate. Under pines on limestone. Edible and very good but peel off the gelatinous cuticle before cooking. E3.

Hygrophorus hypothejus (Fr.) Fr.
Medium stature, cap 5-7cm, olive-bistre, sometimes tinged with orange at the margin. Gills yellow, then orange. Stipe 8×0.6cm, with a brownish sleeve-like annular zone, finally yellowing throughout. Spores 9×5μm. Common under conifers throughout Britain. E3.

H. lucorum Kalchbr. is entirely lemon yellow, not very viscid, and occurs under larch. E2.

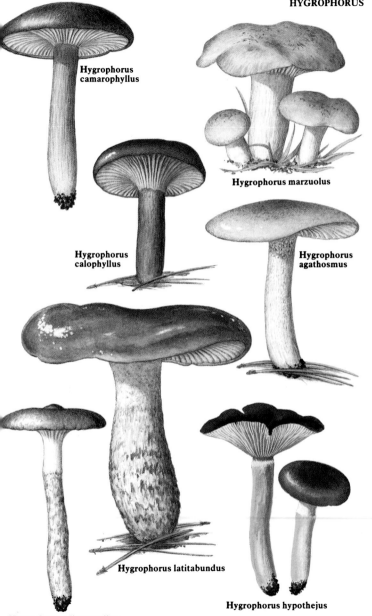

Hygrophorus
camarophyllus

Hygrophorus marzuolus

Hygrophorus
calophyllus

Hygrophorus
agathosmus

Hygrophorus latitabundus

Hygrophorus hypothejus

Hygrophorus olivaceoalbus

Family *Pleurotaceae*. Stipe excentric, lateral or absent. Spore print white to pinkish-lilac but neither ochraceous nor rust colour. Tribe *Pleuroteae*. More or less fleshy fungi, not leathery, gill edge even, gills thin and not noticeably forked except sometimes near the stipe, flesh not gelatinised; thick-walled cystidia absent, spores non-amyloid.

Genus *Pleurotus*. Relatively large fleshy fungi with cylindrical spores.

Pleurotus ostreatus (Jacq.) Kumm. OYSTER FUNGUS
Cap 8-15cm, convex or fleshy, bluish grey to sometimes slaty, fading brownish, smooth. Gills white, unbranched or scarcely interconnected at the base; peacock blue in var. *columbinus*. Stipe short, about 1×1cm, lateral, often velvety, or lacking. Flesh white, smell fungoid. Spores 11×3.5μm, cylindric, print pale lilac; wavy marginal cystidia. On dead trunks and branches of all kinds, often late in the year, commonly in clusters. A good edible fungus, abundant throughout Britain. E3.

P. pulmonarius (Fr.) Quél. is thinner and flatter, with cap pale beige to whitish. E2.

Pleurotus cornucopiae (Paul.) Gill.
Cap 5-12cm, soon becoming depressed, finally even funnel-shaped, whitish to pale beige or greyish yellow at the centre. Gills anastomosing near the base and prolonged as a network on the stipe. Stipe length variable, sometimes only slightly excentric, not downy but often reticulate. Flesh white with a strong smell, sometimes rather unpleasant. Spores 10×5μm, ± elliptical. Common especially on elm stumps in Britain. Edible but not of high quality. E4.

Pleurotus eryngii (DC.) Quél.
Cap 5-12cm, first convex then broadly umbonate and finally slightly depressed, margin incurved and wavy, surface dry to ± scaly, grey brown to pale beige, sometimes mottled or streaked sooty-russet on a pale ground. Gills arched, whitish to greyish. Stipe ± central, 4×1cm, whitish to pale beige. Flesh white, with pleasant fungoid smell. In grassland, isolated or in small tufts, appearing terrestrial but springing from roots of *Eryngium campestre*; cap often regular enough to suggest a *Clitocybe*. Spores 15×5μm. A popular edible fungus in Europe but not found in Britain, in absence of the host. sE2.

Pleurotus dryinus (Pers.) Kumm. [*P. corticatus*]
Cap sometimes reminiscent of *P. cornucopiae* but more fleshy and scarcely depressed, cuticle slightly scaly or cracking outwards from the centre, downy, creamy ochraceous, sometimes yellowish, or in var. *tephrotrichus* more greyish; margin ± appendiculate. Gills white, then yellowing, rather distant, slightly anastomosing at the base. Stipe lateral, often very short, downy, ± reticulate near the gills or down to a fugacious ring, whitish, yellowing at the base. Flesh white, smell pleasant. Spores 15×4.5μm, cylindrical. Common in Britain, especially on oak trunks. E2.

Genus *Nothopanus* [*Pleurocybella*]. Similar to *Pleurotus* but less fleshy and spores globose or broadly oval.

Nothopanus porrigens (Pers.) Sing.
On coniferous stumps and dead trunks, in overlapping clusters, cap sessile, flat or tongue-shaped, 2-6cm, smooth except for a hairy base, pure white or milky white. Gills crowded, soft, white then slightly glaucous. Smell fungoid but rather unpleasant. Not edible. Spores globose, 5-6μm. In Britain confined to the Scottish Highlands, where it is abundant, and the Borders. Em3.

N. lignatilis (Pers.) Bon [*Clitocybe lignatilis*]
Differs from *P. porrigens* in having a distinct lateral or excentric stipe, up to 2cm, with adnate gills; smell mealy. Spores 6×4μm. Common in Britain on stumps and dead trunks of broadleaved trees, especially beech and elm. Perhaps better regarded as a *Clitocybe*, but then exceptional in being on wood. E1.

Phyllotopsis nidulans (Pers.) Sing.
In habit like *Nothofagus porrigens* but cap more kidney-shaped, surface felted to hairy, at first yellowish white, soon becoming orange. Gills crowded orange to cinnamon. Stipe dorsal or absent, shaggy. Flesh orange yellow. Spores pink, 6×3μm, kidney-shaped. On coniferous wood, often in winter or spring. Uncommon. Em2.

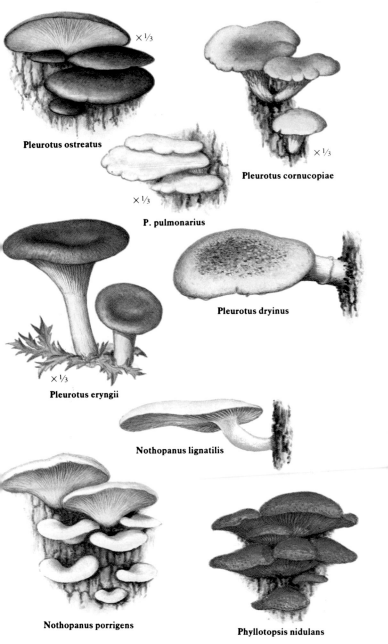

Pleurotus ostreatus

× 1/3

Pleurotus cornucopiae

× 1/3

× 1/3

P. pulmonarius

Pleurotus dryinus

× 1/3

Pleurotus eryngii

Nothopanus lignatilis

Nothopanus porrigens

Phyllotopsis nidulans

121

Tribe *Resupinateae*. Flesh gelatinous or with a gelatinous layer under the cuticle.

Genus *Resupinatus*. Small, sessile, gelatinous-fleshed, without thick-walled cystidia.

Resupinatus applicatus (Batsch) S.F. Gray
Cap 0.5-1cm, bell-shaped or rather conical and attached by the apex, at first whitish but soon greyish to violaceous, rather striate at the margin and downy at the base. Gills radiating from the point of attachment, thick and fairly distant, greyish. Spores spherical, 5-6μm. On twigs and dead wood of all kinds, abundant everywhere. E2.

R. silvanus (Sacc.) Sing. is similar but darker, with elliptical spores 8×4μm. E1.

Genus *Hohenbuhelia*. Small to medium size, flesh with a gelatinous zone under the surface, cystidia present, typically thick-walled and pointed.

Hohenbuehelia geogenia (DC.) Sing.
Cap 4-12cm, often trumpet-shaped or twisted at first, surface rather felted, beige brown to greyish, covering a gelatinised layer. Gills whitish, downy under a lens. Stipe lateral or sometimes almost absent, spout-like, pale. Flesh white, smell slightly mealy. Spores 7×5μm; cystidia thick-walled, encrusted. On soil, often among leaves. Not uncommon. E3.

H. petaloides (Bull.) Schulz. is similar but more elongated and spatulate and grows on stumps. E1.

Hohenbuehelia atrocaerulea (Fr.) Sing.
Cap smaller, 3-5cm, sessile, shaggy hairy to hoary, greyish white passing into dark bluish or blackish at the base. Gills creamy white to yellowish. Spores 9×5μm; cystidia thick-walled, encrusted. Clustered on dead wood, not uncommon. E2.

H. culmicola Bon is more stipitate and occurs on culms of marram grass on sand dunes. Known from Wales. E2.

Tribe *Lentineae*. Flesh leathery or elastic, not-gelatinised. Spores non-amyloid.

Genus *Lentinus*. Stipe ± central or only slightly excentric, gill edge ± toothed.

Lentinus lepideus (Fr.) Fr.
Cap fleshy, thick, 10-15cm, covered with rather large thick scales, ochraceous then rather russet on a creamy ivory ground. Gills arched, slightly decurrent at first, ochraceous cream, sometimes tinged russet or pinkish. Stipe 8×1cm, hard, slightly scaly up to a ring-zone, concolorous. Flesh leathery or compact, smell of cinnamon or toothpowder. Spores variable: 8-17×4-6μm. On stumps of conifers and coniferous timber when not treated with fungicide, fairly common in Britain, especially in the north. sE3, nE1.

Lentinus cyathiformis Bres. [*L. degener*, *L. variabilis*]
A large fungus, cap up to 15-25cm, often depressed, fawn to rust colour. Gills narrow, even fold-like, forked or anastomosing towards the base, creamy ochraceous with an irregular edge. Stipe short, 5×2cm, pale to almost concolorous. Spores 13×5μm. On stumps of willows, poplars or conifers. Not in Britain. E1.

Lentinus tigrinus (Bull.) Fr.
Cap 4-7cm, thin, elastic, rather umbilicate, dotted or striped over the centre with tiny dark brown scales on a whitish ground. Gills decurrent, white. Stipe slender, 6×0.3cm, pallid, smooth or cobwebby, more elongated and spotted in var. *dunalii*. Spores 10×3.5μm. In clusters on stumps and dead branches of poplar and willow, uncommon in southern Britain. E3.

Panus conchatus (Bull.) Fr. [*P. torulosus*]
Cap 8-12cm, convex to slightly depressed, tomentose or glabrous, ochraceous fawn tinged towards the margin with violaceous lilac, at least at first. Gills decurrent, tinged lilac at first; edge not toothed. Stipe scarcely lateral, 3×1cm, pallid to concolorous. Flesh leathery or elastic, pale, odourless. Spores 5×3μm. On stumps and dead wood of various broadleaved trees, rather common throughout Britain. E2.

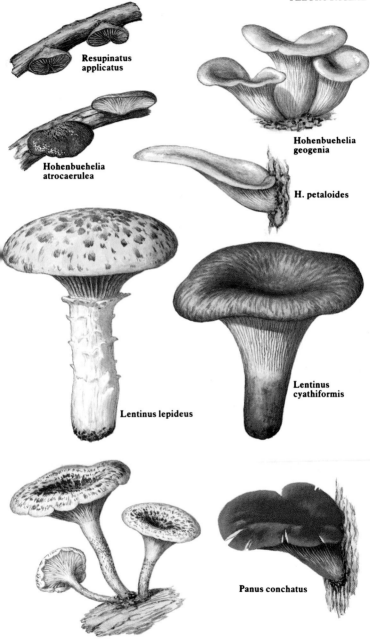

Resupinatus
applicatus

Hohenbuehelia
geogenia

Hohenbuehelia
atrocaerulea

H. petaloides

Lentinus
cyathiformis

Lentinus lepideus

Lentinus tigrinus

Panus conchatus

123

Tribe *Leptoglosseae*. Gills forked or anastomosing, sometimes no more than ridges.

Genus *Arrhenia*. Cap thin-fleshed, translucent, bearing rudimentary anastomosing ridges.

Arrhenia lobata (Pers.) Kühn. & Lamoure [*Leptoglossum lobatum*]
Cap tongue-shaped, 3-5cm, often lobed or jagged, thin, horizontal, pale beige to grey bistre, glabrous, under surface bearing similarly coloured gill-like ridges, sometimes forming alveoli towards the base. Flesh insignificant, odourless. Spores 10×6μm, ovoid to pear-shaped; hyphae clamped. On damp moss or plant debris in bogs. Uncommon. E2.

Arrhenia spathulata (Fr.) Redh. [*Leptoglossum muscigenum*]
Similar but smaller, cap 1-2cm, more circular or often rather trumpet-shaped at first, somewhat zoned, sometimes ± stalked. Spores 8×5μm; hyphae without clamps. On moss. Uncommon. E2.

Faerberia carbonaria (A. & S.) Pouz. [*Geopetalum carbonarium*]
Cap 3-5cm, funnel-shaped, resembling *Cantharellus* (p. 306), blackish to slaty bistre with inrolled margin. Gills very decurrent, fold-like, repeatedly forked, greyish ochre. Stipe short, 1cm, almost central, pallid to almost concolorous. Flesh greyish, almost odourless. Spores 10×4μm, cylindrical; cystidia as in *Hohenbuehelia* but pseudo-amyloid. On burnt ground. Uncommon. E2.

Tribe *Panelleae*. Leathery, not readily putrescent; spores amyloid.

Genus *Panellus*. Stipe lateral or absent, gill margin entire; spores narrow.

Panellus stipticus (Bull.) Karst.
Cap 2-4cm, shell-shaped, surface felted or floccose, brownish ochre or fawn to pale beige. Gill colour similar. Stipe very thick below the gills. Flesh ochraceous, tough, taste bitter. Spores 5×2.5μm, cylindrical. On dead wood of broadleaved trees, ash, birch, beech and especially oak, often in overlapping clusters. Very common throughout Britain especially in late autumn. E4.

P. mitis (Pers.) Kühn. Paler, nearly smooth, with gill edge slightly gelatinous, stipe small, not enlarged at the apex, taste mild. Uncommon in Britain. E2.

Panellus serotinus (Hoffm.) Kühn.
Cap 6-13cm, ± tomentose, greenish to yellowish brown or bronze, darker towards the centre. Gills yellow to orange. Stipe lateral, short, 1×1cm, strigose or spotted dark brown on a greenish yellow ground. Mycelium orange. Flesh pale, odourless, taste milky. Spores narrow, 4×1.5μm. On wood of broadleaved trees and conifers, not uncommon, throughout Britain. E2-3.

Genus *Lentinellus*. Gill edge finely toothed, stipe variable. Spores ± globose to broadly elliptical, often finely ornamented; anatomy suggestive of Aphyllophorales, and probably related to *Auriscalpium* (p.312).

Lentinellus cochleatus (Hoffm.) Karst.
Cap 3-8cm, funnel-shaped, somewhat inrolled, often densely clustered or deformed by mutual pressure, russet brown. Gills deeply decurrent, terminating in a line or furrow on the stipe. Stipe 3×0.6cm, gutter-like, concolorous. Flesh pale with strong smell of aniseed, absent in var. *inolens*. Spores ± globose, 4-5μm. Common on old stumps of all kinds, throughout Britain. E4.

L. omphalodes (Fr.) Karst. is similar but smaller, paler and isolated, odourless. Spores up to 7×4μm, ornamented. On twigs or soil. sE2.

Lentinellus ursinus (Fr.) Kühn.
Cap 2-5cm, lateral, ± imbricate, surface strigose or velvety, russet brown, margin more glabrous. Gills pale, fan-shaped. Stipe absent. Spores 3×2μm, finely warted. On stumps of broadleaved trees, especially beech. Rare in Britain. E1.

L. vulpinus (Fr.) Kün. & R. Mre., more densely clustered, shows paler cap surface, more glabrous but distinctly more glabrous or radially strigose. Rare. E1.

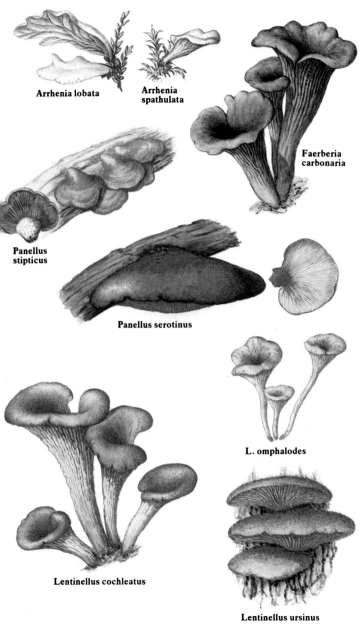

Arrhenia lobata

Arrhenia spathulata

Faerberia carbonaria

Panellus stipticus

Panellus serotinus

L. omphalodes

Lentinellus cochleatus

Lentinellus ursinus

Family *Tricholomataceae*. Stipe central, flesh fibrous.

Tribe *Clitocybeae*. Gills decurrent or broadly adnate. Spores non-amyloid.

Genus *Omphalina*. Small fungi with depressed or umbilicate cap. Tramal hyphae interwoven.

Key to *Omphalina* and similar genera

1a	Brightly coloured fungi, pink or somewhat orange: **2**
1b	Ochraceous to russet or yellowish, sometimes bright yellow in gills only: **4**
1c	Brown, grey or blackish: **11**
1d	White to whitish from the start: **26**

2a Bright orange, gills pale, deeply decurrent, stipe slender ≫ *Rickenella fibula* 128
2b Some shade of pink: **3**
2c Only gills bright yellow or orange: **10**

3a Lilaceous pink, smooth, gills sloping, stipe short; mossy lawns ≫
    Omphalina rosella, 128
3b Surface somewhat frosted to scurfy; on dunes ≫   *O. lilacinicolor*, 128
3c If there is a strong mealy smell ≫   see *Pseudoomphalina compressipes*, 130

4a Russet to reddish brown or pinkish: **5**
4b Yellowish or with yellow gills: **9**

5a With the leathery texture of a *Marasmius*: **6**a
5b Normal agaricoid texture or a little cartilaginous: **7**

6a On wood ≫   *Xeromphalina campanella*, 130
6b In *Sphagnum*; margin more yellow: *X. cornui*, not described here.

7a Stipe compressed or furrowed, strong mealy smell, cap pinkish brown ≫
    Pseudoomphalina compressipes, 130
7b Stipe not compressed: **8**

8a Bright fawny russet to reddish brown; on lawns ≫   *Omphalina pyxidata*, 128
8b Pale ochraceous russet; on mossy dunes ≫   *O. galericolor*, 128

9a Ochraceous-yellowish beige, margin striate or fluted, flesh soft ≫
    Gerronema ericetorum, 128
9b Yellow colour confined to the gills; on rotting wood: **10**

10a Gills pale lemon yellow, cap more livid, wrinkled ≫ *Cuphophyllus grossulus*, 102
10b Gills bright yellow, distant, strongly contrasting with the chestnut brown
    umbilicate cap; stipe ± yellow to russet ≫   *Chrysomphalina chrysophylla*, 128

11a Gills forked: **12**
11b Gills not forked: **14**

12a Colour pale slaty grey with lilaceous or pinkish tinge, umbilicus with an umbo ≫
    Cantharellula umbonata, 130
12b Colour persistently greyish brown: **13**

13a Dark grey-brown fading to whitish; smell slightly fruity or of pelargonium; in
    lawns ≫   *Phaeotellus griseopallidus*, 128
13b Dull grey-brown, not fading much; odourless; sandy or stony pastures ≫
    Phaeotellus rickenii, 128

14a Cap surface smooth, neither viscid nor scaly: **15**
14b Cap surface viscid: **22**
14c Cap surface scaly at least in the middle, elsewhere felted or striped: **24**

15a Margin striate, cap soon expanded: **16**
15b Margin not striate or barely so when young: **20**

16a Hygrophanous, drying whitish: **17**
16b Not hygrophanous so not paling much during drying: **18**

17a Cap *c.* 5cm, gills rather grey when dried; in grassy thickets »
Pseudoclitocybe expallens, 130
17b Cap *c.* 2cm, slightly viscid at first, gills with pinkish tinge when dried; calcareous pasture »   *Gamundia pseudoclusilis*, 130

18a With brown gill edge, stipe pruinose; in troops on stumps »
Hydropus marginellus, 130
18b Not as above: **19**

19a Grey-brown with concolorous gills; under conifers or in *Sphagnum* »
Fayodia gracilipes, 130
19b Slightly paler with white gills »   *F. leucophylla*, 130

20a Rather fleshy fungus, 4(7)cm, resembling a *Clitocybe* but dark slaty brown to blackish; stipe with a reticulum of blackish lines; smell of new mown hay; copses
Pseudoclitocybe cyathiformis, 130
20b More slender, cap 1-2cm: **21**

21a Stipe short; colours dark blackish brown; lawns »   *Omphalina obscurata*, 128
21b Stipe taller, somewhat velvety, gills deeply decurrent; colour violaceous brown at least at top of stipe »   *Rickenella swartzii*, 128

22a On bare ground especially after a fire, gills arched, white »
Myxomphalia maura, 130
22b Not associated with fires: **23**

23a In pastures on limy soil, cap brown ochre, fading, margin striate; gills eventually tinged pinkish »   *Gamundia pseudoclusilis*, 130
23b On mossy dunes, cap dark grey-brown fading whitish, smell mealy »
Omphalina barbularum, 128

24a Centre umbilicate and speckled, remainder of cap grey-brownish radially striped on a white ground; gills scarcely decurrent »   *Clitocybula lacerata*, 130
24b Umbilicus with blackish grey scales, remainder of cap somewhat matted: **25**

25a Scales dark bistre on a paler ground; in *Sphagnum* »
Omphalina sphagnicola, 128
25b Scales almost concolorous or smaller; often not in *Sphagnum* »   *O. oniscus*, 128

26a Small mycenoid fungi, cap about 1cm: **27**
26b Medium sized fungus, grey at first then pale » see *Phaeotellus griseopallidus*, 128

27a Pure white, on humus or rotting wood »·   see *Delicatula*, 186
27b Slightly greyish white at the centre; in lawns »   *Hemimycena mairei*, 186

Omphalina pyxidata (Bull.) Quél.
Cap 1-4cm, umbilicate, margin incurved, striate or fluted; surface smooth or glabrous, russet brown to rusty beige or reddish. Gills arched, moderately spaced, pale to nearly concolorous. Stipe 3×0.3cm, almost concolorous or paler. Flesh pale, inodorous. Spores 9×5μm, ± elliptical. Lawns or bare soil with mosses. Common. E3.
  O. galericolor (Romagn.) Bon. Paler; on fixed dunes. Spores globose, 8×7μm. E2.

Omphalina obscurata Kuhn. ex Reid
Cap 1-2cm, slightly depressed, margin not incurved, scarcely striate, dark grey to blackish, slightly paler when dried. Gills arched to almost horizontal, paler. Stipe 1×0.3cm, smooth, dark. Flesh grey, odourless. Spores 14×6μm. On bare soil or lawns. Uncommon. E2.

O. barbularum (Romagn.) Bon [*Clitocybe barbularum*]. A little more viscid and becoming paler, with smaller spores. Among mosses on fixed coastal dunes. E4.

Omphalina sphagnicola (Berk.) Moser
Cap 3-5cm, umbilicate, with grey-black scales on a paler ground. Gills greyish, deeply decurrent. Stipe 5×0.4cm, quite slender, concolorous. Flesh pale, almost odourless. Spores 13×5μm, ± fusiform. Springing from *Sphagnum* or other bog mosses. Uncommon, more so in the north and west of Britain. E2.

O. oniscus (Fr.) Quél., with more delicate or less contrasting scales and shorter broader spores, 9×6μm, occurs less often in similar situations. E2.

Omphalina rosella (Lange) Moser [*Mycena carnicolor*]
Cap 1cm, only slightly depressed, pink to lilac brown, smooth, not striate. Gills pinkish. Stipe 3×0.3cm, slender, concolorous or pinkish ochre. Flesh pale pink, odourless. Spores 9×5μm; cheilocystidia slightly clavate. Among short grass or with mosses. Uncommon. E1.

O. lilacinicolor Bon, with more hoary cap and shorter spores. Among moss on coastal dunes. E2.

Phaeotellus griseopallidus (Desm.) Kuhn. & Lamoure [*Omphalina griseopallida*]
Cap 3-5cm, slightly depressed, margin wavy or ribbed, surface matt, hygrophanous, dark grey, drying whitish beige. Gills arched, sometimes anastomosing or puckered, greyish beige, paling. Stipe 2×0.3cm, often short or excentric, almost concolorous. Flesh whitish with slight smell of pelargonium. Spores 10×5.5μm, rather tear-shaped. In lawns. Uncommon in Britain. E3.

P. rickenii (Sing. ex Hora) Bon [*Omphalia muralis* p.p.], drying less pale and distinguished by absence of clamp connections on the hyphae, occurs on gravelly soil or old walls. E1.

Gerronema ericetorum (Pers.) Sing. [*Omphalina umbellifera*]
Cap 1-2cm, convex or depressed, pale yellowish brown to ochraceous beige, striate or fluted. Gills widely spaced, yellowish. Stipe 3×0.3cm slender, concolorous. Flesh pale, almost odourless. Spores 9×6.5μm, no clamp connections. In damp moss on moors and heaths or on rotten wood; often with *Coriscium* lichen. Very common. E2.

Chrysomphalina chrysophylla (Fr.) Clmç. [*Gerronema chrysophyllum*]
Relatively fleshy, cap 4-7cm, dark brown in contrast to the bright yellow gills, which are widely spaced and rather thick like those of a *Hygrophorus*. Stipe (3×0.5cm) and flesh yellow. Spores 10×5μm. On rotten wood. Rare. E2.

Genus *Rickenella*. More slender fungi with distinctive cystidia.

Rickenella fibula (Bull.) Raithel. [*Mycena fibula, Omphalina f.*]
Cap deeply umbilicate, 0.5-2cm, bright orange. Gills very deeply decurrent, pale orange. Stipe 8×0.15cm, concolorous. Flesh pale, odourless. Spores narrow, 6×2μm. On lawns, pastures and among small mosses. Very common. E4.

R. swartzii (Fr.) Kuyper [*Omphalina setipes*] is greyish with a violaceous tint at the apex of the stipe. E3.

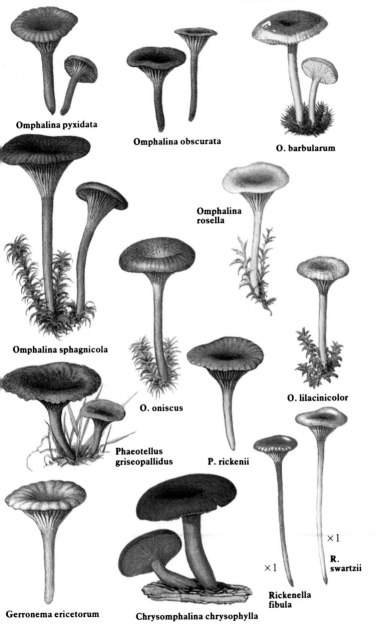

Omphalina pyxidata

Omphalina obscurata

O. barbularum

Omphalina rosella

Omphalina sphagnicola

O. oniscus

O. lilacinicolor

Phaeotellus griseopallidus

P. rickenii

×1

×1

R. swartzii

Rickenella fibula

Gerronema ericetorum

Chrysomphalina chrysophylla

129

The fungi on this page are from various groups (*Marasmiaceae, Fayodiae, Leuco-paxilloideae* etc.) but are covered together here for convenience because of their superficial resemblance to *Omphalina*. They are difficult to distinguish without recourse to microscopic characters. All have amyloid or ornamented spores.

Fayodia gracilipes (Britz.) Brsky. & Stangl
Cap 2cm, convex or a little umbilicate, brownish grey with margin striate and soon extended. Gills arched, greyish. Stipe 3×0.2cm, concolorous. Flesh pale, smell slightly mealy or of cocoa. Spores round, 8µm, spiny and ± reticulate, amyloid. Under conifers or in *Sphagnum*. Rare. E1.

F. leucophylla (Gill.) M. Lange & Siv. [*Clitocybe striatula*], paler with white gills and more elongated minutely spiny spores about 7×4µm. Rare in Britain in roadside grass under conifers. E2.

Myxomphalia maura (Fr.) Hora
Cap 3-6cm, umbilicate, surface shining or viscid, separable, grey-brown blackish with only slightly striate margin. Gills white, arched. Stipe 5×0.4cm, nearly concolorous, smooth. Smell mealy. Spores 6×4.5µm, smooth, amyloid. On burnt ground or with the moss *Funaria*. Common. E2.

Gamundia pseudoclusilis (Joss. & Konrad) Raithel. [*Fayodia p.*, *Omphalina p.*]
Cap 2cm, convex to ± umbonate then depressed, greyish, dark at the centre then paling to dingy ochraceous beige. Gills adnate or slightly arched, pale or with pinkish tinge. Stipe 3×0.3cm, greyish, as is the flesh; smell faint. Spores 8×5µm, ± punctate but nonamyloid. Lawns, E1.

Pseudoclitocybe cyathiformis (Bull.) Sing.
Cap 5-8cm, deeply cup-shaped with inrolled margin, smooth, surface rather shiny, blackish or slate coloured. Gills sloping or arched, not crowded, almost concolorous. Stipe 9×0.8cm, slightly club-shaped, concolorous, surface finely reticulate. Flesh greyish with slight smell of hay, melilot, Sweet Vernal-grass (*Anthoxanthum odoratum*) or *Marasmius oreades* (p. 174). Spores 10×7µm, smooth and amyloid; clamp connections absent. In copses of broadleaved trees in late autumn and winter. Common. E3.

P. expallens (Pers.) Moser is more striate and paler when drying, and rather less common. E2.

Pseudoomphalina compressipes (Peck) Sing. [*Omphalina graveolens*]
Cap 2-5cm, convex then depressed, pinkish brown with margin smooth, slightly incurved, more yellowish, sometimes wavy. Gills cream, arched and ± distant. Stipe 4×0.4cm, often furrowed, almost concolorous. Flesh pale, with strong mealy smell. Spores 7×4µm, smooth, amyloid; hyphae with clamp connections. Lawns. Rare. E2.

Cantharellula umbonata (Gmel.) Sing.
Cap 3-5cm, umbonate, then sunk in a deep umbilicus with the umbo at the base, silky to ± velvety, grey-violet, margin inrolled, smooth. Gills deeply decurrent, forked, white with a pinkish tinge. Stipe 7×0.4cm, rather spindle- or club-shaped, nearly concolorous. Flesh pale, odourless, reddening slightly. Spores fusiform, 9×4µm, smooth, amyloid. Often in tufts among moss under broadleaved trees or mixed woods. Rare in Britain. E1.

Xeromphalina campanella (Batsch) R. Mre.
Cap 1-2cm, umbilicate, pellucidly striate, bright yellowish brown to almost orange. Gills decurrent, yellowish, fairly distant and ± interveined. Stipe leathery, concolorous above, dingy and velvety at the base. Flesh tough like a *Marasmius*. Spores 7×3.5µm, smooth, amyloid, cystidia fusiform. On rotten wood. Rare in Britain, more frequent in the Highlands. E1.

Clitocybula lacerata (Scop.) Métr.
Cap 3-5cm, convex then umbilicate, greyish white, speckled with grey-brown at the centre, surface fibrillose or cracked towards the margin. Gills ± adnate, pale. Stipe 6×0.4cm, fibrillose, becoming hollow, almost concolorous. Flesh pale, smell variable, sometimes fruity. Spores nearly globose, 7µm, amyloid. On branches of conifers, sometimes clustered. Very rare in Britain. E1.

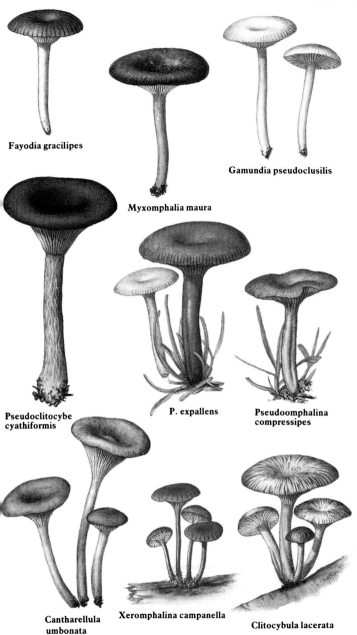

Fayodia gracilipes

Gamundia pseudoclusilis

Myxomphalia maura

Pseudoclitocybe
cyathiformis

P. expallens

Pseudoomphalina
compressipes

Cantharellula
umbonata

Xeromphalina campanella

Clitocybula lacerata

Genus *Clitocybe*. Rather fleshy fungi with decurrent or downward sloping gills and often a funnel-shaped cap. Spores smooth, print white or tinged pink.

Key to *Clitocybe* - principal species

1a Cap rather fleshy or umbonate and tardily depressed and/or surface smooth or hoary, frosted, neither matt, velvety nor hygrophanous. Gills often only slightly sloping or barely decurrent : **2**
1b Cap soon funnel-shaped or rather thin-fleshed, surface not distinctive or felted to matt or somewhat scaly, not hygrophanous; gills distinctly decurrent: **11**
1c Thin-fleshed fungi with hygrophanous cap, cuticle sometimes pruinose : **21**

2a White to pinkish cream or speckled ochraceous : **3**
2b Distinctly coloured fungi : **8**

3a Cap mottled or hoary appearing more ochraceous when wiped : **4**
3b Cap smooth or frosted, uniform : **7**

4a Cap 5 (10) cm, in woods : **5**
4b Cap 3 (5) cm, in lawns or grassy verges of copses : **6**

5a White, somewhat zoned with sodden spots; gills pale » *C. phyllophila*, 136
5b More pinkish ochraceous; gills pink » *C. martiorum*, 136

6a Cap obtuse, somewhat mottled; gills almost adnate » *C. dealbata*, 136
6b Cap more depressed, eventually concentrically cracked; gills more markedly sloping or decurrent » *C. rivulosa*, 136

7a Frosted, pure white, smell faint; in copses » *C. candicans*, 136
7b Smooth, creamy white, smell pleasant, then earthy; on lawns »
C. graminicola, 136
(If there is a smell of aniseed, may be a discoloured variety of *C. odora*, 136)

8a Colour green, smell of aniseed » *C. odora*, 136
8b Colour beige or ochraceous to brownish; smell different or none : **9**

9a Cap margin ribbed, smell fruity then fishy » *C. inornata*, 136
9b Cap margin even or inrolled, smell fungoid to slightly mealy : **10**

10a Gills almost adnate, cap pale yellowish grey; smell slight » *C. nebularis*, 136
10b Gills more sloping to decurrent and anastomosing, cap more ochraceous grey-brown often slightly zoned with sodden spots; smell strong »
C. alexandri, 136

11a Smell mealy or of cucumber, corduroy etc : **12**
11b Smell slight or of new mown hay (cyanic) : **15**

12a Colours greyish : **13**
12b Colours orange to pinkish : **14**

13a Dark grey, slightly scaly » *C. trullaeformis*, 134
13b Slightly paler, more slender and omphalinoid » *C. font-queri*, 134

14a Brick-orange, matt, smell strong » *C. sinopica*, 134
14b Pinkish ochraceous, slightly scaly to fleecy, smell faint » *C. squamulosa*, 134

15a Gills soft, a peculiar creamy yellowish; stipe club-shaped, cap yellowish brown or greyish, slightly funnel-shaped or with a spongy slightly umbonate centre; smell faint » *C. clavipes*, 134
15b Gills white or concolorous : **16**

16a Big, rather fleshy or stocky fungi, cap 10-25 cm, russet ochre or pallid : **7**
16b Medium size, 5 (10)cm, or thin-fleshed : **18**

17a Cap with a distinct umbo persisting in the centre of the depression, stipe rather slender; distinct smell of new mown hay » *C. geotropa*, 134
17b Cap with umbo slight or absent, up to 25cm, stipe short stout » *C. maxima*, 134

17c Cap whiter, with slightly furrowed margin, gills separable from flesh and aromatic smell » see *Leucopaxillus giganteus*, 162

| 18a | Colour predominantly ochraceous or rufous : **19** |
| 18b | Colour grey-brown to blackish : **20** |

19a Pale creamy ochraceous, slightly umbonate then flexuous, cuticle matt; distinct smell of new mown hay »   *C. gibba*, 134
19b More ochraceous-chamois, margin ribbed »   *C. costata*, 134
    (If colours are more brightly rufous or yellowish, with a glabrous or shining cuticle, see *Lepista* section *Inversae*, 142)

20a Greyish to dull bistre, cap surface slightly velvety or fleecy »
                                         C. squamulosoides, 134
20b Blackish slate-grey, suface smooth, stipe with a network of blackish lines, fruity in late autumn »   see *Pseudoclitocybe cyathiformis*, 130

21a Gills white or pale, concolorous, not greyish : **22**
21b Gills greyish, dark or not becoming as pale as the cap : **28**

22a Smell of aniseed : **23**
22b Smell different or none : **25**

23a Margin smooth or scarcely striate : **24**
23b Margin persistently strongly striate, pale, cap centre dingy yellowish brown »
                                           C. fragrans, 138

24a Colours yellowish brown, tinged pinkish on drying; smell strong and sweet »
                                         C. perplexa, 138
24b Brownish clay to pale ochraceous beige; smell slight »   *C. obsoleta*, 138

25a Colours somewhat pinkish, smell fruity »   *C. diatreta*, 138
25b Colours beige to brownish : **26**

26a Cap quickly depressed, gills crowded; smell slight »   *C. angustissima*, 138
26b Cap remaining convex, gills rather distant : **27**

27a Stipe short, smell finally rather earthy; in pastures, with debris and cowpats »
                                         C. nitrophila, 138
27b Stipe longer and hollow; in the mountains »   *C. fragilipes*, 138

28a Smell mealy, of cucumber etc : **29**
28b Stinking like the inside of a hen-house or wet hens, sometimes more pleasant like iris or honey, finally earthy; cuticle matt, like putty, when dry »
                                    C. phaeophthalma, 140
28c Smell nitrous; cap hollow or umbilicate, gills decurrent »   *C. nitriolens*, 140
    (If the gills are only slightly decurrent or cap convex go to choice **29** below).
28d Smell none or slightly earthy; colours dull greyish brown to dingy ochraceous : **31**

29a Dark grey to olivaceous, margin slightly striate, cuticle smooth »
                                         C. pausiaca, 140
29b Colours greyish, cap surface somewhat bloomed : **30**
29c Dark grey-brown, somewhat viscid; on mossy dunes »
                          see *Omphalina barbularum*, 128

30a Pruina abundant, whitening on drying, margin not striate, stipe short; strong smell of cucumber »   *C. ditopa*, 140
30b Pruina fleeting, margin slightly striate, smell rather rancid »   *C. vibecina*, 140

31a Stipe persisting pale greyish brown »   *C. metachroa*, 140
    (See also *Pseudoclitocybe expallens*, in grassy thickets and wood margins, 130
31b Stipe blackish or browning : **32**

32a Stipe with blackish striations; smell earthy »   *C. atrostriata* (not described here)
32b Stipe not striate : **33**

33a Stipe dark brown; smell earthy, taste unpleasant »   *C. fritilliformis*, 140

33b Stipe pale brownish from the base; cap persisting with a clearly delimiting dark grey-brown central area when faded; smell slight or only developed late »
                                         C. decembris, 140

Subgenus *Clitocybe*. Not hygrophanous; ± fleshy.

Section *Hygroclitocybe*. Gills soft or rather thick and distant, suggestive of some *Hygrophorus* species. Tramal hyphae somewhat interwoven, pigment predominantly vacuolar.

Clitocybe clavipes (Pers.) Kumm.
Cap 5-10cm, scarcely depressed or with a pad of compressible spongy tissue at the centre forming a low umbo, surface matt, yellowish grey or sometimes tan. Gills decurrent, rather broad, soft, slightly thickened towards the base, a distinctive creamy yellowish tint. Stipe 6×0.5cm, typically club-shaped, soon flabby at the base, nearly concolorous. Flesh white with faint fruity smell and pleasant taste. Spores 9×5μm, slightly tear-shaped. Common under broadleaved trees. Edible but poor. E4.

Clitocybe geotropa (Bull.) Quél.
Cap 10-18cm, typically depressed around a small central umbo; surface glabrous and matt, pale tan to slightly flesh colour, paler with age. Gills arched to decurrent, ± distant and pale. Stipe slightly club-shaped, 16×3cm, almost concolorous or paler. Flesh whitish, strong smell of new-mown hay or Sweet Vernal-grass (*Anthoxanthum odoratum*), or like *Marasmius oreades* (p. 174). Spores 8×5μm, ovoid. Common under broadleaved trees, especially on calcareous soils. Edible and good. E3.

Large specimens with whitish cap lacking the umbo and a short thick stipe have been called **C. maxima** (Fl. Wett.) Kumm.

Section *Infundibuliformes*. Only slightly or moderately fleshy fungi with ± funnel-shaped cap and often deeply decurrent gills. Trama regular.

Clitocybe gibba (Pers.) Kumm. [*C. infundibuliformis*]
Cap 5-8cm, slightly umbonate at first, then depressed and wavy, cream to ochraceous, sometimes tinged pinkish. Gills white, deeply decurrent. Stipe 4×0.8cm, whitish. Flesh whitish, smelling of *Anthoxanthum* or *Marasmius oreades*. Spores 7×4.5μm, tear- or pear-shaped. Widespread but especially under broadleaved trees. Edible. E4.

Clitocybe costata K.-R.
Similar to *C. gibba* but more strongly coloured, even ochraceous brown or chamois, with margin distinctly notched and ribbed. Gills pale. Stipe 5×1cm, concolorous, streaked or silky. Smell as in *C. gibba* or fruity. Spores as in *C. gibba*. Grassy places under conifers especially on calcareous soil. Uncommon. Edible. E2.

Clitocybe squamulosa (Pers.) Kumm.
Cap somewhat resembling *C. gibba* but with fibrillosely scaly or fleecy surface, pinkish brown to rusty ochre. Gills crowded, sloping or arched, pale beige. Stipe 6×0.8cm, slightly club-shaped, nearly concolorous, fibrillosely striate. Flesh pale, smell slightly mealy. Spores 7×4μm, slightly tear-shaped. Grassy places under conifers but not in Britain. E2.

C. squamulosoides Orton differs in its dingier duller colour, greyish bistre, with a more cyanic smell and more elliptical spores. E1.

Clitocybe sinopica (Fr.) Kumm.
Cap 3-6cm, remaining flat but soon wavy, surface matt or peeling a little towards the centre, browning orange, gills sloping or slightly decurrent, cream. Stipe 5×1cm, thickset, pale to nearly concolorous, often with a few rootlets. Smell strong, mealy. Spores 9×5.5μm, elliptical. On bare ground, footpaths or burnt soil. Uncommon. E1.

Clitocybe trullaeformis (Fr.) Karst. [*C. parilis* p.p.]
Cap 4cm, funnel-shaped, sometimes papillate, uniformly dark grey, granulate or speckled or ± scaly. Gills whitish, crowded, scarcely decurrent. Stipe 2×0.4cm, pale to almost concolorous. Flesh pale, smell mealy. Spores 5×3μm, elliptical; pigment vacuolar. Under broadleaved trees. Uncommon. E1.

C. font-queri Heim seems to be the corresponding species in the Mediterranean region, more slender and omphalinoid, under *Cistus* or on grassy slopes. Rare. sE2.

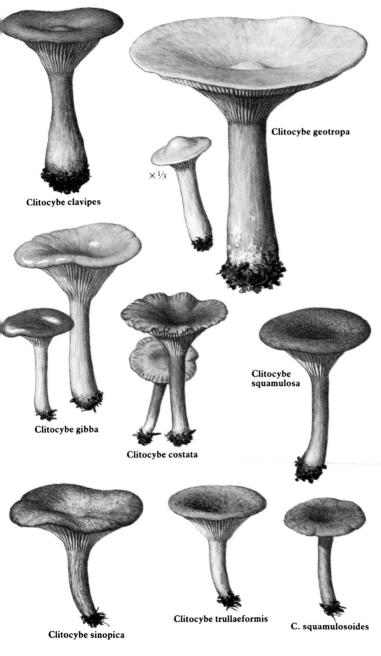

Clitocybe geotropa

× 1/3

Clitocybe clavipes

Clitocybe squamulosa

Clitocybe gibba

Clitocybe costata

Clitocybe sinopica

Clitocybe trullaeformis

C. squamulosoides

135

Section *Clitocybe* [*Disciformes*]. Robust or fleshy fungi, not umbilicate or only so in age, gills often almost horizontal, cap surface smooth, ± coloured.

Clitocybe nebularis (Batsch) Kumm. [*Lepista nebularis*]
Cap 12-20cm, fleshy, convex, broadly umbonate, a distinctive yellowish grey, glabrous or slippery. Gills cream to yellowish, rather crowded, remaining ± adnate. Stipe 10×3cm, almost equal or slightly club-shaped, cream ochraceous to nearly concolorous. Flesh pale, smell like *Pleurotus*, eventually unpleasant. Spores 7×4μm, elliptical, yellowish. Very common throughout Britain under various broadleaved trees, especially in late autumn and winter. Apparently eaten with impunity by some people, causing mild illness to others, best avoided. E4.

C. alexandri (Gill.) Konrad. Darker coloured or brownish ochraceous, with fleshier umbo, and more decurrent gills, often anastomosing at the base. Under broadleaved trees in warm situations, especially under holm oak. Very rare in Britain. sE2.

Clitocybe inornata (Sow.) Gill.
Cap 6-10cm, margin wrinkled or eventually ribbed, colour of milky coffee to brownish beige, surface very finely tomentose. Gills nearly horizontal, with a pinkish grey tinge. Stipe 8×1cm, almost concolorous. Flesh pale, smell faint, becoming fruity and finally unpleasant, of fish. Spores 9×5μm, fusiform. Under broadleaved trees and pines. Uncommon in Britain. E2.

Clitocybe odora (Bull.) Kumm.
Small to medium sized fungus, cap 5-8cm, only slightly depressed, greenish (rarely white) and tending to discolour. Gills ± adnate, white to greenish. Stipe 4×0.8cm, pallid or tinged greenish. Flesh pale with strong smell of aniseed (Subsection *Odorae*). Spores 9×5μm, elliptical. Under broadleaved trees, less often conifers. Common. Edible and fragrant. E3.

Section *Candicantes*. Generally fleshy fungi, cap surface whitish, hoary or glossy.

Clitocybe phyllophila (Pers.) Kumm.
Cap 7-12cm, circular with a low umbo then slightly depressed, surface hoary, whitish then ± zoned with moist beige or ochraceous stains (looking waxy). Gills rather adnate or sloping, crowded, white or with a pinkish tint. Stipe 8×1cm, white to ochraceous russet towards the base. Flesh whitish with a complex mealy or spermatic smell. Spores 6×4μm, slightly pink in the mass. Under broadleaved trees. Common. Edibility suspect. E3.

C. martiorum Favre. More coloured from the outset, pinkish ochre or spotted pale brick, with similarly coloured gills, occurs under conifers. Not yet found in Britain. Em2.

Clitocybe dealbata (Sow.) Kumm.
Cap 3cm, remaining convex or flattened with incurved margin, which is sometimes notched; surface rather glossy, cream on a pinkish ochraceous ground. Gills scarcely sloping, creamy white with ochraceous or flesh coloured tints. Stipe 2×0.4cm, almost concolorous. Flesh pale with mealy-spermatic odour. Spores 4×3μm, almost spherical. Common on lawns and grassy places generally. **Toxic**, with muscarin. E3.

C. rivulosa (Pers.) Kumm. More slender and with cap soon becoming depressed, has the surface developing concentric cracks in the whitish outer layer; equally common in similar situations, roadside grass and maritime grassland. E2.

Clitocybe graminicola Bon
Cap 2-3cm, not fleshy, soon depressed, with glabrous surface, slightly hygrophanous so changing from white to creamy ochre on drying. Gills sloping or arched, white, not crowded. Stipe 3×0.4cm with an ochraceous base, ± pink in f. *roseipes*. Smell slightly cyanic or of melilot, becoming earthy. Spores 5×3.5μm. On lawns and in thickets. Fairly common but not yet distinguished in Britain. Edibility suspect. E3.

C. candicans (Pers.) Kumm., with glossy pure white surface, is almost odourless and occurs mainly in copses. Rather common. Toxic, with muscarin. E2.

136

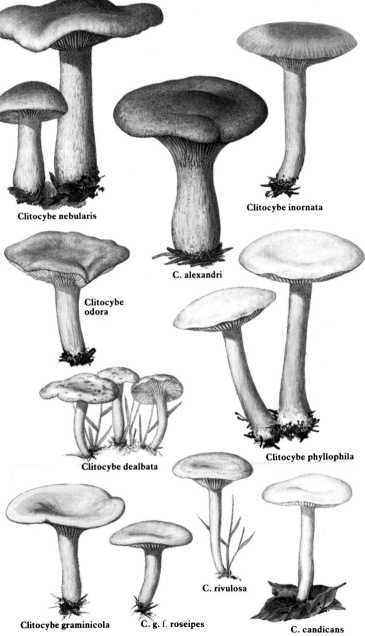

Clitocybe nebularis

Clitocybe inornata

C. alexandri

Clitocybe odora

Clitocybe phyllophila

Clitocybe dealbata

Clitocybe graminicola

C. g. f. roseipes

C. rivulosa

C. candicans

137

Subgenus *Pseudolyophyllum*. Hygrophanous fungi, not particularly fleshy.
Section *Epruinatae*. Gills white or pale, not greyish.

Clitocybe diatreta (Fr.) Kumm.
Cap 4-8cm, pinkish brown or reddish ochre, flesh colour, margin not striate but sometimes pruinose. Gills scarcely decurrent, pale or flesh coloured. Stipe 3×0.7cm, smooth, almost concolorous. Flesh pale, smell fruity. Spores 5×2.5µm, pinkish in the mass. In moss under conifers and other trees. Toxic, contains muscarin. Quite common. E3.

Clitocybe angustissima (Lasch) Kumm.
Cap as in *C. diatreta* or more depressed, 3-5cm, brownish beige without pink tint. Gills pale, very crowded and decurrent. Stipe slender, 7×0.3cm, white. Smell faint. Spores as in *C. diatreta*, but not or scarcely pinkish. Thickets and copses of broadleaved trees. Uncommon. E2.

Clitocybe mortuosa (Fr.) Gill.
Cap 2-4cm, only slightly depressed, dark chocolate brown, only slightly paling. Gills ± adnate, crowded, white. Stipe 3×0.4cm, smooth, similar colour to cap. Smell faint. Spores 5×3µm, white. In grassy thickets. Not likely in Britain. E1.

Clitocybe brumalis (Fr.) Quél.
Cap 2-4cm, slightly umbilicate, dark olive-grey, fading to dull beige. Gills pale, eventually ochraceous, decurrent. Stipe 4×0.5cm, pale. Flesh whitish, odourless. Spores 4×3µm, white. Under conifers and on heaths. Fairly frequent but a poorly known species in Britain. E2.

Clitocybe nitrophila Bon
Cap 3-6cm, convex-flattened, margin often lobed; dull ochraceous brown tints, sometimes tinged pink; like *C. diatreta*. Gills pale to nearly concolorous, sloping slightly. Stipe 4×0.4cm, concolorous, often compressed or tubular. Flesh pale, smell and taste eventually earthy. Spores 7×4µm, elliptical, white. In rough grassland, parks, gardens, reclaimed meadows, sometimes in clusters. Common in Europe but not known in Britain. E2.

C. fragilipes Favre. Fleshier, with very hollow stipe up to 10×1cm and longer spores. Occurs more in woods or hill country. Not in Britain. E1.

Section *Fragrantes*. Smell pleasant or of aniseed (Pernod).

Clitocybe deceptiva Bigelow [*C. suaveolens*]
Cap 3-6cm, slightly depressed, pale, in part uniformly dull yellowish brown with a pinkish tinge, fading to creamy pink, margin only slightly striate, sometimes pruinose. Gills white, slightly decurrent. Stipe 4×0.3cm, pale, tough. Flesh white, smell of aniseed or merely fruity and pleasant. Spores 7×3.5µm, pale pinkish in the mass. In mossy or moist places under broadleaved trees or grassy thickets. Common. E3.

Clitocybe obsoleta (Batsch) Quél.
Cap 4-7cm, convex, wavy, not striate, uniformly clay or brownish flesh colour, fading to ochraceous beige. Gills dingy white, crowded, scarcely decurrent. Stipe 5×0.5cm, similar colour to cap, elastic, hollow. Smell of pure aniseed but rather faint. Spores like *C. deceptiva* or shorter. Under conifers. Uncommon. E2.

Clitocybe fragrans (With.) Kumm.
Cap 3-6cm, soon markedly depressed or umbilicate, margin striate, paler than the persistently dingy yellowish brown centre. Gills cream to pale pinkish, sloping. Stipe 7×0.4cm, concolorous, darker at the base. Smell strong, of aniseed only. Spores 9×5µm, white in mass. Under broadleaved trees, often among grass. Common. E3.

C. subalutacea (Batsch) Kumm. is more fleshy and browner and belongs rather in *Disciformes* (p. 136). E1.

A rare white variety of *C. odora* (p. 136) may also be confused with species of this section.

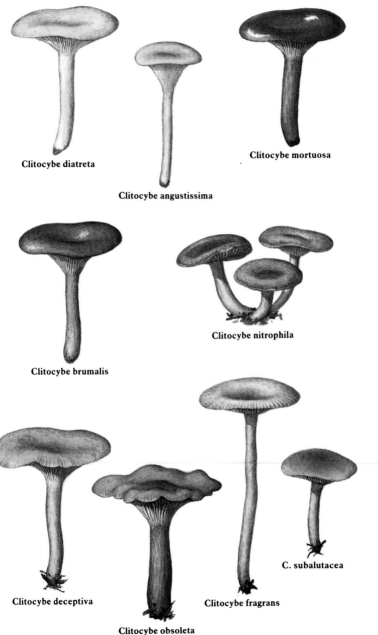

Clitocybe diatreta

Clitocybe angustissima

Clitocybe mortuosa

Clitocybe brumalis

Clitocybe nitrophila

Clitocybe deceptiva

Clitocybe obsoleta

Clitocybe fragrans

C. subalutacea

Section *Ditopae*. Gills grey, smell mealy.

Clitocybe ditopa (Fr.) Gill.
Cap up to 6-10cm, sightly convex, not depressed, pruinose or cracking, margin not striate, colours greyish, a little darker under the pruina, whitish and hoary on drying. Gills slightly decurrent, ± concolorous. Stipe short, 3×0.8cm, ± concolorous. Strong smell of meal or cucumber or water melon. Spores ± globose, 4×3μm. Under spruce or broadleaved trees in wet places, such as alders, in rings. In Britain, more a species of coniferous woodland. Common. E3.

Clitocybe pausiaca (Fr.) Gill.
Cap 3cm, only slightly depressed, dark grey with olivaceous tinge, margin striate. Gills rather crowded, almost concolorous, then pale and dingy. Stipe 3×0.4cm, slightly compressed, similar colour. Smell and taste strong when cut, becoming less pleasant. Spores 6×4μm. Under conifers on acid soils, sometimes on heaths and moors. Uncommon. E2.

Clitocybe vibecina (Fr.) Quél.
Cap 4cm, ± umbilicate, has colour and pruina like *C. ditopa* but more fleeting and margin slightly striate. Gills sloping, similar colour. Stipe 6×0.3cm, smooth or a little fleecy. Flesh greyish, smell mealy but a trifle rancid or oily. Spores 8×4.5μm, elliptical. Under conifers and broadleaved trees, especially in damp places. Common. E3.

C. langei Sing. ex Hora has a more felted yellowish brown surface, a rather more alkaline smell and shorter or slightly tear-shaped spores. Less common, in similar situations. E2.

Section *Metachroae*. Gills grey but odour earthy or none.

Clitocybe decembris Sing. [*C. dicolor* p.p.]
Cap 3-6cm, convex then slightly umbilicate, darker at the centre, remaining so while the margin turns whitish as it dries. Gills arched, not crowded, greyish. Stipe 7×0.7cm, pale greyish or browning at the base, often with a whitish band below the gills. Smell none at first, later rancid or earthy. Spores 8×5μm, elliptical. Under broadleaved trees in late autumn and winter. Common. E4.

C. metachroa (Fr.) Kumm. Has been variously interpreted, usually as a species with smooth margin, only slightly paling and with stipe not browning. E2.

Clitocybe fritilliformis (Lasch) Gill.
Cap 2-5cm, soon depressed, brownish grey, margin slightly striate. Gills narrow and decurrent, grey. Stipe 4×0.4cm, dark or blackish towards the base, not striate or scarcely so. Smell earthy, taste unpleasant, tart or bitter. Spores 5×3μm. Among moss under broadleaved trees. Rare. E1.

Clitocybe nitriolens Favre [*Gerronema nitriolens*, *C. concava*]
Cap 5-8cm, distinctly umbilicate with incurved margin, slightly striate; colour yellowish brown. Gills deeply decurrent, similar colour. Stipe 6×0.8cm, slightly compressed, elastic, similar colour, with a zone of white fibrils below the gills and white tomentum at the base. Smell nitrous. Spores 8×4.5μm. Under conifers in the Alps, rare in Britain. E2.

Section *Bulliferae*. Enlarged protruding cells present in the cuticular hyphae.

Clitocybe phaeophthalma (Pers.) Kuyper [*C. hydrogramma*]
Cap 4-7cm, only slightly depressed, margin slightly wavy, strongly striate when moist; surface hygrophanous but matt, becoming ± velvety on drying, dull greybrown, sometimes yellowish, drying whitish. Gills pale. Stipe 5×0.5cm, pale, smooth or a little strigose towards the base. Smell of a henhouse or sodden feathers, finally earthy. Spores 7×4μm, elliptical. Under broadleaved trees. Uncommon. E3.

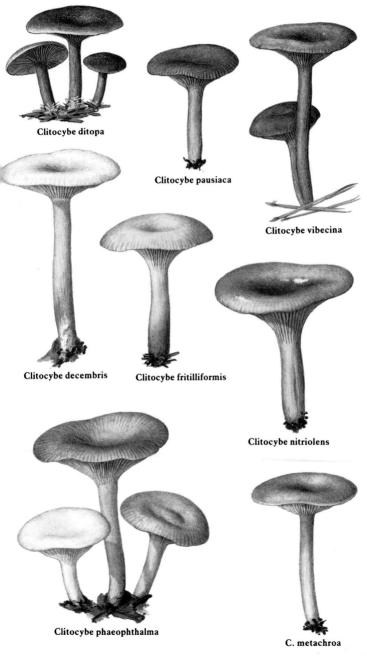

Clitocybe ditopa

Clitocybe pausiaca

Clitocybe vibecina

Clitocybe decembris

Clitocybe fritilliformis

Clitocybe nitriolens

Clitocybe phaeophthalma

C. metachroa

Genus *Armillaria*. Gills adnate or slightly decurrent, cap ± scaly, fruit-bodies with a ring or clustered.

Armillaria mellea (Vahl) Kumm.   HONEY FUNGUS
Cap 4-7cm, umbonate, at the centre covered with small yellowish brown scales on a honey yellow ground, margin incurved, fibrillose. Gills slightly arched, decurrent by a tooth, creamy white. Stipes clustered, 12×1cm, sometimes slightly bulbous, with a ± yellow shaggy or membranous ring with scales like those on the cap on its under side. Blackish brown rhizomorphs present, resembling long leather bootlaces. Flesh pale, smell fungoid. Spores 8×6μm, elliptical. No clamps. On stumps, buried branches and dead roots of trees of all kinds, a destructive parasite in woods, plantations and gardens. Edible when young, old or poorly preserved specimens may prove toxic. Very common throughout Britain. E4.

A. obscura (Sch.) Herink., without honey-colours, is more obscurely warted, almost up to the margin. Spores up to 10x7mu; clamps rare. Em3.

Armillaria tabescens (Scop.) Emel
Closely resembling *A. mellea*, caps sometimes smaller or closely packed and soon depressed, with brownish beige streaky-fibrillose surface ± dotted with brown warts towards the centre. Gills slightly arched, sometimes pinkish. Stipe slender, 10×0.8cm, without a ring, slightly spindle-shaped, fibrillose, similarly coloured. Spores 10×6μm. In dense tufts on stumps or woody debris, especially of oak. A southern species found occasionally in southern England. E3.

A. ectypa (Fr.) Lamoure. Occurs singly in *Sphagnum* bogs and is rather pinkish brown, sometimes with vinaceous tints especially on the rather distant gills and is not yet verified as British. E1.

Tribe *Lepisteae*. Spores ornamented.

Genus *Lepista*. Spores minutely warted, white or pale pink in mass. Gills often readily separable from the flesh.

Section *Inversae*. Colours russet to yellow, gills decurrent, spore print white.

 Lepista inversa (Scop.) Pat. [*Clitocybe inversa*]
Cap 7-10cm, rather fleshy, soon umbilicate or with margin remaining incurved; surface smooth, bright tawny to reddish brown or rusty orange. Gills crowded, deeply decurrent, narrow, ochraceous russet. Stipe 4×0.7cm, smooth, similar colour. Flesh pale, smell fungoid. Spores round, 4-5μm. Under conifers, often in rings. Good edible fungus. Common. E4.

 Lepista gilva (Pers.) Roze [*Clitocybe gilva*]
Closely resembling *L. inversa* but more yellowish ochre with zones of droplets or sodden ochraceous spots. Gills pale, arched. Stipe colour similar. Spores as in *L. inversa*. Thickets or copses of broadleaved trees. Common. E2.

Section *Lepista* [*Spongiosae*]. As *Inversae* but colour white or brownish, spore print pink, pigment predominantly vacuolar.

 Lepista densifolia (Favre) Sing. & Clmç.
Cap regular, 5-8cm, with a low umbo, surface white, glossy like the white Clitocybes. Gills arched, crowded, creamy pink, sometimes as bright as in a *Clitopilus*. Stipe 6×1cm, white to pinkish. Flesh white, smell fungoid. Spores short, 5×3μm. Under beech and fir on acid soils in the mountains. Rare in Europe. Not found in Britain. Em2.

Lepista rickenii Sing.
Cap 12-20cm, soon depressed about a central umbo, surface smooth or veined, yellowish beige to dingy leather-brown, sometimes zoned or with droplets. Gills arched, dingy pinkish grey. Stipe 8×1.5cm, concolorous, fibrillose. Flesh pale, smell slightly mealy like *Clitocybe nebularis*. Spores 7x4mu. Under conifers or woodland glades. E1.

Armillaria
mellea

× ⅓

Armillaria
tabescens

× ⅓

A. ectypa

Lepista
densifolia

Lepista inversa

Lepista gilva

Lepista rickenii

143

Section *Rhodopaxillus*. Aspect of a *Tricholoma*, gills horizontal, ± sinuate. Pigment predominantly membranal.

Lepista irina (Fr.) Bigelow

Cap 8-13cm, convex, fleshy or umbonate, margin incurved; surface smooth, ochraceous beige, sometimes with a pinkish tinge. Gills crowded, creamy white to pinkish ochre. Stipe 8×2cm, coloured like the cap but streaked with brownish fibrils from the base. Flesh pale, smell of iris or violets (eau de Cologne or orange flower water); taste mild. Spores 9×5μm, nearly smooth. Mixed woods in sheltered places. Considered edible but an alpine form (f. *montana*) has an unpleasant smell and taste. Uncommon in Britain. E2.

Lepista panaeolus (Fr.) Karst. [*L. luscina*]

Cap 10-15cm, plano-convex, soon becoming expanded or depressed, surface typically flecked with watersoaked spots, then punctate or cracked at the centre, spots sooty brown on a beige ground which may be rather pale ochraceous or pinkish towards the margin. Gills adnate, becoming sloping with age, dingy greyish beige then dull pinkish. Stipe 5×1.5cm, coloured similarly or mottled brown. Flesh whitish, smell fruity. Spores 7×4μm, finely granular. Pastures, woodland glades or grassy copses. Edible and good. Uncommon in Britain. E3.

var. **nimbata** is paler and slightly hoary so as to be readily confused with toxic species of *Clitocybe* (p. 132). E2.

Lepista nuda (Bull.) Cke.   WOOD BLEWITS

Cap 8-15cm, convex then expanded, surface smooth or sometimes pruinose, at first bluish lilac, becoming russet brown to ochraceous from the centre outwards. Gills lilac then pinkish ochre. Stipe 10×2cm, violaceous lilac, fibrillose, sometimes white-pruinose at the apex. Flesh bluish, then russet, smell faint and fruity except in var. *pruinosa* which has a strong or somewhat nauseous smell of Vitamin B pills or babies' cereals. Spores 8×5μm. Ubiquitous in woods, gardens compost heaps in late autumn and winter. Very common throughout Britain and a good edible fungus. E4.

L. glaucocana (Bres.) Sing. has paler colouring, bluish to greyish flesh-colour, with aromatic smell resembling menthol. Uncommon. E2.

Lepista saeva (Fr.) Orton [*Tricholoma personatum*]   BLEWITS

Cap 10-15cm, fleshy, convex, greyish rather like *Clitocybe nebularis* but paler, sharply incurved at the margin. Gills adnate or sinuate, pinkish beige. Stipe short 5×2cm, typically streaked bright amethyst. Flesh a little lilaceous at the surface, smell strong, not always pleasant. Spores 8×5μm. Pastures and woodland glades. A good edible fungus, less common than *L. nuda*. E3.

Lepista sordida (Fr.) Sing. [*Clitocybe tarda*]

Cap 4-10cm, not very fleshy, soon expanded or wavy, margin thin and slightly striate; hygrophanous, surface smooth, pale bluish violet then pinkish beige with tinge of olive at the centre and in concentric zones on drying. Gills pale lilac to pinkish. Stipe 4×0.6cm, similar colour, often fragile. Flesh pale with strong smell and slightly bitter taste. Spores 7×4μm, very finely warted. Manured places, among litter, in parks, often clustered. Uncommon in Britain. E3.

A variable species. Among named varieties are: var. *umbonata*, more slender and umbonate; var. *obscura*, dark blackish violet; var. *lilacea*, with bright colours; var. *aianthina*, without any lilac tint. Luxuriant forms may develop enormous clusters on compost. All E2-3.

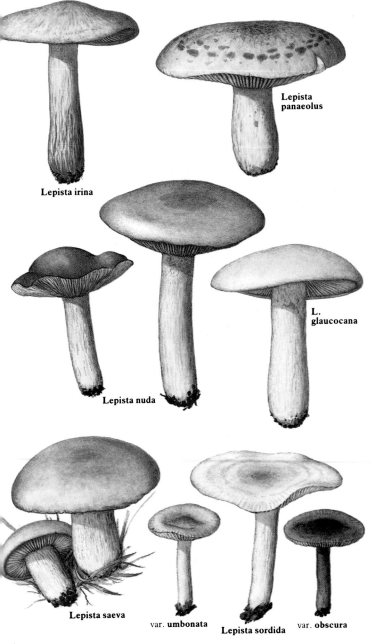

Lepista irina

Lepista panaeolus

Lepista nuda

L. glaucocana

Lepista saeva

var. umbonata

Lepista sordida

var. obscura

145

Genus *Ripartites*. Gills sloping, pinkish ochre. Resembles an *Omphalina* (p. 128) or a *Clitocybe* (p. 132), but spores with rather prominent or truncate spines, and pinkish ochre in the mass.

Ripartites tricholoma (A.-S.) Karst.
Cap 4-7cm, convex to slightly depressed; margin typically fringed, surface frosted or fleecy-fibrillose, white, then cracking and greyish ochre. Gills sloping, dingy pinkish ochre. Stipe 4×0.6cm, pale ochre. Flesh pale, smell faint, slightly mealy. Spores ± globose, 5×4μm, with obtuse spines. In coniferous woods, especially spruce. Uncommon in Britain. E2.

R. strigiceps (Fr.) Karst. has been distinguished by a more hairy surface, with concentric zones of hairs like a small *Lactarius torminosus*. E1.

Ripartites metrodii Huijsm. [*R. helomorphus* p.p.]
Cap 2-4cm, soon depressed and like an *Omphalina*, margin naked or slightly fibrillose, surface satiny, creamy white, centre pinkish ochraceous. Gills and stipe as in *R. tricholoma*. Odour slight. Spores 6×5μm, with taller cylindrical or truncate spines. Under broadleaved trees. Rare in Britain. E2.

R. helomorphus (Fr.) Karst. is a little more fleshy or umbonate, with smaller spores, 4.5μm, bearing obtuse warts. Rare. E1.

Genus *Laccaria*. Gills horizontal or with decurrent teeth, rather thick or distant as in *Hygrophorus*. Spores usually spiny, print white.

Laccaria laccata (Scop.) Bk.& Br.
Cap 1-3cm, soon depressed, smooth, margin ± striate, reddish brown to russet pink, fading to dull ochraceous or russet. Gills pallid to pinkish. Stipe 5×0.4cm, smooth or slightly fibrillose, similar colour. Flesh pale, odourless, taste mild. Spores 10×7μm, elliptical, covered with slender spines 0.5-1μm long. For British authorities *L. laccata* is a species with globose spores, 8μm. [var. *anglica*]. Rather variable, abundant in diverse situations throughout Britain. E4.

var. **moelleri** [*L. proxima* p.p.]
More robust or fleshy, cap 5-8cm, scaly at the centre, warm reddish brown, paling only slightly. Stipe 10×1cm, tough, fibrous, concolorous or a little rusty. Spores as in var. *laccata*. Widely distributed and common. Edible but leathery. E3.

L. affinis (Sing.) Bon has more fluted margin, hygrophanous cap and round spores and occurs on peat moors. E3.

Laccaria tortilis (Bolt.) Cke.
Cap 1-2cm, usually distorted, margin striate and wavy, often contorted; surface smooth, pinkish ochre with lilaceous tints. Gills pale, pinkish, irregular or wrinkled. Stipe short or twisted, 1×0.2cm, dark russet. Spores globose, variable, 15-18μm with prominent spines about 2μm long. On mud of cart ruts, edges of ponds or muddy willow woods. Umcommon in Britain. E2.

Laccaria bicolor (R. Mre.) Orton
Cap 2-6cm, convex, pale ochraceous with vague lilaceous tints, slightly flecked or ± scaly. Stipe 6×0.4cm. Gills and stipe distinctly amethyst in contrast to the cap. Spores 8×7μm, with stout spines. Often under conifers. E1 (m2).

Laccaria amethystea (Bull.) Murr.
Cap 5-8cm, convex, then flat with wavy margin, surface matt, bright amethyst throughout but fading to blue-grey or dingy whitish on drying. Gills irregular, bright violet. Stipe 8×0.7cm, striate, dark amethyst-violet, fading little. Flesh colour similar. Spores globose, 9μm, with spines of medium length. As ubiquitous as *L. laccata* and more abundant, but preferring shady woods. Edible. E4.

L. maritima (Teod.) Sing. More brick red colour, with virtually smooth elliptical spores, occurs on coastal dunes, especially the Culbin sands, Morayshire. nE2.

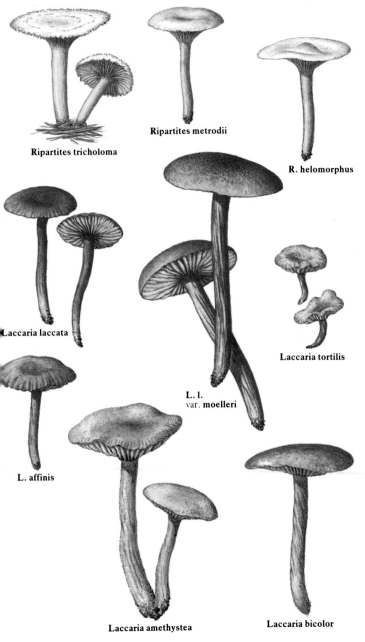

Ripartites metrodii

Ripartites tricholoma

R. helomorphus

Laccaria laccata

Laccaria tortilis

L. l.
var. **moelleri**

L. affinis

Laccaria amethystea

Laccaria bicolor

Tribe *Tricholomateae*. Rather thickset; gills horizontal or sinuate, cap often umbonate fleshy or conical, seldom depressed. Spores hyaline, smooth, non-amyloid.

Key to *Tricholoma* and similar genera

1a Colours white to whitish, very pale: **2**
1b Colours grey to blackish: **9**
1c Colours russet to brownish, ochraceous, fawn or reddish: **19**
1d Colours yellow or greenish: **30**
1e Colours somewhat lilaceous, violaceous or purple, sometimes on a yellow ground: **34**

2a Taste and/or smell unpleasant: **3**
2b Smell none or mealy; taste mild: **7**

3a Taste bitter, smell slight ≫   see *Collybia maculata*, 178
3b Taste acrid or peppery; gills crowded ≫   group of *T. album*, 150
3c Taste mild or in accordance with the smell: **4**

4a Gills distant, cap surface matt, finally rather creamy beige; smell earthy or rather nauseating ≫   *T. inamoenum*, 152
4b Gill spacing normal: **5**

5a Gills somewhat arched, irregular, cap surface matt, rather rugulose at the centre; smell characteristic ≫   see *Leucopaxillus paradoxus*, 162
5b Gills adnate, sinuate, cap surface smooth: **6**

6a Surface yellowing when bruised; smell fruity to nauseous ≫
                                                      T. sulphurescens, 150
6b Less yellowing, often smaller, cap surface more fibrillose, smell unpleasant ≫
                                                      T. inocybeoides, 154

7a Smell faint, not distinctive: **8**
7b Smell of meal or strongly mealy-fungoid, pleasant ≫   see *Calocybe*, 166
7c Smell fruity-soapy ≫   see white forms of *T. saponaceum*, 150

8a Cap somewhat conical or umbonate, silky; stipe often spotted greenish blue or pinkish, not yellowing ≫   *T. columbetta*, 156
8b Cap expanded, flattened or with low umbo ≫   see *Melaleuca*, 164

9a Taste acrid or bitter, unpleasant ≫   *Tricholoma* section *Virgata*, 152
9b Taste mild or mealy: **10**

10a Cap surface ± scaly: **11**
10b Cap surface fibrillosely fleecy or streaky: **12**
10c Cap surface smooth or greasy: **16**

11a Cap 10-20cm, rather flattened, with often wellmarked, trapezoidal, concentric scales; gills tinged glaucous; smell rather nauseous ≫   *T. pardinum*, 152
11b Cap 6-15cm, ± umbonate, with radial black scales only distinct towards margin (cog-wheel); smell strong, aromatic or mealy ≫ group of *T. atrosquamosum* . 154
11c Cap soon expanded with beige bistre scales on a whitish ground; gills slowly yellowing; smell and taste mealy ≫   group of *T. scalpturatum* . 154

12a Smell none or fungoid ≫   group of *T. terreum*, 154
    (If gills broad and distant, stipe with long rooting and ± branched white rhizoids, see *Megacollybia platyphylla*, 176)
12b Smell and/or taste mealy or peculiar: **13**

13a Some yellow or olivaceous tinge present: **14**
13b No tinge of yellow at first: **15**

14a Gills white with tinge or yellow ≫   *T. portentosum*, 156
14b Gills grey; smell strong, mealy; under conifers ≫   *T. luridum*, 156

15a Smell and taste mealy, gills yellowing with age ≫   *T. argyraceum*, 154
15b Distinctive smell of washing, then of celery ≫   *T. josserandii*, 152
15c Insipid slightly nauseous smell ≫   forms of *T. pardinum*, 152

16a Cap hygrophanous, with a low umbo ≫ see *Melanoleuca*, 164
16b Cap not hygrophanous, convex, sometimes blackening: **17**

17a Blackening species ≫ see *Lyophyllum*, 166
17b No colour change or flushing pink: **18**

18a Smell soapy ≫ *T. saponaceum*, 150
18b Smell slightly fruity ≫ see *Lepista panaeolus*, 144

19a Ochraceous to pale russet; cap surface smooth or tardily pulled apart: **20**
19b Colours brown to fawn, pinkish brown or more definitely reddish: **24**

20a Stipe pruinose, concolorous, up to a defined annular line ≫ *T. psammopus*, 158
20b Stipe naked or with scales scattered throughout: **21**

21a Margin furrowed; taste sharp or harsh ≫ *T. acerbum*, 158
21b Margin even: **22**

22a Smell distinctive, often strong: **23**
22b Smell faint or merely fungoid ≫ see *Melanoleuca*, 164

23a Smell of celery ≫ *T. apium*, 158
23b Smell fruity or of face powder ≫ *T. lascivum*, 150

24a Cap surface dry: **25**
24b Cap surface viscid: **29**

25a Stipe with sheathing ring of similar nature to the cap surface, colours often bright orangey or reddish ≫ *Tricholoma* subsection *Caligata*, 160
25b Stipe naked or with illdefined commonplace scales: **26**

26a Taste very bitter; cap smooth or pruinose ≫ *Leucopaxillus gentianeus*, 162
26b Taste mild or slightly bitter; cap somewhat fleecy-fibrillose to scaly : **27**
(If smooth see *Lyophyllum loricatum*, 166)

27a Smell none or merely fungoid; flesh russeting slightly ≫
Tricholoma subsection *Imbricata*, 158
27b Smell fruity or mealy: **28**

28a Smell fruity or jasmine, flesh yellowing; cap margin shaggy or bearded ≫
see *Porpoloma spinulosum*, 162
28b Smell and taste mealy, yellowing only with age ≫ *T. scalpturatum*, 154

29a Stipe naked or without a defined annular zone ≫ *T.* subsection *Pessundata*, 158
29b Stipe with ± ringed or with a well-defined zone ≫
T. subsection *Subannulata*, 160
29c Stipe with sheathing ring similar to cap surface ≫ *T.* subsection *Caligata*, 160

30a Cap surface smooth, barely greasy, smell soapy ≫ *T. saponaceum*, 150
30b Cap surface matt or scaly to fibrillose and greasy to viscid: **31**

31a Taste or smell unpleasant; fungus yellow throughout: **32**
31b Taste mild, mealy or becoming rather bitter: **33**

32a Taste acrid, cap outline somewhat conical ≫ *T. aestuans*, 152
32b Smell of gas tar, gills distant ≫ *T. sulphureum*, 152

33a Stipe naked or with generally dispersed scales ≫ *T.* section *Tricholoma*, 156
(For fungus of this kind on wood see *Tricholomopsis decora*, 150)
33b Stipe with sheathing ring ≫ *Floccularia straminea*, 162

34a Strong smell as in *T. sulphureum*, gills distant ≫ *T. bufonium*, 152
34b Smell faint or pleasant, aromatic; gills crowded: **35**

35a Cap speckled purple on yellow ground; on conifer stumps ≫
Tricholomopsis rutilans, 150
35b Smooth, lilac to violet-brown, smell fruity or nauseous ≫ see *Lepista nuda*, 144
35c With dark red-brown or vinaceous scales, also on sheathing ring ≫
T. caligatum, 160

Tribe *Tricholomateae*. Gills horizontal; aspect of *Tricholoma*. Spores smooth, non-amyloid. Genus *Tricholomopsis*. On wood; gill edge fringed with large cystidia visible under a hand lens. Clamp connections numerous.

Tricholomopsis rutilans (Sch.) Sing.
Cap 8-15cm, convex, speckled with fine purplish scales on a bright yellow or golden ground, finally turning a little rusty. Gills rather broad, yellow with concolorous edges. Var. *variegata* has been distinguished by its more scaly surface and a more rusty edge to the gills. Stipe 8×1cm, ± curved in relation to its situation, fibrous, concolorous. Flesh yellow, smell faint of damp wood, taste becoming bitter; pink reaction with ammonia. Spores 8×6μm, smooth. On stumps of conifers and fence posts, common throughout Britain. Edible but poor. E4.

Tricholomopsis decora (Fr.) Sing.
Cap 3-8cm, less fleshy or a little more depressed than *T. rutilans*, surface fibrillosely scaly, yellow ochre to golden with a few ± olivaceous flecks, especially towards the centre. Stipe 4×0.5cm. Gills and stipe yellow, shape sometimes rather like a *Pleurotus*. Spores 7×5μm, elliptical. On stumps, fallen branches, or sawdust of conifers. Uncommon in Britain, chiefly in the Highlands. Edible but poor. Em3.

Callistosporium xanthophyllum (Malç. & Bert.) Bon [*Collybia x., Tricholoma exsculptum*]
More like a *Collybia* (p. 178). Cap 3-6cm, thin-fleshed, flat or a little depressed, margin thin or wavy, surface smooth, shining, then hygrophanous, yellowish bistre with olivaceous tints, drying a little bronze-grey. Gills rather crowded, adnate, sinuate, concolorous or yellower, tinged pink with age. Stipe 8×0.6cm, fibrillose, soon hollow, concolorous. Flesh concolorous, smell weakly aromatic, taste slightly bitter; pinkish with ammonia, especially on gills. Spores 7×4μm, yellowish, reddening with age or in ammonia, as does content of basidia. Clamp connections absent. On twigs and stumps, especially of conifers. Not in Britain. E2.

Genus *Tricholoma*. On ground. Fleshy or with gills lacking a fringed margin, at most splitting slightly. Clamp connections scanty or absent.

Section *Saponacea* [Subgenus *Contextocutis*]. Cap cuticle commonplace, smooth or silky; smell and taste rather unpleasant. Clamp connections present.

Tricholoma saponaceum (Fr.) Kumm.
Cap 10-15cm, fleshy or convex, surface smooth, slightly greasy then rimose, cracking into scales in dry weather, pale grey brown with a greenish tinge, or yellowish, leaden, becoming tinged pinkish from the margin inwards. Gills fairly distant, whitish to glaucous or yellow olivaceous, reddening slightly. Stipe 12×2cm, often spindle-shaped or tapered and rooting, whitish or tinged pink at the base. Flesh pallid, tinged pink in the base, smell typically soapy, then of laundry or iodine. Spores 7×4μm, elliptical. Widespread but mainly under trees. Common. Edibility questionable. E4.

Tricholoma sulphurescens Bres.
Aspect of *T. saponaceum* but white then yellowing rather as in *Agaricus silvicola*. Gills narrow, often eroded as though aborted. Smell fruity to nasty or nauseating; taste mild. Spores 6×4.5μm, short elliptical. In sheltered places especially under holm oak. Rare in Britain. E2.

T. lascivum (Fr.) Gill. has more ochraceous or milky coffee colour, not yellowing, ± decurrent gills and a smell of *Philadelphus*. Fairly common in Britain, mainly under broadleaved trees. E2.

Tricholoma album (Sch.) Kumm.
Cap 4-7cm, convex to flat or irregular, wavy, silky, pure white then ochraceous. Gills fairly distant, irregular, white. Stipe 6×0.5cm, fragile, white. Flesh white, smell mealy-aromatic then sweet like jasmine, taste acrid. Spores 6×3.5μm. Under broadleaved trees on acid soils. Not edible. Common. E2.

T. pseudoalbum Bon. More robust, with 6-12cm ± fluted cap, regular gills and strong earthy odour. Common on neutral to calcareous soils but not distinguished by British authors. E3.

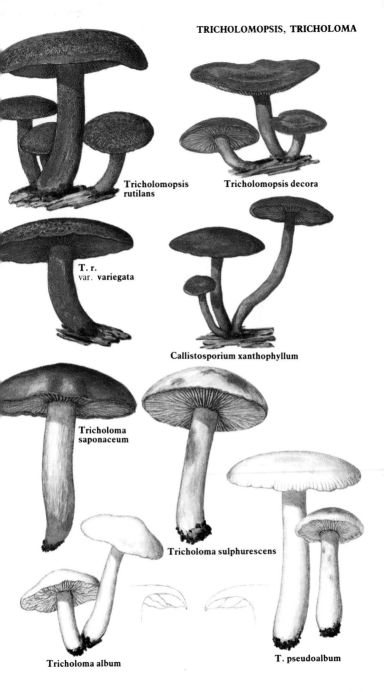

Tricholomopsis
rutilans

Tricholomopsis decora

T. r.
var. variegata

Callistosporium xanthophyllum

Tricholoma
saponaceum

Tricholoma sulphurescens

Tricholoma album

T. pseudoalbum

151

Section *Inamoena*. Cap surface more matt to almost velvety; gills distant. Smells distinctive and unpleasant. Basidia elongated with large spores, about 10µm or over; clamp connections rare.

Tricholoma inamoenum (Fr.) Gill.
Similar to *Tricholoma album* (p. 150) but with more matt surface, coloured dingy white or weak milky coffee to ochraceous. Gills concolorous, distant, rather thick. Stipe 8×0.7cm, equal or club-shaped, whitish, fibrillose. Flesh white; smell strong, rather like jasmine then earthy or of coal gas. Spores 12×7µm. Under spruce in the mountains above (600) 1000m, often among bilberries. Rare. Em3.

Tricholoma sulphureum Kumm.
Cap 6-12cm, convex, then flattened with incurved margin, sometimes lobed; surface matt to velvety-fibrillose, sulphur yellow, flushed lilac at the centre in var. *coronarium*. Gills distant, bright yellow. Stipe 10×1cm, equal or slightly club-shaped, concolorous, fibrillose. Flesh yellow; strong smell of coal gas. Spores 11×7µm, yellowish. Under broadleaved trees, beech, oak, holly etc, mainly on acid soils. Common. E4.

T. bufonium (Pers.) Gill. is doubtfully distinct, but smaller (cap 3-5cm, stipe 2×0.5cm) and with reddish-brown cap and dingy yellow gills and stipe. Smell fruity or sweet at first but soon becoming nauseating. Not uncommon in similar situations to typical *T. sulphureum*. E2.

Section *Virgata*. Cap streaky-fibrillose to scaly. Taste acrid or bitter, smell rather unpleasant. Clamp connections absent, pigment membranal.

Tricholoma virgatum (Fr.) Kumm.
Cap conical, 5-7cm, fibrillose (silky in var. *montana*), eventually ± streaked with innate fibrils, silvery grey then leaden blackish. Gills rather narrow, waxy looking or yellowish grey. Stipe 8×1cm, ± bulbous at the base, 1.5cm across, or truncate; fibrillose, pallid or pinkish in f. *roseipes*. Flesh greyish white with faint earthy or radishy smell, taste bitter, soon becoming acrid or peppery. Spores 7×5µm, elliptical. Under broadleaved trees and conifers especially in the variety and form. Common. Harmless but inedible. E3.

Tricholoma bresadolanum Clemç. [*T. sciodes* p.p.]
Cap convex, 7-12cm, with rounded concentric scales slate grey on a silvery ochre ground. Gills irregular, greyish white, margin dotted blackish. Stipe 8×1.5cm, slightly scaly, similar colour. Flesh pale or greying, smell faint, taste ± bitter. Spores 7×6µm; gill edge bearing fascicles of brownish cells. Under broadleaved trees. Uncommon. E2.

T. sciodes (Pers.) Martin s.str. has outline of *T. virgatum* but gills and taste of *T. bresadolanum* and a tendency to redden. E2.

Tricholoma aestuans (Fr.) Gill.
Like *T. virgatum* but with yellow colouring reminiscent of *T. equestre*. Gills rather ascending, pale yellow, edge splitting. Stipe 8×1cm, ± spindle-shaped, fibrillosely scaly. Flesh pale, taste bitter then acrid. Spores 7×4.5µm, some clavate marginal cells present. Among bilberries under spruce. Rare. Inedible. E1.

Tricholoma josserandii Bon [*T. groanense*]
Cap 5-8cm, convex then deformed, almost smooth to streaky, pale greyish, sometimes silvery, to whitish beige or bluish. Gills ± distant, white or tinged glaucous. Stipe 7×1cm, narrowed at the base, whitish, russet or pink at the base. Flesh pale with mingled smell of rancid meal, *Lactarius quietus*, celery or nauseating-fruity. Taste unpleasant. Spores 7×5.5µm; clamp connections absent. Oak woods on sandy soil, moors and heaths. Not British. **Poisonous**. E2.

Section *Pardinocutis*. Cap surface with distant scales. Hyphae with encrusting membranal pigment and clamp connections.

Tricholoma pardinum (Pers.) Quél. [*T. tigrinum*]
Cap fleshy, rather truncately conical, 15-25cm, with incurved margin; surface covered with broad round or trapezoidal blackish brown scales on a pale ground. Gills dull whitish, slightly glaucous. Stipe stout or swollen, 12×5cm, nearly smooth, pallid. Flesh whitish, smell rather mealy-spermatic becoming unpleasant to earthy. Spores 10×7µm. Beech and fir woods. **Poisonous**. Not in Britain. E2-3.

152

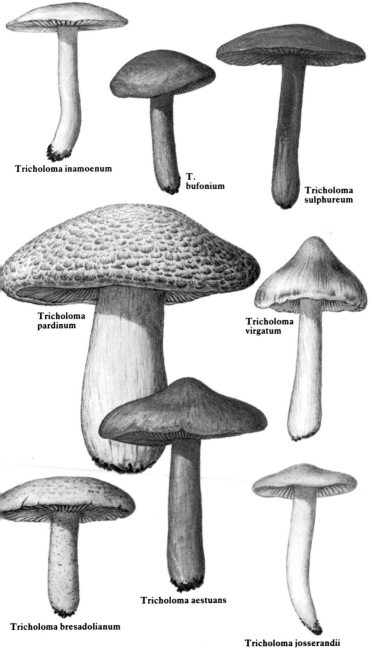

Tricholoma inamoenum

T. bufonium

Tricholoma sulphureum

Tricholoma pardinum

Tricholoma virgatum

Tricholoma bresadolianum

Tricholoma aestuans

Tricholoma josserandii

Section *Atrosquamosa*. Surface tomentose to scaly-fibrillose, blackish grey to bistre. Taste mild. Clamp connections absent, pigment mainly membranal.

Tricholoma atrosquamosum (Chev.) Sacc.
Cap 7-10cm, convex to broadly umbonate, typically covered with dark sepia-grey or blackish bistre scales on a pale ground, margin fleecy. Gills dull cream to greyish or dotted black on the edges. Stipe 6×1cm, cylindrical, whitish and ± scaly (entirely concolorous in var. *squarrulosum*). Flesh whitish, smell mealy then aromatic, peppery or of basil. Spores 8×5.5µm, elliptical; some pigmented cells present on gill edge. Under broadleaved trees on limestone, beech-fir woods and sometimes spruce. Edible. Uncommon. E3.

Tricholoma orirubens Quél.
Similar to *T. atrosquamosum* in stature but with more fibrillose surface, dark at the centre and paler at the margin, which is sometimes smooth. Gills white, reddening from the edges, sometimes only with age. Stipe 6×1cm, white, fibrillose, springing from yellowish mycelium and sometimes spotted steely blue at the base; reddening quickly inside and out in var. *basirubens*. Taste and smell mealy, slightly aromatic, fruity or sweet. Spores as in *T. atrosquamosum* or broader; marginal cells colourless or pink. Beech woods. Uncommon in Britain. Edible. E2.

Tricholoma terreum (Sch.) Kumm.
Cap rather conical or umbonate, 6-10cm, surface fibrillose with slate or almost black fibrils. Gills pale grey. Stipe 8×1cm, rather spindle-shaped, smooth, pure white. Flesh whitish, smell and taste weak, not mealy. Spores 7×5µm, subcuticular hyphae with ± globose cells. Under pines, especially on limestone. Common. Edible. E3.

Lowland records with white gills and cap fleecy enough to yield a slight cortina have been called **T. myomyces** (Pers.) Lange. .

Tricholoma gausapatum (Fr.) Quél.
Similar in stature to *T. terreum* but less umbonate or more fleshy, cap surface more felted and matted. Gills broad, deeply sinuate and slightly veined. Stipe fibrillose or pruinose at the apex above a fleeting annular zone. Spores as in *T. terreum* or broader; subcutis less clearly differentiated. In grassy broadleaved woods, parks. Common. Edible. E2.

Tricholoma triste (Scop.) Quél.
Cap 4-7cm with low umbo, fibrillose or speckled slaty grey-brown on an ochraceous ground. Gills grey. Stipe short, 4×1cm, tinged greyish or slate around the middle, paler elsewhere, with a sparse cortina. Flesh white, smell and taste weak, fungoid. Spores 4-6×3-4µm, rather variable. Copses of broadleaved trees, often in wet places. Uncommon. Edible. E1.

Tricholoma scalpturatum (Fr.) Quél.
Cap 4-8cm, thin-fleshed, surface scaly, pale or silvery with small grey scales varying to grey-brown or brownish scales on a beige ground. Gills white, staining bright lemon yellow with the onset of decay. Stipe 4×0.6cm, pure white with some trace of a cortina. Flesh white, smell and taste distinctly mealy. Spores 6×3µm, rather elongated; no ± cellular subcutis present. Ubiquitous, often in copses of broadleaved trees or along grassy margins. Common. Edible. E4.

T. inocybeoides Pears. Similar or more conical and whitish but lacks scales and has an unpleasant smell. Rare. E1.

T. argyraceum (Bull.) Gill., more whitish or silvery, is fibrillous. Uncommon. E3.

Tricholoma cingulatum (Almf.) Jacob.
Cap similar to *T. scalpturatum* or more obtuse, margin incurved, surface with beige to pale greyish scales. Gills ± distant and similarly yellowing. Stipe more slender, 6×0.8cm, white with a ± yellowish membranous annular zone. Flesh white, smell and taste mealy. Spores like those of *T. scalpturatum* or slightly longer. In damp broadleaved woods, mainly under willows. Not uncommon in Britain. E2.

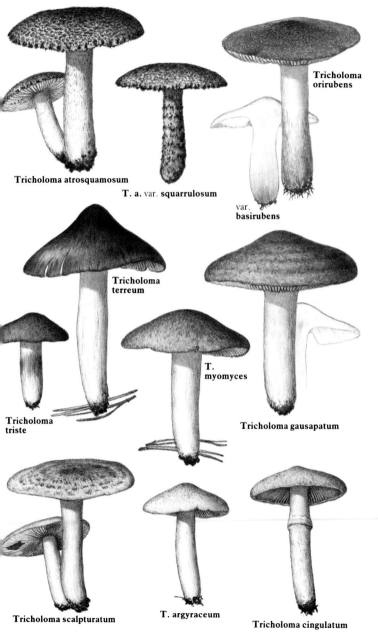

Tricholoma atrosquamosum

T. a. var. **squarrulosum**

Tricholoma orirubens

var. **basirubens**

Tricholoma terreum

T. myomyces

Tricholoma triste

Tricholoma gausapatum

Tricholoma scalpturatum

T. argyraceum

Tricholoma cingulatum

155

Section *Tricholoma* [*Equestria, Sejuncta*]. Caps ± viscid and bright coloured, yellow or greenish, seldom white or greyish. Clamp connections absent.

Tricholoma columbetta (Fr.) Kumm.
Cap 7-12cm, typically obtusely conical or umbonate, then expanded, becoming deformed with lobed margin; surface silky satiny or viscid, pure white or spotted pinkish. Gills irregular, white. Stipe 10×1cm, slightly spindle-shaped, fibrous, white or with bluish blotches near the base. Flesh white, smell faintly mealy. Spores 7×5μm, elliptical. Sandy oak woods and heaths. Common. Edible but to be distinguished carefully from white capped forms of the lethal Amanitas (p. 298). E3.

Tricholoma sejunctum (Sow.) Quél.
Cap 6-9cm, rather conical or umbonate, surface streaky fibrillose, greenish, sometimes more bronze at the centre and yellowish towards the margin. Gills ± distant, sinuate, whitish. Stipe 8×1cm, slightly spindle-shaped, white or tinged yellow. Flesh white, smell mealy, taste slightly bitter. Spores 8×5.5μm. Under various broadleaved trees, also conifers (var. *coniferarum*, more greyish). Uncommon in Britain. Edible but still rather bitter when cooked. E3.

Tricholoma viridilutescens Moser
General aspect of *T. sejunctum* but with yellower margin and gills typically yellow towards the outside with edges eroded or notched. Flesh ± yellow, taste and smell mealy. Spores 8×5μm. Under broadleaved trees on acid soils. Rare in Britain. E2.

T. arvernense Bon is similar but the cap is more yellow to orange, smoother and lobed; spores 5×3μm and clamped basidia. Not known in Britain. Em1.

Tricholoma fucatum (Fr.) Gill. var. **subglobisporum**
Cap 4-6cm, slightly conical or umbonate, surface fibrillose, slightly viscid, dark bronze at the centre, more olivaceous elsewhere. Gills yellowish white. Stipe 9×1cm, whitish, base attenuated and darkened by olive-bistre fibrils. Flesh dingy white with strong smell of meal or cucumber. Taste mild. Spores ± globose, 7×6μm, basidia without clamps. Among bilberries under spruce in the mountains. Not in Britain. E2.

The type species (var. *fucatum*) is not so dark-coloured and has ± elongated spores. Mainly Scandinavian and E. European, seems to be unknown in W. Europe.

T. joachimii Bon & Riva [*Tr. fucatum* p.p.] is more fleshy, cap 6-10cm, greenish olive, with a faint smell, more elongated spores and clamped basidia. Occurs under pines on calcareous soil. **T. viridifucatum** Bon is the more greenish yellow homologue under broadleaved trees. E2.

Tricholoma auratum Gill.
Cap 10-15cm, convex or with a fleshy umbo, viscid, and russet or orange at the centre, slightly scaly and brighter yellow further out, margin smoother. Gills ± distant, sulphur yellow. Stipe 7×1.5cm, rather thickset, whitish or yellow at the base. Flesh pale yellow or brighter towards the surface; pink with ammonia. Smell fungoid, taste nutty and pleasant. Spores 7×4.5μm. Sandy pine woods. Not known in Britain. Edible and good. E3.

T. equestre (L.) Quél. [*T. flavovirens*] differs in its drier and more scaly umbo with brighter yellow tints, especially on the stipe and in the flesh. Under broadleaved trees and conifers. Uncommon, but present throughout Britain and especially in the Highlands. E2.

Tricholoma portentosum (Fr.) Quél.
Cap 10-15cm, slightly conical or umbonate, surface covered with ± dark grey fibrils on a pale yellowish ground. Gills white with tinge of lemon. Stipe 10×1.5cm, white, ± tinged lemon in places. Flesh white, slightly yellowish at the surface. Smell and taste mealy. Spores 7×5μm, elliptical. Under conifers, with a paler slender form under broadleaved trees. In Britain mainly in the Highlands. Edible. E4.

T. luridum (Sch.) Quél is more olive-brown, with greyish gills and a strong smell of cucumber. Spores 11×7μm. Doubtfully British. E1.

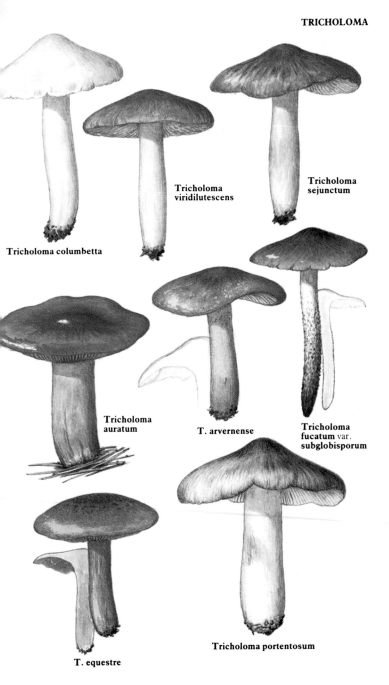

Tricholoma columbetta

Tricholoma
viridilutescens

Tricholoma
sejunctum

Tricholoma
auratum

T. arvernense

Tricholoma
fucatum var.
subglobisporum

T. equestre

Tricholoma portentosum

Section *Imbricata*. Colours brown to russet ochre. Cap cuticle dry and ± fibrillose-scaly.

Tricholoma imbricatum (Fr.) Kumm.
Cap 8-12cm, broadly umbonate, surface fibrillose, slowly separating into scales, velvety reddish brown over the disk, paler or progressively becoming ochraceous to the margin, sometimes tinged olivaceous. Gills crowded, rather broad, cream to pinkish. Stipe 13×2cm, spindle-shaped, attenuated below or rooting, whitish, fibrillose or ± reddish-brown scaly. Flesh whitish or creamy russet, smell faint, taste rather bitter. Spores 7×5μm; epicuticular hyphae clavate. Under pines, less often poplar or holm oak. Common. Barely edible after blanching: not worth it. E3.

T. vaccinum (Sch.) Kumm. Less robust, with a more fleecy surface and bearded margin. In similar situations, but in Britain far less common than *T. imbricatum*. E2.

Tricholoma psammopus (Kalchbr.) Quél.
Cap similar to *T. imbricatum* or smaller, surface smoother or granulate, slowly becoming scaly, uniformly pale russet ochre. Gills irregular, soon speckled pinkish. Stipe 10×1cm, almost cylindrical, typically concolorous or granulate up to an often narrow white annular zone below the gills. Flesh pale, almost odourless, taste bitter. Spores 7×5μm; epicuticular hyphae capitate or constricted. Under conifers. Uncommon. E3.

Tricholoma acerbum (Bull.) Quél.
Cap 10-15cm, convex, margin incurved, typically fluted or furrowed, surface nearly smooth or matt, pale yellowish brown, scarcely more russet at the centre. Gills cream, slightly dotted reddish. Stipe 8×2cm, pale beige, dotted yellow at the apex. Flesh pale, smell faint, taste sharp or tart. Spores 5.5×4μm, short-elliptic; epicuticular hyphae equal, russet, with mucilaginous sheath. Under broadleaved trees. Rare in Britain. Edible but poor quality. E2.

T. apium J. Schaef. has similar stature and colouring but a smooth margin and a smell of celery or chicory. In Britain only known from the Highlands, and there extremely rare. E1.

Section *Albobrunnea*. Colour brown, cap-cuticle smooth, viscid.

Subsection *Pessundata*. Stipe smooth or without a distinct annular zone.

Tricholoma fulvum (D.C.) Sacc. [*T. flavobrunneum*]
Cap 6-10cm, convex or with a low umbo, margin striate at first, surface viscid, then matt, orange brown or yellower towards the margin. Gills yellow, then russet. Stipe 8×1cm, fibrillose, yellow to brownish. Flesh yellow, smell strong, mealy, taste rather bitter. Spores 6×4μm, elliptical. Under birch, abundant throughout Britain. E4.

T. pseudonictitans Bon, with smooth margin and only internal yellow tints, occurs under conifers. E3.

Tricholoma populinum Lange
Cap 10-15cm, convex, sometimes deformed, surface viscid, smooth, dark brown, sometimes with pinkish or olivaceous tints. Gills pale, ± rufescent with age. Stipe 10×2cm, whitish, almost smooth or slightly scaly, with yellowish mycelium. Flesh pale, smell strong of meal or cucumber; taste mild. Spores 6×3.5μm, elliptical. Often in clusters, associated with poplar. Rare in Britain. Edible and good. E3.

T. pessundatum (Fr.) Quél. is smaller, very viscid, speckled over the centre with darker spots. Under pines and spruce. Uncommon in Britain, chiefly in the Highlands. E3.

Tricholoma ustale (Fr.) Kumm.
Cap medium size, 6-9cm, almost smooth or slightly viscid, chestnut colour at the centre, margin paler. Gills becoming rufescent. Stipe 6×1cm, white, browning towards the base. Flesh whitish, smell faint, taste slightly bitter. Spores 7×4.5μm, elliptical. Under broadleaved trees. Common. Edible but of poor quality, after blanching. E3.

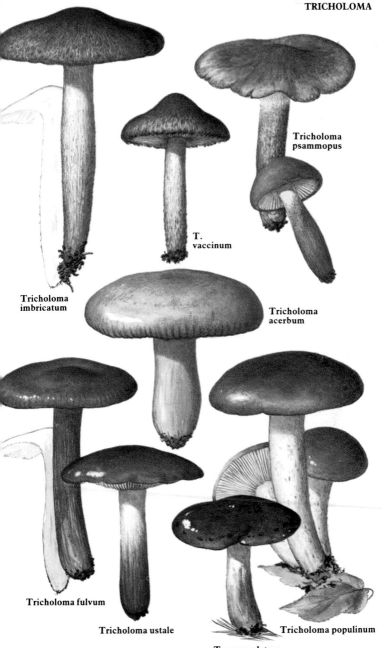

Tricholoma psammopus

T. vaccinum

Tricholoma imbricatum

Tricholoma acerbum

Tricholoma fulvum

Tricholoma ustale

Tricholoma populinum

T. pessundatum

Subsection *Subannulata*. Annular zone on the stipe ± membranous or at least clearly defined.

Tricholoma fracticum (Britz.) Kreis. [*T. batschii, T. subannulatum* p.p.]
Cap 10-15cm, fleshy, convex, margin smooth or incurved, surface slightly viscid or silky, chestnut brown. Gills cream to pinkish or speckled reddish. Stipe short, 8×2cm, whitish, base brownish as far up as a pale, fugaceous, ± membraneous annular zone. Flesh cream to russet, with fleeting mealy smell and very bitter taste. Spores 5.5×4.5μm. Under pine especially on calcareous soil. Edible after blanching but poor quality. E2.

T. striatum Sacc. [*T. albobrunneum* p.p.] is more slender, with striate margin and surface a little fibrillose has a less bitter flavour and occurs in the mountains, under conifers. E1.

Tricholoma ustaloides Romagn. [*T. albobrunneum* auct.]
Cap 6-10cm, convex, margin striate or slightly furrowed at first, surface very viscid, uniformly chestnut brown, drying russet. Gills whitish or speckled reddish. Stipe 10×1cm, cylindrical or slightly club-shaped, zoned with russet up to a well defined but not raised annular zone; apex white pruinose. Flesh white, almost unchanging; smell strong, mealy or of cucumber, water melon, corduroy etc. Taste immediately very bitter. Spores 7×5μm, epicutis strongly gelatinised. Under broadleaved trees. Common. E3.

Tricholoma colossus (Fr.) Quél.
Large fungus, cap 20-28cm, convex and fleshy, smooth or slightly viscid, pinkish beige ± spotted with reddish brown or eventually vinaceous. Gills pinkish russet, bruising salmon or vinaceous. Stipe stout, 15×5m, slightly swollen, zoned vinaceous brown from the base up to an annular zone like a fleecy cushion. Flesh whitish then salmon, smell faint, taste rather mild. Spores 10×7μm, the largest in the group. Under conifers, in Britain under pine in the central Highlands. Edible. E1.

Subsection *Caligata*. A ring the same colour as the cap sheathing the stipe.

Tricholoma aurantium (Sch.) Ricken
Cap medium size, 7-10cm, convex, soon flattened, surface very viscid then flecked, a bright fawnish orange darkening to russet brown. Gills white to russet orange. Stipe 5-10×1-2cm, covered with zones concolorous with the cap up to a floccose ring zone. Flesh white, tinged orange near the surface, smell strong of meal or cucumber; taste ± bitter. Spores 5.5×4μm, ± globose. Under conifers, in Britain under pine in the Highlands. E2.

Tricholoma robustum (A.-S.) Ricken
Cap 6-12cm, convex and fleshy, only slightly viscid or a little silky, fibrillosely streaked with coppery reddish brown. Gills cream to russet. Stipe short 5×2cm, concolorous with the cap up to a shaggy ring, apex white. Flesh white, compact, smell mealy or of cucumber; taste almost mild. Spores 6×3.5μm. Generally calcareous soil. Under pines in the Highlands, less often in England. Edible. E2.

T. focale (Fr.) Ricken is more slender, brighter coloured, reddish orange; stipe girdled with concolorous fleecy flakes. In Britain under pines in the central Highlands. In southern Europe there is var. *caussetta*, more robust, with fleecy bright red scales, under holm oak and Aleppo or maritime pines. E2.

Tricholoma caligatum (Viv.) Ricken
Cap 10-20cm, convex, fleshy, with circular reddish brown scales on a ± contrasting paler ground. Gills cream, crowded. Stipe 18×3cm, typically sheathed with a ring of similar nature to the cap surface, up to a membranous ring. Flesh white to russet, smell strong, aromatic or fruity, sometimes of chloride or nauseating in the end; taste sweetish. Spores 7×5.5μm, short-elliptic; epicuticular hyphae strongly pigmented. Under conifers, sometimes holm oak or in maquis. In Britain with pine in the Highlands. Edible, slightly euphoriant, much appreciated in Japan. sE1-2.

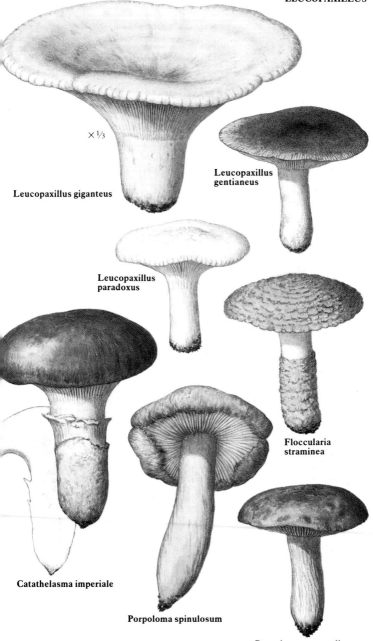

× ⅓

Leucopaxillus giganteus

Leucopaxillus gentianeus

Leucopaxillus paradoxus

Floccularia straminea

Catathelasma imperiale

Porpoloma spinulosum

Porpoloma metapodium

Genus *Melanoleuca*. Cap thin-fleshed or with a low umbo, often hygrophanous; gills somewhat adnate, colours dull. Spores warted, distinctive cystidia frequent, clamp connections absent. All species seem to be edible, but they are inadequately known and difficult to distinguish.

Melanoleuca vulgaris (Pat.) Pat. [*M. melaleuca* p.p.]

Cap medium size, 6-10cm, with low umbo, smooth to shining, dark brown, fading to dull grey-brown from the margin. Gills white, rather crowded. Stipe 8×0.8cm, slightly club-shaped, whitish. Flesh white or pallid, slightly brownish at the base; smell and taste not distinctive. Spores 8×5µm, with rather elongated warts; cystidia fusiform. Meadows, pastures and under broadleaved trees. Common. E3.

Melanoleuca cognata (Fr.) K.-M.

Cap 10-12cm, convex to broadly umbonate and obtuse; colour bright for the genus, yellowish brown to golden ochre, milky coffee or copper, sometimes orange. Gills crowded, pale cream, sometimes flushed pink. Stipe 13×1.5cm, often bulbous, colour similar. Flesh pallid, more coloured like the cap towards the base; smell and taste not distinctive. Spores 10×7µm, with isolated warts; cystidia fusiform. Woodland glades, sometimes in the spring. Not uncommon. E1 (m3).

Melanoleuca subpulverulenta (Pers.) Sing.

Cap 5-8cm, soon flattened or thin-fleshed, surface matt or pruinose, pale ashy grey to silvery. Gills white, crowded, brittle. Stipe 6×0.6cm, ± cylindrical, whitish, apex pruinose. Flesh white, smell and taste slight. Spores 8×5.5µm, warts slightly elongated; cystidia flask-shaped. In grassy pine woods especially on calcareous soils. Uncommon. E2.

M. strictipes (Karst.) Murr. is more fleshy, with smooth surface and has a stiffer or fibrous-cartilaginous stipe. E2.

Melanoleuca grammopodia (Bull.) Pat.

Cap 12-18cm, distinctly umbonate with incurved margin; surface smooth, brownish to yellowish grey. Gills crowded, rather broad, adnate or sloping, dull white or tinged yellowish brown (spore print cream). Stipe 15×1.5cm, slightly bulbous, striate or with twisted brownish fibrils on a pale ground. Flesh pallid, browner in the base; smell strong, mealy becoming aromatic with age. Spores 10×6µm, with rather elongated warts; cystidia nettle-hair type, i.e. short with broad base and slender pointed or barbed apex. Woodland glades and grassy copses. Common. E3.

Melanoleuca brevipes (Bull.) Pat.

Cap 8-12cm, much as in *M. grammopodia*, sometimes deformed, rather darker at the centre. Gills rather broad and crowded, tinged yellowish brown. Stipe thickset, scarcely half as long as the cap is wide, 3×1cm, slightly striate, similar colour. Flesh brown in the base. Smell and taste not distinctive. Spores 9×6µm with small regular warts; cystidia nettle-hair type. Among grass under broadleaved trees, in parks, waste ground etc. Not uncommon. E2.

Melanoleuca pseudoluscina Bon

Slender with flat cap 2-3cm, grey-brown, paling. Gills whitish or cream. Stipe rather slender 6×0.4cm, similar colour or rusty with vinaceous tint in var. *rufipes*. Flesh brownish in the base; smell and taste not distinctive. Spores short-ovoid, 8×6.5µm with isolated warts; cystidia nettle-hair type. Spinneys or thickets, often in sand. Not yet recognised in Britain. E2.

M. excissa (Fr.) Sing. is more variable in colour, with stipe pale or shorter and has the spores elongated or narrow. E2.

Melanoleuca verrucipes (Fr.) Sing.

Medium size, cap 5-10cm, creamy white with a brownish disk; gills whitish, slightly sloping. Stipe 8×0.8cm, distinctly warted or roughened, resembling a *Krombholziella*. Flesh white, smell fruity, then mealy-earthy; taste mild. Spores narrow, 11×5µm, ± reticulate; cystidia nettle-hair type. Among grass and in copses of broadleaved trees. Rare, not known in Britain. E1.

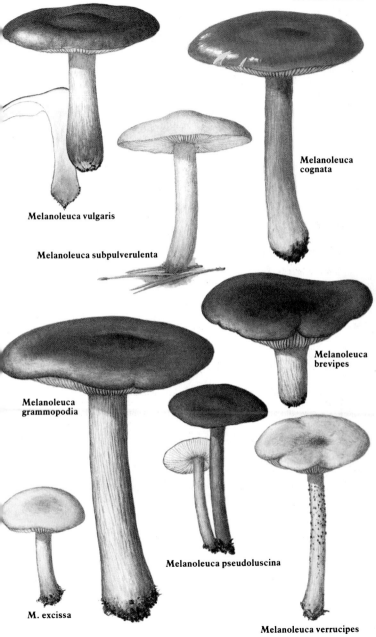

Melanoleuca vulgaris

Melanoleuca subpulverulenta

Melanoleuca cognata

Melanoleuca brevipes

Melanoleuca grammopodia

M. excissa

Melanoleuca pseudoluscina

Melanoleuca verrucipes

Tribe *Lyophylleae*. Distinguished microscopically by presence in the basidia of granules stained blackish red by aceto-carmine (=siderophilic).

Genus *Lyophyllum*. Fruit-bodies robust, clustered or blackening.

Lyophyllum leucophaeatum (Karst.) Karst. [*L. fumatofoetens*]
Cap 6-10cm, fleshy, convex, slightly fibrillose radially, brownish grey or dull ochraceous. Gills greyish or greying, sometimes bluing on the margin, adnate. Stipe 6×1cm, fibrillose, whitish, bruising grey-brown. Flesh greying, sometimes finally blue-black; smell faint, taste mild. Spores 9×4μm, cylindrical, somewhat warty. Mixed woods. Uncommon. E2.

Some superficially similar species are distinguished by the shape of their smooth spores, such as: **L. transforme** (Britz.) Sing. [*L. trigonosporum*]. Spores triangular. E2. **L. deliberatum** (Britz.) Kreis. [*L. infumatum*]. Spores diamond-shaped. E2. **L. semitale** (Fr.) Kühn. Spores elliptical. Also has a strong, rancid smell. E3.

Lyophyllum decastes (Fr.) Sing. [*L. aggregatum*]
Cap 6-10cm, convex then flat, brownish ochre, smooth. Gills white to ochraceous, sometimes flushed pinkish. Stipe 12×1.5cm, fibrillose, whitish. Flesh white, unchanging, smell slightly mealy. Spores globose, 5.5μm, smooth. Grassy copses, gardens etc, in dense clusters. Common throughout Britain. Edible but beware of possible confusion with *Entoloma lividum*. E4.

L. loricatum (Fr.) Kühn. is similar but with a thick or leathery surface layer on the cap and more often occurs singly. Quite common. E2.

Lyophyllum ulmarium (Bull.) Kühn. [*Pleurotus ulmarius*]
Cap 15-20cm, convex, umbonate or deformed, ochraceous to grey-brown, sometimes olivaceous, slightly streaky, eventually cracking. Gills adnate or sinuate, white. Stipe curved or excentric, 8×2cm, whitish, felted. Flesh white, smell slightly mealy. Spores globose, 4.5μm. On trunks of broadleaved trees, especially elm. Uncommon. E1.

Lyophyllum connatum (Schum.) Sing.
Cap 5cm, convex, slowly becoming depressed, pure white, glossy. Gills arched to ± decurrent, crowded, white. Stipe white, 12×0.8cm. Flesh white, smell and taste not mealy, rather like green peas. Spores 7×4μm. Gills Fe reaction violet. In dense clusters on lawns, woodland glades etc. Fairly common. E1 (m3).

Genus *Calocybe*. Rather stout, white, solitary fungi or more slender, *Collybia*-like, brightly coloured species.

Calocybe gambosa (Fr.) Donk. [*Tricholoma gambosum, T. georgii*]
ST. GEORGE'S MUSHROOM
Cap 10-13cm, convex or fleshy, rounded at first, with incurved margin; surface smooth, white to creamy ochre. Gills crowded, narrow, whitish to pale buff. Stipe 6×1.5cm, white. Flesh firm, white, with agreeable rather mealy smell like the common mushroom. Spores 5x3μm, smooth. Among grass along margins and in clearings in woods, under hedges, or in grassy sand-dunes. April-June. The English name refers to its traditionally fruiting around St. George's Day, 23rd April. Common throughout Britain. Edible and excellent. E3.

C. constricta (Fr.) Kühn. Autumnal, with a strong mealy smell, like cucumber, has a ring on the stipe, spiny spores, and occurs on manured ground. E2.

Calocybe carnea (Bull.) Donk
Cap 2-5cm, flat or only slightly fleshy, pink or creamy-flesh colour with brick centre. Gills horizontal, white. Stipe 4×0.5cm, pink. Flesh white, smell slight. Spores 5×2.5μm. Common on lawns. E2-3.

C. ionides (Bull.) Donk differs especially in its purplish violet cap and occurrence under conifers. Uncommon in southern Britain, under beech on chalk. E1.

Calocybe chrysenteron (Bull.) Sing. ex Bon & Contù
Cap 6-7cm, soon expanded or depressed, almost velvety, bright yellow with a ± fawn centre. Gills very crowded, yellow. Stipe 5×0.5cm, concolorous, often compressed. Flesh sulphur yellow; smell mealy, taste becoming bitter. Spores 4×2.5μm. Under conifers, rare. E1.

166

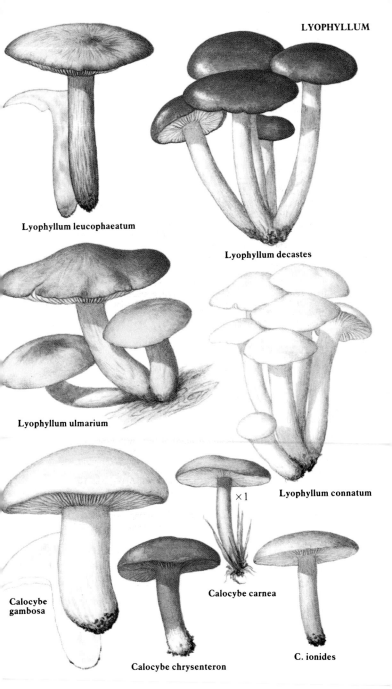

Lyophyllum leucophaeatum

Lyophyllum decastes

Lyophyllum ulmarium

×1

Lyophyllum connatum

Calocybe gambosa

Calocybe carnea

Calocybe chrysenteron

C. ionides

167

Genus *Tephrocybe*. Like *Lyophyllum* but more slender, *Collybia*- or *Mycena*-like, colours dull; gills adnate or sinuate.

Tephrocybe atrata (Fr.) Donk [*Collybia atrata*]
Cap 3-5cm, rather fleshy or umbonate, not striate, dark brown to blackish, hygro-phanous, becoming paler concentrically. Gills greyish. Stipe short, 2×0.5cm, similar colour. Smell rather mealy to rancid. Spores 7×4μm, smooth. On burnt ground, often in tufts. Common. E2.

Superficially similar and equally common on burnt ground are: **T. anthracophila** (Lasch) Orton [*Collybia carbonaria*], spores round, smooth, 5-6μm. E2; **T. ambusta** (Fr.) Donk, more slender, with striate cap, spores round but rugulose. E2.

Tephrocybe palustris (Peck) Donk [*Collybia leucomyosotis*]
Cap 1-3cm, convex, margin striate, smooth, olive brown, drying livid beige. Gills pallid, ± distant. Stipe slender, 10×0.3cm, pale and brittle. Smell strong of cucum-ber. Spores 8×5μm, smooth. Abundant everywhere in *Sphagnum* bogs from May to September. E3.

Tephrocybe rancida (Fr.) Donk [*Collybia rancida*]
Cap 3-5cm, rather conical or deformed, slaty grey, centre darker, margin paler with a silvery pruina. Gills ± distant, greyish. Stipe 7×0.4cm, similar colour, cartilaginous and prolonged into a whitish pointed root 2-5cm long. Flesh pallid with strong smell of rancid oil. Spores elliptical, 8×4μm, smooth. In copses of broadleaved trees on heavy soils. Quite common. E2.

Tephrocybe boudieri (K.-R.) Derbsch
Cap similar to *T. rancida* or flatter, ochraceous grey or silvery sooty, margin rather silky. Stipe 6×0.4cm, not rooting but typically speckled with whitish flecks on a violet-grey ground. Gills ochraceous. Flesh pallid, smell strong of cucumber, taste sharp. Spores 8×4μm, smooth. Under broadleaved trees in copses on calcareous soil. Rare. E2.

Tephrocybe putida (Sacc.) Moser [*Collybia putidella*]
Cap 5-7cm, slightly umbonate, fleshy enough to suggest a *Lyophyllum* but not black-ening, greyish, tinged olivaceous on drying. Gills broad and crowded, greyish. Stipe 5×0.8cm, compressed or furrowed, soon hollow, similar colour. Strong smell of meal. Spores 9×5μm, cylindrical, smooth. Under broadleaved trees. Uncommon. E2.

Tephrocybe graminicola Bon
Cap 1-3cm, rather mycenoid but margin not striate, silvery silky with lead grey centre. Gills greyish. Stipe 2×0.3cm, similar colour, powdery above. Faint smell of rancid oil or grease. Spores 8×5.5μm, with short spines. Lawns. E1.

T. tylicolor (Fr.) Moser [*Collybia tesquorum*] is similar, growing under broadleaved trees, with spiny ± globose spores 7×6μm. Common in Britain from May to Decem-ber. E2.

Tephrocybe misera (Fr.) Moser
Slender fungus with the aspect of a *Mycena*, cap hemispherical, greyish, 1-2cm, margin striate. Gills ascending, ashy. Stipe pallid, 4×0.2cm. Smell none. Spores ± fusiform, 7×3μm, smooth. Under broadleaved trees. Uncommon. E1.

Genus *Asterophora* [*Nyctalis*]. Confined to old fruit-bodies of *Russulaceae*.

Asterophora lycoperdoides (Bull.) Ditm. [*Nyctalis asterophora*]
Cap 2-5cm, convex, covered with ochraceous to chocolate brown powder, composed of chlamydospores. Gills aborted or rudimentary. Stipe short, 1×0.5cm, pallid. Smell unpleasant. Spores 6×4μm; chlamydospores star-shaped, 15μm. Fairly common, especially on decaying *Russula nigricans*. E4.

Asterophora parasitica (Bull.) Sing.
Cap 1-3cm, thinner, smooth, silvery or whitish, slightly striate. Gills distant, normal, greyish. Stipe 4×0.3cm, pallid. Smell mealy. Spores as above, but chlamydospores absent. Fairly common on decaying specimens of various *Russula* spp. in Section *Compactae* (p. 54) or on white *Lactarius* (eg *vellereus*, p.94). E3.

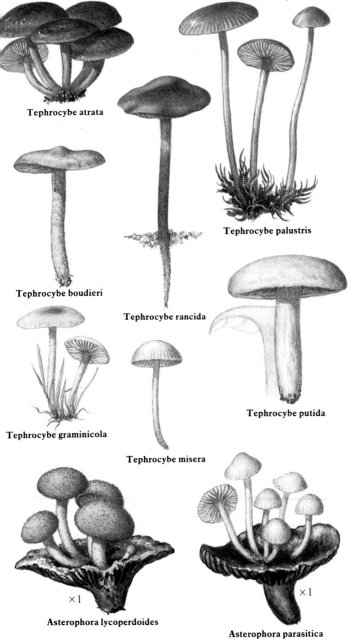

Tephrocybe atrata

Tephrocybe boudieri

Tephrocybe rancida

Tephrocybe palustris

Tephrocybe graminicola

Tephrocybe misera

Tephrocybe putida

×1

Asterophora lycoperdoides

×1

Asterophora parasitica

Tribe *Dermolomateae*. More or less collybioid fungi with cap surface wrinkled, sometimes viscid or powdered. Cuticle ± cellular, palisadic or formed of dermatocystidia or sphaerocysts. Genus *Dermoloma*. Aspect of small *Tricholoma* with wrinkled cap surface; smell rather mealy. Epicutis palisadic, of clavate hyphae with membranal pigment.

Dermoloma atrocinereum (Pers.) Orton
Cap 3-6cm, convex or slightly umbonate, dark grey to sooty. Gills sinuate, greyish. Stipe whitish, 6×0.6cm. Flesh pallid, strong smell of meal. Spores 8×5μm, non-amyloid. In grassy broadleaved woods and glades, lawns etc. Common. E2.

Dermoloma pseudocuneifolium Herink ex Bon [*D. cuneifolium* p.p.]
Cap 2-4cm, rather fleshy, grey bistre or brownish, soon becoming cracked over its surface. Flesh pallid, smell of meal or cucumber. Spores 6×4μm, amyloid; epicutis with ± globose cells. Lawns. Common. E3.

Genus *Camarophyllopsis* [*Hygrotrama*]. Gills ± decurrent, recalling *Hygrophorus*.

Camarophyllopsis atropuncta (Pers.) Arnolds
Cap 1-3cm, dark olive-brown. Gills greyish ochre. Stipe 4×0.5cm, pale, the upper part dotted black. Flesh pallid, smell mealy-spermatic. Spores 6×4μm. Epicutis with ± globose hyphae. Grassy copses. Uncommon. E1.

Camarophyllopsis foetens (Phill.) Arnolds
Cap 1-3cm, somewhat umbilicate, dark brown to yellowish grey. Gills distant, ochraceous. Stipe 5×0.5cm, tapered below. Flesh pallid, smell foetid. Spores 7×5μm; epicutis palisadic. Grassy copses. Rare. E1.

Hydropus marginellus (Pers.) Sing.
Cap 2cm, ± umbilicate, brownish, margin pale, striate or pruinose. Gills ± decurrent, whitish, edge brown. Stipe 2×0.2cm, dark brown, powdered. Smell faint. Spores 7×5μm, amyloid; cuticle a palisade of dermatocystidia. On stumps of conifers, especially *Abies*. Rare in Britain. Em2.

Genus *Oudemansiella* [*Mucidula*]. Fruit-bodies fleshy or with elongated stipe, some with a ring; cap surface ± viscid. Spores non-amyloid.

Oudemansiella mucida (Schrad.) V. Hohn.
Cap convex, 8-10cm, fluted and very viscid, hyaline white or tinged greyish. Gills distant, arched, white. Stipe 6×0.6cm, white with a viscid ring. Flesh hyaline. Spores 16×13μm, cuticle with gelatinised dermatocystidia. On standing dead trunks or lightning scars and fallen branches of beech. Common throughout Britain. E4.

Oudemansiella radicata (Relh.) Sing.
Cap 3-8cm, convex or slightly umbonate, wrinkled, viscid, ochraceous grey, milky coffee colour or pale beige. Gills ± distant, white, edge brown in var. *marginata*. Stipe elongated, 15×0.8cm, without a ring, fibrous, white to concolorous, with a buried whitish rooting portion which may be as long and attached to a root. Flesh pallid, odourless. Spores 13×10μm, cystidia very large, 120×30μm; cuticle palisadic. Under beech. Very common everywhere. Edible. E4.

Oudemansiella longipes (Kumm.) Moser [*Xerula pudens*]
Stature similar to *O. radicata* but cap dry, pubescent, grey-brown to russet. Gills cream, distant. Stipe long but not markedly rooting, 13×1cm, covered throughout with velvety red-brown hairs. Taste becoming bitter. Spores 9×6μm; cystidia as in *O. radicata* but cuticular hairs thick-walled, ± brown. Under broadleaved trees. Uncommon. E2. **O. badia** (Lucand.) Moser has darker brown hairier cap and ± globose spores 12μm. Rare. E1.

Flammulina velutipes (Curtis) Karst. [*Collybia v.*]
Cap 5-10cm, flat, viscid, orange yellow to bright fawn. Gills broad, ± distant, creamy ochraceous. Stipe 6×0.5cm, velvety dark brown to blackish below, apex yellowish. Flesh pallid, odourless. On trunks and dead branches, especially gorse and elm, in late autumn, winter and spring. Edible but flabby and tasteless (though cultivated in Japan). Spores 8×5μm, non-amyloid; dermatocystidia and hairs gelatinised. Very common everywhere. E4.

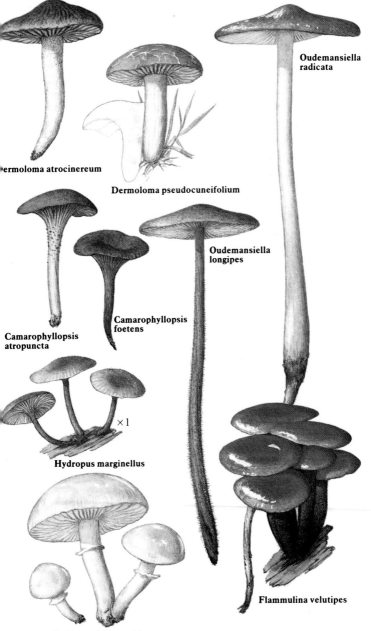

Oudemansiella
radicata

ermoloma atrocinereum

Dermoloma pseudocuneifolium

Oudemansiella
longipes

Camarophyllopsis
foetens

Camarophyllopsis
atropuncta

×1

Hydropus marginellus

Flammulina velutipes

Oudemansiella mucida

171

Genus *Cystoderma*. Cap surface powdered. Stipe with sheathing ring, concolorous with cap. Sphaerocysts in chains, spores amyloid or not.

Cystoderma amianthinum (Scop.) Fayod
Cap 2-5cm, convex or umbonate, surface powdery, bright ochraceous yellow to fawn, ± wrinkled or veined (f. *rugulosoreticulatum*) Gills white to cream. Stipe 7×0.4cm, sheath powdery, concolorous, annular zone shaggy, apex smooth and white. Flesh whitish, smell earthy. Spores 5×3.5µm, amyloid. Under conifers, on lawns, heaths and moors, very abundant. E4.

C. jasonis (Cke. & Mass.) Harmaja [*C. amianthinum* var. *longisporum*]. Differs in its more russet colour and longer spores, 8×4µm. E2.

Cystoderma carcharias (Pers.) Fayod
Cap 5-7cm, fleshy or umbonate, granulate or powdery, dingy whitish (f. *album*) to pale pinkish grey. Gills pallid, ± adnate. Stipe 6×1cm, concolorous below the narrow membranous sheathing ring. Flesh white, smell strong, earthy. Spores 5×4µm, amyloid. Under conifers, often spruce with bilberries, and open moors. Less common than *C. amianthinum*, and chiefly in the Highlands. E1 (m3).

Cystoderma terrei (Bk. & Br.) Harmaja [*C. cinnabarinum*]
Cap 5-10cm, soon flat, matt to pruinose, brick red or vermilion orange (pale ochraceous orange in var. *claricolor*). Gills cream, slightly sinuate. Stipe 7×1cm, slightly bulbous, basal sheath concolorous, poorly delimited above. Flesh white, odourless. Spores 5×3µm, non-amyloid; marginal and facial cystidia nettle-hair type. Under broadleaved trees. Rare. E2.

C. granulosum (Batsch) Fayod has a more reddish brown cap, punctate, and lacks the facial cystidia. Rare in Britain. E2.

Phaeolepiota aurea (Matt.) R. Mre.
Large fungus with cap 15-25cm, umbonate or fleshy hemispherical, surface powdery or granulose, bright orange brown or fawn, dotted brown. Margin often appendiculate with remnants of the veil. Gills russet ochre, almost free. Stipe stout, 15×4cm, sheathed below like a *Cystoderma*, ending in a funnel-shaped ring. Flesh white, odourless. Spores 13×5µm, ochraceous; epicuticular hyphae clavate, diverticulate. Roadsides, parks and nettle beds. Throughout Britain but rare. E1.

Rhodotus palmatus (Bull.) R. Mre.
Cap 8-13cm, convex, pleurotoid, margin incurved, surface wrinkled or reticulately veined, a pretty pink to orange. Gills pale pink. Stipe excentric or lateral, 5×1.5cm, pinkish. Flesh pallid, smell fruity. Spores round, 7µm, warty, pink; cuticular hyphae globose or palisadic, strongly gelatinised. On dead wood, especially elm, sometimes in clusters. Common in England. E2.

Squamanita schreieri Imb.
Cap 5-7cm, umbonate or convex, golden yellow with radial ochraceous brown fibrils, concentrated as a dark cap on the disk, margin appendiculate. Gills whitish, adnate. Stipe 4×1cm, enlarged at base to form a tuber-like bulb 3-4cm across, its upper edge volva-like and toothed, dark ochraceous. Flesh whitish, smell earthy or of decay. Spores 6×4µm, non-amyloid; protocarpic chlamydospores 7-9µm. Lawns, especially in damp places, sometimes in clusters from a common basal bulb (protocarp). Very rare. E1.

Leucocortinarius bulbiger (A.-S.) Sing.
Superficially resembles *Cortinarius multiformis* (p. 210) but the spores are white, hence gills creamy white to pale ochraceous even at maturity. Cap 5-8cm, surface scarcely viscid, with pale scales from the veil. Stipe 8×1cm, with a bulb like that in the subgenus Bulbopodium (p. 210). Flesh white, almost odourless, blue with sulfoformol. Spores 8×4.5µm, wall thick, smooth and colourless. Epicuticular hyphae ± filamentous. (Systematic position doubtful.) Under conifers on calcareous soil. Very rare in Britain, chiefly in the Highlands. E1 (s3).

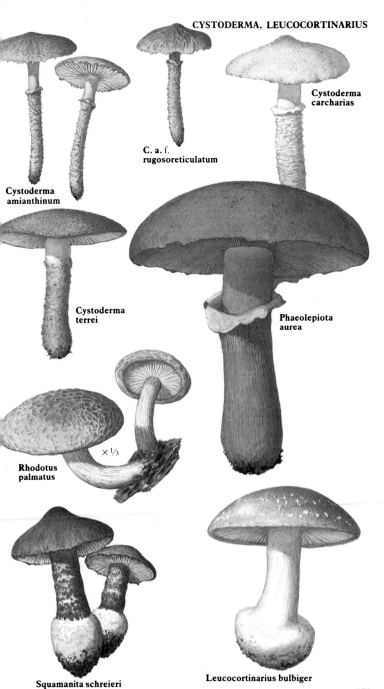

C. a. f. rugosoreticulatum

Cystoderma carcharias

Cystoderma amianthinum

Cystoderma terrei

Phaeolepiota aurea

× ⅓

Rhodotus palmatus

Squamanita schreieri

Leucocortinarius bulbiger

173

Family *Marasmiaceae*. Thin-fleshed or with leathery-elastic flesh, cartilaginous or shrivelling without rotting. Genus *Marasmius*. Withering and/or with a matt wrinkled cuticle; cuticle with ± cellular palisadic or brush-cells.

Marasmius androsaceus (L.) Fr.
Cap 1-1.5cm, radially furrowed and fluted (like a parachute), russet brown to chocolate. Gills ± distant, adnate, brownish. Stipe 3×0.1cm, wiry, dark red-brown or blackish, smooth and shiny. Smell none. Spores 7×4µm, cuticle non-cellular but with brush-like hyphae. On woody debris and fallen needles of conifers and especially on stems of heather, on which it has been claimed to be parasitic. Very abundant throughout Britain. E4.

Marasmius rotula (Scop.) Fr.
Aspect similar to *M. androsaceus* but slightly more robust; cap white and gills adnate to a tubular collar enclosing the stipe apex. Stipe 3×0.2cm, wiry, smooth, dark brown below. Smell none. Spores 9×4µm; cap cuticle a palisade of diverticulate cells. On fallen twigs and bark at base of trunks. Very common. E4.

M. graminum (Lib.) Bk. & Br. has a small reddish brown cap and occurs on stems of grasses and cereals on lawns, dunes, pastures etc. Common throughout Britain. E3. **M. epiphyllus** (Pers.) Fr., white throughout, on fallen leaves, with gills not attached to a collar, is one of a group of small species hard to recognise without the microscope. E2.

Marasmius alliaceus (Jacquin) Fr.
Cap 2-5cm, flat to slightly umbonate, dingy cream-ochraceous or whitish, surface matt or wrinkled. Gills distant, whitish sinuate. Stipe long, 13×0.4cm, thickening towards the base, velvety throughout, blackish except for a paler apex. Flesh brownish, smelling of garlic. Spores 11×7µm, slightly diamond-shaped; cystidia variable, fusiform or swollen; cap cuticle of smooth, clavate cells. Among fallen leaves, especially of beech. Common in southern England. E4. **M. scorodonius** (Fr.) Fr., more slender with stipe shining and equal thickness throughout. E2.

Marasmius wynnei Bk. & Br. [*M. globularis*]
Cap 3-7cm, hemispherical then convex, obtuse, matt or wrinkled, milky white, then tinged greyish violet from the margin inwards. Gills distant, thick, white then greying. Stipe 7×0.3cm, smooth reddish-brown to blackish below, white to violaceous grey at the apex. Smell of hay or melilot. Spores 8×4µm, marginal cystidia lobed; cuticle with smooth sphaerocysts. Under broadleaved trees, often in clusters. Common. E2.

Marasmius cohaerens (Pers.) Cke. & Quél. [*M. ceratopus*]
Cap 2-4cm, convex, matt or velvety, ochraceous russet to fawn. Gills ± distant, cream ochraceous with darker fringed margin. Stipe 8×0.5cm, shining, horny, ± furrowed, dark reddish brown at base passing through ochraceous orange to whitish at the apex; base strigose. Flesh pallid, odourless. Spores 10×5µm; cystidia thick-walled, brown and pointed, cap surface with brush-cells mingled with cystidia. Fairly common. E3.

Marasmius oreades (Bolt.) Fr. FAIRY RING
Cap 3-7cm, convex to flat with lobed margin; surface matt, often cracking, creamy with a pinkish tinge at first becoming dingy whitish. Gills distant, cream. Stipe 6×0.5cm, fibrous and tough so as to be twistable without breaking, elastic, similar colour. Flesh pallid with a slight smell of hay or Sweet Vernal-grass, *Anthoxanthum odoratum*. Spores 10×6µm, tear-shaped; cap cuticle a palisade of smooth cells. In lawns and pastures throughout the year, usually in rings and associated with "fairy rings" in turf. Very common. Edible and easily preserved dry, but can be confused with the white poisonous *Clitocybe* species (p. 136). E4.

Crinipellis stipitarius (Fr.) Pat.
Cap 1-2cm, convex or slightly depressed, surface shaggy, brownish on a cream ground. Gills ± distant, adnate, cream. Stipe 3×0.2cm, furrowed, russet. Texture like *Marasmius*. Spores 8×7µm; cap cuticle with long, wavy, pseudoamyloid, thick-walled brown hairs. On dead grass stems, twigs etc. especially in hedge bottoms. Fairly common. E3.

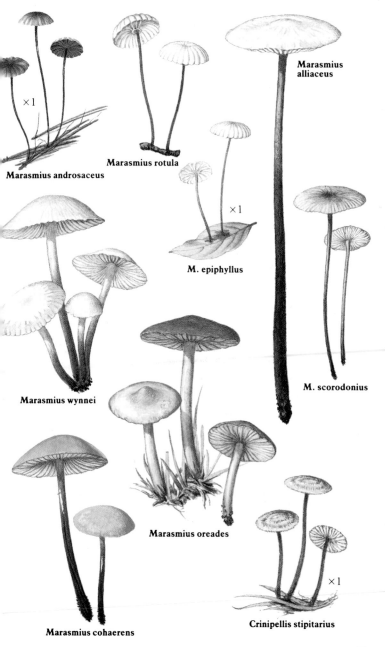

×1

Marasmius
alliaceus

Marasmius androsaceus

Marasmius rotula

M. epiphyllus

×1

M. scorodonius

Marasmius wynnei

Marasmius oreades

Marasmius cohaerens

Crinipellis stipitarius

×1

Strobilurus esculentus (Wulf.) Sing. [*Pseudohiatula esculenta*]
Cap 2-3cm, convex, smooth, matt or wrinkled, dark reddish brown, tinged olivaceous or yellowish when young or on drying. Gills slightly greyish, ± distant, sinuate. Stipe 5×0.3cm, yellowish brown, arising from a copious ochraceous mycelium. Flesh pallid, smell fungoid, taste mild. Spores 6×3µm; cystidia swollen below, cap cuticle a palisade; clamp connections absent. On fallen or buried cones especially spruce, in spring. Common. Edible. E3.

S. tenacellus (Pers.) Sing.is more slender with crowded gills, a sharp or bitter taste and narrower cystidia. On cones, especially pine. E2. **S. stephanocystis** (Hora) Sing. has mild flesh, and peculiar capitate cystidia with a ring of crystals round the head. Chiefly N. Europe. E2.

Baeospora myosura (Fr.) Sing. [*Collybia conigena*]
Similar especially to *Strobilurus tenacellus* with crowded gills but with powdered stipe and mild tasting flesh and commonly fruiting in autumn; microscopic characters diagnostic. Spores 4×2µm, amyloid; cap cuticle filamentous, hyphae with clamp connections. On fallen or buried cones. Common. Edible. E2.

Genus *Micromphale*. Cap surface somewhat viscid, smell foetid; cuticle filamentous, ± gelatinised.

Micromphale perforans (Hoffm.) S.F. Gray
Resembling *Marasmius androsaceus* (p. 174) but with less furrowed cap, velvety stipe and a ± striking smell of garlic when bruised. Spores 6×3µm, cap surface without brush-cells. Attached to fallen conifer needles, one to a needle, epecially spruce. Uncommon in Britain. E2 (m4).

Micromphale foetidum (Sow.) Sing.
Cap 2-5cm, soon flattened, deeply striate-furrowed half way to the centre, smooth or viscid, pinkish russet or reddish brown with more beige or livid centre. Gills distant, similar colour. Stipe 4×0.4cm, typically compressed with a widened apex, dark brown, velvety. Flesh colour similar, smell strong of rotten cabbage or stagnant water. Spores 9×5µm. On fallen broadleaved twigs and branches. Uncommon. E3.

Micromphale brassicolens (Romagn.) Orton
Rather similar to *M. foetidum* but with much less deeply striate cap, brighter yellowish brown, sometimes tinged orange-fawn. Gills whitish. Stipe 5×0.4cm, almost equal, apex fawn, base blackish, finely downy. Flesh colour similar, smell of cabbage or radish. Spores 6×3µm; cuticle downy with variable ± thick-walled hairs. Among fallen beech leaves, not uncommon in southern England. E2.

Genus *Marasmiellus*. Small tough fungi on woody substrates, with dry downy caps; cuticle with lobed and interlocking hyphae.

Marasmiellus ramealis (Bull.) Sing.
Cap 1-2cm, hemispherical then flattened, greyish cream, sometimes tinged pinkish, scarcely striate at the margin. Gills ± distant, similar colour. Stipe 2×0.2cm, concolorous or darker at the base, slightly shaggy. Flesh tough, pallid, odourless and insipid. Spores 9×4µm, cystidia and cuticular hairs somewhat lobed or brush-like. Abundant everywhere on fallen twigs of broadleaved trees, dead brambles and juniper. E4.

M. candidus (Bolt.) Sing. [*M. albus-corticis*] differs in its crinkled white cap with somewhat fold-like gills. E2.

Megacollybia platyphylla (Pers.) Kotl. & Pouz. [*Tricholomopsis, Collybia, Hydropus p.*]. Cap 6-10-15cm, hemispherical or convex with straight slightly splitting margin and surface typically radiately streaky-fibrillose or cracking, brownish on a paler ground. Gills very broad, 1-2cm, ± distant, white, sometimes grey on the edges, adnate or emarginate. Stipe 8×1cm, fibrous, cartilaginous, cream to nearly concolorous, passing at the base into a network of long whitish rhizoids ramifying in the litter or surface layer of soil. Flesh pallid, odourless or insipid. Spores round, 8µm, non-amyloid; cuticular cells ± clavate. In litter and decayed wood of broadleaved trees, mainly beech and oak, less often conifers, from May onwards. Common. Just edible. E4.

MARASMIACEAE

Strobilurus esculentus

Baeospora myosura

Micromphale perforans ×1

Micromphale foetidum

Micromphale brassicolens

Marasmiellus ramealis

M. candidus

Megacollybia
platyphylla

177

Genus *Collybia*. Cartilaginous or elastic fungi; cap surface smooth. Cuticular hyphae filamentous or with lobed cells.

Section *Striipedes*. [Subgenus *Rhodocollybia*]. Rather fleshy, *Tricholoma*-like species with a fibrous or striate stipe; spore print somewhat pinkish.

Collybia maculata (A.-S.) Kumm.
Cap 5-10cm, convex or umbonate to deformed, smooth, white then with rusty pink spots. Gills very crowded, edge denticulate, creamy white, reddening. Stipe 12×1cm, very fibrous, corticate, white or with russet stripes. Flesh whitish to pinkish, taste bitter. Spores 6×5μm; marginal cells numerous. Under trees, especially birch, and on open heaths and moors. Very common. E4.

Collybia distorta (Fr.) Quél.
Cap a little smaller or less fleshy than in *C. maculata*, 6-8cm, dark reddish brown from the start and remaining unaltered. Gills rather crowded, white or reddening (pink with ferrous sulphate). Stipe 8×0.7cm, with twisted fibrils, concolorous. Flesh white, thin. Spores globose 4μm; no cystidia. Under conifers. Rare in Britain and chiefly in the Highlands. E3.

Collybia fusipes (Bull.) Quél.
Cap 5-10cm, fleshy or umbonate with inrolled margin; surface matt or becoming cracked, pale reddish brown sometimes with rusty spots. Gills distant, thick, often crinkled, whitish then flecked reddish-brown. Stipe spindle-shaped or rooting, commonly arising in clumps from a false sclerotium of stipe bases from the previous year, 15×2cm, furrowed, concolorous. Flesh pallid, smell fungoid or of damp wood. Spores 5×4μm. On stumps or attached to roots, especially of beech and oak. Caps only are edible when young. Common in southern England, less so in the north. E4.

Collybia butyracea (Bull.) Kumm.
Cap 5-8cm, umbonate to convex, feeling greasy especially over the umbo, very hygrophanous, dull yellowish brown, drying paler, dark grey-brown to blackish in f. *asema*. Gills pallid, rather crowded. Stipe 8×1cm, conical or enlarged towards the base, spongy, similarly coloured or striped with pruinose whitish lines. Flesh pallid, odourless. Spores 8×4μm, slightly tear-shaped. Under broadleaved trees and conifers, especially spruce. Very common. E4.

Section *Vestipedes*. Stipe pruinose or shaggy at the base.

Collybia peronata (Bolt.) Kumm. [*Marasmius urens*]   WOOD WOOLLY-FOOT
Cap 3-5cm, shallowly convex, ochraceous brown, sometimes sulphur yellow at first. Gills ± distant, boxwood yellow then concolorous. Stipe 7×0.6cm, concolorous, typically covered with fleecy buff or yellowish hyphae especially in lower half. Flesh almost concolorous, smell of vinegar when bruised, taste peppery. Spores 8×4μm, cystidia fusiform, cap hyphae diverticulate. Very common everywhere in woods of all kinds. E4.

Collybia confluens (Pers.) Kumm.
Cap 3-5cm, beige flesh colour to brownish. Gills very crowded, whitish to pinkish brown, edge denticulate. Stipe slender, 12×0.5cm, typically furrowed or compressed, covered with a distinctive lilac grey pruina. Flesh thin, smell rather of melilot or hay. Spores 8×4μm, tear-shaped; cystidia numerous, coral-like. Abundant in woods of all kinds, often in clusters. E3.

Section *Laevipedes*. Stipe smooth or shining, without strigose hairs at the base.

Collybia dryophila (Bull.) Kumm.
Cap 2-5cm, flat, smooth, bright russet fading to ochraceous. Gills white, commonplace, but yellow in var. *funicularis*. Stipe 5×0.3cm, cylindrical, a beautiful bright orange fawn. Flesh thin, smell fungoid. Spores 6×3μm, slightly tear-shaped; cystidia and cuticular hyphae lobed. Abundant everywhere in woods of all kinds, especially oak, and among bracken on heaths. Edible. E4.

Collybia kuehneriana Sing. [*C. marasmioides, Marasmius erythropus*]
Rather similar to *C. dryophila* but stipe purplish red-brown. Spores 8×4μm, cystidia fusiform, seldom lobed. Often in tufts on woody debris. Common. E3.

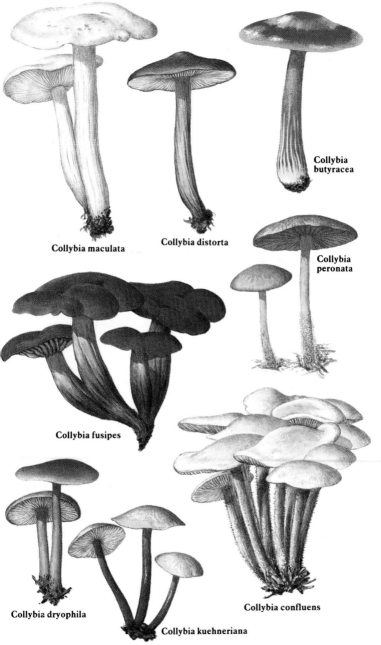

Collybia butyracea

Collybia maculata

Collybia distorta

Collybia peronata

Collybia fusipes

Collybia dryophila

Collybia kuehneriana

Collybia confluens

Section *Collybia* [*Cirrhatae*]. Small white fungi saprophytic on old agarics.

Collybia cirrhata (Pers.) Kumm.
Cap 1-2cm, flat, thin, pure white. Gills crowded, white. Stipe 2×0.1cm, white, felted. Flesh very thin, white. Common. Spores 5×2μm. In woodland litter, on old decayed mushrooms. E3.

C. tuberosa (Bull.) Kumm. has a black sclerotium at base of stipe and in **C. cookei** (Bres.) Arn. there is a yellow sclerotium. Both are common. E3.

Genus *Mycena*. Slender fungi with cap often hemispherical and striate.

Section *Lactipedes*. Broken stem exudes drop of white or coloured milk.

Mycena galopus (Pers.) Kumm.
Cap 2-3cm, hemispherical, greyish (pure white in var. *alba* or entirely black in var. *nigra*). Gills white, Stipe 4x0.2cm, grey, milk white. Smell faint or of radish. Spores 15×6μm; cystidia rather long, ± fusiform and pointed, occasionally forked above. Very common in woods of all kinds. E4.

Mycena crocata (Schrad.) Kumm.
Cap 2cm, somewhat umbonate, greyish white tinged brownish orange. Gills pallid or spotted with bright orange. Stipe 10×0.4cm, ochraceous or stained orange by the bright saffron milk. Spores 10×6μm; cystidia clavate, brush-like. Especially under beech. Rare in Britain, chiefly in the South. E3.

Mycena sanguinolenta (A.-S.) Kumm.
Cap 1cm, becoming flat, pinkish ochre. Gills white with pink edge. Stipe thread-like, 6×0.1cm, pinkish brown, pale vinaceous at the base, milk vinaceous red. Spores 10×7μm, cystidia fusiform, smooth. Under broadleaved trees, often in moss, in litter under conifers and with rushes and heather on heaths and moors. Very abundant everywhere. E4.

M. haematopus (Pers.) Kumm. is similar but more fleshy, cap 2-4cm, stipe pruinose, juice red-brown and occurs on stumps and fallen branches. Common. E2.

Section *Calodontes* [including *Luculentae*]. Gill edge coloured.

Mycena aurantiomarginata (Fr.) Quél. [*M. elegans*]
Cap 3-4cm, umbonate or soon expanded, brownish with olivaceous tint and bright orange margin. Gills greyish with orange edges. Stipe 5×0.5cm, yellowish grey. Smell slight. Spores 9×5μm; cystidia brush-like. Under conifers. Uncommon. E2.

Mycena rosella (Fr.) Kumm.
Cap 1cm, convex, bright pink. Gills adnate, pinkish with reddish edges. Stipe 2×0.2cm, concolorous. Spores and cystidia similar to the preceding species but facial cystidia smooth. Under conifers. E1 (m3).

M. seynii Quél. is stouter and occurs on fallen cones of pine, with spores 13×8μm and cystidia not brush-like. Rare in Britain. E2.

Mycena capillaripes Peck
Cap 2cm, convex, dingy whitish to pink, pruinose. Gills pallid with pinkish-brown edges. Stipe very slender, 8×0.2cm, brownish grey. Strong smell of chlorine. Spores 10×6μm, cystidia fusiform, smooth. Common in troops under conifers. E2.

Mycena pelianthina (Fr.) Quél.
Cap 3-5cm, convex then expanded, grey-violet or lilac. Gills whitish with lilaceous-grey tinge and dark violaceous brown edges. Stipe 6×0.6cm, nearly concolorous. Smell strong, of radish. Spores 8×4μm, cystidia fusiform, smooth. Under broad-leaved trees especially beech. Quite common. E2.

Mycena pura (Pers.) Kumm.
General aspect similar to *M. pelianthina* but the gills lack the dark edge. Colour varies from bluish violet in the typical form to pink in var. *rosea*, which tends to be more fleshy, or lilac and yellow in var. *lutea*. Smell unpleasant, of radish. Spores 7×4μm, cystidia fusiform, occasionally branched. Common under various conifers, var. *lutea* chiefly in fixed sand-dunes and var. *rosea* often also under beech. E4.

Collybia cirrhata ×1

C. tuberosa ×1

Mycena galopus ×1

Mycena crocata

Mycena sanguinolenta ×1

M. haematopus

Mycena aurantiomarginata

Mycena rosella

Mycena capillaripes

Mycena pelianthina ×1

Mycena pura

M. p. var. rosea

181

Section *Hygrocyboideae* [including *Viscipelles*]. Viscid species.

Mycena epipterygia (Scop.) S.F. Gray
Cap bell-shaped, 1cm, margin scalloped, surface viscid, grey-brown to yellowish. Gills white, with a lemon tinge. Stipe 10×0.3cm, viscid, pale lemon yellow. Flesh colour similar, smell faint, taste slightly mealy. Spores 11×5.5μm, cystidia brush-like with long, often branched, processes. Among moss especially under conifers and under bracken on moors. Very common. E3.

M. viscosa R. Mre. differs in being a little less fragile, with rusty spots on cap and gills. **M. epipterygioides** Pearson is like a stout, more greenish version of *M. epipterygia* on rotting stumps. E2.

Mycena vulgaris (Pers.) Kumm.
Cap convex, 1-1.5cm, greyish with a separable gelatinised pellicle. Gills arched to ± decurrent, whitish, edges gelatinised. Stipe 5×0.3cm, greyish, viscid. Smell faint. Spores 10×5μm, cystidia clavate brush-like embedded in gelatine of the gill edge. In beds of needles under conifers. Uncommon. E2. **M. rorida** (Scop.) Quél. has cap only 0.5cm on a thread-like stipe with hyaline gelatinous sheath very conspicuous when damp. On fallen twigs. Not uncommon in Britain. E2.

Mycena amicta (Fr.) Quél.
Cap convex, 1-2cm, slightly viscid, rather fibrillose, striate, yellowish to greenish or bluish (var.**iris**). Gills ascending, crowded, greyish. Stipe 8×0.2cm, somewhat rooting, greyish with bluish base, downy-hoary. Flesh bluish, odourless. Spores 10×5μm, cystidia smooth, subcylindrical, obtuse. On plant debris, especially under conifers. Occasional in Britain. E1.

Mycena stylobates (Pers.) Kumm.
Cap 0.5-1cm, whitish, gelatinous with a few granular excrescences. Gills pallid, adnate. Stipe 4×0.1cm, arising from a flat disk, hairy. Spores 8×3μm, cystidia clavate with a few processes. On dead twigs and leaves. Not uncommon. E2.

Section *Adonidae*. Colouring bright, spores non-amyloid.

Mycena adonis (Bull.) S.F. Gray
Cap 0.5-2cm, ± conical, bright salmon pink to bright red, very striate. Gills pink. Stipe 3×0.1cm, thread-like, pale to nearly concolorous like the flesh. Spores 10×5μm, cystidia fusiform with long slender neck, smooth. Under conifers in damp moss. E1.

M. acicula (Sch.) Kumm. Differs only in bright orange colour. Gills ascending, and so differs from the superficially similar *Rickenella fibula*. Spores 12×5μm, fusiform; cystidia inconspicuous, clavate, smooth. E2.

Mycena flavoalba (Fr.) Quél.
Cap 1-2cm, conical to convexly expanded, white with ± bright yellow tinge at the centre. Gills white. Stipe 5×0.2cm, white to yellowish. Spores 9×4μm; cystidia flask-shaped with long neck, smooth. In grass and moss. Very common. E3.

Section *Filipedes*. Slender fungi with thread-like stipe and ± distinct smell of iodine. Spores amyloid, cystidia brush-like.

Mycena metata (Fr.) Kumm. [*M. vitrea* var. *tenella*, *M. phyllogena*]
Cap 1-3cm, campanulate to convex, markedly striate, pale pinkish brown to whitish flesh colour. Gill colour similar. Stipe 8×0.1cm, similar to dingy brownish. Smell of iodine on drying. Spores 10×6μm; cystidia clavate, brush-like with short processes. Among dead leaves and needle beds under conifers. Common. E2.

Mycena filopes (Bull.) Kumm. [*M. amygdalina*]
Cap hemispherical, dark grey-brown with paler or whitish striate margin, somewhat pruinose. Gills whitish. Stipe 4×0.2cm, grey. Developing a smell of iodine or green soap. Spores 11×7μm; cystidia clavate with rather longer processes. Under broadleaved trees, usually in moss. Common. E3.

M. arcangeliana Bres. [*M. olivascens*, *oortiana*] has a greenish yellow to olivebronze cap and occurs in tufts on dead branches and logs. Fairly common. E2.

Mycena epipterygia

Mycena vulgaris

M. viscosa

var. iris

Mycena amicta

M. rorida

Mycena adonis

M. acicula

cena stylobates

Mycena flavoalba

Mycena filopes

M. arcangeliana

Mycena metata

All ×1

183

Section *Fragilipedes*. Slender fungi with amyloid spores and smooth fusiform cystidia.

Mycena alcalina (Fr.) Kumm.
Cap 2-3cm, campanulate, brownish grey, sometimes olivaceous, margin paler, striate. Gills ascending, greyish. Stipe 7×0.2cm. Smell strong, alkaline. Spores 12×6μm; cystidia fusiform, obtuse. Often in tufts on stumps and fallen branches. Very common. E4.

Mycena leptocephala (Pers.) Gill.
Cap 1-1.5cm, soon expanded, ochraceous grey, sometimes slightly greenish, rather pruinose and scarcely striate when dry. Gills pallid. Stipe thread-like, 8×0.1cm, similar colour. Smell alkaline or sour like poppy petals. Spores 11×5μm; cystidia somewhat flask-shaped, sometimes forking at the apex. In clusters, especially in pine-needles. Very common. E4.

Mycena aetites (Fr.) Quél.
Cap 1-2cm, hemispherical or umbonate, blackish grey-brown, margin with black striae on a pale ground. Gills greyish, tapered at the ends. Stipe 4×0.2cm, similar colour. Inodorous. Spores 10×5μm; cystidia varying from flask-shaped and smooth to clavate with a few stout apical processes. Among short grass on lawns etc. Common. E2.

Mycena zephirus (Fr.) Kumm.
Cap 2-3cm, soon expanded or umbonate, pale beige to brownish grey or with rusty spots. Gills beige with rusty spots or pinkish. Stipe 7×0.3cm, concolorous with rusty brown base. Flesh pallid to pinkish, smell faint. Spores 12×5μm; cystidia obtusely fusiform to somewhat lobed or branched above. In troops under conifers. Uncommon. E1 (m3).

Section *Mycena* [*Rigidipedes*]. Rather more fleshy or less fragile fungi, often in tufts.

Mycena vitilis (Fr.) Quél. [*M. filopes* ss. Ricken]
Cap 2-3cm, convex or umbonate, dull yellowish grey, ± striate. Gills whitish. Stipe 13×0.2cm, tougher than it appears, white, slightly greasy. Flesh pallid, odourless. Spores 10×6μm; cystidia often forked above or with a few long processes. Under broadleaved trees and hedges, often solitary. Common. E4.

Mycena galericulata (Scop.) S.F. Gray
Cap 5-7cm, slightly umbonate, margin undulating, surface matt or wrinkled, pale beige grey to whitish. Gills ± distant, somewhat interveined, often flushed pink. Stipe 13×0.4cm, compressed or furrowed, often rooting, stiff, smooth, greyish. Smell and taste mealy. Spores 11×6μm, basidia commonly 2-spored; cystidia clavate, brush-like with rather long processes. More or less tufted on stumps and dead branches. Very common. E4. **M. tintinnabulum** (Fr.) Quél. is like a miniature *M. galericulata*, with ± decurrent gills and small spores 5-6×3μm, on stumps of broadleaved trees in winter. Uncommon. E1.

Mycena polygramma (Bull.) S.F. Gray
Cap 2-5cm, convex, pruinose, greyish. Gills greyish. Stipe 10×0.5 cm, marked with fine greyish lines throughout. Flesh pallid, odourless. Spores 10×7μm; marginal cystidia slender and smooth. Tufted, on stumps. Common. E3.

M. laevigata (Lasch) Quél., with a more whitish cap, somewhat fulvous with age, and smooth stipe, is rarer or only common in mountains. Spores smaller, 8×4μm. E1 (m3).

Mycena inclinata (Fr.) Quél.
Cap 3-5cm, convex or umbonate, margin typically extending a little beyond the gills, scalloped, markedly striate; surface smooth, slippery, yellow-brown to reddish at the centre. Gills pale. Stipe 10×0.5cm, whitish above, becoming progressively darker yellow to bright reddish brown towards the base. Smell and taste of candle grease or rancid oil. Spores 10-12×6-7μm; cystidia rather narrow and brush-like, with long processes. In dense clusters on stumps, especially oak – in Britain almost exclusively so. Common. E3.

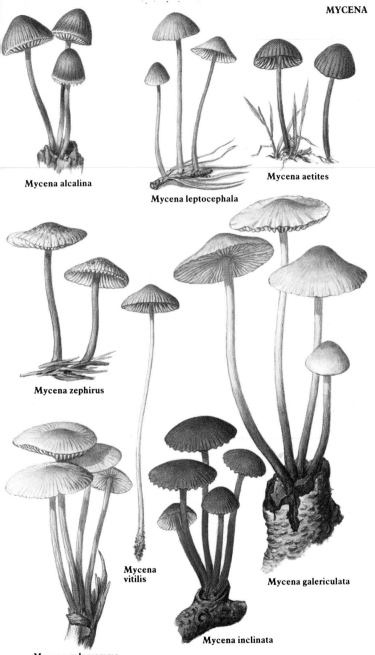

Mycena alcalina

Mycena leptocephala

Mycena aetites

Mycena zephirus

Mycena vitilis

Mycena galericulata

Mycena polygramma

Mycena inclinata

185

Section *Hiemales*. Spores non-amyloid, colours dull.

Mycena hiemalis (Osb.) Quél.
Cap 1-2cm, brownish grey with whitish striate margin. Gills sinuate to ± adnate, pallid. Stipe 4×0.1cm, whitish or concolorous at the base. Smell slight. Spores 9×7μm; cystidia obtusely fusiform, smooth. Among moss on dead branches and bark of living trees. Locally common. E2.

M. speirea (Fr.) Gill. differs in its decurrent gills and narrow spores 10×5μm. Common everywhere. E2.

Mycena olida Bres. [*M. minutula*]
Cap 2-3cm, campanulate, white, yellow at the centre. Gills tapered or sinuate, white. Stipe 3×0.2cm, white, velvety. Smell rather rancid. Spores 8×5μm; cystidia fusiform, smooth. On bark of broadleaved trees. Common everywhere in Britain. E1.

Section *Supinae* [*Insititiae* p.p.]. Spores amyloid. On bark of living trees or fallen leaves.

Mycena pseudocorticola Kühn.
Cap 0.5-1cm, hemispherical, striate, surface pruinose, steel blue-grey or indigo to purplish or mauve-pink. Gills sinuate, pallid. Stipe 1×0.1cm, often curved, colours similar. No smell or taste. Spores ± globose, 10-11μm; cystidia brush-like. On bark of living trees, common in western districts of Britain. E2.

Mycena capillaris (Schum.) Kumm.
Cap 0.5cm, grey-brown, pale. Gills almost free, dingy white. Stipe 3×0.1cm, whitish, rather powdery. Spores narrow, 10×4μm; cystidia brush-like. On fallen leaves of beech. Common. E1.

Genus *Mycenella*. Spores globose, ± ornamented, non-amyloid.

Mycenella bryophila (Vogl.) Sing. [*Mycena lasiosperma*]
Cap 2-3cm, brownish grey, pruinose. Gills amost free, white. Stipe 4×0.2cm, rooting, concolorous, powdery. Spores 6×7μm, warty; cystidia smooth. Often among moss. Uncommon in Britain. E1.

M. margaritispora (Lange) Sing. is more slender, with non-rooting stipe and slender cystidia diverticulate at the tip. E1.

Genus *Hemimycena*. White, Mycena-like or Omphalina-like. Spores non-amyloid.

Hemimycena cucullata (Pers.) Sing. [*Mycena gypsea*]
Cap 2cm, campanulate, slightly striate, matt, white. Gills adnate. Stipe 6×0.2cm, white, smooth. Smell none. Spores 11×4μm; cystidia conical to flaskshaped. On trunks and leaf-beds of broadleaved trees. Common. E2.

Hemimycena delicatella (Peck) Sing. [*Mycena lactea*]
Cap 1cm, soon expanded or umbonate, creamy white. Gills adnate or ± decurrent. Stipe 3×0.1cm, pruinose. Spores 9×3μm, ± fusiform; marginal cystidia capitate. In needle beds under conifers. Common. E2.

Hemimycena mairei (Gilb.) Sing.
Cap 1-1.5cm, slightly umbilicate, white with greyish centre. Gills whitish, slightly decurrent. Stipe 4×0.2cm, smooth, white. Inodorous. Spores 10×4.5μm; cystidia scanty or absent. Among short grass in parks. Not common. E3.

H. delectabilis (Peck.) Sing. has a strong nitrous or chlorinated smell. In conifer needles, Em3.

Genus *Delicatula*. White, funnel-shaped with decurrent gills. Spores amyloid.

Delicatula integrella (Pers.) Fayod
Cap 1-2cm, irregular, umbilicate, white. Gills narrow, ± decurrent, forked or anastomosing. Stipe 1×0.1cm, white, smooth or with a velvety basal bulb. Spores 8×5μm; cystidia absent. In humus or on rotten wood. Uncommon. E2.

D. cuspidata (Quél.) Cejp is more bell-shaped or conical, with narrow spores ×3μm. E1.

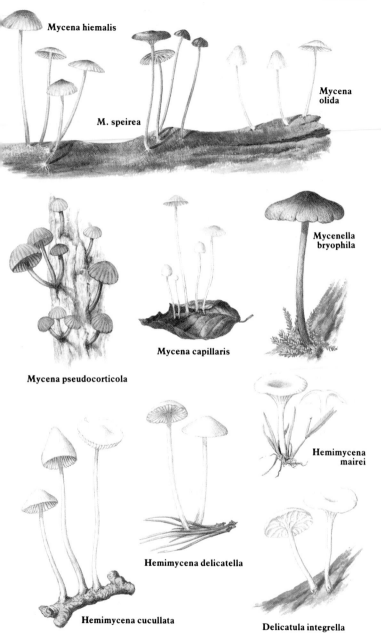

Mycena hiemalis

M. speirea

Mycena olida

Mycena pseudocorticola

Mycena capillaris

Mycenella bryophila

Hemimycena mairei

Hemimycena delicatella

Hemimycena cucullata

Delicatula integrella

All ×1

Order *Pluteales*. Spores and gills pink or reddish brick colour.

Family *Entolomataceae* [*Rhodophyllaceae*]. Cap not separable from stipe, gills adnate, decurrent or almost free. Spores polyhedral or longitudinally angled. Genus *Clitopilus*. Gills decurrent, spores longitudinally angled.

Clitopilus prunulus (Scop.) Kumm. THE MILLER
Cap 5-12cm, fleshy, umbonate then depressed with ± wavy incurved margin and matt to ± velvety surface, whitish or tinged greyish over the centre. Gills decurrent, bright pink at maturity. Stipe 3×1cm, white. Flesh white with strong smell and taste of fresh meal. Spores 10-13×6μm, typically with six longitudinal angles. Common under various broadleaved trees. Edible and good, but do not confuse with toxic white species of *Clitocybe* (p. 132). E4.

Clitopilus hobsonii (Bk. & Br.) Orton [*C. pleurotelloides*]
Cap 1-2cm, kidney-shaped or excentric, *Pleurotus*-like, white, slightly velvety. Gills fan-like, pinkish. Stipe lateral or almost absent, whitish. No smell or taste. Spores 9×5μm, angles less conspicuous. On dead branches of broadleaved trees. Fairly common. E1. **C. cretatus** (Bk. & Br.) Sacc. occurs on the ground, with a funnel-shaped but often asymmetrical cap. E1.

Genus *Rhodocybe*. Rather fleshy fungi with adnate to decurrent gills and spores with numerous facets, appearing warted.

Rhodocybe truncata (Gill.) Sing. ex Bon
Cap 8-12cm, fleshy, smooth or slightly frosted, pale pinkish ochre or blotched russet, margin somewhat inrolled, sometimes notched. Gills adnate, sloping or decurrent, pinkish ochre. Stipe variable, 3-8×1-2cm, whitish to concolorous. Flesh pale, smell aromatic to mealy, or similar to *Lepista nuda* (p.144). Taste oily or nutty. Spores 7×4μm, clamp connections absent. Mixed woods and rather grassy thickets. Rare in Britain. Edible. E3. **R. nitellina** (Fr.) Sing. is more slender, bright orange-brown with strong smell of meal and has clamp connections (Subgenus *Rhodophana*). E2.

Rhodocybe popinalis (Fr.) Sing.
Cap 4-7cm, slightly umbonate but soon flattened, surface matt then cracking concentrically, yellowish grey-brown. Gills sloping to almost decurrent, crowded, pinkish grey. Stipe 3×0.8cm, nearly concolorous or paler. Flesh pale, smell of rancid meal, taste bitter. Spores round, 6μm. Pastures. Uncommon. E2. **R. mundula** (Lasch) Sing. has dull pale greyish cap tending to blacken. E1.

Genus *Entoloma* [*Rhodophyllus*]. Spores polyhedral. Subgenus *Eccilia* [including *Omphaliopsis*, *Claudopus*]. Funnel-shaped or excentric; gills decurrent.

Entoloma undatum (Quél.) Moser [*Eccilia sericeonitida*]
Cap 3-5cm, depressed or funnel-shaped, surface slightly zoned or undulate, somewhat fibrillose, grey-brown, darker at centre. Gills sloping or arched, dingy pinkish grey. Stipe 2×0.4cm, similar colour. Flesh pale, ± odourless and tasteless. Spores 10×7μm, 6-10-angled, basidia clamped at the base. Lawns, pastures. Frequent. E2.

Entoloma leptonipes (K.-R.) Moser
Cap 2-4cm, soon depressed to umbilicate with margin expanded, wavy or splitting, surface smooth or silky-fibrillose, grey-brown with a bluish-lilac tint, blackish at the centre. Gills arched or decurrent, ± distant, rosy pink. Stipe 3×0.3cm, steel blue to slaty violet, silky or shining. Flesh similar colours with mealy-spermatic smell. Spores 11×7μm, 5-7-angled, clamp connections absent. In damp places under broadleaved trees. Uncommon. E1.

Entoloma sericellum (Fr.) Kumm.
Cap 3-5cm, at first convex with slight umbo but becoming umbilicate, surface silky, creamy white or yellowish at the centre. Gills adnate and somewhat decurrent, slightly broader in the middle, bright pink. Stipe 6×0.3cm, stiff, pure white. Spores 12×8μm, 6-8-angled, clamp connections present and rather variably shaped cystidia. Moors, damp grassy woods and under willows. Very common. E3.

E. byssisedum (Pers.) Donk has a greyish excentric cap, like a *Crepidotus*. E1.

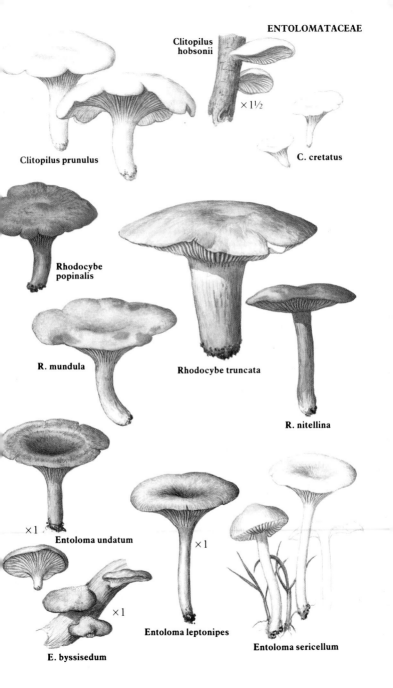

Clitopilus
hobsonii

× 1½

C. cretatus

Clitopilus prunulus

Rhodocybe
popinalis

R. mundula

Rhodocybe truncata

R. nitellina

× 1

Entoloma undatum

× 1

Entoloma leptonipes

× 1

E. byssisedum

Entoloma sericellum

Subgenus *Nolanea*. Slender or thin-fleshed fungi, cap often conico-campanulate, gills almost free or sinuate.

Entoloma papillatum (Bres.) Dennis. Cap 2-4cm, conico-campanulate with papillate umbo, hygrophanous, dark brown or blackish sepia becoming brownish or creamy beige, margin deeply striate. Gills ascending and almost free, pale pinkish grey. Stipe 4×0.2cm, smooth, colour similar or pale above. Flesh colour similar, smell and taste mealy. Spores 12×8μm, 6-8-angled, clamp connections numerous, cap hyphae with encrusting pigment. Lawns, pastures, roadsides. Common. E2. **E. infulum** (Fr.) Noord. differs in its white gills and lack of mealy taste or smell. E2.

Entoloma minutum (Karst.) Noord.
Very like *E. papillatum* but cap not or scarcely papillate and paler, grey-brown flesh colour, whitish on drying. gills pale pinkish grey. Stipe 6×0.2cm, similar colour or tinged orange-yellow. Smell and taste slight. Spores 10×8μm, 5-7-angled, clamp connections and pigment as *E. papillatum*. Damp broadleaved woods. Uncommon. E1. **E. juncinum** (K.-R.) Noord., with furrowed stipe and strongly mealy taste, occurs in copses with deep humus or grass. Uncommon. E2.

Entoloma sericeum (Bull.) Quél.
Cap 5-7cm, slightly fleshy, soon expanded but often retaining an umbo, more slender and campanulate in var. *nolaniforme*, surface silky, dark russet-brown, hygrophanous and paling concentrically to whitish beige as it dries; margin somewhat striate when moist. Gills sinuate, pinkish grey, edge irregular and toothed. Stipe 6×0.3cm, cylindrical, ± silky-fibrillose or with silvery striations on a brownish ground. Flesh almost concolorous, smell and taste strongly mealy. Spores ± globose, 8-10μm with 5-8 blunt angles. Clamp connections present, pigment clearly encrusting. The commonest member of the genus on lawns. Doubtfully edible. E4. **E. hirtipes** (Schum.) Moser has more elongated spores, somewhat capitate marginal cystidia and a mealy smell mingled with that of cucumber or fish. Common. E3.

Entoloma conferendum (Britz.) Noord. [*Nolanea staurospora*]
Cap 3-5cm, conico-campanulate, obtuse, hygrophanous, margin deeply striate, dark grey-brown drying reddish to pale ochraceous. Gills ascending, broadest at the middle, slightly greyish pale pink. Stipe 6×0.7cm, fragile, slightly club-shaped, typically lined with silvery fibrils on a yellowish brown ground. Flesh pale, smell ± mealy, taste rancid. Spores cuboid or stellate, 8-13μm diameter, no clamp connections, pigment vacuolar. In grassy woods, wet pastures and very abundant on moorland. E4. **E. vernum** Lund., with smoother stipe and no smell, may grow in similar habitats, but chiefly alpine or northern, in spring. Spores not stellate, 10×8μm. Edibility suspect. E1 (m3).

Entoloma cetratum (Fr.) Moser
Cap 2-5cm, conical becoming expanded, typically striate up to a small central area like the pupil of an eye, yellowish brown or ochraceous yellow, brighter towards the margin. Gills nearly free, yellowish then salmon. Stipe 8×0.5cm, yellowish with silky silvery fibrils. Flesh pale, odour slight or faintly mealy. Spores 13×8μm, basidia 2-spored, no clamp connections. Woods, particularly conifer plantations, and heaths. Fairly common. E3.

Entoloma icterinum (Fr.) Moser
Cap 2-4cm, campanulate-convex or umbonate, margin only slightly striate, surface hygrophanous, smooth, olivaceous yellow-brown, paler to lemon olivaceous towards the margin and on drying. Gills adnate, sinuate, yellowish white becoming pinkish ochre. Stipe 6×0.3cm, yellowish or olivaceous. Flesh colour similar with strong smell of amyl acetate. Spores 10×7.5μm, 5-6-angled, clamp connections numerous, pigment intracellular. Lawns, parks, nettle-beds etc. Uncommon. E2.

Entoloma araneosum (Quél.) Moser [*Leptonia babingtonii*]
Cap 2-3cm, obtusely conical, felted-fibrillose, silvery or bluish grey. Gills ascending, brownish grey. Stipe 5×0.3cm, silvery, fibrillose. Smell complex, mealy earthy. Spores 11×7μm, 6-10-angled, cystidia present, clamp connections frequent, pigmentation mixed. Damp broadleaved woods and moors. Not uncommon. E1. **E. versatile** (Fr.) Moser is more olivaceous and odourless. Rare. E1.

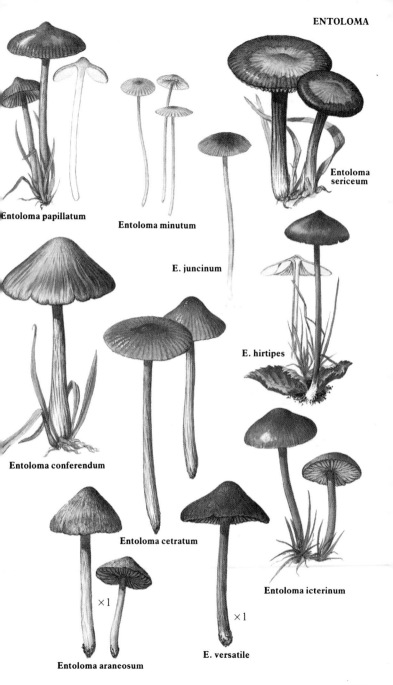

Entoloma papillatum

Entoloma minutum

E. juncinum

Entoloma
sericeum

E. hirtipes

Entoloma conferendum

E. versatile

×1

Entoloma cetratum

Entoloma araneosum

×1

Entoloma icterinum

Subgenus *Entoloma*. Rather fleshy fungi with *Tricholoma-* or *Collybia*-like outline and horizontal, often sinuate gills.

Entoloma lividum Quél. [*E. sinuatum* p.p.]
Cap 8-20cm, fleshy or broadly umbonate with incurved margin, surface smooth, creamy yellow to beige or milky coffee colour, often somewhat mottled, pruinose or streaky. Gills typically yellowish at first, then salmon. Stipe 12×2cm, whitish, fibrillose. Flesh white, firm, strong mealy smell. Spores 9×8μm, 5-7-angled, clamp connections numerous. Under broadleaved trees on heavy calcareous soils. Throughout Britain to the Moray Firth but mainly in southern England, not common. **Poisonous**. E3.

Entoloma nitidum Quél.
Cap 4-6cm, plano-convex to umbonate, smooth, violaceous blue-grey, paler or greying with age. Gills pink. Stipe 7×0.5cm, concolorous, smell faint. Spores 9×7μm, with 5-7 blunt angles. Clamp connections present. Mixed woods, often under conifers. Rare in Britain. E3.

Entoloma bloxamii (Bk. & Br.) Sacc. [*E. madidum*]
Cap 6-10cm, fleshy or umbonate, violaceous blue-grey with cream or ochraceous umbo, finely wrinkled or streaky. Gills broader at the middle, cream, then rose-pink. Stipe 7×1cm, fibrillose, concolorous with creamy yellow base. Flesh yellowish, smell mealy-spermatic or slightly fruity. Spores 9×8μm, with numerous blunt angles, clamp connections present. Pastures on calcareous soil and woodland glades. Uncommon. E2.

E. inopiliforme Bon occurs in similar situations but has the aspect of an *Inocybe*, lacks blue pigment and its mealy smell is sometimes aromatic. Uncommon. E2.

Entoloma clypeatum (L.) Kumm.
Cap 8-12cm, flat, regular, with a broad umbo ("shield-shaped"), hygrophanous, often eventually cracking at the centre, dark grey-brown, paling to dingy ochre, margin incurved, then undulate. Gills commonplace. Stipe 12×2cm, slightly club-shaped, whitish or with brownish grey striations. Flesh pallid, smell and taste mealy. Spores 10×9μm, with 5-6 blunt angles. Among grass in hedge bottoms, often under hawthorn or blackthorn. March-June (-August). Common. Edible. E3.

Entoloma nidorosum (Fr.) Quél.
Cap 4-8cm, convex then expanded or depressed, hygrophanous, yellowish brown fading to dingy white, margin somewhat striate. Gills whitish, then pink. Stipe 10×0.8cm, whitish, fibrillosely striate. Flesh pallid with strong nitrous or chlorinated smell, taste unpleasant. Spores 9×7.5μm, 5-7-angled, clamp connections numerous. Damp places under broadleaved trees, especially willow. Edibility suspect. Common. E4.

E. lividoalbum (K.-R.) Kub. is a little more fleshy, slightly greyer and has a mealy smell. Common in woods. E2.

Subgenus *Trichopilus*. Cap surface felted to fleecy; marginal cystidia present, clamp connections absent, pigment vacuolar.

Entoloma porphyrophaeum (Fr.) Karst.
Cap 5-8cm, fleshy or umbonate, surface fibrillosely fleecy, violaceous grey to lilac-brown. Gills greyish then dingy pinkish lilac. Stipe 12×1cm, fibrillose or felted, greyish, flushed purplish over the middle portion. Flesh pallid, smell faint. Spores 12×6.5μm, cystidia capitate. Grassy thickets and mossy meadows. Fairly common throughout Britain but replaced in the north and on moorland by the usually smaller darker **E. jubatum** (Fr.) Karst. E2.

E. helodes (Fr.) Kumm. is browner with little or no violet tint and occurs in *Sphagnum*. E2.

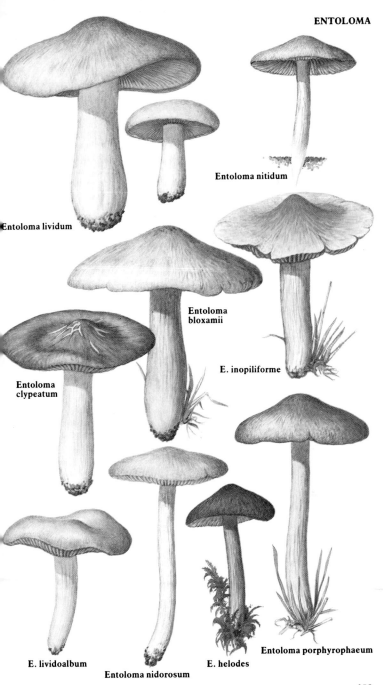

Entoloma nitidum

Entoloma lividum

Entoloma
bloxamii

E. inopiliforme

Entoloma
clypeatum

E. lividoalbum

Entoloma nidorosum

E. helodes

Entoloma porphyrophaeum

Subgenus *Leptonia*. Collybioid ± umbilicate fungi with adnate or sinuate gills; spores usually elongated with 5-7 angles.

Section *Lampropodes* Fr. Cap shaggy or scaly; clamp connections present.

Entoloma euchroum (Pers.) Donk.
Cap 2-3cm, entirely bright violaceous blue. Gill sometimes paler, but always with bright blue edge. Stipe 3×0.4cm, concolorous. Smell spermatic or sweetish. Spores 10×7μm, clavate marginal cystidia. On stumps and twigs. Occasional in Britain, especially in the South. E1.

Entoloma lampropus (Fr.) Hesl.
Cap grey-brown or slate, ± speckled, occasionally tinged bluish. Stipe 4×0.5cm, a contrasting ± dark violaceous blue, smooth. Gills pink. Flesh pallid, odourless. Spores similar to *E. euchroum* but marginal cystidia absent. On the ground, in humus or mossy lawns. Fairly common. E1.

E. dichroum (Pers.) Kumm. occurs on dead wood, especially beech, with cap surface texture like *Tricholoma terreum* and distinctive marginal cystidia. Rare. E1.

Section *Roseocaules*. Colours bright green or pink.

Entoloma incanum (Fr.) Hesl.
Cap 2-3cm, slightly depressed, finely striate, soft olive-green. Gills whitish or tinted olivaceous. Stipe 4×0.3cm, a fine blue-green, intensified by bruising toward the base. Flesh concolorous. Smell strong, of mouse-droppings. Spores 14×7μm, 7-12-angled. Pastures especially on chalk and limestones. E2.

Entoloma roseum (Longyear) Moser
Cap 2-3cm, convex to ± umbilicate, smooth or felted, margin incurved, bright pink becoming pinkish brown or vinaceous. Gills white to pinkish. Stipe 3×0.6cm, pink. Flesh pale, odourless. Spores 10×7μm, marginal cells variable. Lawns, on calcareous soils. Rare. E1.

E. catalaunicum (Sing.) Noord. has pinkish-brown to lilac-blue tints. Not uncommon in Scotland. E1.

Section *Paludocybe*. Cap smooth or striate, rarely a little scaly at the centre; colours brownish to ± violaceous blue. Cap cuticle a trichoderm, clamp connections absent, marginal cystidia frequent.

Entoloma mougeotii (Fr.) Hesl. [*E. ardosiacum*]
Cap 3-6cm, slightly depressed, slate grey, not striate, slightly speckled at the centre. Gills eventually slightly decurrent, not bluish. Stipe 7×0.5cm, slate-lilac, dotted at the apex. Flesh pallid, smell faint. Spores 12×7μm, marginal cells scanty on gill. Lawns, grassy fringes of woods. Uncommon, perhaps less so in Scotland. E2.

E. caelestinum (Fr.) Hesl. has a slightly striate cap and gills tinged blue but not fringed. Uncommon. E2.

Entoloma serrulatum (Pers.) Hesl.
Resembles *E. mougeotii* in its dark slaty cap but has gills fringed with dark blue dots. Cap smooth or fibrillose, blackish blue, often quite dark, finely striate when fresh, opaque bistre when dry. Stipe 5×0.3cm, not dotted. Odourless. Spores 9×6μm, marginal cells coloured. In grass and on fallen twigs. Common. E2.

E. querquedulum (Romagn.) Noord. has a pretty greenish-blue cap and blue-grey gill edge; in damp coppices. There are many other species common on heaths and moors with ± bluish to slaty caps, difficult to distinguish. E2.

Entoloma sarcitum (Fr.) Noord.
Cap 1-3cm, russet-grey to yellowish brown without a trace of violaceous blue, surface almost smooth, margin striate. Gills not fringed (except in var. *spurcifolium*). Stipe 4×0.5cm, colour similar or yellowish. Flesh pallid, smell faint. Spores 10×7.5μm, marginal cells inconspicuous. Thickets and woodland glades. Common. E3.

E. turci (Bres.) Moser has a more tomentose cap without striations and a rather velvety stipe ± tinged pink and occurs in mossy meadows. Uncommon. E2

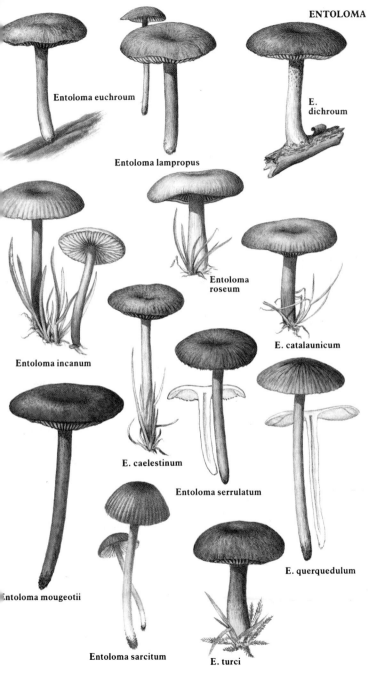

Entoloma euchrum

Entoloma lampropus

E. dichroum

Entoloma roseum

E. catalaunicum

Entoloma incanum

E. caelestinum

Entoloma serrulatum

Entoloma mougeotii

E. querquedulum

Entoloma sarcitum

E. turci

All ×1

Family *Macrocystidiaceae*. Only one genus: spores smooth, tramal hyphae parallel and cystidia distinctive.

Macrocystidia cucumis (Pers.) Joss.
Cap 3-6cm, campanulate, dark brown, surface matt or pruinose, margin paler, not striate except in var. *latifolia*. Gills narrowly adnate to almost free, broader in the middle, whitish then brick-ochre. Stipe 8×0.5cm, attenuated at the base, velvety, blackish brown with paler apex. Flesh pallid, smell strong, of cucumber, becoming fishy. Spores 8×3.5μm, cystidia conical, pointed, up to 80×25μm. Skirts of woodland, roadsides and bare soil under broadleaved trees and conifers. Quite common. E2.

Family *Pluteaceae*. Cap and stipe separable, gills free, trama inversely bilateral.

Genus *Pluteus*. Volva absent.

Section *Pluteus* [*Trichodermi*]. Cap surface fibrillose to ± scaly, cystidia spiny.

Pluteus cervinus (Batsch) Fayod [*P. atricapillus* auct.]
Cap 8-15cm, convex or umbonate, brownish, ± speckled blackish towards the centre. Gills broadest in the middle, white then pink, crowded. Stipe 10×1cm, thickened at the base, white with brown fibrils. Flesh pallid, faint smell of radish. Spores 8×5μm, clamp connections rare. On stumps. Very common throughout Britain. E4.

P. atromarginatus (Konrad.) Kühner[*P. tricuspidatus, nigrofloccosus*] has a darker cap and the gill edge dotted black. E2.

Pluteus petasatus (Fr.) Gill. [*P. patricius*]
Remarkable for its great stature, cap 15-20cm, and growth in tufts on rotten wood and sawdust heaps. Cap whitish, mottled or speckled grey-brown at the centre, sometimes finely cracked. Gills as in *P. atricapillus* or broader. Stipe 12×2cm, white, slightly streaked brownish. Flesh pale with stale smell of elder blossom. Microscopic details as in *P. cervinus*. Edible but poor quality. Uncommon. E2.

P. pellitus (Pers.) Kumm. is more slender, 5-7cm, white throughout and occurs singly on woody debris. E2.

Pluteus salicinus (Pers.) Kumm.
Cap 4-7cm, brownish grey with glaucous greenish tints. Gills commonplace. Stipe 8×0.8cm, whitish, tinged ± dingy grey green towards the base. Flesh glaucous. Spores 8×5.5μm, clamp connections numerous. On dead wood of broadleaved trees. Common. E3.

Section *Hispidodermi*. Cap surface velvety or shaggy. Cystidia smooth, cap cuticle a trichoderm.

Pluteus umbrosus (Pers.) Kumm.
Cap 5-10cm, convex to umbonate, shaggy or checkered with dark scales on a brownish ground, especially over the centre. Gill edge brown. Stipe 5×1cm, shaggy with brownish hairs towards the base. Flesh pale, smell of garlic or *Lepiota cristata* (p.284). Spores 7×5μm, cystidia with brown contents. On stumps and logs of broadleaved trees. Fairly common. E2. **P. plautus** (Weinm.) Gill., with gill edge not brown and stipe more punctate or pruinose, occurs on wood of conifers. E1.

Pluteus semibulbosus (Lasch) Gill.
Cap 4-5cm, slightly umbonate, whitish, discolouring grey brown over the centre, margin faintly pinkish-striate. Gills dingy pink. Stipe slender, 6×0.2cm, white, base somewhat bulbous. Flesh pale, odourless. Spores 7×6μm, cystidia clavate or narrowed below the tip, brownish. On small dead branches of broadleaved trees and among their leaves. Uncommon. E2.

Pluteus leoninus (Sch.) Kumm. [*P. fayodii*]
Cap 3-7cm, ± conical to umbonate, bright yellow, with ± blackish tomentum towards the centre or a tinge of olivaceous. Gills pink with ± yellow edge. Stipe 6×0.5cm, yellowish, flesh similar colour. Spores 7×6μm, cystidia not coloured. On debris and fallen branches of broadleaved trees and conifers. E3.

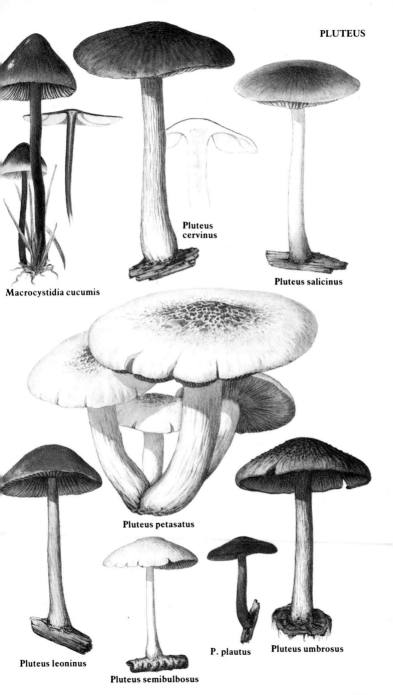

Macrocystidia cucumis

Pluteus
cervinus

Pluteus salicinus

Pluteus petasatus

Pluteus leoninus

Pluteus semibulbosus

P. plautus

Pluteus umbrosus

Section *Cellulodermi*. Cap surface matt or wrinkled, sometimes dotted or veined. Cuticle a palisade or ± cellular, cystidia smooth.

Pluteus aurantiorugosus (Trog) Sacc. [*P. coccineus*]
Cap 3-5cm, matt or wrinkled, a splendid orange-red. Stipe 4×0.5cm, golden towards the base. Inodorous. Spores 6×4μm, facial and marginal cystidia present. Stumps and logs of broadleaved trees, especially elm. Uncommon. E1.

P. luteovirens Rea is yellow or mustard colour, superficially like *P. leoninus* (p. 196). E1.

Pluteus romellii (Britz.) Sacc. [*P. lutescens*]
Cap 3-6cm, sepia brown, contrasting with a yellow stipe, and flesh. Stipe 5×0.5cm. Gills broadest at the middle, pale yellow at first. Flesh yellow at the surface, odourless. Spores ± globose, 7×6μm, facial and marginal cystidia present. On dead logs and branches of broadleaves trees. Common. E3.

Pluteus phlebophorus (Ditm.) Kumm.
Cap similar to *P. romellii*, without a trace of yellow, but surface much more veined, even reticulately wrinkled. Gills pinkish. Stipe 4-0.5cm, white, striate, rarely tinged yellow at the base only. Flesh white, odourless. Spores as in *P. romellii*. On dead branches, plant debris and humus. Common. E3. **P. chrysophaeus** (Sch.) Quél. is doubtfully distinguished by possessing some tint of yellow and a lumpier, irregular brain-like cap surface. E2.

Pluteus podospileus Sacc. ex Cub.
Cap 2-4cm, granulate-wrinkled, russet brown or sepia, margin striate. Gills commonplace. Stipe 4×0.3cm, typically dotted brown on a dingy whitish ground. Flesh pale, smell slight. Spores 6×4.5μm, cap cuticle mixed, pyriform cells mingled with tall fusiform ones. On rotten wood. Uncommon. E1. **P. seticeps** (Atk.) Sing. [*P. minutissimus*], scarcely more slender, has an almost smooth or slightly floccose stipe. Uncommon. E1-2.

Pluteus cinereofuscus Lange
Cap 3-5cm, rather fleshy, greyish brown, sometimes glaucous or dull. Gills pallid, margin often toothed. Stipe slender, 7×0.5cm, silvery-silky. Flesh pallid, odour faint. Spores 8×6μm, facial and marginal cystidia present. On humus and rotten wood of broadleaved trees. Uncommon. E2. **P. thomsonii** (Bk. & Br.) Dennis [*P. cinereus*] has a darker cap and ash-grey stipe but lacks facial cystidia. Common on logs and fallen branches of broadleaved trees. E2.

Genus *Volvariella*. Like *Pluteus* but with a membranous volva as in *Amanita*.

Volvariella speciosa (Fr.) Sing.
Cap 8-15cm, viscid, whitish to greyish, olivaceous grey-brown in var. *gloiocephala*. Gills broadest at the middle, crowded, pallid then pinkish brick colour. Stipe 15×1cm, white, thickened to 3cm at the base; volva white to brownish, fragile. Spores 16×19μm. On rotting straw, manured ground, flowerbeds, rich pastures and marram-grass on coastal dunes. Common. Edible. E3.

Volvariella bombycina (Sch.) Sing.
Cap 10-20cm, with silky whitish surface, becoming felted-shaggy and yellowish. Gills broad. Stipe 10×2cm, often curved, white; volva large often lobed, ochraceous then russet. Spores 9×5μm. On stumps and logs especially elm. Fairly common in southern England. E2.

V. surrecta (Knapp) Sing. is a small fungus growing on old *Clitocybe nebularis*. Rare. E1.

Volvariella murinella (Quél.) Moser
Cap 3-6cm, greyish, smooth. Gills pale. Stipe 6×0.6cm and volva white. Smell slight, of pelargonium. Spores 7×4.5μm. Lawns, pastures, under brambles etc. Occasional in Britain. E2.

There are several other small whitish species difficult to distinguish from one another, e.g. *V. hypopythis* (Fr.) Moser. E2.

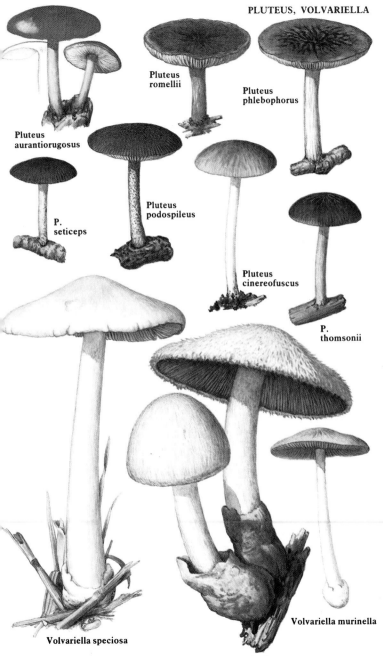

Pluteus romellii

Pluteus phlebophorus

Pluteus aurantiorugosus

P. seticeps

Pluteus podospileus

Pluteus cinereofuscus

P. thomsonii

Volvariella murinella

Volvariella speciosa

Volvariella bombycina

199

Order *Cortinariales*. Spore print and mature gills rusty or brownish to blackish. Stipe and cap not easily separable.

Family *Cortinariaceae*. Spore print and gills rusty, not blackish. Gills adnate or sinuate.

Genus *Cortinarius*. Partial veil a cortina, occasionally coherent enough to form a ring or series of rings. Spore print rusty. The genus is difficult to study, and the species have been much confused. In most cases they can only be named when fresh specimens of all ages are available. The species are very numerous and this key has been simplified to lead to groups of them.

Key to *Cortinarius* – principal species

1a	Cap and stipe both viscid; subgenus *Myxacium*: **2**	
1b	Cap viscid but stipe dry: **5**	
1c	Cap dry, at most a little slippery in damp weather: **11**	
1d	Cap surface hygrophanous, usually smooth; subgenus *Telamonia*: **16**	

2a	Taste mild: **3**	
2b	Taste bitter, ± elongated with slender or rooting stipe ≫	section *Ochroleuci*, 204

3a	Stipe strongly ornamented or annulate, scaly: **4**	
3b	Stipe fusiform, cortina viscid, cap somewhat fluted ≫	section *Elatiores*, 202

4a	Brown to russet, stipe rather thickset ≫	section *Myxacium*, 202
4b	Yellow to lilac, stipe more slender or club-shaped ≫	section *Delibuti*, 202

5a	Stipe ± slender, or club-shaped but not bulbous; subgenus *Phlegmacium*: **6**	
5b	Stipe base abruptly bulbous or marginate ("Scauri" aspect); subgenus *Bulbopodium*: **10**	

6a	Stipe slender or equal, taste often bitter ≫	group of *C. infractus*, 204
6b	Stipe stout, somewhat club-shaped ("Cliduchi" aspect): **7**	

7a	Colours somewhat lilaceous or blue-violaceous in cap or stipe but also and especially in the young gills ≫	section *Variecolores*, 208
7b	Colours yellow to russet or brownish, gills sometimes lilaceous: **8**	

8a	Gills white or lilaceous at first: **9**	
8b	Gills yellow ≫	section *Percomes*, 206

9a	Stipe whitish or not annulate ≫	section *Phlegmacium*, 206
9b	Stipe ± annulate or garlanded ≫	section *Triumphantes*, 206

10a	Gills white at first ≫	section *Leucophylli*, 210
10b	Gills greenish to olivaceous or khaki yellow ≫	section *Virentophylli*, 210
10c	Gills bright yellow ≫	section *Xanthophylli*, 212
10d	Gills bluish or lilaceous ≫	section *Cyanophylli*, 214

11a	Cap surface silky to micaceous or powdery-punctate, colours bluish or dull ≫	subgenus *Sericeocybe*, 216
11b	Cap surface somewhat fibrillose-fleecy to tomentose or scaly: **12**	

12a	Dark violaceous, tomentose to shaggy ≫	*Cortinarius violaceus*, 222
12b	Colours green, yellow to orange, or russet: **13**	

13a	Cap surface fleecy-velvety to scaly, gills concolorous; subgenus *Leprocybe*: **14**	
13b	Cap surface fibrillosely fleecy; gills often brightly coloured; bright ± red reaction with KOH; subgenus *Dermocybe*: **15**	

14a Colours green, olivaceous or bronze ≫   group of *C. venetus*, 222
(If surface is more fibrillose, and there is no smell, see section *Dermocybe*, 226)
14b Colours yellow, orange or fawnish ≫   group of *C. limonius*, 222
14c Colours russet to rusty or somewhat reddish ≫   group of *C. orellanus*, 224

15a Gills bright red ≫   section *Sanguinei*, 224
15b Gills orange-yellow or greenish ≫   section *Dermocybe*, 226

16a Stipe annulate or flushed bright red, at least towards the base ≫
      section *Armillati*, 220
16b Stipe without any trace of red, at most lilaceous violet to pinkish: **17**

17a Slender or elongated fungi, stipe 0.2-0.5cm thick ≫   section *Tenuiores*, 220
17b Large, rather fleshy fungi, stipe 1-3(5)cm thick; section *Firmiores*: **18**

18a Colours ± lilaceous or blue-violaceous: **19**
18b Colours yellow, russet or brown: **20**

19a Stipe fusiform, ± garlanded or naked ≫   group of *C. evernius*, 218
19b Stipe with sheathing ring ≫   group of *C. torvus*, 218

20a Gills distant: **21**
20b Gills ± crowded: **22**

21a Colour dark brown, smell faint or none, ring ± inconspicuous ≫
      group of *C. brunneus*, 218
21b Colour fulvous, smell earthy; ringed ≫   group of *C. hinnuleus*, 218

22a Stipe fusiform, naked; smell of iodine ≫   *C. duracinus*, 218
22b Stipe equal or ± bulbous, somewhat garlanded ≫   group of *C. privignus*, 218

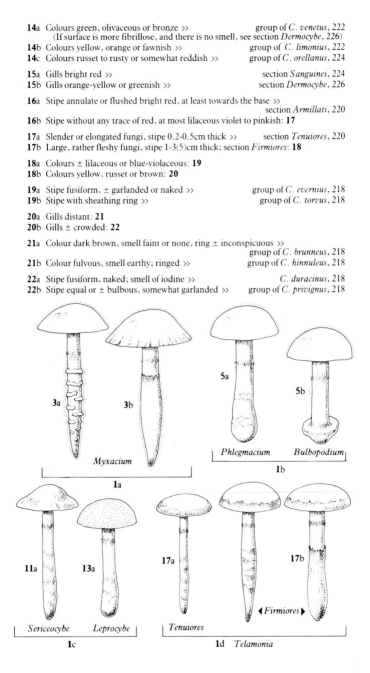

3a   **3b**

Myxacium

1a

5a   **5b**

Phlegmacium   *Bulbopodium*

1b

11a   **13a**

Sericeocybe   *Leprocybe*

1c

17a   ◀*Firmiores*▶   **17b**

Tenuiores

1d   *Telamonia*

Subgenus *Myxacium*. Cap and stipe both viscid.

Section *Myxacium* [*Triviales*]. Stipe ± annulate or sculptured.

Cortinarius trivialis Lange
Cap 5-10cm, conical or umbonate, dull olive-ochre to dingy brown, margin smooth, somewhat incurved. Gills pallid, lilaceous in var. *subolivascens*. Stipe 12×1cm, almost equal, coarsely sculptured by ± anastomosing rings of gluten, brownish on a paler ground. Flesh pallid, smell faint, rather like honey. Spores 13×7μm, no marginal cystidia. Under broadleaved trees. Common. E3.

Cortinarius collinitus (Sow.) Fr.
Cap 8-12cm, convex, brownish ochraceous to dull orange fawn or rusty. Gills white at first. Stipe 13×2cm, bluish, slightly bluish in the stipe, smell slight. Spores 13×7μm, gill edge fertile, without cystidia. Under mixed broad leaved trees. Fairly common. E3.

Cortinarius mucosus (Bull.) Kickx
Cap 6-10cm, fleshy, a fine fawn orange, sometimes quite bright. Gills white, then rusty clay colour. Stipe 12×1.5cm, pure white, scarcely scaly below the cortina. Under conifers, especially pine, also birch. Fairly common. Microscopic details as in *C. collinitus*. E3.

Section *Elatiores* [*Defibulati*]. Stipe somewhat spindle-shaped with viscid cortina. Cap ± fluted, clamp connections absent, marginal cystidia well developed.

Cortinarius elatior Fr.
Cap 10-15cm, campanulate or umbonate, margin strongly fluted, colour olive-brown or ochraceous to dark purplish brown. Gills clay colour, interveined or wrinkled, margin paler, floccose. Stipe 15×2cm, spindle-shaped, ± violaceous at least beneath the viscid cortina, apex striate. Flesh pallid, smell none or faintly of honey. Spores 15×7μm, marginal cystidia balloon-shaped. Under beech. Common. Good edible fungus. E4.

Cortinarius pseudosalor Lange [*C. mucifluoides* p.p.]
Cap 6-10cm, grey brown, sometimes tinged violet, margin not or slightly fluted. Gills clay colour, little veined. Stipe 10×1cm, ± equal or only slightly enlarged at the level of the cortina, entirely blue-violaceous or white at the base. Flesh bluish, smell of honey or *Mahonia*. Spores 14×7μm, cystidia slightly clavate. In mixed copses. Common. E2.

C. mucifluus Hry., with white stipe, occurs under conifers. E2.

Section *Delibuti*. Stipe equal or club-shaped, colours yellow or violaceous. Taste mild.

Cortinarius delibutus Fr.
Cap 4-7cm, convex, yellow or ochraceous, becoming paler or eventually dull brownish ochre. Gills lilaceous. Stipe 8×1cm, slightly club-shaped, whitish at the summit, lilaceous with some yellow flecks below the cortina. Flesh pallid, odourless. Spores ± globose, 8×7μm, marginal cells inconspicuous. Under various broadleaved trees. Very common. E4.

Cortinarius salor Fr.
Cap 5-10cm, very convex, a striking blue-violet with the centre finally becoming ± ochraceous. Gills lilaceous. Stipe 8×1cm, similar colour or whitish. Flesh pallid, odourless. Spores 7×6μm. Under broadleaved trees in warm places, also under conifers. Rare. E2.

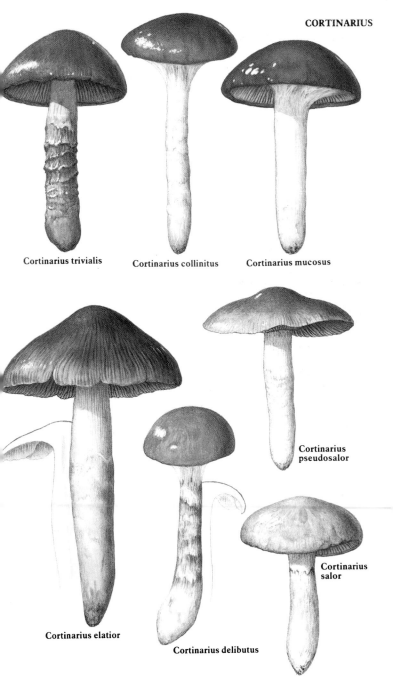

CORTINARIUS

Cortinarius trivialis

Cortinarius collinitus

Cortinarius mucosus

Cortinarius elatior

Cortinarius delibutus

Cortinarius pseudosalor

Cortinarius salor

Section *Ochroleuci* [*Amarescentes*]. Taste bitter.

Cortinarius croceocaeruleus (Pers.) Fr.
Cap 3-5cm, convex, lilaceous blue or amethyst with the centre, eventually fading to ochraceous. Gills ochraceous to saffron. Stipe 7×0.6cm, slightly spindle-shaped or rooting, whitish to ochraceous, cortina evanescent. Flesh creamy white, bitter, smell of radish then of honey. Spores 8×5µm. Under broadleaved trees on calcareous soils. Southern England, uncommon. E2.

Cortinarius vibratilis (Fr.) Fr.
Cap 5-7cm, bright golden yellow becoming rather orange, shining with gluten and slightly streaky. Gills ochraceous, rather crowded. Stipe 6×1cm, pure white. Taste very bitter, especially the gluten, smell faint. Spores 8×4µm. Mixed woods on calcareous soils. Uncommon. E2.

Cortinarius causticus Fr.
Similar stature to *C. vibratilis* but less viscid, surface with a slight creamy white frosting over an orange-russet ground, only exposed by wiping. Gills pale clay-colour to rusty yellow. Stipe 5×0.7cm, white, usually somewhat kinked. Flesh pale, smell slight, taste mild apart from the cuticle which is bitter. Spores 7×4µm. On calcareous soils under broadleaved trees and conifers. Not common, mainly in southern England. E2.

Cortinarius ochroleucus (Sch.) Fr.
Cap 3-5cm, creamy white verging on ochraceous, no deeper colour when wiped, scarcely viscid. Gills pale ochraceous. Stipe 6×0.8cm, spindle-shaped or rooting, white. Flesh pale, bitter, smell slight of radish or honey. Spores 8×5µm. Under broadleaved trees. Not uncommon in England. E2.

C. eburneus (Vel.) Hry ex Bon [*C. crystallinus* p.p.] is more viscid and whitish. Less common. E1.

Subgenus *Phlegmacium*. Cap viscid, stipe dry.

Section *Elastici*. Stipe equal, neither club-shaped nor bulbous, recalling the previous section.

Cortinarius decolorans (Pers.) Fr.
Size and colouring similar to *C. delibutus* but the stipe is dry. Cap pale yellowish ochraceous. Gills pinkish lilac. Stipe white, rarely flushed lilac at the apex and with basal yellowish scales vague or wanting. Flesh white, odourless, taste mild. Spores ± globose, 8×6.5µm. Under birch and conifers. Uncommon. E2.

Cortinarius infractus (Pers.) Fr.
Cap 5-12cm, convex with oblique margin or sharply incurved, olive-grey-brown, sometimes slightly violaceous, dark and distinctive, often zoned with remnants of a marginal veil and radially striped. Gills dark dingy brown. Stipe 8×2cm, pale brownish or violaceous at the apex. Flesh white or bluish, taste bitter, smell faint. Spores short-elliptical, 9×6µm. Under broadleaved trees. Fairly common. E4.

There are several colour variants; those illustrated here are var. *obscurocyaneus* and var. *olivellus*. E2.

Cortinarius subtortus (Pers.) Fr.
Cap 5-7cm, convex, margin incurved, surface slightly matt, dull olivaceous yellow or dingy greenish ochraceous. Gill colour similar or more dingy, gills ± distant. Stipe 8-10×0.5-1cm, pale ochraceous to almost concolorous, rarely slightly zoned yellowish. Flesh pale, smelling of cedar oil (pencil wood), taste bitter or tart. Spores 8×6µm, numerous fusiform facial and marginal cystidia present, up to 100×15µm, even visible under a hand lens. On moors with *Sphagnum*, often under spruce or birch. Uncommon. E2.

CORTINARIUS

Cortinarius
causticus

Cortinarius
vibratilis

Cortinarius croceocaeruleus

Cortinarius
ochroleucus

C. i. var. olivellus

Cortinarius decolorans

Cortinarius infractus
var. **obscureocyaneus**

Cortinarius subtortus

Section *Phlegmacium* [*Claricolores*]. Colouring ± yellow to russet, gills whitish or violaceous; stipe spindle-shaped or club-shaped, ("*Cliduchi*" aspect), whitish or not garlanded.

Cortinarius claricolor (Fr.) Fr.
Cap 8-15cm, fleshy, pale yellow or rather more russet at the centre with the margin rendered paler by the white veil and floccose. Gills white to pale milky coffee colour. Stipe 8×1cm, whitish, fleecy. Flesh pale with slight smell of pastry. Spores 9×4.5μm, ± fusiform and only slightly warted. Under spruce and deciduous trees. Not definitely known in Britain, where the name *C. claricolor* has been applied to *C. rufoalbus* Kühn. and to *C. durus* Orton, both with larger spores. E2.

C. turmalis (Fr.) Fr. only slightly smaller, is more reddish-brown with spores 12×6μm. E3.

Cortinarius rufoalbus Kühn.
Cap 10-12cm, creamy ochraceous to fawn russet or bruising reddish brown, surface only slightly viscid, margin whitish silky and ± fleecy. Gills tinged lilaceous. Stipe 10×1.5cm, with concentric white silky scales below a conspicuous ring zone near the apex, yellowing a little at the base. Flesh bluish at the surface, smell slightly earthy, becoming cheesy. Spores 14×8μm, almond-shaped. Under beech on chalk. Uncommon. E2.

C. fraudulosus Britz. is paler with distant non-lilaceous gills and occurs under conifers. E2.

Section *Triumphantes*. Stipe garlanded by a yellowish to russet veil.

Cortinarius triumphans Fr.
Cap 10-15cm, a beautiful yellow verging on fawn, margin slightly russet-appendiculate. Gills beige with a bluish tinge. Stipe 13×2cm, club- or spindle-shaped, garlanded by the russet-ochre veil, sometimes in a zigzag. Flesh pale, smell slight. Spores 14×7μm, elongated lemon-shaped. In damp woods on acid soils, especially birch. Rare in Britain where it is replaced under birch by the very similar *C. crocolitus* Quél. with smaller spores 11×6μm. E3.

C. olidus Lge. [*C. cephalixus* auct.] is a little less fleshy, with very viscid duller coloured cap, minutely darker-scaly at the centre, with a strong earthy smell. Uncommon. E3.

Cortinarius varius (Sch.) Fr.
Cap 8-12cm, fawn yellow to bright orange, margin without a veil. Gills bright lilac at first. Stipe club-shaped, 12×2cm, with pale fleeting band of white veil below a rust coloured annular zone. Flesh pale, smell slight. Spores 11×6μm, almond-shaped. Under conifers on calcareous soils. Uncommon in Britain. E1 (m4).

Section *Percomes*. Gills yellow.

Cortinarius percomis Fr.
Cap 10-15cm, a beautiful yellow, finally rather golden orange or rust colour from the centre. Gills bright yellow then rusty orange ochre. Stipe 12×2cm, somewhat yellow, veil inconspicuous or concolorous. Flesh yellowish with strong smell of muscatel, tangerine or eau de cologne, eventually sometimes unpleasant. Spores 12×7μm, subelliptical. Under conifers on calcareous soils. Rare. E2.

Cortinarius nanceiensis R. Mre.
Cap 5-10cm, ± thin-fleshed, at the centre speckled purplish brown on a yellowish or rust-brown ground, sometimes olivaceous, margin more lemon yellow. Gills ± decurrent, lemon yellow to greenish. Stipe 10×1.5cm, almost equal or club-shaped to ± bulbous, lemon yellow, with remnants of a purplish brown veil near the base. Flesh yellow, smell slight or rather fruity. Spores 11×6μm, slightly lemon-shaped. Under broadleaved trees on calcareous soils. Not known in Britain. E2.

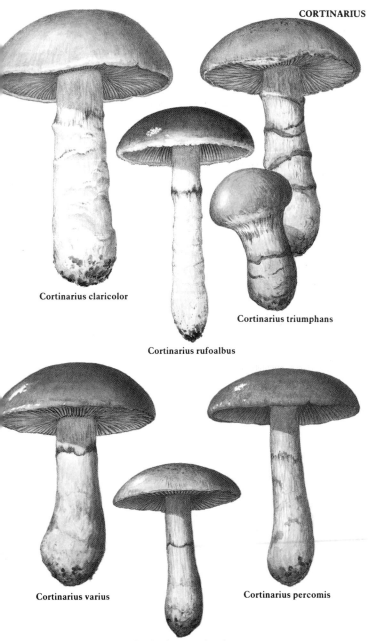

Cortinarius claricolor

Cortinarius rufoalbus

Cortinarius triumphans

Cortinarius varius

Cortinarius nanceiensis

Cortinarius percomis

Section *Variecolores*. Colours strikingly blue, violet or purplish-brown; gills lilaceous or whitish at first, not yellow.

Cortinarius largus Fr.
Cap 10-15cm, ± convex with inrolled margin, smooth or silvery silky, bluish lilac becoming whitish or brownish ochraceous from the centre. Gills pale bluish. Stipe almost straight-sided, 10×1.5cm, nearly concolorous or paler, smooth, without a veil. Flesh lilaceous, fading white when cut, odourless; ammonia reaction yellow. Spores 10×6μm, almond-shaped. Under broadleaved trees on calcareous soils. Edible. Not uncommon. E3.

C. lividoviolaceus (Hry.) Moser has a fruity smell and is more distinctly lilaceous violet in gills and stipe. Not known in Britain. E2.

Cortinarius variecolor (Pers.) Fr.
Cap 12-18cm, rather dark violet-brown with a fibrillose or streaky margin. Gills violaceous. Stipe 12×2cm, with fleeting bluish-brown zones in the lower part. Flesh nearly concolorous, smell strong and earthy; ammonia reaction bright yellow. Spores 11×6μm, almond-shaped. Under conifers in the mountains. Edible. Rare in Britain. E1 (m4).

C. nemorensis (Fr.) Lange is very similar but rather paler coloured and quite common in Britain especially under beech. E3.

Cortinarius balteatus (Fr.) Fr.
Cap 10-12cm, convex, fleshy, fawnish brown, distinctly violaceous at the margin which is incurved and sometimes bears remnants of a whitish general veil. Gills pallid or with a trace of lilac. Stipe 8×2cm, ± bulbous, white, without a coloured veil. Flesh white, smell weak, fruity becoming rather earthy; ammonia reaction yellowish brown. Spores 10×6μm. Under conifers. Rare in Britain, where it is replaced by *C. balteato-cumatilis* Hry., with a more blue-violet stipe, under beech. E2.

C. cumatilis Fr. has violaceous garlands on the stipe as in *C. praestans* (below) but lacks its fluted margin. Coniferous woods, rare in Britain. E1.

Cortinarius praestans (Cordier) Gill. [*C. berkeleyi*]
A massive fungus with fleshy cap 15-25cm, violet-brown to purplish grey or chocolate, margin incurved, typically fluted-furrowed and often bearing whitish remnants of the universal veil, like the scales on an *Amanita*. Gills whitish clay colour or with a vague trace of lilac. Stipe massive, 15×4cm, somewhat bulbous, pale violet with thick silky zones of the veil, becoming paler or brownish. Flesh lilac at the surface, smell slight; ammonia reaction negative. Spores 17×9μm, lemon-shaped. Deciduous woods on calcareous soils. Edible. Rare in Britain. E2.

C. herculeus Malç. occurs under cedar, has similar massive stature but more ochre or brown than lilaceous tints and a strong smell of *C. variecolor*. Not known in Britain. E1.

Cortinarius cyanites Fr.
Cap 6-10cm, persistently hemispherical, only slightly viscid, rather fibrillose or streaky, violaceous grey or dull lilaceous and bluing. Gills concolorous or bluish. Stipe 10×1cm, club-shaped to ± bulbous, dull lilac or reddish, slightly zoned violaceous towards the base. Flesh bluish, reddening when cut. Spores 11×6μm, elliptical. Under broadleaved trees on heavy soils, less often with conifers. Not uncommon with birch and pine in Scotland. E2.

C. spadiceus Fr. occurs under conifers with equally dry but more scaly cap, ochraceous grey with fleeting violaceous tint and bluish non-reddening flesh. Doubtfully British. E2.

NOTE. Some species or forms in the following subgenus *Bulbopodium* may have a narrowly or scarcely marginate bulb and so be confused with this group.

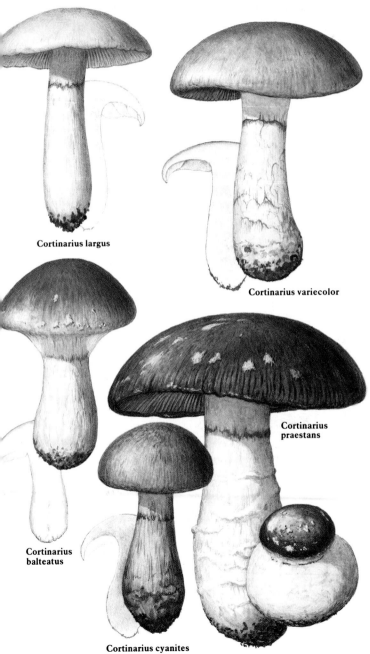

Cortinarius largus

Cortinarius variecolor

Cortinarius praestans

Cortinarius balteatus

Cortinarius cyanites

209

Subgenus *Bulbopodium*. Species with "*Scauri*" aspect i.e. stipe with marginate bulb.

Section *Leucophylli* [*Multiformes*]. Gills white or pallid at first.

Cortinarius multiformis Fr.
Cap 5-10cm, plano-convex, a bright ochraceous fawn becoming rather reddish milky coffee colour, somewhat streaky-fibrillose with smooth creamy ochraceous margin, paler at first. Gills pallid to ochraceous beige. Stipe 6×1cm, whitish to slightly ochraceous, yellowing when rubbed, with a narrow or obtuse whitish basal bulb 2cm across. Flesh white, bruising yellow and then smelling more strongly of honey or Mahonia. Spores 11×6μm, almond-shaped, only slightly warted. Under broadleaved trees especially beech. Uncommon. There is a f. *coniferarum* under spruce in Europe, more thickset, deeper coloured and almost odourless. E2.

C. herbarum Hry. is more robust, with warmer colouring and less marginate bulb, flesh less yellowing, in grassy places under conifers in Europe. E2.

Cortinarius subturbinatus Hry. ex Orton
Cap 8-15cm, rather brighter yellow than *C. multiformis*, eventually speckled russet over the centre. Gills creamy ochraceous. Stipe 8×2cm, persistently white with a yellowish broad or pointed basal bulb 4cm across, sometimes concave. Flesh pale, smell slight. Spores 12×7μm, somewhat lemon-shaped, coarsely warted. Under beech, locally common on chalk. E3. **C. langei** Hry. is more slender with spores 8×.5μm, in similar situations. E2.

Cortinarius rapaceus Fr.
Cap 5-8cm, not very fleshy or umbonate, pale cream, hardly becoming ochraceous even when old. Gills white then cream. Stipe 8×1.5cm, dingy white with an often oblique basal bulb 2cm across. Flesh white, smell weak, of turnip then of honey. Spores 10×5μm, elliptical. Mixed woods. Rare. E2. **C. aleuriosmus** R. Mre. is a little more thickset, with stipe sometimes bluish and a strong smell of slightly rancid meal. Not known in Britain. E1.

Section *Virentophylli*. Gills greenish or olivaceous. .

Cortinarius rufoolivaceus (Pers.) Fr.
Cap 8-13cm, soon expanded, a beautiful purplish to carmine shade hard to describe but distinctive. Gills bright olive. Stipe 9×1.5cm, pale violaceous, bulb 4cm, edged reddish. Flesh violaceous in the stipe, smell faint, sometimes rather bitter; KOH reaction dark green. Spores 12×7.5μm. Under broadleaved trees, especially beech, not uncommon on chalk. E3.

C. orichalceus (Batsch) Fr. has only a coppery red hue scarcely turning purplish or vinaceous brown when old and is mainly with conifers. Rare. E2.

Cortinarius atrovirens Kalchbr.
Cap 6-10cm, fleshy, blackish green, darkest at the centre with more olivaceous or sometimes lemon margin. Gills greenish yellow then olivaceous. Stipe thickset, 7×2cm, greenish yellow, with lemon-coloured scarcely marginate bulb. Flesh lemon-coloured, smell peppery. Spores 11×6μm. Under conifers on calcareous soils. Rare. E3.

Cortinarius odoratus (Joguet ex Moser) Moser
Cap 6-10cm, plano-convex, bright lemon-green, slightly fibrillose, centre ± fawnish-scaly. Gills greenish yellow. Stipe 8×1cm, clear green or lemon with a more sulphur yellow marginate basal bulb 3cm across. Flesh pale to greenish lemon near the surface with strong smell of orange blossom, acacia or honeysuckle. Spores 10×6μm. Under broadleaved trees on heavy calcareous soils. Not known in Britain. E2.

C. odorifer Britz. has cap coppery red at the centre, lemon or olivaceous yellow gills and a smell of aniseed or fennel. Not known in Britain. E2.

NOTE. All the above species give a negative reaction with Henry's Tl-4 Reagent. Other species which give a positive reaction and have duller colours include *C. herpeticus* Fr. [*C. aureopulverulentus*] in beech woods, and *C. scaurus* (Fr.) Fr. in damp coniferous woods. E2.

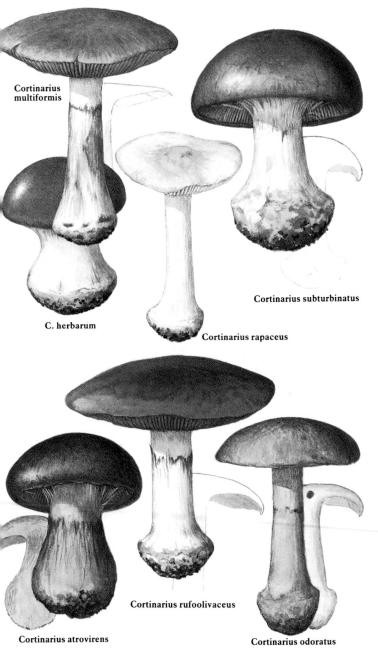

Cortinarius
multiformis

C. herbarum

Cortinarius rapaceus

Cortinarius subturbinatus

Cortinarius atrovirens

Cortinarius rufoolivaceus

Cortinarius odoratus

Section *Xanthophylli*. Gills yellow.

Cortinarius elegantissimus Hry. [*C. aureoturbinatus*]
Cap 5-12cm, fleshy, a striking chrome yellow slightly flushed orange fawn at the centre. Gills bright yellow. Stipe 12×2cm, pale yellow with a rather more fawn spreading basal bulb, 4-5cm. Flesh pale, slightly blue at the stipe apex. Smell pleasant; KOH reaction carmine red, especially on the cuticle. Spores 15×8μm, strongly roughened, lemon-shaped. Under beech, fairly common on chalk. E3.

C. suberetorum R. Mre. seems intermediate between *elegantissimus* and *C. orichalceus* (p. 210) in its rather more coppery colour and lemon gills with olivaceous tinge. Not known in Britain. E1.

Cortinarius splendens Hry.
Cap 5-7cm, thin-fleshed, bright chrome yellow, centre sometimes discoloured by fawnish scales. Gills bright yellow or slightly russet. Stipe 4×1cm, bright yellow with marginate bulb 3cm across. Flesh bright yellow with an orange tinge, odourless. (KOH reaction reddish pink). Spores 11×6μm. Under beech on chalk, locally common. **Toxic** and not to be confused with yellow species of *Tricholoma*. E2.

var. *meinhardii* [*C. vitellinus*] occurring under conifers, is more robust, rather more fawn coloured with unpleasant smell. Not known in Britain. **Toxic**. E2.

Cortinarius sulphurinus Quél.
Cap 7-10cm, fleshy, sulphur yellow, paler than the above species, discolouring russet olivaceous. Gills sulphur yellow. Stipe 8×1cm, pale yellow, bulb 2cm, edged brownish. Flesh whitish, smell slight or faintly of aniseed. Spores 12×7μm. Mixed woods. Not known in Britain. E1.

Cortinarius elegantior (Fr.) Fr.
Cap 10-15cm, dingy yellow to orange fawn or olivaceous, speckled with whitish spots over the centre. Gills yellow to olive brown. Stipe 8×2cm, straw yellow with a more dingy ochraceous bulb 3cm across. Flesh pale to whitish, smell faint; KOH reaction pink. Spores 15×8μm, somewhat lemon-shaped with coarse warts. Under conifers in the mountains. Rare. Em3.

var. **quercilicis** is more fleshy, with russet-brown tinge to the cap centre or bulb and brighter yellow stipe and flesh, occurs under holm oak. Not known in Britain. sE2.

Cortinarius fulmineus (Fr.) Fr.
Cap similar to that of *C. elegantior* but more fawn, especially at the centre which is dotted with rusty remnants of the universal veil, margin bright yellow or orange, darkening to reddish brown. Gills pale yellow. Stipe 7×1cm, pale yellowish then russet with a concolorous bulb 4-5cm across. Flesh whitish to almost concolorous at the surface and in the base. Spores 9-11×6μm. Under broadleaved trees especially beech. Uncommon. E2.

C. subfulgens Orton [*C. fulgens* ss. Cke.] differs in its smooth cuticle with brighter, ± orange-fawn colours, and yellower gills. E2.

Cortinarius xanthophyllus (Cooke) Hry.
Cap 6-8cm, fleshy, a beautiful purplish lilac, discoloured ochraceous or lemon cream at the centre. Gills bright lemon yellow. Stipe 5×1.5cm, light yellow with a rather more rusty basal bulb 2-3cm across. Flesh pale to almost concolorous beneath the cuticle; KOH reaction orange red. Spores 11×6μm. Under broadleaved trees on warm calcareous soils. Rare. E2.

C. splendificus Chev. & Hry., with cap spotted purplish brown and brighter yellow stipe and flesh; KOH reaction negative. Occurs under holm oak. Not in Britain. sE 2.

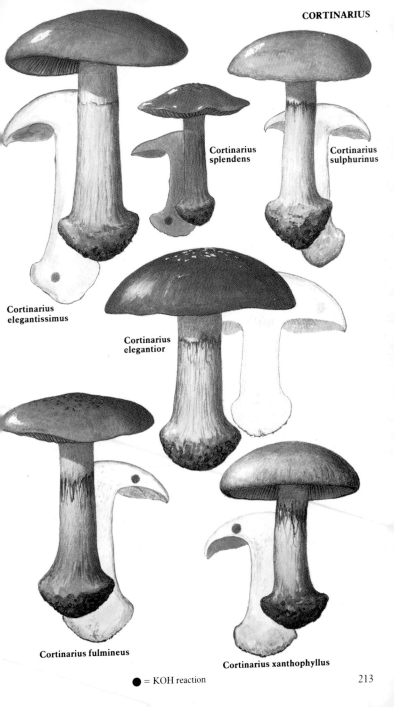

CORTINARIUS

Cortinarius
splendens

Cortinarius
sulphurinus

Cortinarius
elegantissimus

Cortinarius
elegantior

Cortinarius fulmineus

Cortinarius xanthophyllus

● = KOH reaction

213

Section *Cyanophylli*. Gills blue, lilaceous or violaceous.

Cortinarius purpurascens (Fr.) Fr.
Cap 10-15cm, fleshy, streaky-fibrillose, russet-brown to grey violet, margin sometimes bruising lilac or violet. Gills lilac, dark violet where damaged. Stipe 10×2cm,
similar colour, ± stained bright violet by rubbing, basal bulb marginate, 4cm across,
or onion-shaped in f. *largusoides*. Flesh pale or dingy lilac, smell fruity and agreeable
to nauseating; reaction to Henry's Tl-4 Reagent and iodine deep violet. Spores
10×5.5μm. Common under broadleaved trees and conifers throughout Britain.
E3. **C. porphyropus** (A.-S.) Fr. is smaller (5cm), lighter coloured, cap somewhat
ochraceous, stipe silvery amethyst. Not uncommon under birch. E2.

Cortinarius glaucopus (Sch.) Fr.
Cap 8-12cm, streaky-fibrillose, with russet on a reddish orange ground, margin
somewhat lobed, paler or olivaceous in f. *olivaceus*. Gills bluish or lilaceous. Stipe
8×2cm, slightly fibrillose, apex glaucous or vaguely bluish, bulb obtuse, 3cm across,
pale or ochraceous. Flesh pale to blue-grey in the stipe-apex. Smell earthy in var.
submagicus, ± distinct or delayed; reaction to KOH brownish, Henry's Tl-4 Reagent
negative. Spores 8×5μm, elliptical, punctate. Mainly under conifers but not exclusively so. Uncommon. E3.

Cortinarius amoenolens Hry. ex Orton [*C. cyanopus* p.p.]
Cap 10-15cm, fleshy, ochraceous with olivaceous tint, streaky or fibrillose towards
the margin. Gills violaceus blue then chocolate. Stipe 10×2cm, fleetingly bluish at
the summit, elsewhere livid ochraceous; bulb rounded, 3cm across, pale or glaucous.
Flesh white to bluish in the stipe; smell fruity but sometimes delayed, taste ± bitter
in the cuticle; KOH reaction negative. Spores 11×6μm, somewhat lemon-shaped,
very rough. Common in Britain under broadleaved trees, especially beech. E3. **C.
suaveolens** Bat. & Joach. is brighter coloured, pinkish with more distinctly marginate bulb and a strong smell of orange blossom. Rare. E1.

Cortinarius calochrous (Pers.) Fr.
Cap 5-7cm, soon expanded, yellow ochre, brighter yellow at the margin, somewhat
speckled reddish orange at the centre. Gills an attractive lilac pink or amethyst. Stipe
4×1cm, ochraceous, basal bulb whitish, 3cm across, often depressed with an acute
margin. Flesh white. Top of stipe in f. *caroli* is violaceous with lilac flesh. Smell
faint; KOH reaction indefinite. Spores 10×6μm. Common especially under beech
on calcareous soils but in Europe there is a f. *coniferarum*, rather fleshier and more
brownish yellow, under conifers. E3. **C. arquatus** (A.-S.) Fr. is more robust, cap
brighter yellow, stipe often violaceous above, bulb often fringed with volva-like
remnants of yellow veil; KOH reaction pinkish. Coniferous woods. Rare. E1.

Cortinarius sodagnitus Hry.
Cap 4-6cm, at first entirely violaceous blue, discolouring yellowish to buff from centre
outwards, fading to silvery lilac especially round the margin. Gills bright lilac. Stipe
6×1.5cm, concolorous, discolouring like the cap except at the extreme tip, bulb
small, 2.5cm across, marginate. Flesh whitish to bluish, smell faint, mild but cap
cuticle bitter; KOH reaction bright red on cuticle, negative on flesh. Spores 12×7μm,
almond to lemon-shaped, rough. Under beech, fairly common on chalk. E2. **C.
dibaphus** Fr. is rather similar but cap and flesh are both very bitter and the latter
turns rose-red with KOH. Conifer woods, doubtfully British. E2. **C. fulvoincarn-
atus** Joach. is much paler, cap ochraceous fawn mingled with flesh colour, flesh
very bitter. Not known in Britain. E1.

Cortinarius caerulescens (Sch.) Fr.
Cap 8-12cm, a beautiful blue-grey tinged a little violaceous by ± streaky radial fibrils,
discolouring from the centre to ochraceous buff, sometimes eventually entirely pale
ochre. Gills bluish. Stipe 10×2cm, concolorous, bulb marginate, 4cm across, white,
then ochraceous. Flesh bluish becoming creamy ochraceous, with faint mealy smell.
Spores 10×5.5μm. Under broadleaved trees on heavy calcareous soils. Uncommon.
E2. **C. caesiocyaneus** Britz. is deeper violaceous blue, discolouring, stipe concolorous and bulb concolorous at first. Smell sometimes earthy. Under beech on chalk.
Rather common. E2.

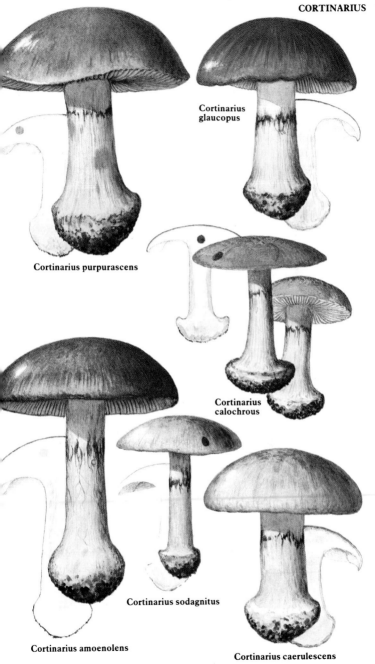

Cortinarius
glaucopus

Cortinarius purpurascens

Cortinarius
calochrous

Cortinarius sodagnitus

Cortinarius amoenolens

Cortinarius caerulescens

● = KOH reaction

Subgenus *Sericeocybe*. Cap surface silky to micaceous or punctate, somewhat greasy but neither truly viscid nor fleecy. Colours dull or bluish.

Cortinarius alboviolaceus (Pers.) Fr.
Cap 5-8cm with broad umbo often like a military "tin hat", bluish lilac, becoming paler, silky. Gills pale greyish lilac. Stipe 8×1cm, somewhat club-shaped, bluish with fleeting concolorous zones towards the base. Flesh white tinged lilac or bluish, smell slight. Spores 9×5.5µm. Under broadleaved trees, especially beech and oak. Fairly common throughout Britain. E4.

Cortinarius camphoratus (Fr.) Fr. [*C. hircinus* p.p.]
Cap 10-15cm, violaceus blue or amethyst at first, fading to a nondescript dull ochraceous with age. Gills lilaceous. Stipe 12×2cm, club-shaped to ± bulbous, similar colours becoming a little rusty at the base, not or scarcely zoned. Flesh violaceous amethyst, fading to bluish grey; smell strong, of cheese then sweaty feet, burnt horn or he-goat. Spores 11×6µm, marginal hairs ± differentiated. Under pine on acid soil, with *Sphagnum*. Rare. E2.

C. traganus (Fr.) Fr. differs mainly in its saffron yellow flesh, whitish gills and different smell, of ripe pears in var. *finitimus*, but typically of acetylene. Spores 9×5µm. Not uncommon under pine in Scotland. E2.

Cortinarius anomalus (Fr.) Fr.
Cap 5-8cm, clay-brownish with a violaceous tinge, surface typically with a micaceous sheen like a snail track and somewhat finely wrinkled, finally dull ochraceous beige. Gills notably tinged violaceous. Stipe 10×1cm, almost equal, whitish or slightly violaceous, with ochraceous ring-zones towards the base at first, more coloured in f. *lepidopus*, which is suggestive of *C. spilomeus*. Flesh pallid to almost concolorous, smell faint, sickly-sweet. Spores ± globose, 8×7µm. Very common throughout Britain under broadleaved trees and conifers, E4; f. *lepidopus* especially with birch and pine. E2.

C. azureovelatus Ort., with a more bluish tint, chiefly in the veil on the stipe, has larger spores and occurs only under conifers. E2.

Cortinarius caninus (Fr.) Fr.
Cap 7-12cm, soon expanded, surface similar to *C. anomalus* but a warmer uniform russet brown, sometimes tinged violaceous. Gills pallid or vaguely bluish to lilaceous. Stipe 10×1cm, whitish to ochraceous, sometimes tinged with violet above a simple, ± membranous, rather brownish annular zone. Flesh pallid, giving pink reaction with formalin or phenol, smell weaker than in *C. anomalus*. Spores as in *C. anomalus* or slightly larger. In grassy woodlands. Uncommon. E1 (m3).

Cortinarius pholideus (Fr.) Fr.
Cap 6-10cm, umbonate, surface typically speckled with bistre-brown scales on a russet ground. Gills violaceous, fading. Stipe 10×1cm, somewhat club-shaped, silvery to violaceous at the top, elegantly zoned with russet-bistre scales towards the base, below a well-defined annular zone. Flesh almost concolorous near the surface; faint, pleasant smell of tangerines. Spores 8×6µm, short-elliptical. Under oak and especially birch on heaths and moors. Common throughout Britain. E2.

Cortinarius spilomeus (Fr.) Berk.
Cap 4-6cm, rather thin-fleshed, soon expanded, surface similar to *C. anomalus* but margin typically speckled with remnants of a reddish universal veil. Gills reddish violaceous. Stipe 8×0.8cm, zoned or speckled towards the base with saffron or blood red on a pale ground which may be lilaceous, especially near the top. Flesh colour similar, smell not distinctive. Spores 8×5.5µm, short-elliptical, faintly punctate. Under spruce, pine and birch on heaths. Uncommon. E1.

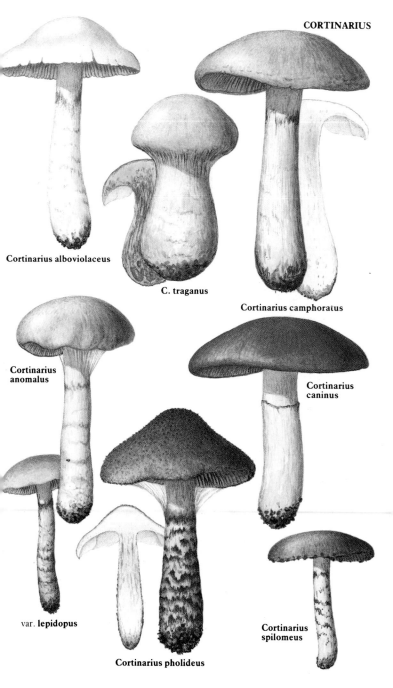

CORTINARIUS

Cortinarius alboviolaceus

C. traganus

Cortinarius camphoratus

Cortinarius
anomalus

Cortinarius
caninus

var. **lepidopus**

Cortinarius pholideus

Cortinarius
spilomeus

Subgenus *Telamonia*. [including *Hydrocybe*]. Hygrophanous fungi with stipe finely zoned or naked.

Section *Firmiores*. Rather robust stature with stipe over 1cm thick; colours dull, dingy or violaceous.

Cortinarius torvus (Fr.) Fr.
Cap 6-10cm, slightly fibrillose, russet brown fading to livid ochraceous or greyish. Gills broad, rather distant, ochraceous to lilaceous grey. Stipe 9×1.5cm, rather club-shaped, summit somewhat violaceous, lower part sheathed by a pallid or brownish "stocking" with an almost annulate upper edge, rarely breaking apart into wreaths. Flesh almost concolorous with weak aromatic smell like camphor. Spores 10×6μm. Under various broadleaved trees. Common, especially with beech and oak, throughout Britain. E4.

Cortinarius evernius (Fr.) Fr.
Cap rather umbonate, 6-10cm, margin slightly notched, surface silky, a beautiful ± purplish reddish brown, fading to greyish yellow. Gills distant, ochraceous to somewhat amethyst. Stipe elongated, 13×1cm, spindle-shaped, violaceous but fading, silky, slightly zoned, more strongly in var. *pseudoscutulatus*. Flesh violaceous in apex of stipe, whitish elsewhere, smell of runner beans. Spores 10×6μm. Under conifers on mossy ground or in *Sphagnum*. Rare, though not uncommon in Scotland. E2.

C. bicolor Cke. differs in its smaller, obtusely convex cap and nearly equal almost naked stipe. E2.

Cortinarius brunneus (Pers.) Fr.
Cap 6-12cm, abruptly umbonate, finely fibrillose, dark sepia brown, sometimes tinged violet or blackish. Gills broad, thick and distant, surface veined, colour similar. Stipe 12×2cm, concolorous or with one or two whitish annular zones. Flesh colour similar, smell faint rather like *C. torvus*. Spores 10×6μm. Under conifers in damp places, especially in the Highlands. E2.

Cortinarius hinnuleus Fr.
Cap 5-8cm, umbonate, rather bright yellowish fawn, fading to ochre along radial stripes. Gills distant, concolorous. Stipe 10×1cm, similar colour with a median ± membranous paler ring. Flesh cream to russet, smell strong and earthy. Spores 8×6μm. Under various broadleaved trees. Common. E3.

Cortinarius privignus (Fr.) Fr.
Cap 5-8cm, relatively bright fawn colour but fading to dull ochraceous, margin often bearing silvery fibrils. Gills rusty ochre with pale edges. Stipe 10×1cm, swollen at the base, whitish, rarely tinged violet at the apex, with an indistinct or fleeting whitish sheath below. Spores 9×5μm. Under various broadleaved trees. This is representative of a group of little understood species difficult to distinguish. E2.

Cortinarius laniger Fr.
Aspect of *C. privignus* or stouter (10-15cm), at first with abundant fleecy white remnants of the universal veil on a russet ground. Gills a striking bright cinnamon-russet with reddish tinge. Stipe 12×4cm, ± bulbous, with rather fleecy white zones on a brownish ground. Flesh pallid to concolorous. Spores 10×5.5μm. Under conifers. Rare. E1 (m2).

Cortinarius duracinus Fr.
Cap convex or slightly umbonate, 5-10cm, reddish brown to russet, fading to whitish, with paler silky margin. Gills pale russet with paler rather toothed edges. Stipe 12×1.5cm, typically tapered to the base or somewhat rooting, white and naked. Flesh white, hard, smell somewhat of iodine. Spores 10×5μm. Under broadleaved trees. Uncommon. E2.·

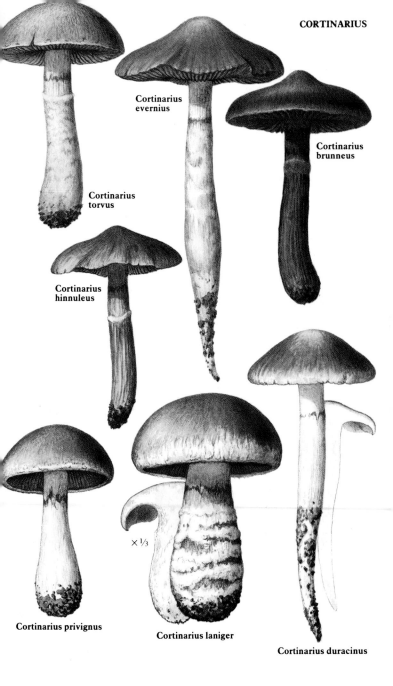

CORTINARIUS

Cortinarius
evernius

Cortinarius
brunneus

Cortinarius
torvus

Cortinarius
hinnuleus

Cortinarius
privignus

× ⅓

Cortinarius laniger

Cortinarius duracinus

Section *Armillati*. Stipe ± red or girdled reddish.

Cortinarius armillatus (A.-S.) Fr.
Cap 8-12cm, fleshy, slightly fibrillose or shaggy like a *Leprocybe* (p. 222), russet fawn to brick colour, fading only slightly, sometimes fringed at the margin with traces of a red veil. Gills russet. Stipe 12×1.5cm, almost cylindrical, russet, decorated with somewhat oblique bright red wreaths of the veil. Flesh pallid, odourless. Spores 11×7μm. Under broadleaved trees on acid soils, with beech, oak and especially birch throughout Britain. Fairly common. E4.

C. veregregius Hry. is similar, with dull pink wreaths on a pale ground. E1.

Cortinarius bulliardii (Pers.) Fr.
Cap 6-8cm, fleshy, smooth, bright chestnut brown, drying livid brownish. Gills tinged lilac then brick russet colour. Stipe 7×1cm, club-shaped or ± bulbous, bright reddish orange (red lead) colour then vinaceous russet at the base, whitish or sometimes lilaceous above. Flesh pallid to lilac-russet; KOH reaction vinaceous on the red areas. Spores 9×5.5μm. Under broadleaved trees on calcareous soils. Uncommon. E2-3.

C. colus Fr., with a pinker stipe, is more slender. Under conifers. Rare. E1.

Section *Tenuiores*. Slender fungi or with an elongated stipe 0.2-0.5cm thick; colours dull or lilaceous to rather pinkish but never bright red.

Cortinarius decipiens (Pers.) Fr.
Cap 3-6cm, dull russet brown, fading to dingy brownish, slightly fibrillose or silvery towards the margin. Gills ochraceous. Stipe 7×0.4cm, with a fleeting bluish lilac tint at the apex, elsewhere brownish grey, watered with silky zones. Flesh almost concolorous, smell faint, but strong and earthy in var. *graveolens*. Spores 10×6μm, marginal hairs wavy or clavate. Under various broadleaved trees. Common. E3.

C. pulchripes Favre, with stipe and flesh blue-violet and ± wreathed with the veil, occurs in wet woods. Not known in Britain. E2.

Cortinarius paleaceus (Weinm.) Fr.
Cap 2-4cm, grey bistre under a veil dotted with evanescent whitish spangles. Gills brownish grey. Stipe 5×0.2cm, pale ochre, wreathed with whitish fibrils, darker at the base. Flesh similar colour with distinctive smell of pelargonium or withered roses. Spores 8x5μm. Under conifers and broadleaved trees, especially birch. Very common. E4.

C. hemitrichus (Pers.) Fr. has a similar aspect, cap and gills paler, with similar fibrillose spangles, but has no smell. Equally common under birch. E3.

Cortinarius helvelloides (Fr.) Fr.
Cap 2-4cm, slightly umbonate, fibrillosely scaly, brownish grey with an olivaceous tinge, margin flecked with yellow. Gills distant or thick, violet grey-brown. Stipe 8×0.4cm, concolorous with the cap and wreathed with fleeting yellowish remnants of the veil, sometimes tinged violaceous above. Flesh similar colour. Spores 10×6μm. Under alder. Common. E3.

C. alnetorum (Vel.) Moser, also under alders, differs in its dirty or obscure colours and white veil on cap and stipe. E2

Cortinarius obtusus (Fr.) Fr.
Cap 3-5cm, convex or obtusely umbonate, russet brown to fawnish ochre, fading greatly on drying, to almost creamy white. Gills pale ochraceous. Stipe spindle-shaped or rooting, 5×0.5cm, whitish, smooth. Flesh pallid or ochraceous with a smell of iodine or phenol. Spores 9×5μm. Often under conifers. Common. E3.

C. acutus (Pers.) Fr. is smaller with a pointed umbo and striate margin, very common in damp places; E2. **C. eustriatulus** Hry., intermediate to *C. obtusus*, is common in muddy spruce plantations. E2.

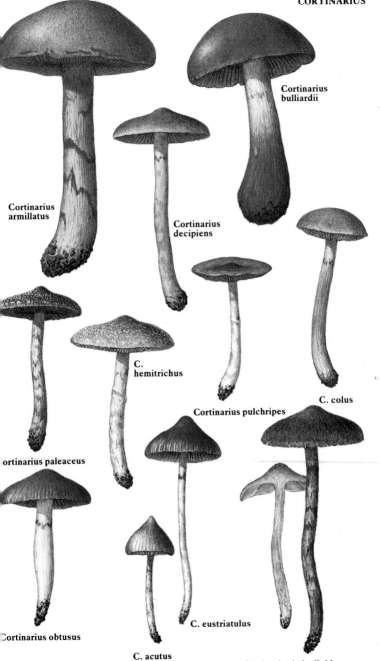

Cortinarius
bulliardii

Cortinarius
armillatus

Cortinarius
decipiens

C.
hemitrichus

Cortinarius paleaceus

Cortinarius pulchripes

C. colus

Cortinarius obtusus

C. eustriatulus

C. acutus

Cortinarius helvelloides

221

Subgenus *Cortinarius*. Cap surface velvety-scaly, dark violaceous with vacuolar pigment and distinctive cystidia.

Cortinarius violaceus (L.) Fr.
Cap 10-15cm, fleshy umbonate, fibrillosely scaly, a striking dark violet colour fading to dark violaceous brown. Gills concolorous, ± distant. Stipe 12×2cm, club-shaped to bulbous, similar colour, fibrillose, with a fleeting woolly violet cortina. Flesh mottled violet with faint smell of cedar wood; KOH reaction red. Spores 15×8µm. Under beech and birch. Rare. E3. **C. hercynicus** (Pers.) Moser is slightly less robust, more bluish, with shorter, rounded spores; under conifers in the mountains. Not known in Britain. E2.

Subgenus *Leprocybe*. Surface velvety to ± fleecy or scaly; colours greenish to yellow, orange or fawnish. Cuticular hyphae 10-20µm wide, pigmentation mixed, somewhat fluorescent.

Cortinarius melanotus Kalchbr.
Cap 3-5cm, slightly umbonate, with fine dark olivaceous scales on a greenish ground. Gills greenish then dark olivaceous. Stipe 6×0.8cm, equal, greenish, zoned with dark olive-brown fibrils up to a well defined ring zone. Flesh greenish to dingy yellow; smell aromatic, rather like parsley, or earthy. Spores 7×5µm. Under broad-leaved trees but not British. E2.

C. venetus (Fr.) Fr. has a more felted surface, more yellow-green colouring, tinged orange russet in var. *montanus*, stalk only slightly decorated with scales towards the base or lacking the ring zone and only a slight smell. Under beech. Rare. E2.

Cortinarius betuletorum (Moser) Moser
Cap 4-6cm, slightly fleshy, dull olivaceous grey-brown, fibrillose. Gills dingy olivaceous brown, thick or distant. Stipe 8×0.5cm, similar colour, with fleeting zonation. Flesh dingy olive brown, odourless. Spores ± globose, 7×6µm. Under birch. Common. E2. **C. valgus** Fr. with violaceous apex to the stipe and spores 9×7µm occurs under various broadleaved trees. Rare, not in Britain. E1.

Cortinarius limonius (Fr.) Fr.
Cap 6-10cm, convex to slightly umbonate, surface quite smooth for this subgenus and slightly hygrophanous, hence the species is sometimes put under *Telamonia* (p. 218), orange-yellow or russet fading to lemon yellow towards the centre. Gills russet yellow, rather distant. Stipe 10×2cm, fleecy-fibrillose, not wreathed, concolorous, browning at the base. Flesh somewhat yellow to orange, smell slight but fruity. Spores 8×6µm. Under conifers in damp places, spruce woods with bilberries. Uncommon but reported from the Highlands. E1.

C. callisteus (Fr.) Fr. has a club-shaped stipe, a more scurfy-scaly cap surface, and a curious smell described as that of (steam) railway engine smoke or of cold mashed potato. E2.

Cortinarius humicola (Quél.) R. Mre.
Cap 5-8cm, somewhat umbonate, yellow with russet scales, shaggy like some *Pholiota* species. Gills well spaced, ochraceous yellow. Stipe 8×0.8cm, rather spindle-shaped or rooting, smooth and pale above, concolorous below where it bears horizontal rows of well-defined scales. Flesh pale, odourless. Spores 10×6µm. Under broadleaved trees on calcareous soils. Not common. E3.

Cortinarius saniosus (Fr.) Fr.
Cap 2-4cm, rather thin-fleshed, soon expanded or with a narrow umbo, fawnish orange to rather rusty, margin at first somewhat yellow-appendiculate. Gills russet ochre, well spaced. Stipe 5×0.4cm, almost equal, concolorous with some fleeting yellowish scales. Flesh concolorous, odourless. Spores 9×5.5µm, elliptical. Under broadleaved trees often in wet places, such as under willows. Common. E3.

C. gentilis (Fr.) Fr. is scarcely more fleshy, rather orange-yellow, with distant gills and better defined garlands round the stipe. Spores shorter and broader, 8×6.5µm. Among bilberries in pine woods and spruce plantations. Uncommon. E2.

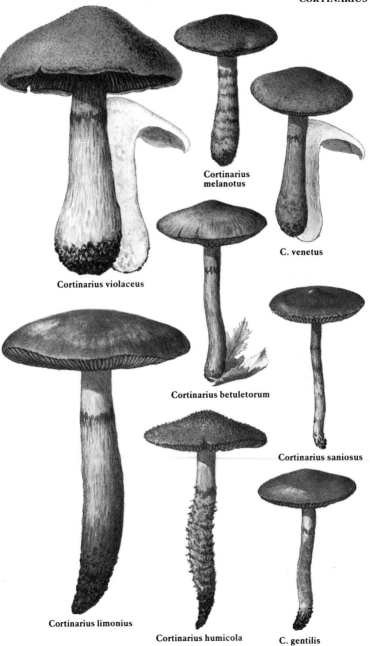

Cortinarius
melanotus

C. venetus

Cortinarius violaceus

Cortinarius betuletorum

Cortinarius saniosus

Cortinarius limonius

Cortinarius humicola

C. gentilis

223

Cortinarius orellanus Fr.
Cap 7-10cm, soon expanded, fleecy-fibrillose to nearly smooth, fawnish orange. Gills distant, orange to bright rusty cinnamon. Stipe 10×1cm, tapered at the base, golden yellow, slightly russet at the base, with no trace of a basal veil. Flesh yellowish, smell slight, ± of radish. Spores 11×6.5μm, almond-shaped. Under broadleaved trees in warm places. Rare. **Deadly poisonous**. E2. **C. orellanoides** Hry. is more umbonate, stipe club-shaped, more rusty, slightly zoned, spores shorter and broader, 10×8μm. Under beech. Rare. **Deadly poisonous**. E2.

Cortinarius speciosissimus K.-R.
Cap 6-12cm, conical or with a rather pointed umbo, orange-brown to reddish, fleecy-fibrillose. Gills thick, rather distant, concolorous. Stipe 8×1.5cm, varying from clavate to slightly spindle-shaped or ± rooting, somewhat wreathed with yellowish fibrils on a russet ground. Flesh orange yellow, smell faint, somewhat of radish. Spores 9×7μm. Under conifers on acid soils, often moors with *Sphagnum*. Rare. **Deadly poisonous**. E2.

Cortinarius bolaris (Pers.) Fr.
Cap 6-8cm, covered with appressed somewhat circular vinaceous red or brick coloured scales on a yellowish or yellowing ground, eventually coppery. Gills clay colour. Stipe 8×1μm, slightly zoned with fine scales coloured as on the cap, on a pale yellow ground, eventually entirely reddish at the base, mycelium saffron. Flesh pale, yellowing in the base, smell faint, peppery, taste slightly bitter. Spores 8×6μm, broadly elliptical. Under beech, birch, oak, occasionally conifers. Quite common. Edibility suspect. E4.

C. rubicundulus (Rea) Pears. [*C. pseudobolaris*]
Entirely yellow ochre at first, fibrillose, becoming reddish brown when bruised but without well-defined scales. Spores narrowly almond-shaped, 8.5×4.5μm. Under birch and oak. Uncommon. E3.

Subgenus *Dermocybe*. Cap felted to fleecy, colours often bright, especially in the gills. Pigments anthraquinones, reaction to bases very bright, marginal cystidia present. Section *Sanguinei*. Gills red.

Cortinarius sanguineus (Wulf.) Fr.
Cap 2-5cm, felted fibrillose to silky, uniformly blood red. Gills bright red or iridescent carmine. Stipe 5×0.4 cm, concolorous, with red cortina and orange base. Flesh vinaceous pink. Inodorous. Spores 8×4.5μm, marginal cystidia septate. Ubiquitous under conifers and broadleaved trees (but British authors distinguish the form under the latter as *C. puniceus* Orton). Edibility suspect. E3.

Cortinarius cinnabarinus (Fr.) Fr.
Cap 6-8cm, fleshy, surface matt or felted, bright red lead colour, hygrophanous, drying brownish orange. Gills ± distant, concolorous. Stipe 7×0.8cm, smooth or silky-zoned, concolorous. Flesh bright brick orange, almost odourless. Spores 10×6μm, marginal cystidia elongated clavate. Under beech and hornbeam. Uncommon. Edibility suspect. E2.

Cortinarius semisanguineus (Fr.) Gill.
Cap 5-8cm, convex or umbonate, fibrillosely scaly, pale brownish fawn or tinged olivaceous ochre. Gills blood red. Stipe 7×0.6cm, yellowish, seldom tinged reddish at the base. Flesh yellow ochre to orange towards the base, smell faint, of radish or iodine. Spores 8×5μm, marginal cells inconspicuous, clavate. Mainly under birch and conifers. Common throughout Britain. Edibility suspect. E4. **C. phoeniceus** (Bull.) R. Mre. is a little more fleshy, yellowish, tinged with red round the margin and with red fibrils on the base of the stipe. Under birch and pine. Uncommon. E2.

Cortinarius purpureobadius Karst. [*C. anthracinus* p.p.]
Cap 3-6cm, silky fibrillose, centre almost smooth, dark purplish brown with carmine pink margin. Gills orange carmine. Stipe 6×0.5cm, almost equal, somewhat wreathed with carmine fibrils on an orange-pink ground, base brownish. Flesh similar colours. Spores 8×4μm, marginal cells inconspicuous. Mainly under birch. Uncommon. Edibility suspect. E2.

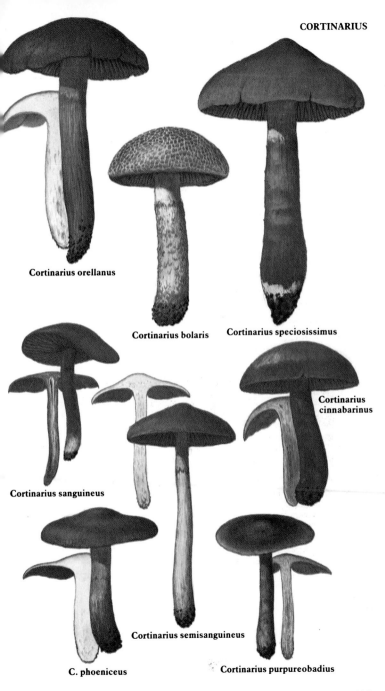

Cortinarius orellanus

Cortinarius bolaris

Cortinarius speciosissimus

Cortinarius cinnabarinus

Cortinarius sanguineus

Cortinarius semisanguineus

C. phoeniceus

Cortinarius purpureobadius

Section *Dermocybe* [*Cinnamomei*]. Gills yellow, orange or greenish but not red.

Cortinarius cinnamomeus (L.) Fr.
Cap 4-7cm, convex or broadly umbonate, russet brown with ochraeous or olivaceous tints. Gills bright orange. Stipe 8×0.8cm, yellowish or tinged olivaceous, sometimes with brownish zones. Flesh bright yellow, duller in the base. Smell slight, of turnip. Spores 8×4.5µm, marginal cells clavate. Under conifers, especially spruce, and birch. Common. E2.

C. croceus (Sch.) Høil. has pale saffron gills, browner-olive cap and smell of iodine. E1.

Cortinarius malicorius Fr.
Cap 3-5cm, bright fawnish, sometimes tinged olivaceous, darker at the centre, more orange at the margin. Gills saffron orange. Stipe 5×0.8cm, rather thickset, 6×1cm, wreathed with an orange cortina on an olivaceous ground. Flesh olive yellow to greenish in the cap, odourless. Spores narrow, subfusiform, 7×4µm. Damp coniferous woods and under alders. Not uncommon in the north. E2.

Cortinarius cinnamomeoluteus Orton.
Cap 5-7cm, slightly umbonate, reddish fawn to olive-brown with ± yellow margin. Gills bright yellow then olive fawn, sometimes saffron. Stipe 8×0.8cm, lemon yellow, naked, or wreathed purplish in var. *porphyrovelatus*. Flesh yellow with slight smell of turnip or iodine. Spores 8×5µm, marginal cystidia narrow, seldom septate. Ubiquitous under broadleaved trees of all kinds. E3.

Cortinarius cinnamomeobadius Hry.
Cap 3-6cm, uniformly chestnut brown, fibrillose. Gills dull fawnish orange. Stipe 6×0.7cm, yellowish brown to fawnish, almost smooth. Flesh yellow, odourless. Spores and marginal cells as in *C. cinnamomeoluteus*. Common, especially under conifers and on heaths. E2.

C. pratensis (Bon & Gaugué) Høil. has a more russet cap and stipe and occurs in lawns and woodland glades; marginal cells articulated like branches of an *Opuntia*. E1.

Cortinarius uliginosus Berk.
Cap 6-10cm, silky, rather bright brick red becoming coppery or mahogany colour. Gills lemon to rusty orange. Stipe 10×0.8cm, apex yellow, base orange, sometimes wreathed with a reddish cortina. Flesh yellow, or russet towards the base. Spores 10×6µm, marginal cystidia septate. Muddy ground under willows and alder. Common. E2.

Cortinarius schaefferi Bres. [*C. olivaceofuscus*]
Cap 4-6cm, fibrillose, russet brown or bronze with a more olivaceous margin. Gills greenish olive. Stipe 5×0.5cm, similar colour. Flesh olive-brown, smell and taste of turnip. Spores 8×4.5µm, marginal cystidia septate. Copses under broadleaved trees, especially hornbeam. Not known in Britain. E2.

Cortinarius palustris (Moser) Nezd.
Cap 5-8cm, greenish brown, slightly fleecy, becoming smooth and bronze or dingy olivaceous. Gill colour similar. Stipe 15×0.5cm, concolorous, ± wreathed with rust coloured cortina. Flesh olivaceous or yellow-brown, smell faint. Spores 9×5µm, marginal cells narrow and elongated. In *Sphagnum*. E2.

C. sphagnogenus (Moser) Nespiak, also in *Sphagnum*, is more russet, with stipe and gills more yellow at first. E3.

NOTE. Subgenus *Dermocybe* is often treated at generic level; hence the names *Dermocybe sanguinea*, *D. cinnamomea* etc.

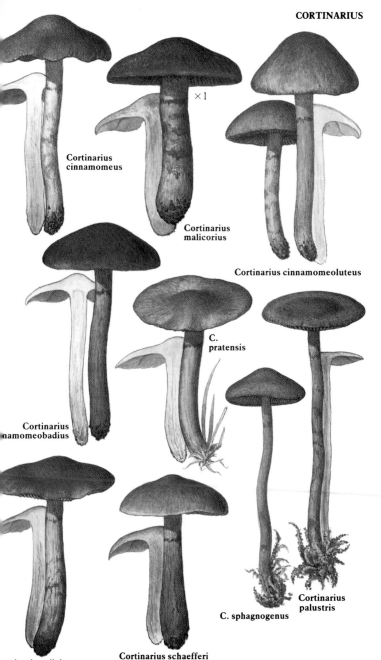

Cortinarius cinnamomeus

×1

Cortinarius malicorius

Cortinarius cinnamomeoluteus

Cortinarius cinnamomeobadius

C. pratensis

C. sphagnogenus

Cortinarius palustris

Cortinarius uliginosus

Cortinarius schaefferi

Genus *Hebeloma*. Caps usually viscid, with dull colours, brownish to whitish. Spores pinkish brown, gills typically milky coffee coloured; spores rough, cystidia on gill edge only.

Section *Denudata*. Without a cortina. Gills sometimes weeping, or with droplets.

Hebeloma crustuliniforme (Bull.) Quél.
Cap 6-10cm, viscid, clay colour to russet brown with paler margin. Gills brownish grey or pinkish clay colour, with opalescent marginal droplets. Stipe 6×1cm, slightly club-shaped, whitish, powdery-pruinose above. Flesh pallid to nearly concolorous; smell of radish, taste rather bitter. Spores 11×6μm, almond-shaped, punctate; marginal cystidia clavate. Under broadleaved trees, very common. Not edible. E4.

H. ochroalbidum Bohus, found under poplar, is more whitish or livid ochraceous, almost devoid of smell and taste, and the only reputed edible member of the genus. Not known in Britain. E2.

Hebeloma leucosarx Orton
Cap 4-7cm, thin-fleshed, pinkish-buff or pale ochraceous-tawny, with ± velvety whitish margin. Gills remaining pale, edged with clear droplets. Stipe 5×0.7cm, whitish, almost naked. Flesh white throughout with faint smell of radish or chocolate.Taste almost mild. Spores 13×7μm, almond-shaped, rugose; cystidia elongated, clavate. Damp places. Common. E3.

H. pusillum Lange, more slender, with browner disk, occurs under willows.

Hebeloma sacchariolens Quél.
Cap 4-7cm, dingy brownish grey or dull ochraceous, eventually stained with russet, viscid or just smooth, rarely velvety (var. *tomentosum*). Gills pale, ± distant, broader at the middle, margin not weeping. Stipe 6×0.5cm, similar colour, fibrillose, fragile. Flesh beige, brownish in the base; smell strong, aromatic, of orange blossom or amyl acetate. Spores 16×9μm, ± fusiform, rugose; marginal cystidia clavate. Damp woods and ditches. Common. E3.

Hebeloma anthracophilum R. Mre.
Cap 4-8cm, fleshy, viscid, centre dark fawnish brown, margin pale beige. Gills dingy beige, not weeping. Stipe 5×0.7cm, almost equal, whitish, fibrillosely striate, very tough and flexible: can be bent without snapping. Flesh pale, browning, smell slight, pleasant. Spores 12×6μm, obtuse, warted; cystidia cylindrical. On burnt ground and charcoal. Uncommon. E2.

Hebeloma sinapizans (Paul.) Gill.
Cap 8-15cm, fleshy, rather lobed or lumpy, surface barely viscid, bright fawn or yellowish russet becoming progressively paler to the margin. Gills pinkish grey to cinnamon, edge not weeping. Stipe 10×1.5cm, strong, base bulbous and 2-3cm thick, whitish, somewhat clothed with horizontal scales, hollow with a hanging wick in the upper part. Flesh pallid, strong smell of radish, taste bitter. Spores 14×8μm, coarsely warted, apically papillate; cystidia bottle-shaped, short or thickset. Under broadleaved trees. Common. Edibility suspect. E4.

H. truncatum (Sch.) Kumm. is smaller, more rufous and the stipe is smoother and neither bulbous nor hollow. E2.

Hebeloma edurum Métrod ex Bon [*H. senescens*]
Similar in stature to *H. sinapizans*, cap more dull beige colour or dingy ochraceous with margin finally somewhat notched. Gills pale clay beige, edge not weeping. Stipe 10×2cm, slightly club-shaped, fibrillosely scaly with hint of a cortina at first, beige to whitish, browning at the base. Flesh similar colour, smell fruity, of pear mingled with chocolate, then nauseous. Spores 10×6μm, scarcely warted; cystidia clavate or enlarged above. Grassy places under pines especially on calcareous soil, less often under broadleaved trees. Occasional in Britain. E3.

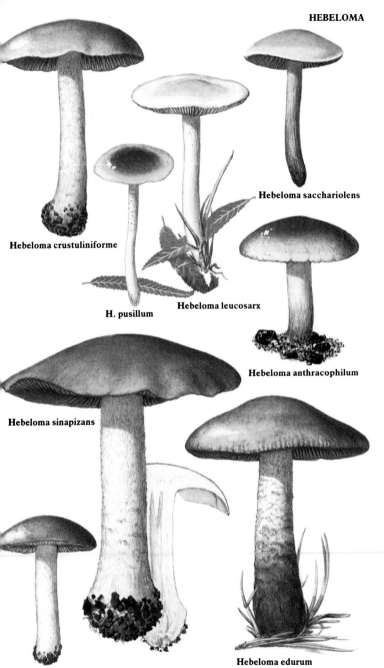

Hebeloma crustuliniforme

H. pusillum

Hebeloma leucosarx

Hebeloma sacchariolens

Hebeloma anthracophilum

Hebeloma sinapizans

Hebeloma edurum

Hebeloma truncatum

Section *Hebeloma* [*Indusiata*]. Stipe with a cortina. Gills without droplets.

Hebeloma mesophaeum (Pers.) Quél.
Cap 5-8cm with low umbo, typically two colours, reddish brown at the centre which is viscid, pale beige at the margin which is fibrillose, often bearing a halo of remnants of a silvery to yellowish veil. Gills normal for the section. Stipe 8×0.6cm, fleecy-fibrillose by the extended greyish white cortina covering a bistre ground, exposed on rubbing, especially towards the base. Flesh similar colour, smell faintly of radish or fruit, taste becoming bitter. Spores 10×6μm, elliptical and almost smooth; cystidia flask-shaped. Under broadleaved trees, especially birch. Very common. E4.

H. strophosum (Fr.) Sacc. has more uniformly coloured cap with an almost membranous cortina forming a ring-zone. E2.

Hebeloma cylindrosporum Romagn. [*H. spoliatum* p.p.]
Cap 5-7cm, with low umbo, cuticle glossy, lacquered when dry, a beautiful reddish brown, sometimes tinged with orange and then rather ochraceous towards the margin. Gills dingy milky coffee colour with white edge. Stipe 8×0.8cm, stiff, tapered to the base, rooting in var. *pseudoradicatum*, whitish, base coloured like the cap. Flesh colour similar, smell and taste not distinctive. Spores somewhat cylindrical, 10×5μm, finely punctate; cystidia cylindrical. Under pine on sandy soils in France. Uncommon. E1. **H. porphyrosporum** R. Mre. has uniformly pinkish ochre cap and gills tinged lilaceous; smell faintly of radish or chocolate, sometimes sweet. Southern. Not known in Britain. sE2.

Section *Myxocybe*. Stipe with a sheathing ring.

Hebeloma radicosum (Bull.) Ricken
Cap 8-12cm, fleshy, brownish cream, very viscid to glutinous, with remnants of the veil round the margin. Gills pallid, clay colour. Stipe 12×1.5cm, swollen at the base and prolonged into a darker root, elsewhere concolorous or whitish with a torn dingy beige ring and concolorous scaly remnants of the veil towards the base. Flesh pale with distinct smell of bitter almonds (frangipani). Spores 10×6μm, almond-shaped, warted; cystidia somewhat capitate. Under broadleaved trees, often round stumps and animal workings, and attached to buried wood. Common. E4.

Genus *Naucoria* [*Alnicola*]. Slender fungi, mostly in swamps.

Naucoria escharoides (Fr.) Kumm.
Cap 2-4cm, fleecy-fibrillose, dull russet brown fading to pale ochraceous. Gills dingy clay-ochre. Stipe 6×0.3cm, pale, browning at the base, fibrillosely silky or with traces of a cortina. Flesh colour similar, odourless and tasteless. Spores 11×5.5μm, almond-shaped with a tapered tip, rough; cystidia flask-shaped with a slender neck. Under alder. Very common. E4. **N. subconspersa** Kuhn., equally common under alder and willow, has a date-brown cap with paler striate margin and dark brown stipe; spores 8-10×5μm. This has been confused with *N. scolecina* (Fr.) Quél. which is rare in Britain. E2.

Naucoria bohemica Vel.
Cap 3-5cm, obtusely campanulate or umbonate, dark slightly reddish brown, fading to chocolate, matt or wrinkled, margin finely striate. Gills russet-ochre. Stipe 6×0.4cm, fibrillosely silky, silvery white, brownish when rubbed. Flesh concolorous, smell and taste not distinctive. Spores 14×7.5μm, broadly lemon-shaped, rough, basidia 2-spored; clamp connections absent, cystidia cylindrical-clavate. Boggy ground under alder, birch and willow. Common. E3. **N. celluloderma** Orton has an ochraceous cap, whitish at the margin, stipe reddish brown below, similar spores and cystidia but abundant clamp connections. Strictly under alder. Fairly common. E1. There are a dozen more British species in this group, all superficially much alike and impossible to separate without critical microscopic study.

Rozites caperata (Pers.) Karst.
Cap 8-12cm, convex or humped, surface radially finely wrinkled, yellowish ochre or pale golden, with rather silvery cobwebby veil covering the centre. Gills pale then clay colour, sometimes tinged lilaceous, margin finely toothed. Stipe 10×1cm, cylindrical to slightly spindle-shaped, whitish with a narrow striate ring. Flesh pale, odourless. Spores 12×8.5μm, punctate. Fairly common under birch and pine in the Highlands, very rare in England. E3.

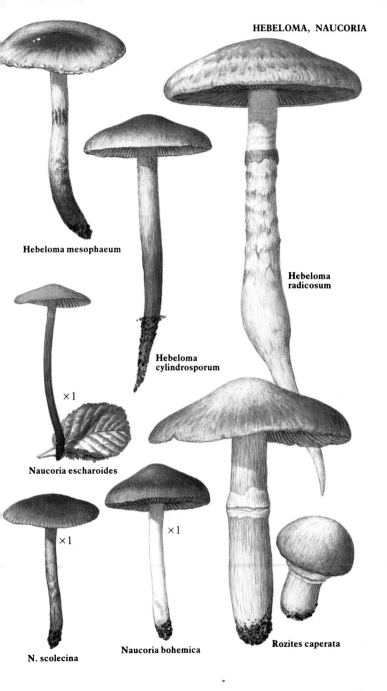

Hebeloma mesophaeum

Hebeloma
radicosum

Hebeloma
cylindrosporum

×1

Naucoria escharoides

×1

×1

Rozites caperata

N. scolecina

Naucoria bohemica

Genus *Inocybe*. Cap often conical or surface fibrillosely fleecy to streaky then splitting; spore print and gills dingy beige to tobacco brown. Many toxic species containing muscarin.

Key to *Inocybe* – principal species

In nearly every case the determination should be confirmed by microscopic examination, but observation with a good hand lens is still quite helpful, especially on the surface characters of the stipe. It is important to collect specimens taking great care not to rub the stipe between the fingers, and to ensure that the base of the stipe is secured intact with any bulb that may be present. The pruina of the stipe and the presence of a bulb are often decisive characters.

1a   Cap convex or not umbonate or with a fleecy surface, shaggy enough to recall some *Pholiota* species: **2**

1b   Cap conical, height = width, or distinctly umbonate, sometimes finally with just a simple low umbo surrounded by a shallow furrow, due to upcurving of the cap margin: **7**

2a   Cap surface felted to appressed scurfy tomentosely fibrillose or almost smooth, russet coloured; stipe with a cortina or garlanded: **3**

2b   Cap surface fleecy-hairy or ruffled to slightly scaly; stipe often concolorous or of similar nature to the cap: **4**

3a   Rusty brown to yellowish fawn or whitish, smell faint or earthy, taste becoming bitter ≫   section *Depauperatae*, 234

3b   Colour beige, stipe white, bloomed at the apex ≫   see *I. flocculosa*, 240

3c   Colour white, reddening ≫   see *I. pudica*, 236

4a   Smell distinctive, balmy fruity or earthy; sometimes reddening ≫   section *Cervicolores*, 234
    (If cap with appressed scales and earthy smell see *I. terrigena*, 234)

4b   Smell merely fungoid or spermatic: **5**

5a   Stipe slightly tomentose without ring zones, base browning ≫   *I. lacera*, 238

5b   Stipe ± garlanded or sheathed: **6**

5c   Stipe pruinose throughout; small fungi, 1-2cm; spores gibbous or stellate ≫   section *Petiginosae*, 242

6a   Cap pale beige, surface hairy ≫   *I. hystrix*, 238

6b   Darker coloured ≫   *I. lanuginosa*, 242

7a   Stipe with a distinct basal bulb, sometimes marginate: **8**

7b   Stipe equal or slightly club-shaped without a distinct bulb: **14**

8a   Stipe not pruinose, sometimes floccose but without fine pruina: **9**

8b   Stipe pruinose throughout: **10**

9a   Colour rather yellowish ochraceous, smell of honey ≫   *I. cookei*, 234

9b   Colour dark brownish ≫   group of *I. umbrina*, 242

10a   Pale, whitish at first, bruising or handled bright reddish ≫   *I. godeyi*, 236

10b   Yellowish to brownish grey, chestnut brown etc, cap surface streaking to splitting radially; spores gibbous; section *Marginatae*: **11**

11a   Stipe russet to reddish; cap chestnut, markedly radiately striped or splitting, spores stellate ≫   *I. asterospora*, 242

11b   Stipe somewhat pink or pinkish ochre: **12**

11c   Stipe white, gills tinged greyish, sometime violaceous grey: **13**

12a   Cap veiled, stipe ochraceous-vinaceous when wiped ≫   *I. decipiens*, 242

12b   Cap naked; stipe bright pink ≫   *I. oblectabilis*, rare: not described here.

13a   Cap 4-5cm, rather dull ochraceous ≫   *I. praetervisa*, 242

13b   Cap 2-3cm, brighter yellow ≫   *I. mixtilis*, 242

14a Lilaceous or violet colours present ≫ section *Lilacinae*, 238
(If cap is nearly smooth with yellow centre see *I. geophylla* var. *lilacina*, 240)
14b Fungus reddening, when cut or rubbed ≫ see p. 236
14c No colour change apart from browning or russet-vinaceous on a rubbed stipe; flesh sometimes mottled pinkish: **15**

15a Stipe not pruinose, sometimes slightly floccose but without fine pruina even at the apex: **16**
15b Stipe pruinose wholly or in part: **23**

16a Smell strong, balmy fruity or aromatic: **17**
16b Smell ordinary or spermatic: **20**

17a Cap greenish at the centre ≫ *I. corydalina*, 236
17b Without green centre: **18**

18a Smell of ripe pears; cap pale ochraceous russet ≫ *I. fraudans*, 236
18b Smell different; darker brown: **19**

19a Cap chestnut brown, smell somewhat like truffles ≫ *I. maculata*, 234
19b Cap greyer, smell or pelargonium. Alpine ≫ *I. geraniodora*, not described here

20a Cap with whitish veil over the centre: **21**
20b Cap with the centre not veiled: **22**
20c Cap a little scurfy to fleecy or ruffled: **24**

21a Disk whitish, stipe slender or twisted ≫ *I. abjecta*, 238
21b Disk greyish, stipe stiffer or pinkish ≫ *I. griseovelata*, 238

22a Cap with dark centre like *Hebeloma mesophaeum* ≫ *I. phaeodisca*, 238
22b Cap uniform colour: **23**

23a Straw yellow, gills tinged olivaceous, edge floccose ≫ *I. fastigiata*, 234
23b Fawnish brown ≫ *I. microspora*, not described here

24a Stipe brownish when wiped; spores gibbous ≫ *I. decipientoides*, 242
24b Stipe dark, rather shaggy, green at the base; spores smooth ≫

25a Pruinose at the apex only; section *Tardae*: **26**
25b Stipe pruinose throughout: **30**

26a Whitish to pale beige fungi: **27**
26b Cap deeper coloured, streaky-fibrillose: **28**

27a With beige scales on pale ground; stipe pinkish ≫ *I. lucifuga*, 240
27b Cap surface more velvety; stipe white ≫ *I. flocculosa*, 240

28a Stipe whitish; cap streaked with russet ≫ *I. fuscidula*, 240
28b Stipe somewhat pink; often under conifers: **29**

29a Cap streaky-splitting; flesh pinkish ≫ *I. nitidiuscula*, 240
29b Cap finely radiately striped, dark brown; flesh pink in the base, somewhat yellow towards the cap ≫ *I. tarda*, 240

30a Colours whitish to pale ochraceous; under conifers: **31**
30b Fawn to brown colours; section *Splendentes*: **32**

31a Big fleshy fungus; spores gibbous ≫ *I. fibrosa*, 242
31b Small to medium size; spores smooth ≫ *I. kuehneri*, 240

32a Stipe white, smell ordinary or spermatic: **33**
32b Stipe white but flushed pinkish at the summit; smell of cherry laurel ≫
32c Stipe almost concolorous with the cap ≫ *I. vaccina*, 240

33a Cap chestnut brown, under broadleaved trees ≫ *I. phaeoleuca*, 240
33b Similar but under conifers, pruina disappearing towards the stipe base ≫
I. abietis, not described here

Subgenus *Inosperma*. No crystal-capped facial cystidia.

Section *Depauperatae*. Cap convex, expanded, surface felted or fleecy.

Inocybe dulcamara (A.-S.) Kumm.
Cap 3-6cm, yellowish ochre, surface felted, becoming somewhat shaggy. Gills slightly arched to ± decurrent with age, similar colour. Stipe 6×0.7cm, equal, concolorous, with a fleeting cortina. Flesh pallid, smell of honey when bruised, taste becoming bitter. Spores ovoid, 10×6μm; marginal cystidia thinwalled, often septate. On bare soil and gravel, sometimes in thickets. Common. E4.

I. heimii Bon [*I.caesariata*] has a more tousled russet cap with copious cortina and longer spores about 12×5.5μm. Common on sand dunes. E2.

Inocybe terrigena (Fr.) Kühn.
Cap 5-8cm, fleshy or slightly umbonate, scaly, beige to brownish ochraceous. Gills tinged olivaceous. Stipe 7×0.8cm, concolorous, clothed with scales like the cap up to a cushion-like ring-zone. Flesh yellowish, smell earthy, taste tart or earthy. Spores 11×7μm, almond-shaped; marginal cystidia clavate. Gravelly soil beside streams and in humus under conifers. Fairly common. E2.

I. agardhii (Lund) Orton is less scaly, nearly odourless, with narrower or conico-cylindrical spores, and occurs under willows. E3.

Section *Cervicolores*. Cap obtuse, somewhat fleecy; colour and smell distinctive.

Inocybe bongardii (Weinm.) Quél.
Cap 6-8cm, relatively fleshy, with shaggy scales brownish beige on an ochraceous ground, eventually somewhat reddish. Gills whitish then pinkish brown. Stipe 8×1cm, whitish to pinkish beige, smooth or slightly wispy towards the base. Flesh pale, reddening, smell fruity, becoming aromatic. Spores 13×7μm, cylindrical to kidney-shaped; marginal cystidia cylindrical-clavate. On heavy soils under broad-leaved trees and conifers. Fairly common. E3.

I. cervicolor (Pers.) Quél. is more slender with an earthy smell like a mouldy barrel. E2.

Inocybe calamistrata (Fr.) Gill.
Cap 3-6cm, somewhat umbonate, surface dark bistre brown, tousled and finally somewhat scaly. Gills ochraceous russet. Stipe 8×0.8cm, garlanded, same colour as cap but with dark green base. Flesh pallid, rather greenish in the base, somewhat pinkish in the apex, smell slightly fruity or resinous. Spores 12×6μm, shaped like a kidney bean; marginal cystidia short, clavate. Under conifers, especially spruce. Common. E3.

Section *Rimosae*. Cap rather conical, surface streaky or radially splitting.

Inocybe rimosa (Bull.) Kumm [*I. fastigiata* auct.]
Cap 5-7cm, covered with yellowish grey to fawnish ochre fibrils on a pale ground. Gills tinged olivaceous. Stipe 8×0.8cm, whitish, fibrillous, somewhat ochraceous at the base. Flesh pallid, smell spermatic. Spores 13-19×5-8μm, very variable; marginal cystidia elongated, obtuse. Ubiquitous under trees of all kinds. Common. E4.

Inocybe maculata Boud.
Similar stature to *I. fastigiata* but with cap a beautiful fawn brown or reddish brown, often bearing white patches of the veil towards the top. Gills beige grey, remaining pale. Stipe 7×1cm, whitish, typically tinged reddish brown about the middle or on one side. Flesh pale, smell aromatic, slightly of jasmine then of truffle. Spores 10×5μm, subelliptic; marginal cystidia clavate. Damp broadleaved woods, especially beech. Common. E4.

Inocybe cookei Bres.
Cap conical or obtusely umbonate, 3-5cm, nearly smooth to fibrillosely splitting, yellow ochre with centre somewhat russet. Gills yellowish grey, a little broader in the middle. Stipe 7×0.7cm, yellowish with a whitish marginate basal bulb, 1cm across. Flesh pallid, smell of honey or *Mahonia* flowers. Spores 9×5μm, slightly bean-shaped; marginal cystidia short, clavate. Under broadleaved trees especially on calcareous soil. Common. E3.

234

Inocybe
dulcamara

I. heimii

Inocybe terrigena

Inocybe bongardii

Inocybe calamistrata

I. agardhii

Inocybe rimosa

Inocybe maculata

Inocybe cookei

Inocybe patouillardii Bres. [*I. erubescens*]

Cap 5-7cm, conical or obtuse, whitish fibrillose, bruising reddish and eventually entirely dingy brick colour. Gills whitish then olive-yellow but soon reddening. Stipe 8×1cm, similar colouring. Flesh white, reddening when cut; smell fruity, becoming rather earthy. Spores 12×7μm, slightly kidney-shaped; marginal cystidia broadly clavate. Among grass at fringe of woods, glades and parks especially on calcareous soils from June to November. Locally common in southern England. **Dangerously poisonous**. E2.

Inocybe adaequata (Britz.) Sacc. [*I. jurana* auct.]

Cap 6-10cm, fleshy with a low umbo, often deformed, fibrillose, dark lilaceous brown. Gills dingy grey brown then similar colour. Stipe 8×1.5cm, rather twisted, fibrous, concolorous. Flesh pinkish ochre, vinaceous when cut; smell like *I. maculata*. Spores 13×7μm, subovoid; marginal cystidia elongated, slightly clavate. Orchards, hedge bottoms, grassy broadleaved woods. Uncommon in Britain. Reputedly edible but to be avoided for fear of confusion with the many allied toxic species. E2.

I. rhodiola Bres., often treated as a variety, is little more than a slender brighter coloured state of *I. adaequata*. E1.

Subgenus *Inocybium*. Spores smooth, facial thick-walled crystal-capped cystidia present.

Section *Lactiferae*. Superficially similar to *Rimosae*, but with ± red or blue bruising, or peculiar odours.

Inocybe fraudans (Britz.) Sacc. [*I. piriodora*]

Cap 5-7cm, convex or umbonate, fibrillose, whitish to pale golden then ochraceous russet, more pinkish to brick colour in var. *incarnata*. Gills remaining pale. Stipe 8×0.8cm, similar colours, silky-fibrillose to shaggy. Flesh pallid, sometimes reddening, smell distinctive of ripe pears. Spores 11×7μm, rather pointed; cystidia with walls 3-5μm thick. Under broadleaved trees of all kinds, occasionally pine, on heavy soils. Common throughout Britain. E3.

Inocybe corydalina Quél.

Cap 5-7cm, obtusely umbonate, dull whitish fibrillose tinged olivaceous to bluish at the top. Gills pallid, greyish. Stipe 9×1.5cm, whitish, slightly bulbous and occasionally greenish at the base. Flesh white, reddening in var. *roseola*. Smell distinctively aromatic. Spores 9×6.5μm, rather lemon-shaped; cystidial wall 1-2μm thick. Under beech, hazel, oak etc. Not uncommon. E3.

Inocybe haemacta (Bk. & Cke.) Sacc.

Cap 4-6cm, obtusely umbonate, surface fibrillose, greenish grey on a pink ground, darker at the centre. Gills greyish, tinged pink especially where bruised. Stipe 7×0.6cm, ± cylindrical, tinged glaucous then pinkish when handled. Flesh pallid, reddening, often bluish towards the base; smell faint but unpleasant, rather like a stable. Spores 11×6μm, conico-cylindrical; cystidial wall 1-2μm thick. Copses, often with ivy. Holowoods. **Toxic**, hallucinogenic. E2.

Inocybe pudica Kühn. [*I. whitei* p.p.]

Cap 4-6cm, obtuse, rather fleshy, silky-fibrillose, white, reddening in patches, sometimes only slowly. Gills white, then grey flesh colour. Stipe 7×0.8cm, slightly club-shaped, silky, slightly powdery at the top, white then ± reddening. Flesh only slightly reddening; smell spermatic. Spores 9×5μm, obtusely elliptical; cystidia commonplace. Mainly under conifers but also beech and oak. Uncommon in Britain. E3.

I. armeniaca Huijsm. is more slender, cap 1-2cm, becoming more orange and perhaps better regarded as a variety of *I. geophylla*. E2.

Inocybe godeyi Gill.

Cap 2-4cm, conical or with a pointed umbo, whitish ochraceous, soon flushed with bright reddish orange, then brick colour, streaky fibrillose. Gills similar colours. Stipe 6×0.5cm, concolorous, powdery throughout, with marginate basal bulb, 0.8cm across. Flesh reddish, smell faint. Spores 11×6μm, pointed; cystidia broadest about the middle, wall 1-2μm thick. Under broadleaved trees, especially beech, on calcareous soils. Fairly common. E2.

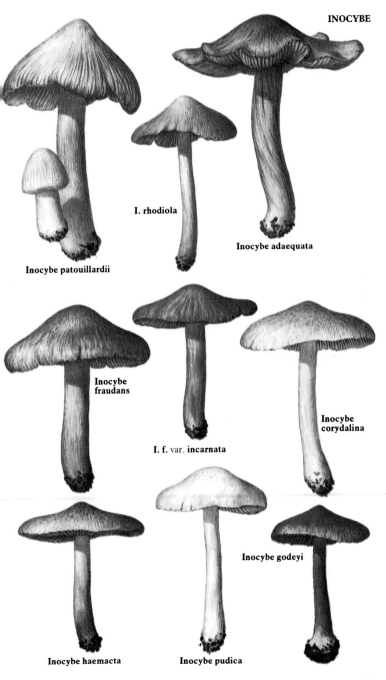

Inocybe patouillardii

I. rhodiola

Inocybe adaequata

Inocybe fraudans

I. f. var. incarnata

Inocybe corydalina

Inocybe haemacta

Inocybe pudica

Inocybe godeyi

237

Section *Lilacinae*. Colour lilaceous and/or surface hairy.

Inocybe hystrix (Fr.) Karst.
Cap 3-5cm, obtuse, covered with erect brown scales on a pale beige ground. Gills ± distant, remaining pale. Stipe 5×0.5cm, equally bristly and concolorous except at the smooth whitish apex. Flesh pallid; smell spermatic. Spores 10-12×6μm; cystidia fusiform. In damp woods, especially beech. Rare in Britain. E2.

I. squarrosa Rea is like a miniature *I. hystrix*, with stature of a *Mycena*, on muddy ground under willows. E1.

Inocybe obscura Gill.
Cap 2-4cm, somewhat hairy, dark brown with violaceous tinge especially in the stipe. Gills dark or with a darker brown edge. Stipe 4×0.5cm, fibrillose, not powdery at the top. Flesh dark lilac; smell sometimes slightly fruity. Spores 9-10×6μm; marginal hairs brownish, facial cystidia elongated, walls 2-3μm thick, turning yellow in ammonia. Under broadleaved trees on heavy calcareous soils. Rather common. E3.

I. phaeocomis (Pers.) Kuyper [*I. cincinnata*] is more elongated with less dark shaggy-tomentose surface. Quite common under broadleaved trees and conifers. E3.

Inocybe griseolilacina Lange
Cap 2-4cm, conical or umbonate, scaly, grey-brown on a lilaceous ground. Gills pallid or white-edged. Stipe elongated, 5×0.3cm, somewhat cortinate, apex lilac, not powdery. Flesh lilaceous; smell spermatic. Spores 10×5.5μm, obtuse; cystidia with thin colourless walls. Copses under beech, hazel and oak. Common. E2.

I. pusio Karst. has a smoother or streaky cap and pruinose top to the stipe; spores slightly papillate. Fairly common. (See also *I. geophylla* var. *lilacina*, p. 240). E2.

Section *Lacerae* [*Inocybium*]. No lilac tint, stipe apex not powdery.

Inocybe lacera (Fr.) Kumm.
Cap 3-5cm, convex, shaggy or fleecy then radially splitting and finally peeling, dingy brownish. Gills tinged dingy brown. Stipe 5×0.3cm, fleecy-fibrillose, concolorous with paler apex and browning base. Flesh browning towards the base, sometimes pinkish; smell faint. Spores narrow and elongated, variable, 12-18×4-7μm; cystidia thin-walled, broadest at the middle. Ubiquitous on bare soil, gravel, footpaths, under broadleaved trees and conifers, common on heaths and moors. Variable with numerous named forms not worth recognition at a higher rank eg. f. *gracilis* dark, slender, in damp places; f. *luteophylla* with yellow gills, f. *subsquarrosa* with scaly cap, on moors etc. E3.

Inocybe abjecta (Karst.) Sacc.
Cap 2-4cm, slightly umbonate, centre silky or veiled whitish, elsewhere somewhat ochraceous, fibrillose then peeling. Gills ± distant, pallid. Stipe 5×0.2cm, whitish, often somewhat twisted. Flesh pallid; smell spermatic. Spores 10×5μm, conico-cylindrical; cystidia fusiform. Under broadleaved trees on heavy soils. Common. E2.

I. griseovelata Kühn. has a cap 5-6cm, with a greyish veil over the centre and a rather bulbous, sometimes pinkish, stipe. Not British. E2.

Inocybe phaeodisca Kühn. [*I. descissa* p.p.]
Cap 3-5cm, convex, finely fibrillose, with dark brown centre and pale margin, rather as in *Hebeloma mesophaeum*. Gills rather broader in the middle, greyish. Stipe 5×0.4cm, fibrillose, white or tinged pinkish. Flesh pallid; smell not distinctive. Spores 10×6μm, pointed at the tip; cystidia commonplace. Under various broadleaved trees and conifers. Common. E2.

I. glabripes Ricken has a more uniformly fawn brown cap and small spores, not exceeding 8×5μm. Common under beech, oak and poplar. E2.

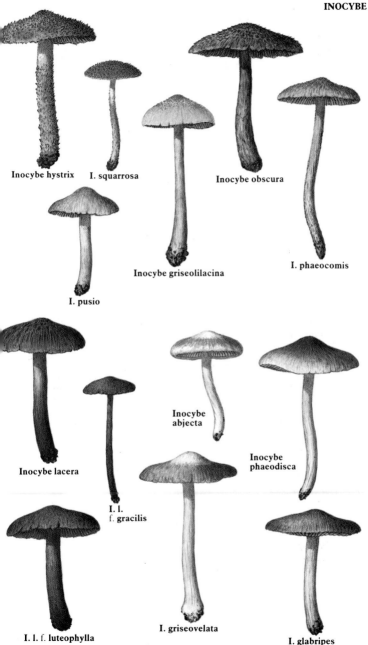

Inocybe hystrix   I. squarrosa   Inocybe obscura

I. phaeocomis

I. pusio   Inocybe griseolilacina

Inocybe lacera   Inocybe abjecta

Inocybe phaeodisca

I. l. f. gracilis

I. l. f. luteophylla   I. griseovelata   I. glabripes

Section *Tardae*. Stipe powdery at the apex only.

Inocybe geophylla (Bull.) Karst.
Cap 3-5cm, umbonate, smooth or silky, pure white or slowly turning ochraceous at the centre. Gills pale ochraceous to clay colour. Stipe 5×0.4cm, white, silky-fibrillose. Flesh pallid; smell spermatic. Spores 10×5.5μm, ovoid, obtuse; cystidia commonplace. Under broadleaved trees of all kinds and conifers, especially on heavy soils. Very common throughout Britain. **Poisonous**. E4. var. **lilacina** (Fr.) Gill. with violaceous cap ± yellow over the umbo often accompanies the typical variety. E3.

Inocybe fuscidula Vel. [*I. virgatula*]
Cap 5-7cm, conical to umbonate, smooth, then with russet brown streaky fibrils radiating on a pale ground. Gills dingy grey-brown. Stipe 8×0.6cm, whitish fibrillose, becoming slightly ochraceous towards the base. Flesh pallid; smell spermatic. Spores 11×6μm, conico-cylindrical; cystidia colourless, walls 1-2μm thick. Under conifers. Uncommon. E4.

Inocybe flocculosa (Berk.) Sacc. [*I. gausapata*]
Cap 3-5cm, convex, felted with a fleecy tomentum, pale greyish beige. Gills remaining pale. Stipe 6×0.4cm, pure white. Flesh pallid; smell spermatic. Spores 10×5.5μm, conico-cylindrical; cystidial walls yellow in ammonia. Under many kinds of broadleaved trees and conifers in woods and parks. Very common. E3. **I. lucifuga** (Fr.) Kumm. has a scalier slightly paler cap and an olivaceous tinge to the gills; cystidia with colourless walls. E3.

Inocybe nitidiuscula (Britz.) Sacc. [*I. friesii*]
Cap 2-4cm, conical or umbonate, streaky-fibrillose to radially splitting, reddish brown or dark chestnut on a pale ground. Gills brownish ochraceous. Stipe 6×0.3cm, whitish, somewhat pinkish ochraceous on handling, more russet towards the base. Flesh white in the cap, somewhat reddish in the stipe; smell spermatic. Spores 12×6μm, conico-cylindrical; cystidia commonplace. Under conifers, also beech. Em4. **I. tarda** Kühn. is more fleshy, surface nearly smooth to finely fibrillose, flesh brown under the cuticle, yellow at the cap centre, whitish elsewhere, fruiting in late autumn. United by some authorities with *I. nitidiuscula*. E3.

Section *Splendentes*. Stipe powdery throughout or at least on the upper two-thirds.

Inocybe kuehneri Stangl & Vesel. [*I. eutheles* p.p.]
Cap 3-5cm, convex or with a low umbo, fibrillose then radially splitting or finally peeling, whitish to ochraceous or dingy beige with age. Gills greyish brown to tobacco brown. Stipe 6×0.5cm, white with some hint of pinkish, fibrillose under the pruina. Flesh pallid; smell rather mealy. Spores 9×5μm, obtuse; cystidial wall 2-3μm thick, slightly yellowed by ammonia. Under conifers but also beech, birch and oak. Common. E3.

Inocybe phaeoleuca Kühn.
Cap similar to *I. kuehneri*, fibrillose, scarcely peeling, but fawnish to chestnut brown, sometimes darker at the centre. Gills remaining pale. Stipe 6×0.8cm, pure white. Flesh whitish; smell spermatic. Spores 12×6.5μm, conico-cylindrical; cystidial walls 3-5μm thick. Under broadleaved trees, especially beech. Not uncommon locally. E2.

Inocybe vaccina Kühn.
Cap 3-4cm, a beautiful warm reddish brown, sometimes dotted reddish or with fine fibrillose scales. Gills ochraceous. Stipe 6×0.6cm, somewhat yellowish to fawn, more concolorous towards the base, the pruina scarcely traceable below the middle. Flesh pallid; smell faint. Spores 10×6μm, obtuse; cystidial wall 3-5μm thick. Under conifers, especially spruce. Uncommon. E2.

Inocybe hirtella Bres.
Cap 3-5cm, conical or slightly umbonate, ochraceous yellow with russet fibrils, centre smooth and somewhat fawn. gills pale ochraceous beige. Stipe 7×0.4cm, white, somewhat pale pinkish at the summit. Flesh similar colour; smell of cherry laurel (the once-familiar white office paste), sometimes delayed. Spores size variable, from 9×5μm to 13-15×7-8μm in bisporous forms; cystidia commonplace. Copses on calcareous soils. Common. E3.

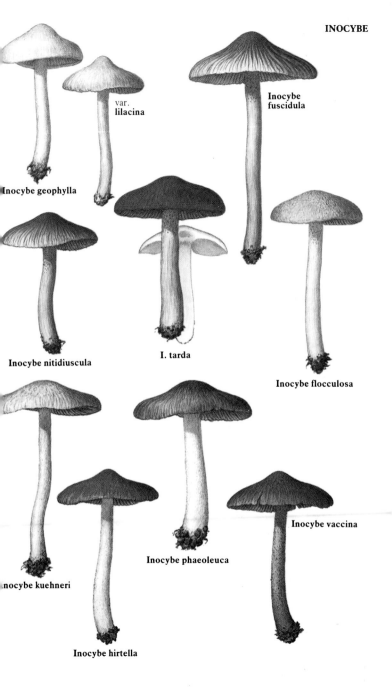

var.
lilacina

**Inocybe
fuscidula**

Inocybe geophylla

Inocybe nitidiuscula

I. tarda

Inocybe flocculosa

Inocybe kuehneri

Inocybe phaeoleuca

Inocybe vaccina

Inocybe hirtella

241

Subgenus *Inocybe* [*Clypeus, Astrosporina*]. Spores with nodules or star-shaped. Section *Cortinatae*. Stipe not powdery or poorly so under the gills.

Inocybe umbrina (Britz.) Sacc. [*I. assimilata*]
Cap 4-6cm, obtuse or umbonate, dark brown, streaky-fibrillose. Gills dingy ochraceous then dull bistre. Stipe 7×0.8cm, similar colour, fibrillose, not powdery, with a rather whitish onion-shaped basal bulb. Flesh brownish; smell rather earthy or like a *Scleroderma*. Spores 10×5.5μm, outline with rather low angular bosses. Under broadleaved trees in damp places. Common. E3. **I. napipes** Lange has a less dingy brown cap, a marginate bulb and spores with more prominent bosses. E2.

Inocybe lanuginosa (Bull.) Kumm.
Cap 5-7cm, convex, surface fleecy or with little upturned scales, rather dark bistre brown. Gills dingy beige. Stipe 7×0.8cm, similar colour, fibrillosely fleecy to scaly. Flesh pallid; smell faint. Spores 9-10×6μm, with numerous hemispherical bosses; cystidia variable (only marginal in **I. casimiri** Vel. E2.) Under many kinds of broadleaved trees and conifers in damp woods. Very common. E3. **I. curvipes** Karst. [*I. lanuginella, I. decipientoides* etc.] is a little less fleecy or paler, fawnish, with stipe browning somewhat when rubbed, and has spores with angular bosses and ovoid cystidia. Equally common. E3.

Section *Petiginosae*. Stipe powdery throughout, but not bulbous.

Inocybe petiginosa (Fr.) Gill.
Small fungus, cap 1-2cm, soon expanded, surface pinkish brown covered with tiny micaceous or silvery-tomentose scales. Gills yellowish. Stipe 3×0.2cm, equal, similar colour, powdery throughout. Flesh pallid; odourless. Spores 8×5μm, with numerous low bosses; cystidia short, 50×12μm, yellow in ammonia. Under broadleaved trees especially beech but also hazel and oak. Occasional. E2. **I. calospora** Quél. with rather similar stature has cap a beautiful dark reddish brown but is especially distinguished by its subglobose spores, covered with narrow, cylindrical, obtuse spine-like lobes. Rare. E1.

Inocybe fibrosa (Sow.) Gill.
The biggest species in the genus, cap 10-15cm, fleshy, whitish. Gills remaining pale. Stipe 9×2cm, white, powdered throughout. The general aspect is that of *Tricholoma columbetta* (p. 156). Flesh whitish; smell spermatic. Spores 10×6.5μm with somewhat angular bosses; cystidia commonplace. Under conifers. Rare. E1.

Section *Marginatae*. Stipe powdery throughout with a basal marginate bulb.

Inocybe praetervisa Quél.
Cap 5-7cm, conico-campanulate, surface streaky fibrillose, yellowish ochraceous brown. Gills tinged lilaceous grey or olivaceous. Stipe 5×0.8cm, entirely white, scarcely becoming ochraceous with age, powdery down to the marginate bulb. Flesh pallid; smell spermatic. Spores 11×8.5μm, with conspicuous angular bosses; cystidia commonplace. Under broadleaved trees. Common. E2. **I. mixtilis** (Britz.) Sacc. is more slender, cap 2-4cm, brighter ochraceous yellow, and more commonly under conifers. Equally common. E3.

Inocybe asterospora Quél.
Cap 4-6cm, somewhat umbonate, centre almost smooth, russet brown to chestnut, surface progressively radially fibrillose and splitting towards the margin. Gills greyish beige. Stipe 6×0.7cm, bright russet fawn, powdery throughout down to the marginate basal bulb. Flesh similar colour; smell spermatic. Spores 12×10μm, with prominent stellate bosses; cystidia broadest in the middle. Under broadleaved trees, especially oak, but also pines. Fairly common throughout Britain, although less frequent in the north. E4.

Inocybe decipiens Bres.
Cap 6-10cm, fleshy, grey-brown, covered with silvery fibrils to which particles of soil may adhere, forming a veil over the centre. Gills greyish. Stipe 7×1cm, whitish to pinkish ochraceous or slightly dingy vinaceous when rubbed, pruinose throughout, with a marginate bulb. Flesh similar colour; smell faint. Spores variable, 12-15×7-9μm, often rhomboidal and scarcely bossed; cystidia commonplace. Under broadleaved trees in moist places. Not known in Britain. E2.

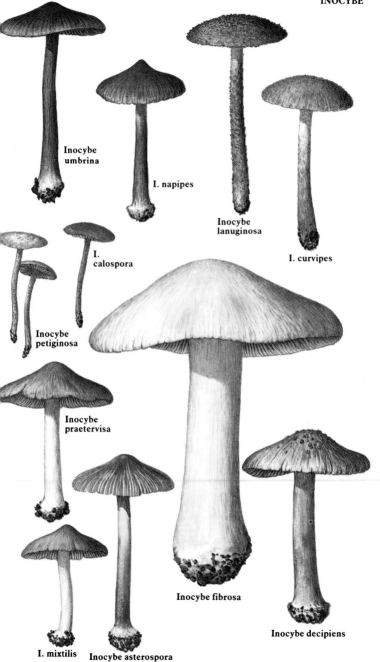

Inocybe
umbrina

I. napipes

Inocybe
lanuginosa

I. curvipes

I.
calospora

Inocybe
petiginosa

Inocybe
praetervisa

Inocybe fibrosa

Inocybe asterospora

I. mixtilis

Inocybe decipiens

243

Family *Crepidotaceae*. Spores and gills ochraceous to rust colour. Gills decurrent to somewhat sinuate. Chrysocystidia absent. Spores smooth or warty, without a germ-pore. Hyphae of cap surface filamentous or jointed.

Genus *Gymnopilus*. Aspect of a *Cortinarius* or *Pholiota*; spores rust coloured, somewhat warty; spores and/or concretions in the trama ± bright yellow in ammonia. Saprophytes on wood, not mycorrhizal.

Gymnopilus spectabilis (Fr.) A.H. Smith
Cap 8-15cm, convex or rounded, fibrillose, rich tawny colour. Gills adnate or sinuate, bright rusty yellow. Stipe very variable, 12-20×2-5cm, slightly club-shaped or spindle-shaped with a short rooting base, fibrous, yellowish, with a membranous but soon shredded ring, tinged rusty by the shed spores. Flesh rather yellow, small woody, taste bitter. Spores 9×5.5µm, coarsely rugose; cystidia swollen or capitate. In dense clusters at base of trunks, stumps or branches of broadleaved trees, stumps or branches of broadleaved trees, occasionally conifers. Common. E3.

var. **junonius** (Fr.) Lange is smaller, more yellow and occurs singly, not in clusters. Rather less common. E2.

Gymnopilus penetrans (Fr.) Murr.
Cap 4-6cm, thin-fleshed or soon flattened, silky-fibrillose, yellowish-ochre to rusty fawn. Gills yellow, often with rusty spots. Stipe 8×0.8cm, fibrous, whitish, with a cortina. Flesh whitish, odourless, bitter. Spores 8×5µm, punctate; cystidia somewhat capitate. On fallen branches, mainly of conifers. Very common. E4.

G. stabilis (Weinm.) K.-R. ex Bon is more fleshy with a persistent cobwebby veil apparent at least around the disc. Uncommon. E1.

Gymnopilus picreus (Pers.) Karst. [*G. satur*]
Cap 3-6cm, convex, thin-fleshed, bright reddish brown, smooth, somewhat hygrophanous. Gills bright yellow, crowded. Stipe 3×0.4cm, often bent, yellowish above but often flushed with reddish brown towards the base, as is the flesh. Taste bitter. Spores 9×6µm, rugulose; cystidia ninepin-shaped. On twigs, often in tufts. Uncommon. E2.

G. bellulus (Peck.) Murr., with gills speckled brownish, has tiny spores, 5×3µm. Rare. E1.

Gymnopilus sapineus (Fr.) R. Mre.
Cap 6-10cm, bearing fawn scales on a yellow ground. Gills yellow, then speckled rusty. Stipe 6×0.5cm, brownish yellow, shaggy-fibrillose, with slight cortina. Flesh concolorous, odourless, slightly bitter. Spores 9×5µm; cystidia rather slender. Often under conifers. Not common. E2.

G. spadiceus Romagn. has the cap rather shaggy or entirely reddish brown, with more broadly capitate cystidia. E2.

Genus *Crepidotus*. Cap with a lateral stipe, or none.

Crepidotus mollis (Sch.) Kumm.
Cap 3-6cm, shell-shaped, pale ochraceous, with a separable gelatinous cuticle, surface smooth or covered with small russet scales in var. *calolepis*. Gills dull, dingy brown. Stipe absent. Flesh pale, odourless or insipid. Spores 9×6µm, smooth. On trunks and stumps of broadleaved trees. Formerly very common in Britain, less so now. E3.

C. applanatus (Pers.) Kumm. is whiter, lacks the separable gelatinous pellicle and has more rounded warted spores. Less common. E2.

Crepidotus variabilis (Pers.) Kumm.
Cap 1-3cm, pure white, surface felted, often attached by the back. Gills pale pinkish ochre. Stipe sometimes visible but always very short, white. Flesh insignificant. Spores 7×3µm, finely warted. Very common everywhere on fallen twigs of broadleaved trees, dead herbaceous stems, even old dung of cattle. E4.

There are several allied species distinguished solely by size, shape and ornament of the spores. **C. luteolus** (Lamb.) Sacc. and **C. cinnabarinus** Peck, however, can be recognised by their distinctive colours, pale yellow and bright red respectively. E1.

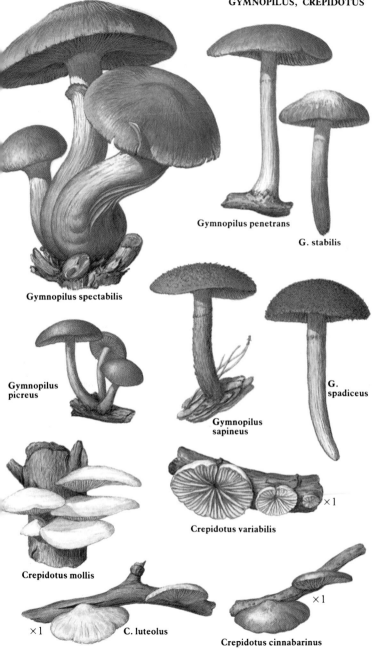

Gymnopilus penetrans

G. stabilis

Gymnopilus spectabilis

Gymnopilus picreus

Gymnopilus sapineus

G. spadiceus

Crepidotus mollis

Crepidotus variabilis

×1

×1   C. luteolus

×1

Crepidotus cinnabarinus

Genus *Tubaria*. Gill. Cap rather flat, gills slightly decurrent; cuticular hyphae filamentous, spores smooth or nearly so.

Tubaria conspersa (Pers.) Fayod
Cap 2cm, slightly convex, russet, at first rendered paler throughout by remnants of a silvery veil. Stipe 4×0.2cm, pale, whitish at the base. Flesh thin, similar colour. Spores 9×5μm, almond-shaped, slightly tapered at the tip, with pale wall. On soil and woody debris. Common. E3.

Tubaria furfuracea (Pers.) Gill.
Much like *T. conspersa* but rather brighter rust colour, margin striate and dotted with fragments of an often fugacious veil. Gills rust colour. Stipe 4×0.2cm, silky-fibrillose, russet. Flesh concolorous, with fungoid smell and taste. Spores 8×5μm, elliptic with obtuse apex and more strongly coloured wall, cheilocystidia 6-(10)μm wide. In grass, on herbaceous debris, or arable soil. E4.

T. hiemalis Romagn. ex Bon with warmer colours but hygrophanous and paling occurs especially in winter on woody debris in thickets. Spores and cheilocystidia larger. E3.

Tubaria autochthona (Bk. & Br.) Sacc. [*T. dispersa*]
Cap 1-2cm, slightly convex, pale ochraceous to fawn. Gills at first clear pale yellow. Stipe 3×0.1cm, whitish. Flesh very thin. Spores 6×3μm, pale, minutely warted. Typically under hawthorn. Quite common. E1.

Flammulaster granulosus (Lange) Watl. [*Naucoria granulosa*]
Cap 1cm, slightly convex, surface mealy with granular scales, russet brown or cinnamon. Gills russet. Stipe 3×0.2cm, similar colour; flesh russet. Spores 9×5μm, almost almond-shaped. Cuticle with short elements, sometimes ± cellular. On soil or debris of broadleaved trees. Fairly common. E2.

Several superficially similar species can only be distinguished by microscopic details of spore shape and cystidia but *F. ferrugineus* (R. Mre. ex Kühn.) Watl. may perhaps be recognisable by being more red-brown with a woolly-scaly disc.

Phaeomarasmius erinaceus (Fr.) Kühn.
Cap 1-2cm, convex, shaggy throughout with dark brown erect scales on an ochraceous russet ground. Gills pale to ochraceous russet. Stipe 1×0.3cm, often curved, concolorous and scaly like the cap. Flesh tough, almost concolorous. Spores 12×8μm, slightly lemon-shaped. On branches of broadleaved trees, especially willow but also ash, beech, hawthorn, rose etc. Quite common. E2.

Genus *Phaeocollybia*. Cap campanulate or conical; spores warted.

Phaeocollybia lugubris (Fr.) Heim
Cap 5-8cm, obtusely campanulate, then umbonate with an irregularly lobed margin, ochraceous grey-brown with reddish or olivaceous tints. Gills ascending with orange tint, fairly spaced. Stipe 13×1cm, ± rooting or narrowed towards the base, pale ochre with vinaceous pink base. Flesh pale to nearly concolorous near the surface; smell earthy or of radish, becoming pleasant. Spores 9×5μm, almond-shaped; cystidia with slender neck and somewhat capitate. Under conifers, especially spruce in the mountains. Rare in Britain. Em2.

Phaeocollybia christinae (Fr.) Heim [*P. lateraria*]
Cap 2-4cm, conical, at first bright reddish recalling *Hygrocybe conica* but fading to dingy reddish ochre. Gills saffron. Stipe 10×0.5cm, rooting, orange with purplish base. Flesh colour similar; smell of radish, taste becoming bitter. Spores 11×5μm, somewhat fusiform, finely punctate; cystidia clavate. Under conifers. Not known in Britain. E3.

P. arduennensis Bon [*P. jennyae* p.p.] is like a small form of the last with darker colouring and smaller spores 6×4×m. E1.

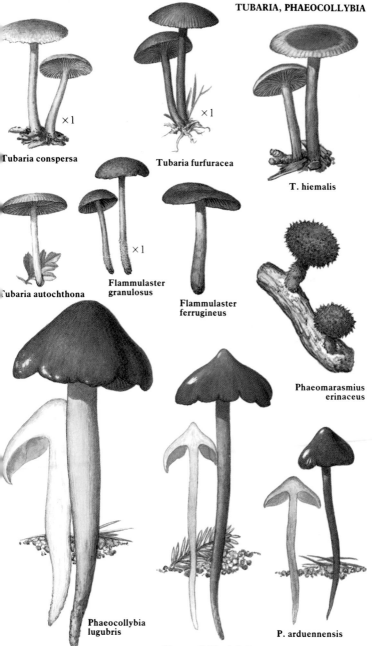

×1

Tubaria conspersa

×1

Tubaria furfuracea

T. hiemalis

Tubaria autochthona

×1

Flammulaster
granulosus

Flammulaster
ferrugineus

Phaeomarasmius
erinaceus

Phaeocollybia
lugubris

Phaeocollybia christinae

P. arduennensis

247

Genus *Galerina*. Cap campanulate or convex with the aspect of a *Mycena*; gills adnate to somewhat sinuate. Spores ± rugose.

Galerina laevis (Pers.) Sing. [*G. graminea*]
Cap 1cm, convex, striate, ochraceous-honey colour to pale fawn, hygrophanous, drying ochraceous cream. Gills yellowish then pale rusty. Stipe 3×0.1cm, pale yellow finely striate or pruinose. Flesh thin. Spores 9×5μm, nearly smooth, rather truncate-conical; cystidia capitate; clamp connections absent (Subgenus *Tubariopsis*). Mossy lawns and pastures, mainly in late autumn. Very common. E3.

Galerina marginata (Batsch) Kühn.
Cap 4-8cm, soon expanded, fawnish brown drying paler to ochraceous, margin slightly striate. Gills rather crowded and narrow, ochre to russet. Stipe 6×0.7cm, equal, almost concolorous, browning at the base, with membranous ring. Flesh colour similar; smell and taste slightly mealy. Spores 10×6μm, almond-shaped; facial and marginal cystidia present. Somewhat clustered on woody debris especially of conifers. Very common everywhere. **Toxic and dangerous**. E4.

G. praticola (Møll.) Orton resembles a slender form of *G. marginata* but more yellowish russet, found commonly in wet meadows and lawns. E2.

Galerina paludosa (Fr.) Kühn.
Cap 2-3cm, hemispherical, dull brownish, margin striate. Gills well spaced, adnate, similar colour. Stipe 10×0.3cm, similar colour, with a whitish, silky or shaggy ring-zone. Flesh pale, odourless or insipid. Spores 10×6.5μm, finely warted; cystidia restricted to gill edge, flask-shaped. Among *Sphagnum* and on peat moss. Very common northwards in Britain. E2.

G. sphagnorum (Pers.) Kühn. has rather brighter colouring, sometimes tinged orange at the disc and no ring zone; taste mealy. Also in *Sphagnum*, as is **G. tibiicystis** (Atk.) Kühn., without mealy taste and distinguished chiefly by more capitate cheilocystidia. E2.

Galerina pumila (Pers.) Lange ex Sing. [*G. mycenopsis*]
Cap 1-2cm, convex, deeply striate, yellowish ochre with fawn centre, fading to ochraceous cream. Gills well spaced, broadest at the middle and almost free. Stipe 5×0.2cm, concolorous, silky, with traces of a whitish veil. Flesh pale, odourless. Spores 13×7μm, almost smooth; cystidia marginal, flask-shaped. Mossy lawns and pastures. Common. E2.

G. mycenoides (Fr.) Kühn. [*G. jaapii*]. Generally similar to *G. pumila* but more slender with a more definite ring and capitate or ninepin-shaped cystidia. Uncommon, on boggy soil among wet mosses. The basidia are two-spored. E2.

Galerina vittaeformis (Fr.) Sing.
Aspect of *G. pumila* but with a more conical cap, a little more reddish brown. Stipe 7×0.2cm, pruinose right to the top with no trace of a veil. Spores 11×6μm, almond-shaped, distinctly warted; facial cystidia present, rather fusiform. Among mosses. Very common. E3.

Galerina sideroides (Bull.) Kühn.
Cap 2cm, convex, viscid, beige-russet brown, slightly striate at the margin, hygrophanous. Gills ochraceous brown. Stipe 4×0.2cm, pale, base reddish brown, zoned with remnants of a silky veil. Flesh concolorous, odourless. Spores 8×4.5μm, smooth; marginal cystidia ninepin-shaped. On stumps and fallen needles of conifers. E2.

G. stylifera (Atk.) A.H. Smith & Sing. differs mainly in larger size, a better defined ring and rather mealy smell. E2.

Galerina uncialis (Britz.) Kühn.
Cap 2-3cm, soon expanded with the aspect of a *Tubaria*, yellowish brown. Gills commonplace. Stipe 3×0.2cm, concolorous, with remnants of a fibrillose silvery veil. Flesh pale; smell and taste somewhat mealy. Spores 10×6μm, rugose; marginal cystidia flask-shaped. On trunks and in mossy lawns. E2.

Galerina laevis

Galerina marginata

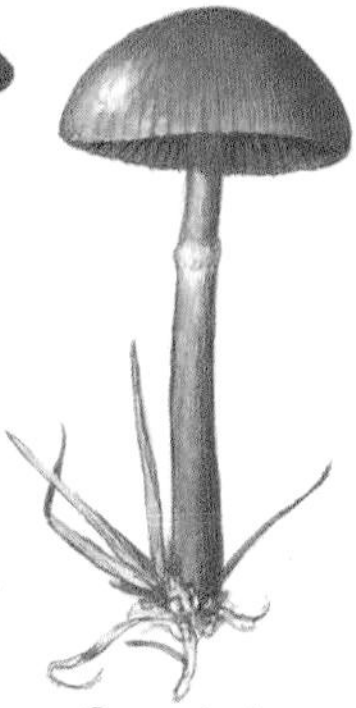

G. praticola

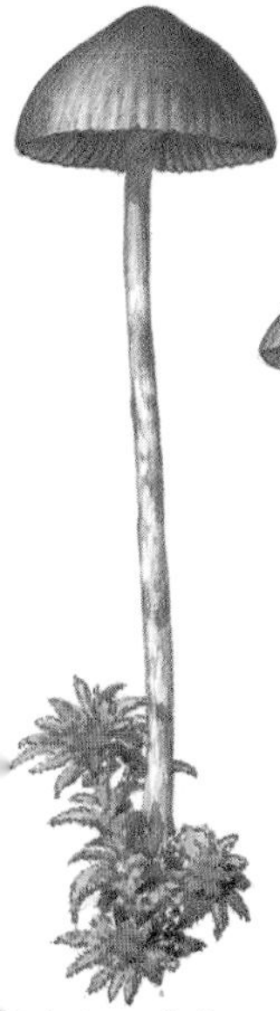

Galerina paludosa

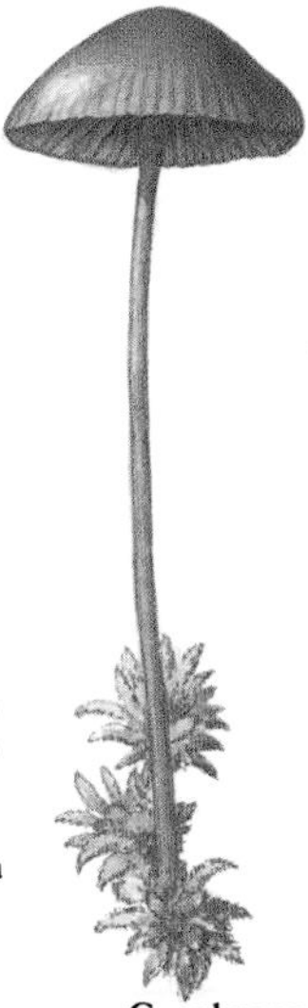

G. sphagnorum

Galerina pumila

G. mycenoides

Galerina vittaeformis

Galerina sideroides

G. stylifera

Galerina uncialis

All × 1

249

Family *Strophariaceae*. Spore print rusty or violaceous; spores smooth, often with a distinct germ-pore; chrysocystidia generally present.

Tribe *Strophariae*. Spores and gills violaceous.

Genus *Stropharia*. Stipe with a ring or bracelet. Cap lacking a cellular hyodermis.

Stropharia aeruginosa (Curt.) Quél. [*S. cyanea* p.p.]
Cap 5-8cm, viscid, bluish green then ± yellowing, with whitish floccose margin. Gills dark grey-violaceous with pale edges. Stipe 6×0.8cm, greenish with white scales and a floccose or membranous ring. Flesh greenish; no distinctive smell but a 'grassy' taste. Spores 8×4.5μm, marginal cystidia hyaline, clavate or constricted and capitate. Woods. Common. Not edible. E4.

S. caerulea Kreis. [*S. cyanea* p.p.] has the veil scanty or almost absent and chocolate brown gills with concolorous edges and occurs in beds of stinging nettles and similar urban habitats. Common. E3.

Stropharia hornemannii (Fr.) Lund. & Nannf. [*S. depilata*]
A large fungus with fleshy cap 10-15cm, viscid, whitish ochraceous then pale violaceous brown, margin white-appendiculate. Gills grey violet. Stipe 12×2cm, white, scaly below a membranous ring. Flesh pale; smell strong, taste unpleasant. Spores 12×6μm; cystidia clavate. In humus and on rotting wood of broadleaved trees. Uncommon. E1-2.

S. ferrii Bres. [*S. rugosoannulata*] is distinguished by the stipe being naked below a fluted ring and the cap reddish grey-brown, scarcely viscid. Edible, sometimes cultivated. Rare. E1.

S.ferrii var. **flavida** has a yellow cap, but in **S. eximia** Bened. the cap is pearly white with ± greyish scales in age, when it resembles an *Agaricus*. E1.

Stropharia inuncta (Fr.) Quél.
Cap 4-7cm, viscid, pale, with beige-violet hue. Gills lilac then purplish grey. Stipe 7×0.5cm, whitish, with fugaceous shaggy ring. Flesh white. Spores 8×5μm; marginal cystidia capitate. Mossy pastures. Common. E2.

Stropharia coronilla (Bull.) Quél.
Cap 4-6cm, convex or fleshy, dry, bright ochraceous yellow or orange. Gills lilaceous then violaceous, with pale edges. Stipe 3-5×0.6-1cm, white, ring striate. Flesh pale. Spores 9×5μm, with narrow pore; marginal cystidia clavate. Among grass of lawns and pastures. Common. E3.

S. melasperma (Bull.) Gill. is very similar but with white or pale ochre cap and blackish grey gills. E2.

Stropharia semiglobata (Batsch) Quél.
Cap 3-5cm, hemispherical, slightly viscid, yellowish ochre. Gills pallid to greyish. Stipe 10×0.5cm, viscid, pale, with a median membranous ring. Flesh pale, smell mealy. Spores 20×10μm, elliptical, with broad germ-pore; cystidia fusiform. In pastures, heaths and moors on dung of cattle, horse and sheep. Very common. E4.

Stropharia squamosa (Pers.) Quél. [*Psilocybe squamosa*]
Cap 4-6cm, convex, scarcely viscid, russet-yellow, with whitish marginal scales. Gills greyish. Stipe 15×0.8cm, white, floccose below a shredded membranous ring. Flesh pale; smell like damp wood. Spores 13×7μm; marginal cystidia tapered; no chrysocystidia. On woody debris of broadleaved trees. Common. E3.

var. **thrausta** differs in its more intense colouring, reddish orange cap and stipe. E1.

L. vulpinus (Fr.) Kün. & R. Mre., more densely clustered, shows paler cap surface, more glabrous but distinctly wrinkled or radially strigose. Rare. E1.

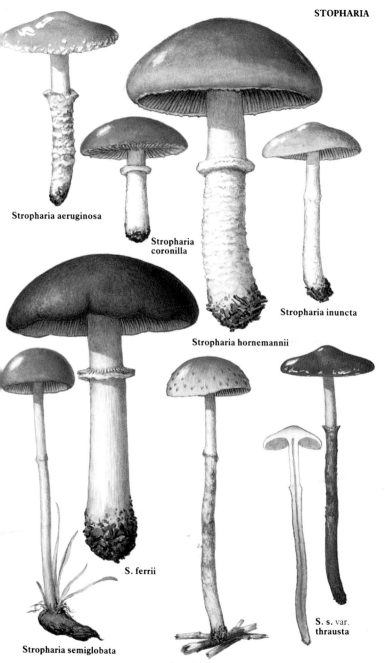

Stropharia aeruginosa

Stropharia
coronilla

Stropharia inuncta

Stropharia hornemannii

S. ferrii

Stropharia semiglobata

Stropharia squamosa

S. s. var.
thrausta

251

Genus *Hypholoma*. Stipe with a cortina; cap with a ± cellular hypodermis.

Section *Fascicularia*. Rather robust fungi, often fruiting in tufts.

Hypholoma fasciculare (Huds.) Kumm.   SULPHUR-TUFT
Cap 4-8cm, with a low umbo, smooth, bright yellow with a slightly fawn-orange
centre; margin incurved, at first with a cortina. Gills sulphur becoming greenish to
olive-grey. Stipe 10×0.8cm, sulphur yellow, with a greenish cortina, base slightly
russet. Flesh yellow, odourless, taste bitter. Spores 7×4µm; marginal cystidia variable. In tufts on stumps, dead branches and from dead roots of conifers and broadleaved trees. Very common. Inedible and suspect. E4.

Hypholoma sublateritium (Fr.) Quél.
Cap 5-10cm, convex, fleshy or umbonate, smooth or fibrillose, pinkish russet to
brick red towards the centre with paler or veiled margin. Gills yellowish then greyish
ochre. Stipe 13×1cm, somewhat russet, cortinate, even ± annulate in var. *pomposa*.
Flesh yellow, often mild. Spores and cystidia similar, or nearly so. In similar situations to *H. fasciculare* but less common. Suspect: do not eat. E3.

Hypholoma capnoides (Fr.) Kumm.
Cap 4-6cm, convex, rather fleshy, yellow ochre, shading to orange-russet at the
centre. Gills greyish, not yellow. Stipe 8×0.8cm, pale, ochraceous russet towards
the base. Flesh whitish; taste mild. Spores 8×5µm; cystidia short, somewhat flask-
shaped. In tufts on wood of conifers. Common. Edible but poor. Em4.

Hypholoma radicosum Lange. [*H. epixanthum* p.p.]
Cap 4-8cm, rather fleshy, dry, marginal zone covered with a whitish silky veil, centre
becoming exposed and yellow ochre to somewhat orange. Gills white to greyish ochre.
Stipe 12×1cm, rooting deeply in the substrate, whitish around the middle, with
sometimes bristling concolorous scales, orange-brown towards the base. Flesh concolorous; smell woody, taste very bitter. Spores 8×4µm; marginal cystidia flask-shaped.
On stumps, mainly of conifers. Rare in Britain outside the Highlands. E1.

Section *Psilocyboides*. Slender fungi, fruiting singly.

Hypholoma marginatum (Pers.) Schroet. [*H. dispersum*]
Cap 3-5cm, slightly umbonate, ochraceous russet, margin with fugacious appendiculate white flaky scales. Gills olivaceous grey-ochre. Stipe 6×0.3cm, dotted or zoned
whitish on a russet ground. Flesh concolorous; odourless, bitter. Spores 8.5×5µm
with truncate pore; cystidia flask-shaped. In troops on rotting wood and debris of
conifers. Common. E3.

Hypholoma subericaeum (Fr.) Kühn.
Cap 3-5cm, ± conical to umbonate, reddish brown to fawnish ochre, then tawny
brown, greasy. Gills pale lilac grey. Stipe 8×0.3cm, whitish, silvery silky-fibrillose,
progressively more russet brown towards the base, especially after handling. Flesh
almost concolorous. Spores 9×5µm; marginal cystidia obtusely flask-shaped. Ditches,
damp woods, swampy pastures. Fairly common. E3. **H. udum** (Pers.) Kühn. is
similar or brighter coloured, especially towards the base of the stipe, which is dark
reddish brown; spores much larger, 18×7µm, ± rugulose. Common on moors. E1-2.

Hypholoma ericaeoides Orton
Stature as in *H. subericaeum*; cap 2-4cm, yellowish ochre, hygrophanous with pale
margin and somewhat orange fawn centre. Gills yellow. Stipe 5×0.2cm, pale, somewhat yellow-brown towards the base. Flesh pale or lemon; smell and taste slight.
Spores 12×7µm; marginal cystidia variable. Cart-ruts, margins of pools and muddy
willow woods. Common. E2.

Hypholoma elongatum (Pers.) Ricken [*H. elongatipes*]
Cap 1-2cm, convex, thin-fleshed, pale glaucous ochraceous or livid. Gills pale, only
slowly becoming dull greyish bistre. Stipe slender, 10×0.2cm, sometimes undulating,
whitish, base tinged ochraceous orange or russet. Flesh pale; odourless, taste becoming bitter. Spores 11×6µm, rather pale; marginal cystidia somewhat swollen. On
moors with peat and especially in *Sphagnum*. Very common in such situations. E3.

Hypholoma fasciculare

Hypholoma sublateritium

Hypholoma radicosum

Hypholoma capnoides

×1

Hypholoma elongatum

×1

Hypholoma marginatum

Hypholoma subericaeum

Hypholoma ericaeoides

Genus *Psilocybe*. Neither ring nor cortina nor chrysocystidia present.

Psilocybe montana (Pers.) Kumm. [*P. atrorufa*]
Cap 1-2cm, convex, somewhat striate, slightly viscid with the cuticle not separable, dark sepia, paler with age. Gills broadly adnate, horizontal, dark grey-bistre or purplish. Stipe 2×0.2cm, concolorous or paler, fibrillose. Flesh concolorous, smell faint. Spores lenticular, 8×5×4μm; marginal cells narrow. Pastures, heaths and moors, especially among mosses on sandy or gravelly soil. Common. E2.

P. muscorum (Orton) Moser, though scarcely more fleshy, has a separable viscid cuticle. Several other species are difficult to distinguish. E2.

Psilocybe crobula (Fr.) M. Lange ex Sing. [*Deconica crobula*]
Cap 2-3cm, olivaceous sepia brown, margin barely striate but somewhat appendiculate. Gills dark russet brown like *Tubaria* (p. 246). Stipe 4×0.3cm, almost concolorous, flecked with fugaceous whitish scales. Flesh pale, odourless. Spores 8×5μm; marginal cystidia tapered. On fallen twigs. Common. E2.

Psilocybe semilanceata (Fr.) Kumm.
Cap 1.5×1cm, pointed like a goblin's cap, greasy, pale yellowish brown to livid olive. Gills ascending, greyish. Stipe 8×0.2cm, often twisted, concolorous, smooth, bluing as does the cap margin in var. *caerulescens*. Flesh pale. Spores 15×7μm; cystidia with slender neck which may fork. Pastures and moors, often associated with dead basal leaves of the larger tufted grasses such as Cocksfoot, *Holcus* etc. Not edible, hallucinogenic and toxic. Very common. E2.

Psilocybe merdaria (Fr.) Ricken [*Stropharia merdaria*]
Cap 2-4cm, olivaceous ochre, fading to dingy cream; margin whitish appendiculate. Gills purplish bistre. Stipe 6×0.3cm, rooting, whitish ochre, diversified by silvery zones, sometimes almost ring-like. Flesh pale. Spores 13×8μm, slightly hexagonal in face view; marginal cystidia wavy. On dung in manured fields and gardens. Fairly common. E1. **P. coprophila** (Bull.) Kumm. is less yellow-olivaceous, lacks the veil and has more blackish gills. Common, on dung. E2.

Tribe *Pholioteae*. Spores and gills brown to rust colour. Stipe with a sheathing ring or cortina.

Kuehneromyces mutabilis (Scop.) Sing. & A.H. Smith [*Galerina mutabilis*]
Cap 5-8cm, convex, very hygrophanous, cinnamon brown drying out to livid ochre from the centre. Gills russet. Stipe 5×0.5cm, sheathed with a floccose-scaly layer up to a membranous ring. Flesh pale. Spores 7x4μm, smooth to very finely warted; marginal cystidia somewhat flask-shaped, no chrysocystidia. In tufts on stumps of broadleaved trees. Very common. Edible, but do not confuse with the poisonous *Galerina marginata* (p. 248) – less hygrophanous and with stipe not sheathed. E4.

Genus *Hemipholiota*. Spores and gills dingy brownish, not rust colour.

Hemipholiota populnea (Pers.) Bon [*Pholiota destruens*]
Cap 10-20cm, fleshy, brownish beige, scaly-woolly or floccose, especially towards the margin. Gills dingy clay colour. Stipe 8×2cm, scaly, similar colour to cap. Flesh pale; smell aromatic. Spores 8×3μm; cystidia contorted or constricted. On stumps or sawdust heaps, especially of poplar. Rare in Britain. E2.

Hemipholiota oedipus (Cooke) Bon
Cap 3-5cm, ± convex or depressed, viscid, hygrophanous, finely striate, ochraceous brown, sometimes with olivaceous tinge, becoming creamy grey. Gills adnate, dull brownish. Stipe 5×0.3cm, with a ± membranous ring. Flesh pale; smell slightly mealy. Spores 8×5μm, with narrow germ-pore; cystidia lobed or constricted. In debris of broadleaved trees and tending to fruit late in the year. Uncommon. E2.

Hemipholiota myosotis (Fr.) Bon
Cap 4-6cm, campanulate or convex with an umbo, viscid, pale russet yellow to olivaceous. Gill colour similar at first, then tinged with dingy purplish grey. Stipe 8×0.5cm, variegated with olive bistre zones on a paler ground, more russet at the base. Flesh pale to russet; smell faint or soapy. Spores 16×9μm; cystidia somewhat flask-shaped. Peat moors, muddy paths and under alder and willow in muddy places. Very common. E3.

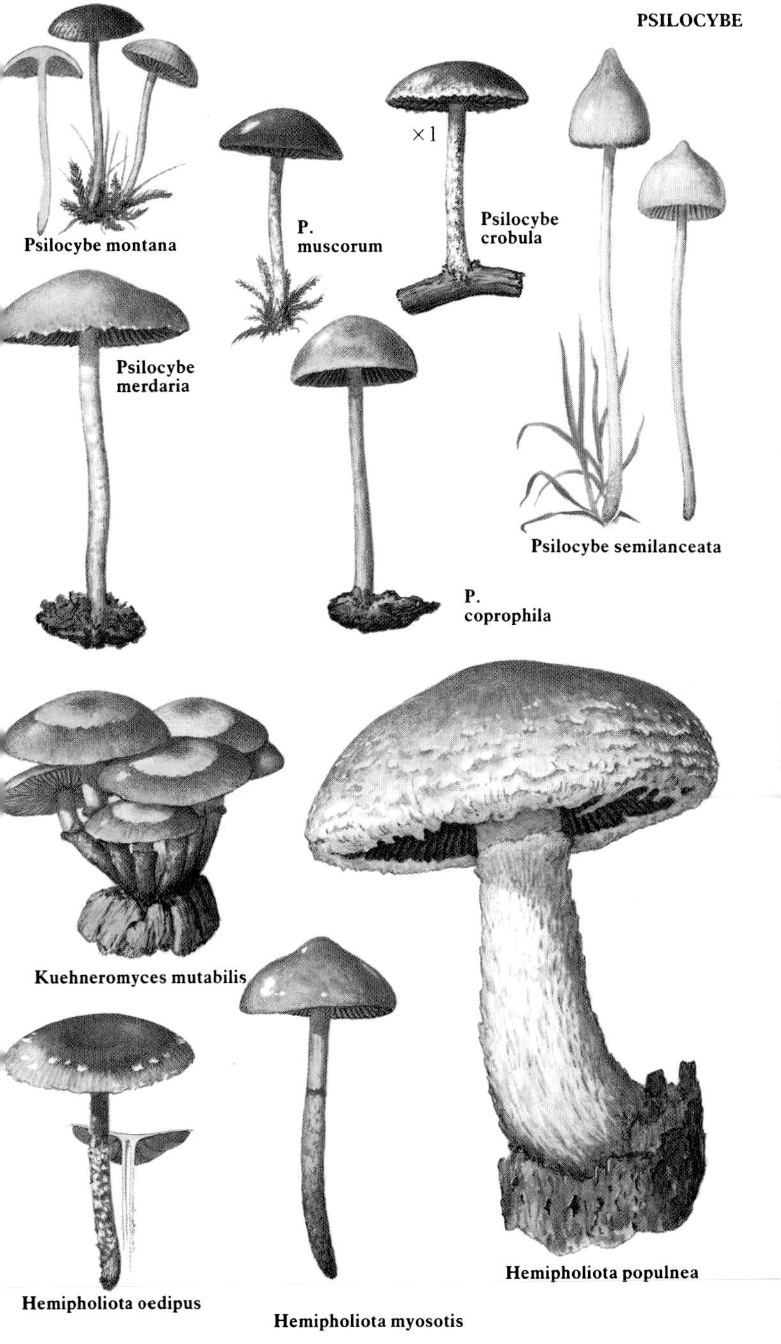

Psilocybe montana

P. muscorum

×1

Psilocybe crobula

Psilocybe merdaria

Psilocybe semilanceata

P. coprophila

Kuehneromyces mutabilis

Hemipholiota populnea

Hemipholiota oedipus

Hemipholiota myosotis

255

Genus *Pholiota*. Spores and gills rust colour, cap and stipe somewhat scaly or viscid, yellow or russet.

Subgenus *Pholiota*. Cap ± scaly. Stipe usually sheathed.

Pholiota squarrosa (Müll.) Kumm.
Cap 10-15cm, fleshy or convex, surface somewhat shaggy with bright russet brown scales on an ochraceous ground. Gills yellowish then olivaceous rusty brown. Stipe 15×1.5cm, clad with scales coloured like the cap. Flesh yellowish; smell ± strong, of straw, taste bitter. Spores 7×4μm; marginal cystidia fusiform or short clavate. In clusters on stumps and at the base of living trunks of broadleaved trees, especially mountain ash, ash and beech. Very common. Edible but poor. E3.

P. ochropallida Romagn. ex Bon is paler, slightly viscid and has a characteristically fruity smell. Rare and not known in Britain. E1.

Pholiota flammans (Batsch) Kumm.
Cap 5-7cm, convex, shaggy with fleecy bright golden yellow scales on a rather orange ground. Gills bright yellow, bruising russet, finally orange. Stipe 8×1cm, concolorous and shaggy like the cap. Flesh bright yellow; smell slightly fruity, taste acrid. Spores small, 4×2μm; marginal cystidia cylindrical. On stumps and branches of conifers. Quite common in Highlands. E2.

Pholiota cerifera (Karst.) Karst. [*P. aurivella*]
Similar stature to *P. squarrosa* but slightly smaller and with a viscid cuticle, showing yellow between flat, appressed, triangular, russet scales which may disappear except round the margin. Gills yellow to russet brown. Stipe 12×0.8cm, concolorous, dry, covered with fibrils which are somewhat coiled and shaggy (smoother in var. *aurivella*), browning at the base. Flesh yellow to brownish; taste almost sweet. Spores 8×5μm; marginal cystidia narrow, yellowish. Clustered on trunks and stumps of most broadleaved trees, especially beech in England. Common. E2 .

P. jahnii Tjal. & Bas. [*P.muelleri*] has erect darker scales, somewhat black at the tips, and smaller spores 6×3.5μm. Rare. nE3.

Pholiota adiposa (Batsch) Kumm.
Similar stature to *P. cerifera*, with viscid golden yellow cap bearing scales that are nearly concolorous or become brown. Gills bright yellow then orange-brown. Stipe 12×1.5cm, viscid, yellow, shaggy with scales and russet at the base. Flesh concolorous; smell pleasant. Spores 6×3.5μm. Clustered on trunks and stumps of broadleaved trees, beech, poplar etc. but less common than *P. cerifera* in England. E1.

Pholiota tuberculosa (Sch.) Kumm.
Cap 3-5cm, golden yellow to orange russet, smooth at the centre, somewhat shaggy-fibrillose towards margin. Gills yellow to russet. Stipe 5×0.5cm, yellow, floccose, reddening when rubbed. Flesh yellow, reddish towards the base. Spores 8×5μm; marginal cystidia capitate, chrysocystidia absent. On branches and twigs of broadleaved trees and sawdust heaps. Fairly common. E2.

P. curvipes (Pers.) Quél. is smaller with rusty finely scaly cap and short, often curved, nearly smooth stipe. Uncommon. E2.

Pholiota lucifera (Lasch) Quél.
Cap 4-7cm, convex or umbonate, waxy, slightly viscid, speckled with russet on a pale yellow ground. Gills pale. Stipe 4×0.5cm, almost concolorous, with russet flakes, browning at the base. Flesh pale; smell of wood, taste bitter. Spores 9×6μm; marginal cystidia rather wavy or appendiculate, chrysocystidia absent. On fallen branches, often buried, mainly poplars and willows. Uncommon. E1.

NOTE. *Cortinarius humicola* (p. 222), with a sheathing ring and shaggy cap, can be confused with *Pholiota*, but usually ocurs singly.

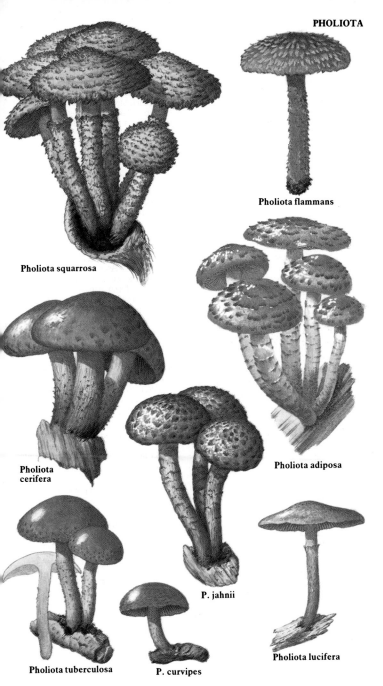

PHOLIOTA

Pholiota flammans

Pholiota squarrosa

Pholiota cerifera

Pholiota adiposa

P. jahnii

Pholiota tuberculosa

P. curvipes

Pholiota lucifera

Subgenus *Flammula*. Stipe with a cortina or at most a narrow ring-zone; gills splitting from the base when the cap is torn apart.

Pholiota lenta (Pers.) Sing.
Cap 6-8cm, soon expanded, viscid, dull ochraceous beige with a few paler scales towards the margin. Gills arched to nearly decurrent, beige, sometimes tinged olivaceous, then rust colour. Stipe 8×0.8cm, equal or club-shaped, concolorous, with a cortina grading into fibrillose scales towards the base. Flesh pale; smell of straw, taste mild. Spores 7×4μm; cystidia fusiform. On woody debris under various broad-leaved trees. Common. E3.

Pholiota gummosa (Lasch) Sing.
Cap 4-8cm, convex, soon expanded, only slightly viscid, with whitish adpressed scales on a greenish ochre ground, more numerous towards the margin. Gills ochraceous beige to orange rust. Stipe 7×0.7cm, almost concolorous, with cortina or loose ring zone, orange-russet at the base. Flesh pale to lemon-russet. Spores 6×3.5μm, marginal cystidia narrowly clavate. Solitary or clustered on woody and herbaceous debris. Common. E4.

Pholiota highlandensis (Peck) A.H. Smith & Hesl. [*Flammula carbonaria*]
Cap 3-5cm, convex to somewhat wavy, only slightly viscid, fawnish russet at the centre, yellower at the margin. Gills yellowish to olivaceous then russet, ± decurrent. Stipe 6×0.8cm, almost equal or constricted beneath the gills, whitish at the apex, yellowish fawn at the base, dotted with russet brown up to a cortinate ring-zone. Flesh pale, mild. Spores 7×4μm; cystidia encrusted. On burnt ground and charred wood. Very common. E2.

P. spumosa (Bolt.) Sing. is very viscid, a brighter yellow colour and found mainly under conifers; cystidia commonplace. E2.

Pholiota graminis (Quél.) Sing. [*P. abstrusa* p.p.]
Cap 3-5cm, convex, fibrillose, only slightly viscid, yellowish ochre to fawnish. Gills clay colour then rusty or tinged orange. Stipe 5×0.3cm, almost equal, concolorous, silky fibrillose with a cortina. Flesh pale; smell of straw. Spores 7×4μm; marginal cystidia bottle-shaped. Among grass in damp places often under alder or willow, or with *Typha*. Not uncommon in such places. E2.

P. muricella (Fr.) Bon has the cap speckled russet and longer narrower spores about 8×3.5μm; on bare damp soil. Uncommon. E1.

Pholiota astragalina (Fr.) Sing.
Cap 4-6cm, convex, only slightly viscid, a beautiful apricot orange or saffron with rosy ochraceous margin. Gills tinged salmon. Stipe 8×1cm, yellow-orange, slightly shaggy about the middle, saffron-fawn at the base. Flesh colours similar; smell slight, taste bitter. Spores 9×5μm; marginal cystidia wavy. On stumps and branches of conifers in the mountains. Rare in Britain. Em3.

Pholiota scamba (Fr.) A.H. Smith & Hesler
Cap 2cm, soon expanded, dry, whitish with a cobwebby or felted veil, rather ochraceous beige when this is rubbed off, margin appendiculate. Gills pale, tinged glaucous, then rusty. Stipe 3×0.2cm, similar colour with small beige scales up to a cortinate ring-zone. Flesh thin, pale. Spores 9×6μm; cystidia swollen below or capitate. On twigs and herbaceous debris, mainly under conifers. Common in Scotland. E1.

Pholiota alnicola (Fr.) Sing.
Cap 6-10cm, remaining hemispherical to convex, greasy, bright yellow then russet-orange towards the centre. Gills yellow then olivaceous rusty brown. Stipe 12×1cm, spindle-shaped, similar colour but rusty fawn towards the base, cortina appendiculate from the cap margin and giving a ring-zone on the stipe at first. Flesh pale; smell pleasant, fruity, taste mild. Spores 10×5.5μm; chrysocystidia absent. In clusters on dead trunks, stumps and debris especially of alder or birch. Very common especially in the Highlands. E2.

P. flavida (Sch.) Sing., odourless, with chrysocystidia, occurs on conifers. Em2.

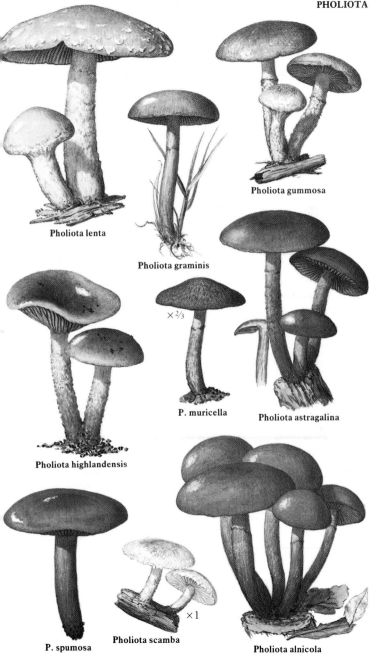

Pholiota lenta

Pholiota graminis

Pholiota gummosa

$\times^2/_3$

P. muricella

Pholiota astragalina

Pholiota highlandensis

P. spumosa

Pholiota scamba

$\times 1$

Pholiota alnicola

Family *Bolbitiaceae*. Cap surface matt, wrinkled or micaceous; cuticle hymeniform or ± cellular.

Genus *Bolbitius*. Fragile, with the aspect of a *Coprinus*.

Bolbitius vitellinus (Pers.) Fr.
Cap 4-6cm, conical, thin-fleshed, viscid, deeply striate or fluted except in the slender var. *fragilis*, bright yellow, fading to ochraceous. Gills narrow, ascending, yellow then ochraceous. Stipe 10×0.5cm, soon becoming hollow, white, yellowish at the apex, silky. Flesh whitish. Spores 12×6μm; basidia stocky, mingled with pseudo-paraphyses. In grassy places, especially where manured, and on compost. Very common. E3.

B. lacteus Lange is white throughout, with elongated cap and seems transitional to *Conocybe*. Grassy places. Not uncommon. E1.

Genus *Conocybe*. Cap thin, ± conical; gills ochraceous to pale rust colour; spores usually with a conspicuous germ-pore.

Conocybe tenera (Sch.) Fayod
Cap 3-5cm, campanulate, striate, ochre to fawnish brown. Gills ascending, ochraceous. Stipe ringless, 10×0.2cm, ochraceous, powdered and finely striate. Flesh pale. Spores 13×7μm; ninepin-shaped cystidia on gill edge and covering the stipe. Pastures. Common. E3. **C. subovalis** Kühn. & Watl. has a bulbous stipe and occurs in manured places. E2.

Conocybe brunneola Kühn. & Watl.
Cap 1cm, more obtuse, somewhat striate, dull brownish ochre. Gills and stipe as in *C. tenera* but only 7×0.1cm, sometimes with a small basal bulb, 0.2cm across. Flesh thin. Spores 8×4μm; cystidia as in *C. tenera*. Mossy lawns and parks. Common. E2.

Conocybe pilosella (Pers.) Kühn.
Cap 3cm, soon expanded, striate, brownish ochre. Gills ringless, very crowded, beige to russet. Stipe 6×0.2cm, ochraceous, not powdered but bearing silky white fibrils. Flesh thin, pale. On Spores 8×4.5μm with inconspicuous germ-pore; ninepin-shaped cystidia confined to gill edge. twigs under broadleaved trees. E2.

C. pseudopilosella Kühn. & Watl. has a more campanulate cap, 1cm, less crowded gills and some ninepin-shaped cystidia on the upper part of the stipe as well as the gill edge. On lawns. E1.

Conocybe intrusa (Peck) Sing.
Unlike the other species in having the aspect of a *Hebeloma*, with fleshy cap 6-10cm, reddish brown. Gills adnate, russet ochre. Stipe 5×1cm, with a thickened ± marginate base, russet ochre, somewhat zoned or cortinate, striate at the apex. Flesh pale. Spores 7×4.5μm; ninepin-shaped cystidia confined to the gill-edge. In manured places, gardens and especially glasshouses, mainly in spring. In Britain known only from glasshouses at R.B.G. Kew and Edinburgh. E1.

Conocybe pygmaeoaffinis (Fr.) Kühn.
Fleshy cap 3-5cm, velvety-fibrillose towards the margin, pale ochraceous. Gills remaining pale, edge velvety with cystidia under a lens. Stipe 6×0.3cm, striate, not powdered. Flesh whitish. Spores 9×5μm; cystidia awl-shaped, with long slender neck. Mossy lawns, gardens etc. sometimes in clusters. Uncommon. E2.

Conocybe arrhenii (Fr.) K. v. Wav. [*Pholiotina togularis* p.p.]
Cap 2-5cm, conical or umbonate, striate, reddish brown, hygrophanous, drying to ochre toffee colour. Gills ochraceous. Stipe 4×0.3cm, bulbous, whitish, with striate ring. Flesh similar colours. Spores 9×5μm; cystidia cylindrical. Grassy places under broadleaved trees. Common. E2.

Conocybe vestita (Fr.) Kühn. [*Pholiotina v.*]
Cap 2-4cm, convex, bright ochre, margin at first conspicuously appendiculate with remnants of a white veil which later disappear. Stipe 6×0.2cm, undulating, floccose, white, bistre when rubbed. Flesh similar colour. Spores 7×4μm with inconspicuous germ-pore; cystidia bottle-shaped. Damp shrubberies. Fairly common. E2.

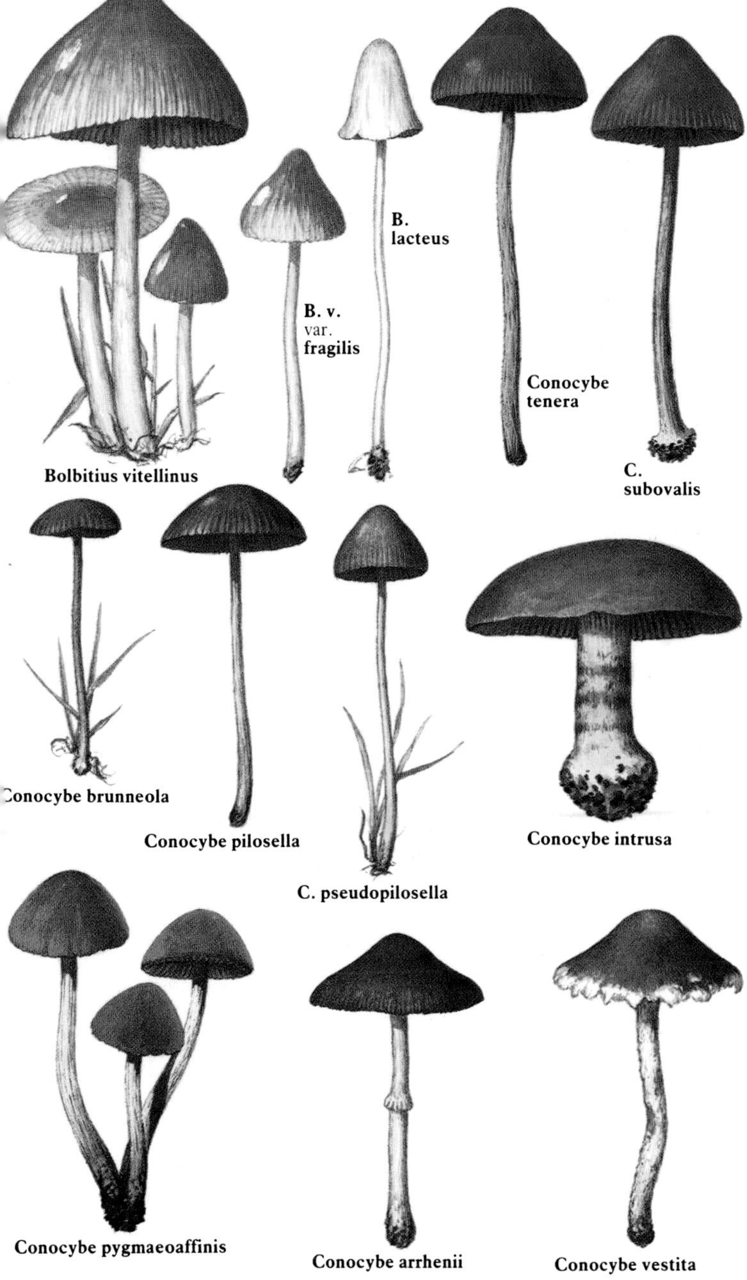

BOLBITIACEAE

B. lacteus

B. v. var. fragilis

Bolbitius vitellinus

Conocybe tenera

C. subovalis

Conocybe brunneola

Conocybe pilosella

C. pseudopilosella

Conocybe intrusa

Conocybe pygmaeoaffinis

Conocybe arrhenii

Conocybe vestita

Genus *Agrocybe*. Spores and gills dull brown or tobacco colour; cap rather fleshy, not striate.

Agrocybe praecox (Pers.) Fayod
Cap 4-6cm, rather thin-fleshed, brownish beige fading to dull greyish ochre. Gills whitish to dingy brown. Stipe 10×0.5cm, whitish, with membranous ring. Flesh pale; smell mealy, taste becoming bitter. Spores 10×6μm, ovoid, with germ-pore; cystidia rather bottle-shaped or bellied. Grassy thickets, commonly but not exclusively in Spring. Edible. Common. E3.

A. sphaleromorpha (Bull.) Fayod is more slender, brighter coloured, ochraceous russet, with ± bulbous stipe and is common in damp or sandy pastures. E2.

Agrocybe molesta (Lasch.) Sing. [*A. dura*]
Cap 6-10cm, convex, fleshy, surface greasy then often cracking, white to pale ochraceous. Gills clay colour then rusty with a grey-lilac tinge. Stipe 10×1cm, slightly club-shaped, ochraceous with a whitish ring. Flesh white; smell like mushroom, taste mild. Spores 12×7.5μm, elliptical, with germ-pore; cystidia swollen in lower part. Gardens, lawns and pastures. Good edible species. Common. E2.

Agrocybe aegerita (Brig.) Fayod [*A. cylindracea*]
Cap 6-10cm, convex, smooth or matt, becoming wrinkled and cracked, livid whitish beige then dingy ochraceous at the disc. Gills pale then clay russet, adnate to ± decurrent. Stipe 10×1cm, white to greyish cream at the base, ring soon becoming torn or shrivelled. Flesh pale; smell and taste pleasant. Spores 10×6μm, pore obscure; cystidia obtusely fusiform. Clustered on stumps or dead trunks of broadleaved trees, ash, oak, poplar, sycamore, willow and often elm in southern England, scarcely reaching Scotland. Good edible fungus. E3.

Agrocybe erebia (Fr.) Kühn.
Cap 4-7cm, somewhat umbonate, russet fawn with somewhat bistre centre. Gills adnate to ± decurrent, beige to dingy rust colour. Stipe 8×0.6cm, slightly club-shaped, concolorous or browning at the base; ring broad and striate; Flesh pale, brownish in the base; taste becoming bitter. Spores 12×6.5μm, ± ovoid without a germ-pore, basidia 2-spored; cystidia elongate. Under broadleaved trees and conifers, on bare damp soil. Occasional. E2.

Agrocybe pediades (Fr.) Fayod
Cap 3-5cm, obtuse, yellowish ochre. Gills beige ochraceous. Stipe 5×0.4cm, whitish, without a ring but sometimes with traces of a cortina. Flesh pale, somewhat bitter. Spores 12×8μm, germ-pore distinct; cystidia bottle-shaped. Lawns, pastures and roadsides. Occasional. E2.

A. semiorbicularis (Bull.) Fayod, more slender with almost campanulate cap, has 2-spored basidia with spores up to 16×9μm and is equally common. E2.

Agrocybe arvalis (Fr.) Sing.
Cap 2-4cm, soon expanded, yellowish brown, hygrophanous, drying beige brown. Gills adnate, brownish. Stipe 8×0.4cm, similar colour, naked, base rooting and commonly arising from a small black sclerotium. Flesh pale. Spores 12×6μm, with germ-pore; cystidia elongated, some bearing finger-like processes. Pastures. Uncommon. E2.

Agrocybe vervacti (Fr.) Sing.
Cap similar to *A. arvalis* but brighter yellow ochre or darker at the centre, scarcely hygrophanous. Gills broadly adnate, brownish yellow. Stipe 3×0.4cm, whitish, somewhat zoned yellowish. Flesh pale. Spores 9×6μm; germ-pore lacking or inconspicuous; cystidia exclusively marginal, with elongated neck. Lawns and pastures. Occasional in England. E2.

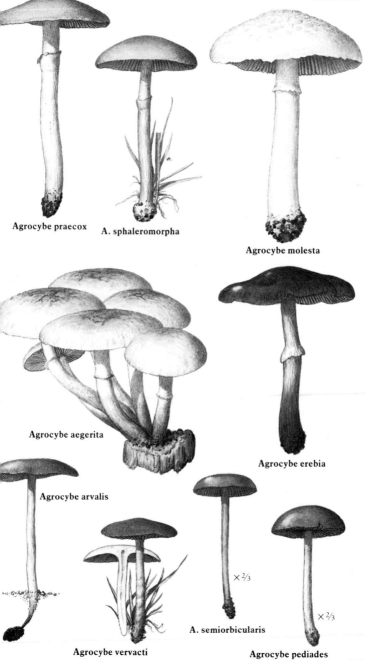

Agrocybe praecox

A. sphaleromorpha

Agrocybe molesta

Agrocybe aegerita

Agrocybe erebia

Agrocybe arvalis

Agrocybe vervacti

× ⅔

A. semiorbicularis

× ⅔

Agrocybe pediades

263

Genus *Simocybe*. Aspect of *Naucoria* (p.230), living on wood.

Simocybe centunculus (Fr.) Karst.
Cap 2-3cm, convex, matt to ± velvety, dingy ochre with olivaceous tinge. Gills dingy yellowish with white edges. Stipe 2×0.2cm, often bent, concolorous, powdery or cottony. Flesh yellowish; taste becoming bitter. Spores 7×4.5μm, kidney-shaped; cystidia clavate; cap surface bearing rather short similar-shaped hairs. On fallen branches of broadleaved trees. Uncommon. E1.

Genus *Panaeolus*. Spores and gills dark brown to blackish, gills generally mottled. Transitional to Coprinaceae and often referred there.

Panaeolus foenisecii (Pers.) Schroet. [*Panaeolina foenisecii*]
Cap 2-4cm, hemispherical then expanded and flat, dark russet brown becoming pinkish ochre. Gills brownish to dark purplish chestnut. Stipe 5×0.3cm, reddish brown or vinaceous at the base. Flesh concolorous. Spores 15×8μm, strongly rugose. Characteristic of mown lawns but also in pastures, sand-dunes and grassy woodland rides. Abundant throughout Britain. E3.

Panaeolus acuminatus Quél.
Cap 1-2cm, pointed, taller than broad, dark brown with a vinaceous tinge, becoming paler but with the margin persisting blackish. Gills nearly free, widest at the middle, blackish. Stipe 10×0.2cm, apex powdered pinkish white on a pinkish brown ground, progressively more vinaceous to blackish towards the base. Flesh colours similar. Spores smooth, ± flattened, 16×11×9μm. Manured pastures and on dung. Common. E2.

P. rickenii Hora has a more obtuse cap, weeping heavily powdered stipe and occurs rather in grassy woods and not on dung. E3.

Panaeolus sphinctrinus (Fr.) Quél.
Cap 3-5cm, ovoid with margin slightly incurved, scalloped or hanging down; surface matt then cracking, greyish clay colour with olivaceous tinge. Gills nearly free, widest at the middle, blackish grey with tinge of olive and white edges. Stipe 12×0.4cm, concolorous or with reddish base. Flesh pale; smell of straw. Spores somewhat flattened, lemon-shaped, 18×12×10μm, with prominent germ-pore. Manured meadows and often on cow dung. Very common. E4.

P. campanulatus (Bull.) Quél. is similar in stature but with less contracted margin and a more russet-brown cap without olivaceous tinge. Equally common. E2.

Panaeolus fimicola (Pers.) Quél.
Cap 1-3cm, conical, sepia to blackish grey-brown, becoming greyish ochre. Gills dark. Stipe 4×0.2cm, brownish with the apex slightly powdered. Flesh colour similar. Spores not flattened, 12×7μm. Lawns and pastures. Common. E3.

Panaeolus ater (Lange) Bon
Cap 1-2cm, hemispherical, soon convexo-expanded, dark purplish black to ochraceous sepia. Gills ash grey to blackish. Stipe 5×0.3cm, powdered, reddish brown at the base. Flesh similar colours. Spores 13×7μm; distinguished by the presence of chrysocystidia. On lawns. Uncommon. E1.

P. obliquoporus Bon is more fleshy, 3-5cm, with warmer pinkish or purplish tints and spores with an oblique germ-pore. Sandy lawns. E1.

Panaeolus semiovatus (Sow.) Wünsche [*Anellaria semiovata, A. separata*]
Cap 3-5cm, ovoid-campanulate, viscid, somewhat wrinkled or uneven, whitish to pale creamy ochre. Gills ascending, widest at the middle, black. Stipe 15×0.5cm, whitish, silky, with membranous ring and ± bulbous base. Flesh pale; smell of straw. Spores 20×10μm, elliptical to ± hexagonal with somewhat oblique germ-pore. Chrysocystidia present. On dung of cattle and horses. Common in the North and West but far less so in S.E. England. E2.

P. phalaenarum (Bull.) Quél. is similar but more slender, cap 2-4cm and lacks the ring. E2.

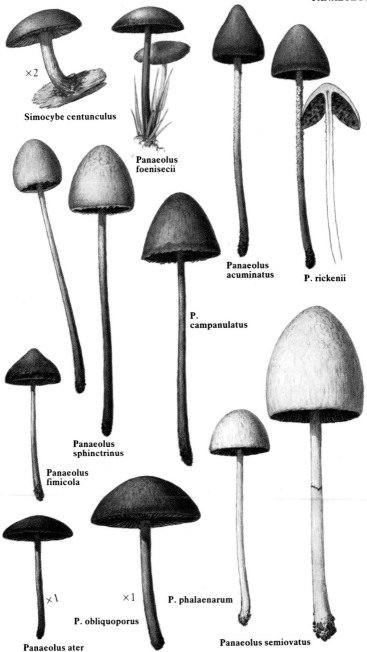

×2

Simocybe centunculus

Panaeolus foenisecii

Panaeolus acuminatus

P. rickenii

P. campanulatus

Panaeolus sphinctrinus

Panaeolus fimicola

P. phalaenarum

×1

P. obliquoporus

×1

Panaeolus ater

Panaeolus semiovatus

Order *Agaricales*. Stipe ± separable from cap. Spores and gills white or blackish.

Family *Coprinaceae*. Spores and gills dark, violaceous brown to blackish, gills not mottled. Somewhat fragile or deliquescent carpophores.

Genus *Psathyrella*. Cap flat or campanulate, non-deliquescent, not or slightly striate. Subgenus *Psathyrella*. Cap campanulate, mycenoid; spores over (10)12μm long, basidia sphaeropedunculate.

Psathyrella gracilis (Fr.) Quél.
Cap 2-4cm, slightly striate, grey-brown to ochraceous clay colour, somewhat pinkish when dried. Gills broad, adnate, brownish grey with somewhat pink edges. Stipe 10×0.3cm, rooting, whitish. Flesh colours similar. Spores 13×6.5μm, with broad germ-pore; cystidia fusiform. Under broadleaved trees, in clearings, often attached to fallen twigs. Common. E3. **P. atomata** (Fr.) Quél. is more slender, not pinkish, and grows on lawns and in pastures. E3.

Psathyrella ammophila (Dur. & Lév.) Orton
Cap 3-5cm, soon expanded, not striate, fawnish ochre to dull greyish brown. Gills adnate, dark brown. Stipe 8×0.5cm, whitish, rooting deep in the sand. Flesh concolorous. Spores 12×7μm; cystidia swollen below or bottle-shaped. On ± fixed sand-dunes with marram-grass – common in such places. E3.

Psathyrella conopilus (Fr.) Pears. & Dennis [*P. subatrata*]
Cap 4-7cm, conico-campanulate, hygrophanous and somewhat striate, dark brown, bright ochre at the centre and dotted under a lens by dark hairs, thick-walled under the microscope. Gills brownish with purplish tint. Stipe 15×0.5cm, whitish, soon hollow. Flesh pale. Spores 17×9μm, pore slightly oblique; cystidia marginal, swollen below. In gardens, parks and copses, among rubbish. Common. E3.

Psathyrella hirta Peck [*P. coprobia*]
Cap convex 2-3cm, chestnut brown, at first covered with white flakes of the general veil, which soon disappear. Gills broad, adnate, greyish brown. Stipe 4×0.2cm, white, floccose. Flesh pale. Spores 13×6μm; cystidia with swollen base and long neck. On dung of cattle and horses. Uncommon. E2.

Subgenus *Psathyra*. Cap plano-convex, often with a veil; spores not exceeding 10μm long unless the basidia are narrow.

Psathyrella artemisiae (Pass.) K.-M. [*P. squamosa*]
Cap 3cm, convex or umbonate, general veil copious, woolly-fibrillose, whitish, universal at first then disappearing from the disc outwards, surface greyish brown. Gills pale to brownish. Stipe 3×0.3cm, white, floccose. Flesh pale. Spores 9×5μm, with germ-pore; cystidia flask-shaped with refringent wall. Under beech. Fairly common. E2. **P. impexa** (Romagn.) Galland takes a pinkish tint on drying and has common-place bottle-shaped cystidia. E2.

Psathyrella hydrophila (Bull.) R. Mre. [*P. piluliformis* auct. p.p.]
Cap 3-6cm, convex, glabrous, very hygrophanous, chestnut brown drying pale ochre in concentric zones; margin whitish appendiculate. Gills brownish to dark chestnut. Stipe 8×0.5cm, fasciculate, white, somewhat cortinate. Flesh pale. Spores 6×3.5μm, pale; cystidia bottle-shaped. In dense clusters on stumps and among debris of broadleaved trees. Very common. E4. **P. multipedata** (Peck) A.H. Smith occurs in dense tufts with numerous slender stipes united at the base. Uncommon. E2.

Psathyrella spadiceogrisea (Sch.) R. Mre.
Cap 4-6cm, slightly umbonate, smooth, somewhat striate but without a veil, rather bright ochraceous fawn, paler at the centre and often chestnut brown at the margin. Gills dingy grey-violaceous to reddish brown. Stipe 8×0.5cm, whitish, soon hollow. Flesh pale. Spores 9×5μm, slightly kidney-shaped, with moderate germ-pore; facial cystidia bottle-shaped, marginal ones sphaeropedunculate. On soil of thickets or among debris of broadleaved trees, especially in Spring. Common. E2.

P. atomata

Psathyrella
gracilis

Psathyrella
ammophila

Psathyrella
artemisiae

P. impexa

Psathyrella
hirta

Psathyrella conopilus

Psathyrella hydrophila

P. multipedata

Psathyrella spadiceogrisea

Psathyrella candolleana (Fr.) R. Mre.
Cap 5-10cm, soon expanded, thin-fleshed, yellowish ochraceous, then pinkish white towards the margin which often eventually splits between the gills. Gills crowded, narrow lilaceous, then brown bistre. Stipe 8×0.5cm, white, striate below the gills. Flesh whitish. Spores 8×4µm, ± cylindrical, pale, with a germ-pore; cystidia on gill edge only, obtuse. Solitary or in troops in copses, nettle beds, gardens etc. Very common. Edible. E4.

P. leucotephra (Bk. & Br.) Orton has greyer gills and a tattered or fugaceous ring which may be appendiculate to the cap margin. E2.

Psathyrella sarcocephala (Fr.) Sing. [*P. spadicea* p.p.]
Cap 5-8cm, convex, a beautiful ochraceous chocolate colour, then pale pinkish brown. Gills tinged flesh colour then chocolate grey. Stipe 10×1cm, whitish with hint of flesh colour, powdered or silky and finely striate. Flesh pale to similarly coloured. Spores 9×6µm, with a pore; cystidia thick-walled, bearing crystals at the apex. In tufts on stumps or at the foot of trunks of broadleaved trees. Quite common. E1.

Psathyrella pygmaea (Bull.) Sing.
Cap 1cm, slightly conical, striate, whitish to brownish grey. Gills crowded, pinkish brown. Stipe 2×0.2cm, pure white, pruinose. Flesh pale. Spores 6×4µm; cystidia short, bearing crystals. In troops on rotten wood, often accompanying *Coprinus disseminatus* which it resembles. Uncommon. E2.

Subgenus *Lacrymaria*. Cap and/or stipe velvety to scaly.

Psathyrella lacrymabunda (Bull.) Moser [*Lacrymaria velutina*]
Cap 5-10cm, convex or umbonate, rather fleshy, fibrillosely velvety or ± scaly, dull ochraceous to brownish grey, margin woolly. Gills brownish then black, weeping. Stipe 8×0.7cm, whitish, with a cortina, fibrillose to scaly like the cap. Flesh brownish ochre. Spores 10×6µm, warted; cystidia somewhat capitate. On bare soil, in fields, beside footpaths, often associated with buried wood or dead roots. Edible. Very common. E4.

P. pyrotricha (Holmsk.) Moser differs in its brighter russet colour and is associated rather with stumps of conifers, especially spruce. Less common. E1.

Psathyrella cotonea (Quél.) K.-M.
Cap 4-8cm, convex or umbonate, fibrillosely woolly, whitish then with pale brownish grey scales. Gills long remaining pale, finally greyish brown. Stipe 12×0.8cm, floccose, whitish, tinged bright yellow at the base by the mycelium. Flesh concolorous. Spores 8×4.5µm, cylindrical, smooth; cystidia flask-shaped or swollen below. In tufts on stumps of broadleaved trees, especially beech. Uncommon. E2.

P. caput-medusae (Fr.) K.-M. occurs on conifers and has more shaggy scales. Rare. E2.

Psathyrella maculata (Parker) Moser
Cap 3-5cm, convex, with trapezoidal or stellate scales, dark brown or blackish on a russet ground, soon blotched with black. Gills violaceous brown. Stipe 5×0.5cm, concolorous with a dark band up to a fluffy annular zone, whitish above this. Flesh colour similar. Spores 5×3µm, without a pore; cystidia flask-shaped with slender beak. In copses of broadleaved trees. Rare, not British. E2.

P. populina (Britz.) K. v. Wav. [*P. sylvestris*] has whitish or slightly scaly stipe, spores 7×5µm and cystidia bearing concretions which turn greenish in ammonia. Rare. E2.

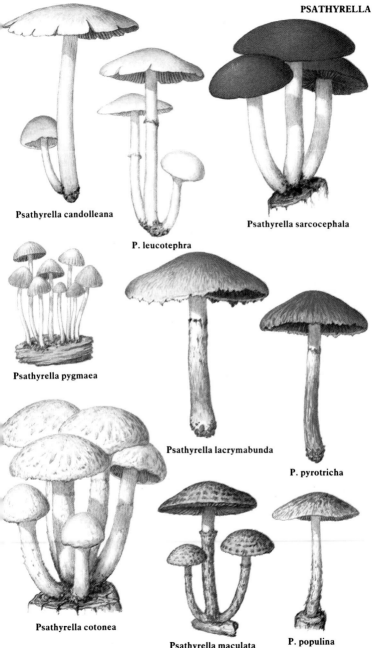

Psathyrella candolleana

P. leucotephra

Psathyrella sarcocephala

Psathyrella pygmaea

Psathyrella lacrymabunda

P. pyrotricha

Psathyrella cotonea

Psathyrella maculata

P. populina

Genus *Coprinus*. Cap ovoid or conical, somewhat thin or fluted or else deliquescent at maturity; stipe often readily separable from the cap.

Section *Coprinus* [*Comati*]. Cap covering woolly or wispy, composed of elongated hyphae. Spores often 3-dimensional.

Coprinus comatus (Müll.) Pers.   LAWYER'S WIG
Cap elliptic-cylindrical, 6-15×2-4cm, not or only tardily expanding, surface fleecy, whitish becoming pink then blackening from the bottom upwards. Gills ascending, free, white then reddening and blackening in pace with the exterior. Stipe 10×0.8cm, thickened below and with a ring near the base, white, hollow. Flesh white, blackening then deliquescent. Spores 15×7µm, with germ-pore. On lawns, pastures, bare soil, waste ground, along footpaths and in rubbish dumps. Very common. A good edible fungus in the young state when quite white (though rather watery alone: best in batter with garlic and parsley) but *not* when blackening. E4. **C. sterquilinus** (Fr.) Fr. resembles *C. comatus* in miniature, shaggier and more quickly blackening, growing on dung; spores 20×12µm. Rare. E1.

Coprinus atramentarius (Bull.) Fr.   COMMON INK CAP
Cap 5-10cm, soon broadly expanded, surface smooth or finely wrinkled, greyish, apex brownish and sometimes peeling slightly. Gills and flesh blackening and quickly deliquescing to a black fluid. Stipe 10×1cm, pale with a rudimentary basal volva. Spores 10×5µm, elliptical, with germ-pore. In clusters on the ground in gardens, parks, commonly near buried or rotting timber. Very common. Edible but causes flushing in the face, sweating and palpitation if eaten with alcohol: best avoided. Antabuse, the drug for treating alcoholics, is derived from it. E4.

Coprinus erythrocephalus (Lév.) Fr.
Cap 3×0.7cm, whitish, becoming pink and eventually brick red throughout, fleecy. Gills pinkish white then grey. Stipe 5×0.3cm, pinkish floccose below. Flesh pale, or pinkish in the base. Spores 9×6µm, ovoid, with narrow germ-pore; cuticular hyphae tinged yellow. On bare soil and rubbish dumps with rotting woody debris. Rare. E1.

Coprinus picaceus (Bull.) Fr.
Cap 6-10cm, ovoid to conical or obtuse, at first whitish, then peeling into white patches on a blackish brown ground. Gills ascending, crowded, blackish then deliquescing. Stipe 15×2cm, whitish, powdered then browning. Flesh colours similar, smell faint at first, later of tar or naphthaline. Spores 18×12µm, elliptical with a broad germ-pore. Under deciduous trees, especially beech. Common only in southern England. E3. **C. gonophyllus** Quél. is like a miniature *C. picaceus* growing on burnt ground, with flattened spores 8×6×4.5µm. Rare. E2.

Coprinus lagopus (Fr.) Fr.
Cap 2-4cm, ovoid, white and fleecy like a small *C. comatus*, then broadly conical, striate and ± peeling to show a brownish ground. Gills ascending, soon black. Stipe 8×0.7cm, slightly club-shaped, fibrillosely scaly, pure white, base smooth without a ring. Flesh white, then greying; inodorous. Spores 12×7µm, ovoid, with a germ-pore. In litter under broadleaved trees and in gardens. Very common. E2. **C. lagopides** Karst. has a fleecy cream-ochre cap, breaking up as in *C. picaceus* and is distinguished by its flattened ± globose spores, 9×7×6µm; not uncommon on burnt ground. E2.

Coprinus cinereus (Sch.) S.F. Gray [*C. macrorhizus*]
Similar size to *C. lagopus*, with fleecy surface, dingy white on a grey ground. Gills ascending, grey then blackish. Stipe ± bulbous and rooting deeply, whitish, smooth to somewhat zoned with ochraceous fibrils towards the base. Flesh pale, greying. Spores 10×6µm, elliptical, with inconspicuous germ-pore. On dung, manure heaps. Very common. E2. **C. radiatus** (Bolt.) Pers. is smaller, 1-2cm at most, shaggy with white fibrils then strongly striate; spores 11-13×6µm. Common on dung. E2.

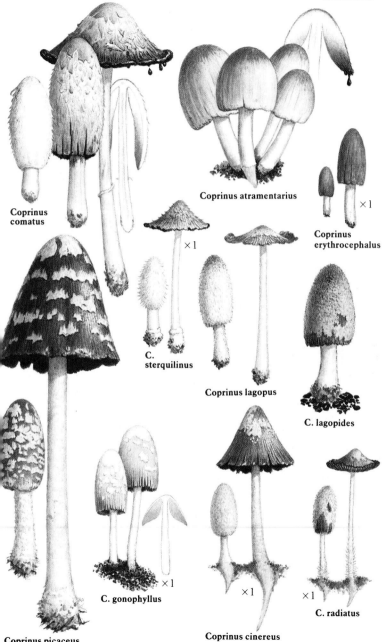

Coprinus
comatus

Coprinus atramentarius

Coprinus
erythrocephalus

C.
sterquilinus

Coprinus lagopus

C. lagopides

C. gonophyllus

Coprinus cinereus

C. radiatus

Coprinus picaceus

271

Section *Micacei*. Cap smooth or striate, veil represented by more or less persistent granules made up of short or spherical cells.

Coprinus micaceus (Bull.) Fr.
Cap 3-5cm, ovoid, then conico-campanulate with a lobed somewhat splitting margin, surface smooth or striate, fawnish ochre, centre sprinkled with fugaceous ochraceous granules. Gills white to brown, becoming purplish black. Stipe 7×0.3cm, whitish, dusted with ochraceous granules towards the base. Flesh pale then blackening. Spores 10×6×5µm, lenticular, somewhat mitre-shaped in face view with a truncate germ-pore. In ± dense clusters on and around stumps, logs and dead roots of broadleaved trees. Very common everywhere. E4.

Coprinus domesticus (Bolt.) S.F. Gray
Similar in stature to *C. micaceus* but rather rusty fawn with more persistent, even shaggy, whiter granules over the apex. Gills pale, then grey with violet tinge. Stipe 10×0.5cm, thicker at the base, floccose, often arising from a bright rusty, shaggy mycelium (*Ozonium*). Flesh pale, not readily deliquescing. Spores 10×5µm, slightly kidney-shaped. On trunks and dead branches of broadleaved trees, worked timber, in cellars and mines etc, sometimes singly. Quite common. E3. **C. xanthothrix** Romagn. is distinguished by its yellowish to fawn pointed cap granules and relatively pale spores. Uncommon, in litter under beech etc. E2.

Coprinus niveus (Pers.) Fr.
Cap 2-5cm, conical to campanulate, obtuse, completely powdered with snow-white granules on a greyish ground exposed by wiping or when blown upon. Gills ascending, greyish. Stipe 6×0.3cm, white, floccose, elongating to 12-15cm at maturity. Flesh pale, blackening. Spores lenticular, 16×12×9µm, with conical apex. On dung of cattle and horses. Common throughout Britain. E3.

Coprinus narcoticus (Batsch) Fr.
Cap 2-3cm, acorn-shaped then expanded, striate to the apex, floccose with greyish russet granules on a beige to light grey ground. Gills pinkish grey to blackish. Stipe 7×0.4cm, spindle-shaped, rather whitish-fleecy. Strong smell of asphalt or some nitrate fertilizers. Spores 12×6µm surrounded by a distinctive colourless envelope (perispore). On soil under broadleaved trees, especially by footpaths. Rare. E1.

Section *Pseudocoprinus*. Veil absent, cap sometimes downy under a hand lens.

Coprinus plicatilis (Curt.) Fr.
Cap 2-3cm, thin, whitish, markedly striate-furrowed up to a small circular ochraceous centre, eventually greyish throughout. Gills distant, attached to a collar round the stipe, apex, white, then grey. Stipe 5×0.2cm, almost equal to ± bulbous, whitish to greyish ochre, smooth. Flesh negligible but scarcely deliquescent. Spores 12×10×7µm, lenticular with an excentric pore; pileus cuticle hymeniform without hairs. Lawns and pastures. Very common throughout Britain. E3. **C. auricomus** Pat. is slightly more fleshy, with the striations somewhat forked, yellowish fawn and bearing velvety hairs towards the centre, thick-walled under the microscope. Uncommon. E3.

Coprinus disseminatus (Pers.) S.F. Gray
Cap 1-2cm, ovoid or conico-campanulate, conspicuously striate, pubescent, pale beige then greyish. Gills ± distant, grey to blackish purple. Stipe 3×0.15cm, whitish or tinged vinaceous, downy. Flesh negligible, not deliquescent. Spores 9×5µm, elliptical with broad truncate germ-pore; cap cuticle beset with erect obtuse colourless hairs. In clusters, though not tufted, on and around stumps or over buried wood. Very abundant in southern England, less so in the north. E3.

Coprinus angulatus Peck [*C. boudieri*]
Cap 2-3cm, ovoid, margin striate, splitting, ± velvety, hygrophanous, chestnut drying to pale ochre, disc brown, sometimes outlined with olive. Gills ash colour with white edges. Stipe 4×0.4cm, pruinose, whitish. Flesh pale, deliquescent. Spores mitre-shaped, lenticular, 10×8×6µm, cap cuticle downy with erect hairs. On burnt soil or charred wood. Quite common. E1.

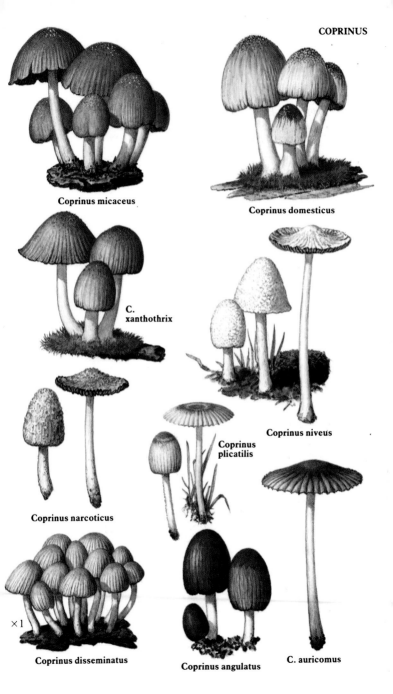

COPRINUS

Coprinus micaceus

Coprinus domesticus

C. xanthothrix

Coprinus narcoticus

Coprinus niveus

Coprinus plicatilis

×1

Coprinus disseminatus

Coprinus angulatus

C. auricomus

273

Family *Agaricaceae*. Gills free. Spore print white or blackish bistre, occasionally greenish or reddish. Partial veil a ring or sheathing ring.

Tribe *Agariceae*. Only one genus in Europe, *Agaricus* [*Psalliota*]. Spore print dark bistre; gills pink then dark brown to blackish at maturity.

Section *Agaricus*. Ring complex, shaggy or doubled by a basal sheath, sometimes like an appressed volva; flesh ± reddening.

Agaricus campestris Linn.   FIELD MUSHROOM
Cap 6-10cm, convex, silky-fibrillose, whitish, tinged ochraceous with age, bearing brown scales in var. *squamulosa* or yellowing in var. *equestris*. Gills crowded, bright pink when young, then bistre, edge concolorous. Stipe 5×1cm, spindle-shaped or attenuated, whitish, ring cottony, fugaceous. Flesh white, turning slightly pink; smell and taste fungoid. Spores 8×5µm, with inconspicuous germ-pore, no sterile cells on gill edge. Pastures. Common. Edible and excellent. E3.

A. cupreobrunneus (Møll.) Pil., vinaceous brown glossy cap with fibrillose margin, short stipe floccose at first and spores up to 10×6µm. Meadows, uncommon. E1.

Agaricus bisporus (Lange) Imbach
Cap 5-10cm, convex, whitish then with russet-brown fibrils, margin fleecy to append-iculate. Gills pink then bistre. Stipe 6×1cm, cylindrical, whitish, ring cottony. Flesh turning slightly pink; smell and taste pleasant. Fields and gardens. Fairly common. Spores 9×6µm, ovoid, basidia 2-spored; gill edge with clavate sterile cells close-packed. Commercially grown mushrooms are mostly races of this species, as is the spawn sold for home cultivation. E3.

Agaricus romagnesii Wasser [*Psalliota radicata* p.p.]
Cap 4-6cm, soon expanded, with brown often star-shaped scales over the centre on a whitish ground and pale fibrillose margin browning slightly. Gills bright pink then dingy brown with paler edges. Stipe 8×0.7cm, whitish, browning, slightly bulbous with white string-like roots; ring fragile. Flesh white to pinkish brown, rather orange towards the base; smell faint. Spores 7×4µm, ovoid; cells of gill edge somewhat septate. Lawns in parks, sometimes under conifers, often in towns. Indigestible or slightly toxic. E2. **A. bresadolianus** Bohus [*A. radicatus* p.p.] is a good edible fungus, though mildly diuretic, close to *A. campestris* in its bright pink gills with fertile edges. E1.

Agaricus bernardii (Quél.) Sacc.
Cap 12-20cm, convex, fleshy, white, cracking, often deeply so at the centre. Gills greyish to purplish brown. Stipe 8×3cm, white; ring broad, thick, somewhat sheath-ing. Flesh white becoming purplish pink or yellowish; smell strong, finally rather fishy. Spores 9×6µm, ovoid; cells of gill edge tufted, cylindrical-clavate or lobed. In pastures, especially near the sea. Edible but poor. Uncommon. E1.

Agaricus bitorquis (Quél.) Sacc. [*A. edulis*]
Cap 6-12cm, convex, fleshy, white, finally often ochraceous in places. Gills pale cinnamon pink then bistre with paler margin. Stipe 8×2cm, whitish, with two rings, the lower narrow and sheathing. Flesh dingy white, slowly turning pale vinaceous fawn; smell acidulous to almond-like. Spores 6×5µm, roundish; cells of gill edge numerous, clavate. Sandy and manured soil beside roads, often beneath pavements, lifting flagstones or bursting through asphalt. Edible and good. Common in S.E. England. E2.

Agaricus subperonatus (Lange) Sing.
Cap 10-15cm, fleshy, rather scaly, yellowish brown with fibrillose somewhat append-iculate margin. Gills dingy pink then bistre with paler edges. Stipe 10×2cm, slightly club-shaped, whitish, bruising tawny; ring thick, duplicated by a basal sheath forming one or two appressed concolorous zones on the lower part of the stipe. Flesh whitish, immediately turning brownish vinaceous when broken; smell fruity, then unpleasant, like chicory. Spores 7×5µm; cells of gill edge elongate-clavate. Gardens, rubbish dumps etc. Uncommon. Edible but poor. E2.

A. vaporarius (Pers.) Cappelli is very similar, darker brown with thick flesh flushing less pink or more orange-brown and smelling strongly of liquorice or chicory. Spores similar, marginal cells less developed. Uncommon in gardens in S.E. England. E2.

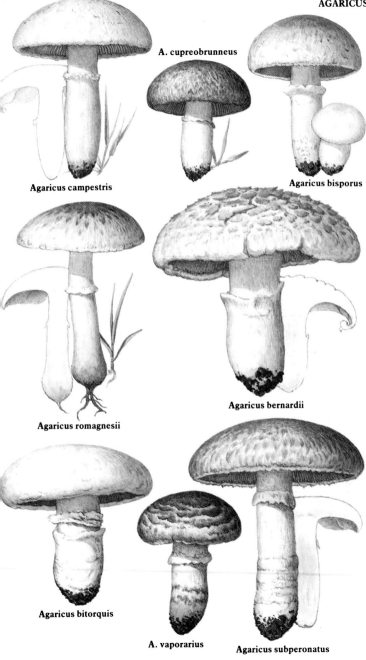

A. cupreobrunneus

Agaricus campestris

Agaricus bisporus

Agaricus romagnesii

Agaricus bernardii

Agaricus bitorquis

A. vaporarius

Agaricus subperonatus

Section *Sanguinolenti*. Flesh reddening, ring simple, pendant.

Agaricus silvaticus Sch.
Cap 6-10cm, not very fleshy, covered with russet brown scales on a pale ochre ground. Several colour variants have been described by some authors. Gills pinkish to greyish brown. Stipe 8×1cm, somewhat bulbous, white, bruising pinkish grey; ring fragile. Flesh white, flushing pale vinaceous red; smell pleasant. Spores 6×3.5µm; cells of gill edge rather inflated clavate. Under conifers. Common. Edible and good. E3.

Agaricus haemorrhoidarius Schulz. ap. Kalchbr.
Cap 10-15cm, fleshy, with close set dark reddish brown fibrillose scales. Gills bright pink, bruising redder. Stipe 10×1cm, slightly bulbous, whitish, brownish grey below, bruising red when handled; ring broad and membranous. Flesh white, flushing blood red. Spores 7×4µm; cells at edge similar to *A. silvaticus*. In woods under broadleaved trees, especially beech and oak. Common. Edible and good. E3.

A. langei (Møll. & J. Schaef.) Møll. differs mainly in its somewhat spindle-shaped stipe and larger spores (9×5µm). Equally common and edible. E3.

Agaricus variegans Møll. [*Psalliota variegata*]
Cap 7-12cm, convex, to umbonate, with somewhat trapezoidal concentric dingy brown scales on a buff ground. Gills dingy pinkish grey then dull brown. Stipe 10×1cm, bulbous, white to dull pinkish; ring whitish or with a line of small brown scales beneath. Flesh flushing dull pink especially in stipe apex; smell of *Lepiota cristata* or *Scleroderma*. Spores 5.5×3µm; cells of gill edge bladder-shaped. Under conifers. Edible but mediocre. Common. E3.

A. koelerionensis Bon has brighter colours, ± lilac, only a slight smell and occurs in grassy or sandy places; spores up to 7×4µm. Uncommon. E2.

Agaricus lanipes (Møll. & J. Schaef.) Sing.
Cap 8-12cm, convex, soon expanded, chestnut brown, nearly smooth or with small woolly reddish brown scales and a pale appendiculate margin. Gills pale then dingy bistre. Stipe 7×2cm, somewhat club-shaped, with concolorous zones below a rather narrow ring, which is white above, scaly brown beneath, base fleecy, somewhat rust coloured, sometimes arising from yellowish cords of mycelium. Flesh becoming pink, apricot yellow in the base; smell of chocolate, becoming sickly. Spores 6×4.5µm; cells of gill edge swollen clavate. In beech woods and parks. Occasional. Edible but poor. E2.

Section *Minores*. Small fungi, ± yellowing or becoming russet; with a simple ring; spores less than 6µm.

Agaricus semotus Fr.
Cap 3-6cm, somewhat umbonate, whitish, smooth but slightly fibrillose at the centre, ochraceous, sometimes tinged lilaceous or vinaceous, yellowing at the margin. Gills narrow, pinkish grey then pale bistre. Stipe 5×0.6cm, slightly bulbous, white, yellowing from the base; ring fragile. Flesh white to ochraceous, sometimes eventually orange; smell of aniseed mingled with bitter almonds. Spores 4-5×3µm; cells of gill edge ± capitately clavate. Under conifers in grassy places. Edible. Common. E3.

A. comtulus Fr. is like a miniature *A. campestris*, having bright pink gills with fertile edges; spores 5×3µm. In meadows. Uncommon. E2.

Agaricus porphyrizon Orton [*Psalliota purpurascens*]
Cap 6-8cm, convex or fleshy, with bright purplish lilac fibrils on a pale somewhat yellowing ground. Gills grey-pink to purplish black, with pale denticulate edges. Stipe 8×1cm, white, with yellowish or eventually orange bulb, often attached to cords of mycelium; ring simple, narrow, pendulous. Flesh white, turning yellowish russet; smell of bitter almonds or slightly of iodine. Spores 5-6×3µm; cells of gill edge bladder-shaped to clavate. In hedges, parks and under conifers and broadleaved trees. Uncommon. E2.

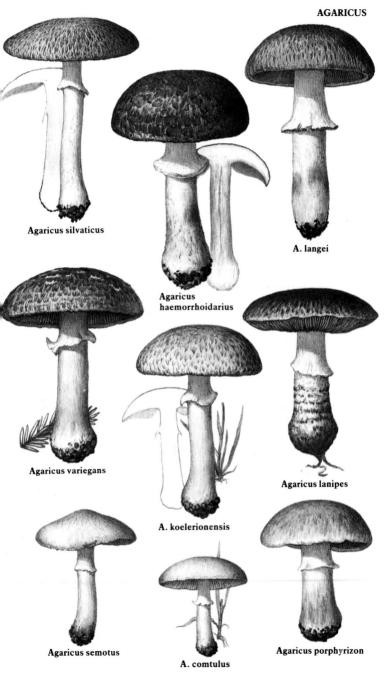

Agaricus silvaticus

Agaricus haemorrhoidarius

A. langei

Agaricus variegans

A. koelerionensis

Agaricus lanipes

Agaricus semotus

A. comtulus

Agaricus porphyrizon

Section *Arvenses*. Large to medium sized fungi, yellowing slow or permanent; ring with a cog-wheel on lower surface. Odours pleasant.

Agaricus arvensis Sch.   HORSE MUSHROOM
Cap 10-15cm, fleshy, convex or a truncate cone, silky, white then yellowing, eventually ochraceous russet, smooth or with crowded floccose scales round the margin. Gills pale pinkish grey to dingy brown. Stipe 13×2cm, almost equal or club-shaped, slightly floccose below the ring, bruising ochraceous; ring with a well-developed cog-wheel. Flesh white, becoming somewhat ochraceous; smell of aniseed. Spores 8×5μm; cells of gill edge clavate. Lawns and meadows. Fairly common. Edible and very good. E3. **A. nivescens** (Møll.) Møll., cap more globose at first, pure white only slightly yellowing, gills long remaining whitish; short to ± spherical spores 6×5μm. Gardens, meadows and pastures, quite common. Edible. E2.

Agaricus silvicola (Vitt.) Sacc.   WOOD MUSHROOM
The woodland analogue of *A. arvensis*, slightly less fleshy. Cap 6-12cm, yellowing slowly but deeply, eventually orange. Gills pinkish grey to bistre. Stipe 10×1.5cm, somewhat bulbous, silky white, yellowing with the typical ring but often torn. Flesh white then ochraceous; smell of aniseed or gingerbread. Spores 6-7×4μm; cells of gill edge balloon-shaped. Woods, esp. under beech and hornbeam but also conifers. Common. Edible and good, but do not confuse with the lethal white *Amanitas*. E4.

Agaricus macrosporus (Møll. & J. Schaef.) Pil.
Cap 20-30cm, very fleshy, white, silky or covered with fine crowded concolorous fibrils, yellowing slightly, eventually slightly ochraceous. Gills pinkish then chocolate bistre. Stipe 18×4cm, stout slightly spindle-shaped, white slightly floccose below a ring which bears shaggy ill-defined teeth. Flesh thick, scarcely yellowing but flushing pinkish in the base, eventually somewhat ochraceous. Smell weakly of aniseed or merely fungoid, sometimes unpleasant when old. Spores 12×6μm, almond-shaped, apex conical; thick-walled; cells of gill edge bladder-shaped. Pastures, the characteristic *Agaricus* of hill pasture in the Highlands and of maritime grassland in coastal Scotland. Edible. E3. **A. excellens** (Møll.) Møll. differs from *A. augustus* in being at first snow-white, from *A. macrosporus* in its taller, slender, striate stipe and in growing also in woods, especially under spruce but also beech. E3.

Agaricus augustus Fr.
Cap 12-18cm, fleshy, ± globose then convex-expanded, covered with pale greyish ochre then golden yellow scales. Gills pinkish grey to dark orange-brown. Stipe 12×3cm, slightly club-shaped, concolorous; ring broad, scaly on lower surface. Flesh white, flushing pink towards the base, yellowing in the cap; smell of bitter almonds. Spores 8×5μm; gill edge covered with rounded cells, usually in short chains. In parks, gardens and under various broadleaved trees, also spruce and yew. Quite common. Edible and good. E2.

Section *Xanthodermatei*. Less fleshy, quickly yellowing then fading again; smell rather unpleasant.

Agaricus xanthoderma Genev.   YELLOW-STAINING MUSHROOM
Cap 5-10cm, typically with a flattened top and a slightly lobed margin, silky, white, quickly turning bright yellow round the margin and where damaged, wholly streaked with grey in var. *griseus*. Gills pale, then bright flesh colour and finally blackish brown. Stipe 8×1cm, bulbous, sometimes with cords of white mycelium, white, yellowing somewhat and strongly so when scratched at the base; ring with a circle of coarse often yellowish teeth below or a downward directed collar. Flesh white, somewhat pinkish in the cap but chrome yellow in the extreme base of the stipe. Smell variously described as of iodine, phenol, ink or soft soap. Spores 6×3μm; cells of gill edge ± globose to pear-shaped. In gardens, parks and copses under broadleaved trees. Quite common. Highly indigestible, causes acute temporary upsets. E4.

Agaricus praeclaresquamosus Freem. [*Psalliota meleagris, A. placomyces* p.p.]
Similar to *A. xanthodermus* but with a *Lepiota*-like cap surface, fibrillose or broken up into dark scales contrasting with a paler or pinkish ground. Gills whitish then dingy pinkish. Yellowing similarly but smelling like ink, sweat or mouldy straw. Spores 5×3μm; cells of gill edge ± globose. Under broadleaved trees in damp places. Uncommon. Not edible. E4.

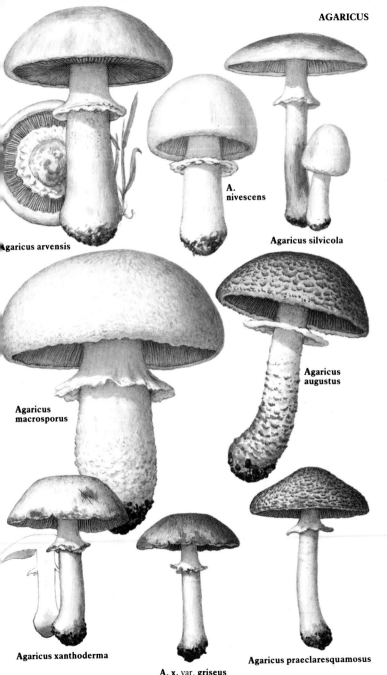

Agaricus arvensis

A. nivescens

Agaricus silvicola

Agaricus macrosporus

Agaricus augustus

Agaricus xanthoderma

A. x. var. griseus

Agaricus praeclaresquamosus

279

Tribe *Lepioteae*, Spore print white or pale.

Key to *Lepiota* and allied genera (condensed).

1a Cap surface powdery to granular or with shaggy points at least over the disc : **2**
1b Cap surface matt or wrinkled at least over the centre under a lens : **3**
1c Cap surface merely fibrillose to silky or slightly velvety, without definite scales or only peeling back near the margin; ring often ascending : **5**
1d Cap surface concentrically scaly round a well defined smooth central patch : **8**

2a Gills distinctly coloured at maturity »   *Melanophyllum*, 282
2b Gills white to cream or pale ochraceous »   *Cystolepiota*, 282

3a Cap entirely glabrous and wrinkled, no well-defined central patch, white to creamy ochraceous or putty colour; stipe with membranous ring and weeping amber droplets, sometimes the gills also. Smell faint »   *Chamaemyces fracidus*, 118
3b Cap soon cracking or scaly apart from a well defined central patch : **4**

4a Smell strong, of *Scleroderma* or fruit; ring whitish »   *Lepiota cristata*, 284
4b Smell slight; ring purplish grey, somewhat oblique »   *Lepiota lilacea*, 286

5a White to pale creamy ochraceous species : **6**
5b Cap pink, at least at the disc »   group of *Leucoagaricus sublittoralis*, 288
5c Cap beige to reddish brown or reddening, turning green with ammonia : **7**

6a Small fungus with fragile ring and slightly clavate stipe
                                                    Leucoagaricus serenus, 288
6b Fleshier, with moveable membranous ring »   *Leucoagaricus leucothites*, 288

7a Cap pale beige to rather reddish brown, reddening strongly then blackening, eventually slightly scaly »   *Leucoagaricus badhamii*, 288
7b Cap reddish brown, slightly velvety from the start, only feebly reddening »
                                                    Leucoagaricus pilatianus, 288
    (If more slender, paler, not reddening, ammonia reaction negative, see *Lepiota laevigata*, 184)

8a Large fleshy fungi, rather russet-brown, ring moveable along the stipe; Macrolepiota : **9**
8b Medium to small fungi with floccose or bracelet-like ring : **14**

9a Colour unchanging or only slowly and weakly reddening : **10**
9b Fungus reddening : **11**

10a Cap umbonate, central patch stellately cracking and peeling at the edge, stipe pale or only faintly zoned, ring simple, not thick »   *Macrolepiota konradii*, 290
10b Concentric scales well defined, ring double or thick and shaggy »
                                                    Macrolepiota procera, 290

11a Solitary, cap with regular recurved scales and complex ring, reddening distinctly and quickly, slightly saffrony : **12**
11b Tufted or in dense groups; ring simple, colouring duller red, vinaceous or yellow; on compost, sawdust etc : **13**

12a Cap 12 (15) cm, often under conifers; stipe rather slender from an onion-shaped bulb »   *Macrolepiota rhacodes*, 290
12b Cap up to 20 (30) cm, stipe stout with broad bulb; in gardens of fringe of woods
                                                    M. rhacodes var. *hortensis*, 290

13a Resembling the last with the same thick bulbous stipe but scales of the cap more stellately peeling »   *Macrolepiota venenata*, 290
13b Rather medium stature with spindle-shaped stipe, slightly zoned, poorly developed concentric scaling; yellowing then reddening orange-vinaceous »
                                                    Leucoagaricus bresadolae, 288

14a	White or pale : **15**
14b	Rather bright yellow : **16**
14c	Beige-ochraceous to brownish : **17**
14d	Brighter colouring, around orange or fawn russet : **18**
14e	Greenish, at least towards the centre : **19**
14f	Colour blackish, at least in the scales : **20**
14g	Pinkish to vinaceous or purplish, at least in the stipe : **22**

15a Cap fibrillose-scaly, ill-defined central patch; stipe rooting or spindle-shaped, membranous at first, later torn » *Leucoagaricus macrorhizus*, 288
15b Cap scarcely scaly with somewhat ochraceous central patch; stipe equal or clavate, rather fleecy below a wad-like ring » *Lepiota alba*, 284

16a Bright yellow throughout with striate margin » *Leucocoprinus birnbaumii*, 288
(If margin not striate and stipe duller, see *Lepiota xanthophylla*, 288)
16b Only the veil bright yellow, cap ground colour ochraceous fawn, stipe whitish *Lepiota ventriosospora*, 284
(If less bright yellow with pleasant smell see *L. ochraceofulva*, 286)

17a Cap fleshy with brown central patch and beige scales; stipe with oblique ring or garlanded, brownish, base reddening, sometimes tardily »
Lepiota ignivolvata, 284
17b More slender fungi or with floccose ring-zone not garlanded »
section *Lepiota*, 284

18a Smell strongly aromatic or pleasant » *Lepiota onchraceofulva*, 286
18b Smell faint or different » *Lepiota castanea*, 284

19a Scales dark greenish grey, margin bronzed; sometimes tinged orange as also the stipe towards the base » *Lepiota griseovirens*, 284
19b Patch over the disc olive-brown, surrounding scales progressively paler; gills often pinkish; smell somewhat like rubber » *Lepiota forquignonii*, 286

20a Margin striate; stipe smooth, ring fragile, white » *Leucocoprinus brebissonii*, 288
20b Margin not striate though sometimes splitting or appendiculate : **21**

21a Stipe somewhat scaly at base, ring dotted black; smell fruity or of pelargonium »
Lepiota felina, 286
21b Stipe whitish, turning pink, ring ascending, whitish; cap speckled with concentric scales » *Leucoagaricus meleagris*, 289

22a Ring absent or doubtful; often with traces or basal zones : **23**
22b Ring membranous or more permanent : **24**

23a Smell faint. Cap scales purple and concolorous zones on stipe »
L. brunneoincarnata, 286
23b Similar, scales smaller, pinkish ochre, central patch ill-defined » *L. kuehneri*, 286
23c Smell strongly aromatic or spirituous» *Lepiota josserandii*, 286

24a Smell strong, pleasant, fruity; rather robust fungus with concentric vinaceous-pink scales and stipe with pinkish zone » *Lepiota helveola*, 286
24b Smell strong and unpleasant, of *Scleroderma* or rubber; more slender fungus with russet central patch and somewhat vinaceous stipe » · *Lepiota cristata*, 284
24c Smell slight; ring often oblique : **25**

25a Cap dark red-brown; ring reddish, scaly » *L. subgracilis*, 284
25b Cap pale pinkish brown with scales and central patch sometimes dull on a pinkish ground; ring pinkish grey » *Lepiota pseudohelveola*, 286
25c Similar but slightly more fleshy, sometimes slightly velvety and lilaceous; ring with greenish grey border. On sand by the sea » *L. brunneolilacina*, 286
25d Disc and scales purplish brown, margin lilac, ring underlined purplish grey. On manured ground » *Lepiota lilacea*, 286

Tribe *Lepioteae*. Spore print white or pale, at most reddich or greenish. Genus *Melanophyllum*. Spores and gills reddish or greenish.

Melanophyllum haematospermum (Bull.) Kreis. [*Lepiota echinata*]
Cap 3-5cm, convex, surface powdery, yellowish grey to dingy brown, margin appendiculate. Gills pinkish then dark vinaceous red. Stipe 5×0.3cm, pruinose, ochraceous grey to reddish. Flesh somewhat concolorous; smell faint. Spores 6×3.5μm, slightly punctate; cap cuticle with sphaerocysts. Roadside rubbish-tips, nettle beds, greenhouse soil etc. Uncommon in S.E. England, extending northwards to the central valley of Scotland. E2. **M. eyrei** (Mass.) Sing. has greenish gills; rather uncommon in southern England under ash, beech, oak. E1.

Genus *Cystolepiota*. Cap powdery or bristly, with sphaerocysts or chains of short cells.

Cystolepiota bucknallii (Bk. & Br.) Sing. & Clemç.
Cap 2-5cm, slightly campanulate then convex or broadly umbonate, powdery, yellowish with somewhat lilaceous margin. Gills dingy yellowish, well spaced. Stipe 8×0.3cm, creamy yellowish, lilaceous violet at the base. Flesh similar; smell strong like *Tricholoma sulphureum*. Spores 10×4μm; cystidia absent. On nitrogen-rich soil and under broadleaved trees. Widespread in S. England and N. to the Borders. E1.

Cystolepiota seminuda (Lasch) Bon
Cap 1cm, convex, soon expanded, white, mealy with appendiculate margin. Gills whitish. Stipe 3×0.1cm, white, base ± lilac-grey. Flesh very thin, odourless. Spores 4×2μm; cystidia absent. Soil of tracks, damp lanes, thickets. Common throughout Britain. E2. **C. sistrata** (Fr.) Bon & Bellù is distinguished by being less slender, 2-3cm, and tinged pinkish ochre on the disc and stipe base but is regarded as a synonym by British authors. E1.

Cystolepiota hetieri (Boud.) Sing.
Cap 3-5cm, felted or mealy, creamy white to ochraceous or pinkish and spotted pinkish brown. Gills white then pinkish brown. Stipe with similar tints, 5×0.4cm, with floccose ring zone. Flesh pale then finally vinaceous brown; smell faint. Spores 5×2.5μm with truncate base; cystidia mainly marginal, appendiculate or with neck constricted several times. Roadside rubbish tips, nettle beds. Rare. E1. **C. cystophora** (Malç.) Bon, whiter or with vinaceous base and dingy ochraceous gills, spores 7×4μm and normal marginal cystidia, occurs under holm oak in Mediterranean area. E1.

Cystolepiota aspera (Pers.) Bon [*Lepiota friesii* p.p., *L. acutesquamosa* var. *furcata*]
Cap 10-15cm, conical or irregularly umbonate, covered with pointed scales, especially over the centre, chestnut brown on a fawnish ground. Gills pallid, very crowded, often forked, edges velvety. Stipe 8×1cm, slightly bulbous, brown and bearing similar scales below the ring, zoned towards the base; ring membranous, thin, white-edged brown. Flesh pale; smell strong of rubber or *Scleroderma*. Spores 9×3μm, almost fusiform; marginal cystidia balloon-shaped. Common in England, especially in beech woods north to the Borders. E2.

Cystolepiota echinacea (Lange) Knuds.
Cap 6-10cm, conico-convex, with dark somewhat bristly and detachable scales on a chestnut brown or reddish ground. Gills well-spaced, creamy or ivory white. Stipe 6×1cm, covered with similar scales below a distinct but non-membranous ring. Flesh pale, smell faint, perhaps of cedarwood. Spores 5×2.5μm; no marginal cells present. In damp woods especially under hazel. Widespread in S. England. E1.

C. eriophora (Peck) Knuds. is smaller, pale ochraceous with somewhat contrasting scales. Less common. E1.

Genus *Chamaemyces*. Cap surface matt or wrinkled.

Chamaemyces fracidus (Fr.) Donk [*Lepiota irrorata*]
Cap 5-8cm, convex, soon expanded, whitish to ochraceous or with reddish-brown blotches. Gills cream, weeping. Stipe 5×1cm, similar colours up to a ± membranous ring, typically speckled with droplets of amber exudate. Flesh pale with faint rubbery smell. Spores 4.5×2.5μm; facial cystidia somewhat swollen; cap cuticle palisadic. Widespread in S. England in grass under broadleaved trees, conifers and yew. E2.

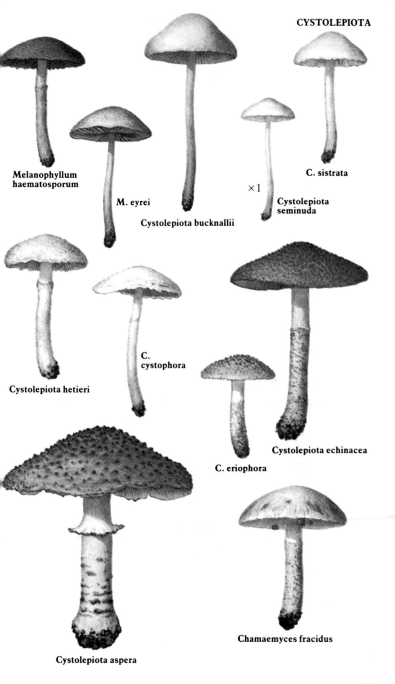

CYSTOLEPIOTA

Melanophyllum
haematosporum

M. eyrei

Cystolepiota bucknallii

×1

C. sistrata

Cystolepiota
seminuda

Cystolepiota hetieri

C.
cystophora

Cystolepiota echinacea

C. eriophora

Cystolepiota aspera

Chamaemyces fracidus

Genus *Lepiota*. Small to medium-sized. Cap with a central patch commonly surrounded by concentric scales. Stipe ringed. Gills broadest at the middle, typically free; marginal cells often present. Section *Lepiota* [*Fusisporae*]. Spores elongated to fusiform.

Lepiota clypeolaria (Bull.) Kumm.
Cap 4-6cm, with a well defined central, smooth, pale brownish patch with peripheral beige to whitish scales. Gills white. Stipe 8×0.7cm, slightly club-shaped, with rather shaggy concolorous zones up to a poorly developed ring-zone. Flesh pale, nearly odourless. Spores 14×6μm; cuticle with elongated hairs. Under broadleaved trees, occasionally conifers and yew, mainly in S. England. Uncommon. E3.

Lepiota ventriosospora Reid [*L. metulaespora* auct.]
Similar in stature to *L. clypeolaria* but with ill-defined disc and more yellowish brown scales on an ochraceous ground; margin fleecy bright yellow or in var. *fulva* orange-fawn. Gills cream. Stipe covered with fleecy yellow scales, becoming concolorous with the cap towards the base. Flesh pale. Spores mummy-shaped, 20×5μm; cuticle as in *L. clypiolaria*. Under conifers but also beech and birch; var. *fulva* under broadleaved trees. Throughout Britain but not common. E2.

Lepiota alba (Bres.) Sacc.
Cap 3-5cm, umbonate, disc ill-defined, rather ochraceous, elsewhere whitish with fleecy-fibrillose or velvety margin. Gills well spaced, white. Stipe often spindle-shaped, 5×0.8cm, whitish with a soft cushion-like ring. Flesh pale. Spores 14×6.5μm; cuticle with variously shaped hairs. Grass under broadleaved trees, lawns, sandy pasture by the sea, throughout Britain. Uncommon. E2. **L. laevigata** (Lange) Rea, more slender, entirely pale ochraceous fawn. Uncommon. E2.

Lepiota subgracilis Kühn. ex Wass.
Cap 2-4cm, slightly umbonate, with dark red-brown disc and scales progressively more widely spaced towards the margin, on a pinkish ground. Gills pinkish white. Stipe 5×0.3cm, basal part coloured as cap; ring membranous, slightly scaly. Flesh pinkish, smell faint. Spores 13×6μm; cuticle with long hairs. Under broadleaved trees especially in damp places. Uncommon. E1. **L. sublaevigata** Bon & Boiff. has a less defined disc and vague ring, in sandy pastures on limestone in warm places. sE1.

Lepiota ignivolvata Joss.
Rather robust fungus, cap 10-13cm, central patch chestnut brown, scales pale beige to whitish near the margin. Gills rather broad, white. Stipe 13×1cm, somewhat bulbous, reddening slowly at the base, wreathed with oblique rings edged brownish. Flesh white with rubbery smell. Spores 12×6.5μm; cuticle bearing long hairs. Under conifers and copses on limestone. Uncommon. E2.

Section *Stenosporae*. Spores spurred or with a lateral apiculus.

Lepiota cristata (Bolt.) Kumm.
Cap 2-6cm, with reddish brown or reddish central patch and similarly coloured concentric scales in a pinkish ground. Gills white, well spaced. Stipe 4×0.2cm, whitish with a somewhat vinaceous base and membranous but often fugaceous ring. Flesh white or vinaceous grey; smell strong, fruity, then rubbery or like *Scleroderma*. Spores 8×3.5μm; cuticle palisadic. On lawns and soil of copses or all kinds. Very common throughout Britain. E4.

Lepiota castanea Quél.
Cap 2-4cm, chestnut brown russet, scales not isolated. Gills whitish or stained russet. Stipe 4×0.3cm, somewhat scaly and concolorous up to an ill-defined ring-zone. Flesh pale or ochraceous; smell faintly fruity. Spores 10×4μm; cuticular hairs septate. In copses under broadleaved trees. Widely distributed in England and Wales but seldom abundant. E2. **L. ignicolor** Bres. is brighter orange or reddish with yellowish gills and a distinctive smell of *Pelargonium* or cedar. Hairs not or scarcely septate. E2.

Lepiota griseovirens R. Mre.
Similar size to *L. castanea* but with dark greenish grey scales and ± bronzed margin. Gills creamy ochraceous. Stipe with concolorous scales at base, and a diffused ring-zone sometimes tinged orange. Flesh whitish or flushed orange, smell slight. Spores 8×4μm; cuticular hairs rather short or swollen, with pigmented walls. Typically under conifers; var. *obscura* is darker or bluish, under broadleaved trees. E1.

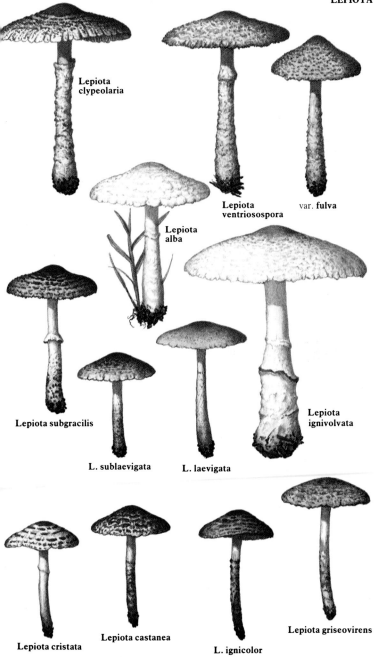

Lepiota
clypeolaria

Lepiota
ventriosospora

var. fulva

Lepiota
alba

Lepiota subgracilis

L. sublaevigata

L. laevigata

Lepiota
ignivolvata

Lepiota cristata

Lepiota castanea

L. ignicolor

Lepiota griseovirens

285

Section *Ovisporae*. Spores elliptical or ovoid. Most toxic *Lepiota* species belong here. Edibility of the others is doubtful: they should *not* be tried.

Lepiota helveola Bres.
Cap 5-8cm, rather fleshy, with concentric rather stellate scales, vinaceous pink on a whitish ground. Gills well spaced, pinkish white. Stipe 5×1cm, lower part somewhat zoned vinaceous pink; ring membranous, fragile. Flesh reddening slightly; smell fruity, of apple or mandarin. Spores 10×5μm; cuticle with elongated hairs without underlying hymeniform layer. In urban copses in warm places. Rare, occasionally reported from S.E. England. **Deadly poisonous.** E1.

L. josserandii Bon & Boiff. [*L.helveola* p.p.] is more slender, with strong sweetish smell, a cortiniform spongy ring and smaller spores 6× 3μm. **Deadly poisonous**. E2.

Lepiota brunneoincarnata Chod. & Mart.
Rather like *L. helveola* but less fleshy, with the scales of the disc more purplish, forming a dark patch. Gills white. Stipe 4×0.8cm, wreathed brownish grey beneath a vague ring-zone. Flesh white to vinaceous; smell faintly fruity. Spores 9×5μm; cuticular hairs arising from an irregular hymeniform layer. Grassy copses, widely distributed in England and Wales. **Deadly poisonous**. E2.

L. kuehneri Huijs. ex Hora is paler, with cap entirely pinkish brown, velvety, lacking a distinct apical patch; subcuticular layer distinctly hymeniform and pigmented. Uncommon. E3.

Lepiota forquignonii Quél.
Cap 3-5cm, slightly umbonate, disc pale olive-brown, becoming progressively paler to a whitish margin. Gills sometimes tinted pink. Stipe 6×0.5cm, pinkish white with olivaceous base. Flesh whitish; smell slightly rubbery. Spores 7×4μm; cuticular hairs rather short with a regular subcuticular layer. Under broadleaved trees especially hazel but var. *coniferarum* is darker, without a pink tint under conifers. E2.

Lepiota felina (Pers.) Karst.
Cap 2-4cm, umbonate, central patch blackish sepia in contrast to the rest of the cap which is speckled dark brown on a white ground. Gills white. Stipe 5×0.3cm, white, with dark brown scales below a rather broad ring which is dotted blackish. Flesh whitish; smell of *Pelargonium* or cedarwood. Spores 8×3.5μm; epicutis with a regular subcuticular layer. Copses and plantations, especially under conifers and yew. Widely distributed but scarcely common in England. E2.

Lepiota pseudohelveola Kühn. ex Hora
Cap 3-5cm, pale pinkish brown or with beige scales on a pinkish ground but scarcely separate from one another. Gills white, well-spaced. Stipe 6×0.5cm, ring oblique, creamy russet, pinkish-grey floccose on its lower surface. Flesh tinged pink; smell fruity. Spores 10×5μm; cuticular hairs arising from a discontinuous subcuticular layer. Under broadleaved trees especially beech but also yew. Widespread in England. **Poisonous**. E2.

L. brunneolilacea Bon & Boiff. is more fleshy, 5-7cm, stipe 1cm thick, the ring edged with greenish grey, and occurs on sand dunes and alluvial soils inland. **Poisonous**. E1.

Section *Lilaceae*. Spores ovoid, cap cuticle hymeniform.

Lepiota lilacea Bres.
Cap 4-7cm, disc matt, purplish brown, margin pale, lilac. Gills whitish. Stipe 5×0.5cm, similar colour at the base, ring rather oblique, pinkish grey. Flesh pinkish; smell fruity. Spores 5×3μm. Gardens and manured soil. Uncommon. **Poisonous**. E2.

L. ochraceofulva Orton
Cap 4-6cm, scales reddish brown to fawn on a somewhat yellowing ochraceous ground. Gills creamy ochraceous. Stipe 8×0.4cm, concolorous or yellowing rusty brown at the base. Flesh similar colour; smell strong, fruity, like jasmine. Spores 7×4μm; epicutis with somewhat short unequal hairs. Under broadleaved trees. Uncommon. E1.

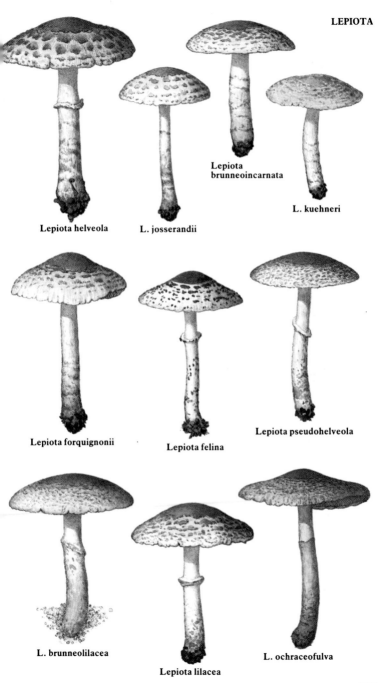

Lepiota helveola

L. josserandii

Lepiota brunneoincarnata

L. kuehneri

Lepiota forquignonii

Lepiota felina

Lepiota pseudohelveola

L. brunneolilacea

Lepiota lilacea

L. ochraceofulva

287

Tribe *Leucocoprineae*. Spores white or pale with an endospore stained reddish by cresyl blue. Clamps rare or none. Genus *Leucoagaricus*. Ring a bracelet or funnel-shaped and often moveable; clamp connections absent.

Leucoagaricus macrorhizus Locq. ex Hora
Cap 8-12cm, convex fibrillosely scaly, dingy grey-beige on a pale ground. Gills crowded, with a collar, white then brownish. Stipe 10×1cm, spindle-shaped or rooting white then browning. Flesh white to brownish. Spores 9×5.5µm; with narrow pore; cuticular hyphae septate. In fields and gardens. Uncommon. E1.

Leucoagaricus serenus (Fr.) Bon & Boiff.
Cap 3-5cm, thin-fleshed, fibrillosely silky or satiny, white or faintly ochraceous at the centre. Gills white. Stipe 8×0.5cm, slightly club-shaped, white or slightly ochraceous; ring a bracelet. Flesh whitish, smell slight. Spores 9×5µm, tapered at the tip; cap cuticle with prostrate, somewhat gelatinised hyphae (subgenus *Sericeomyces*). In copses under various broadleaved trees and yew, with ivy and stinging-nettles. Widespread in southern England. E1.

Leucoagaricus sublittoralis (Kühn. ex Hora) Sing.
Cap 5-8cm, convex, smooth, disc pinkish ochre, margin whitish. Gills white, well-spaced. Stipe 9×0.8cm, slightly club-shaped, white; ring fragile. Flesh white; smell fungoid. Spores 8×4µm, apex conical; cuticular hairs about 20µm wide. In sandy copses away from the sea. Uncommon. E1.

Leucoagaricus badhamii (Berk.) Sing. [*Lepiota meleagroides*]
Cap 6-12cm, convex or umbonate, velvety to fibrillosely scaly or fleecy, beige, reddening then browning. Gills cream, reddening, edge turning brown. Stipe 12×1cm, slightly club-shaped, white, fibrillose, velvety below a bracelet-like ring, reddening from the base upwards and bruising dark blackish brown. Flesh concolorous. Reaction to ammonia green (section *Piloselli*). Spores 8×5µm, apex obtuse; marginal cystidia appendiculate. In gardens, greenhouses, conifer and yew woods but also beech and oak. Widespread in southern England but never common. E1. **L. pilatianus** (Demoulin) Bon & Boiff. is more reddish brown from the first, only slightly reddening and has commonplace cystidia. E2.

Leucoagaricus bresadolae (Schulz.) Bon & Boiff.
Cap 8-12cm, campanulate or umbonate, with reddish brown scales on a pale, somewhat yellowing or orange ground. Gills yellowish. Stipe 12×3cm, rather spindle-shape slightly zoned brown on a pale or yellowing ground; ring thick or cushion-like. Flesh yellowing, then vinaceous orange. Reaction to ammonia green. Spores 10×6µm, with distinct germ-pore; cystidia somewhat constricted. In clusters on compost, sawdust. Often resembling *Macrolepiota* species (p.290). Uncommon. **Indigestible or poisonous**. E2.

L. meleagris (Sow.) Sing. is less robust, cap surface merely speckled grey-brown, and has spores with indistinct pore or none. E1.

Leucoagaricus leucothites (Vitt.) Wasser [*Lepiota pudica*]
Cap 6-10cm, convex, fleshy entirely white, smooth or eventually cracking, sometimes eventually faintly tinged ochraceous at the centre. Gills white to pink. Stipe 5×1 cm, somewhat club-shaped white, ring typical of the genus. Flesh white; smell pleasant, taste fungoid. Spores 9×6µm, ovoid, with a germ-pore. Cystidia commonplace. Meadows. Common in England. Edible and good. E3. **L. holosericeus** (Gill.) Moser is more silky, matt or velvety and distinguished by first yellowing then browning when bruised. Uncommon. E2.

Leucocoprinus brebissonii (Godey) Locq.
Cap 3-5cm, conical or umbonate, fragile, with a striate margin. A blackish brown patch over the disc is surrounded by small dark scales contrasting with a pure white ground. Gills white, very crowded. Stipe 8×0.4cm, white, with fragile thin ring. Flesh white, smell faintly spermatic. Spores 10×6µm, with a germ-spore. Under various broadleaved trees. Uncommon, in southern England. E. **L. birnbaumii** (Corda) Sing. [*Lepiota lutea*] is bright yellow throughout, common in well heated glasshouses as are a number of other tropical species casually introduced into Europe with exotic plants. (Not to be confused with *Lepiota xanthophylla* (p.288), which is far less brightly coloured, smaller, less delicate, not striate, with differing microcharacters and also occurs in woodland.) sE1.

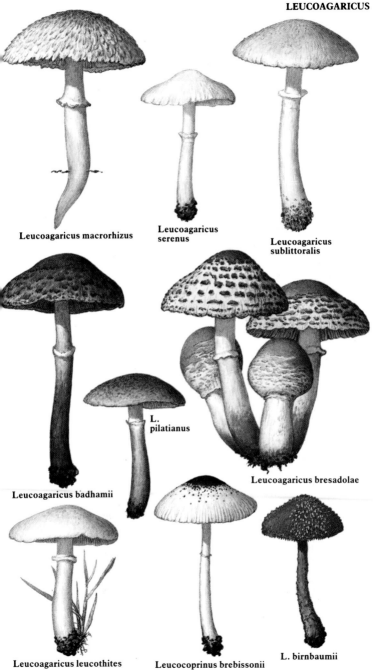

Leucoagaricus macrorhizus

Leucoagaricus serenus

Leucoagaricus sublittoralis

L. pilatianus

Leucoagaricus badhamii

Leucoagaricus bresadolae

Leucoagaricus leucothites

Leucocoprinus brebissonii

L. birnbaumii

Genus *Macrolepiota*. Large or fleshy fungi with cap surface distinctively peeling back or with striking scales, ring ± thick and often moveable on the stipe.

Section *Macrosporae*. Star-shaped excoriation, ring simple; clamp connections none.

Macrolepiota excoriata (Fr.) Wasser
Cap 8-12cm, convex with finely shaggy surface, breaking up towards the margin in a rather stellate fashion, pale cream to milky coffee colour at the centre. Gills white, reddening slightly. Stipe 7×1cm, rather bulbous, smooth, similar colour, ring rather thin. Flesh pale, not reddening. Spores 18×10µm with broad refractive pore. Under broadleaved trees in grassy places. Uncommon. Edible. E3.

Macrolepiota konradii (Huijs. ex Orton) Moser
Cap 6-10cm, umbonate, disc dark greyish brown, margin clearly peeled back in a stellate manner, brownish on a creamy ground. Gills whitish. Stipe 12×1cm, scarcely bulbous with faint russet-bistre zones; ring thick, edged greyish. Flesh pale, reddening slightly. Spores 15×8µm, germ-pore somewhat refractive. Grassy places, woodland glades, hedges. Not uncommon. Edible. E2.

Macrolepiota venenata Bon
A large fleshy fungus. Cap 15-30cm, breaking into broad star-shaped flakes, sometimes eventually ± circular, dark reddish brown on a dull ochraceous creamy ground. Gills dingy white or discoloured dull pinkish. Stipe 18×3cm, with a massive bulb 6cm across, often almost marginate, white, smooth or pruinose, bruising rather dingy reddish; ring simple or slightly scaly. Flesh thick, dense, becoming tinged vinaceous or dingy reddish brown. Spores 12×8µm, ovoid with truncate germ-pore without callus; clamp connections absent. Often in clusters, on heaps of rubbish, compost etc. Not yet reported from Britain. Indigestible or ± toxic. E1.

Section *Procerae*. Scaling concentric, ring complex; basidia clamped.

Macrolepiota procera (Scop.) Sing.   PARASOL
Cap 12-25cm, slightly umbonate, with a continuous brown patch at the centre surrounded by regularly concentric scales, ochraceous beige on a paler ground. Gills creamy white. Stipe 25×2cm, slightly bulbous, 4cm across, closely zoned brownish up to a thick ring with an outer fleecy flange. Flesh pale, not reddening. Spores 16×9µm, with lens-shaped germ-pore. Meadows, grassy glades, hedges and roadside grass. Common. Edible and excellent. E3.

Macrolepiota gracilenta (Krombh.) Wasser
Cap 8-10cm, umbonate with dark centre surrounded by closely crowded scales down to a naked margin which peels back in a slightly stellate fashion. Gills dingy cream. Stipe slender 18×1cm, finely zoned greyish ochre. Flesh white, not reddening. Spores 13×8µm, germ-pore convex. Grassy places under broadleaved trees. Fairly common. Edible. E3.

M. mastoidea (Fr.) Sing. is a little more fleshy, with less slender stipe covered with pale or scarcely discernible zones; spores 16×9µm. Uncommon. E3.

Macrolepiota rhacodes (Vitt.) Sing.   SHAGGY PARASOL
Cap 12-18cm, surface with the texture of wool shoddy, pulled apart to leave only a small dingy beige brown central patch surrounded by discrete concolorous scales concentrically arranged. Gills creamy white, discolouring when handled. Stipe 12×1.5cm, with a broad basal bulb, smooth, without colour zones, creamy white bruising reddish orange. Flesh white, turning saffron when cut. Spores 13×8µm, ovoid with a truncate germ-pore. Typically under conifers. Fairly common. Edible and good. E3.

var. **hortensis** is more robust, with more contrasting reddish-brown scales, found in gardens, grassland or under broadleaved trees, and is liable to confusion with *M. venenata*. Indeed, the so-called species in *Macrolepiota* are so ill-defined and have been so diversely interpreted that no reliance can be placed on existing records of their abundance or distribution. E2.

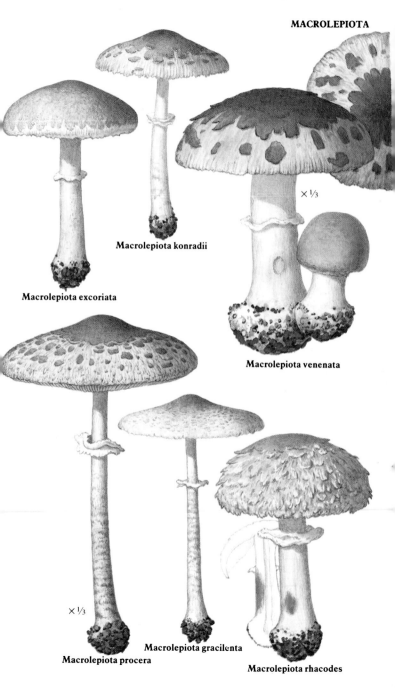

Macrolepiota konradii

Macrolepiota excoriata

× 1/3

Macrolepiota venenata

× 1/3

Macrolepiota procera

Macrolepiota gracilenta

Macrolepiota rhacodes

Key to *Amanita* – species

1a Ring absent, cap margin conspicuously striate, stipe usually tapered upwards; subgenus *Amanitopsis*: **2**

1b Ring present: **7**

2a Volva friable, leaving floccose traces at the same time on cap and stipe base: **3**

2b Volva membranous, generally forming a sack round the base, with only occasional non-friable remnants on the cap: **4**

3a Remnants of the veil dingy grey to blackish, very powdery; big or tall fleshy fungus 15(25)cm, in copses on heavy soils and alluvium »   *A. ceciliae*, 294

3b Remnants of the veil pale greyish, more felted or torn into shreds; on more acid soils, often with *Vaccinium myrtillus* »   *A. submembranacea*, 294

4a Colours somewhat bright, russet or orange: **5**

4b Colours pure white throughout »   *A. vaginata* var. *alba*, 294

4c Cap some shade of brown to grey: **6**

5a Reddish brown reaction with phenol. Cap bright fawn, stipe ± vaguely zoned russet with a fawnish volva »   *A. fulva*, 294

5b Vinous purple reaction with phenol. Cap orange-yellow to saffron, stipe pale or with yellow zones, volva similar colour or whitish »   *A. crocea*, 294

5c If the stipe is white and volva no more than a cushion »   see *A. junquillea*, 296

6a Grey brownish to dingy ochraceous, volva whitish »   *A. vaginata*, 294

6b Yellowish grey to olivaceous, often with a dark band at the base of striae, stipe zoned and volva somewhat concolorous »   *A. battarae*, 294

6c Pale ochraceous grey, sometimes pinkish, volva whitish, stipe zoned »   *A. lividopallescens*, 294

7a Membranous sack-shaped volva present; remnants on cap occasional or none: **8**

7b Volva a hemispherical cushion from which the stipe arises, remnants of the veil as broad scales on the cap: **13**

7c Volva friable; abundant remnants of the veil left on the cap: **15**

8a Margin striate, cap bright orange »   *A. caesarea*, 296

8b Margin not striate: **9**

9a Greenish tints ± dominant; sometimes pale and only at the disc: **10**

9b White throughout: **11**

10a Cap entirely green, rather streaky, stipe zoned greenish »   *A. phalloides*, 298

10b Cap greenish ochraceous at centre, stipe white, ring fragile »   *A. verna*, 298

11a Cap slightly conical or lobed; stipe shaggy »   *A. virosa*, 298

11b Cap regular, convex or expanded; stipe smooth: **12**

12a Ring membranous; fungus medium size, not thick-fleshed; smell none or faint and slightly of roses drying »   *A. phalloides* var. *alba*, 298

12b Ring floccose to creamy; robust fleshy fungus; smell slightly fishy; a southern or Mediterranean species »   *A. ovoidea*, 298

13a Odourless, cap yellow with striate margin »   *A. junquillea*, 296

13b Smell of turnip or raw potato: **14**

14a Cap yellow with whitish or brownish scales »   *A. citrina*, 298

14b Cap entirely white »   *A. citrina* var. *alba*, 298

14c Cap greyish purplish »   *A. porphyria*, 298

15a Margin striate from the outset; subgenus *Amanita*: **16**

15b Margin not striate: **20**

16a Volva crenellate scales, cap bearing abundant regular white or yellow scales when young and fresh: **17**

16b Volva a somewhat helicoid cushion: **18**

17a Cap vermilion to orange ≫ *A. muscaria*, 296
17b Cap dark reddish brown ≫ *A. regalis*, 296

18a Cap yellow, scales variable shreds ≫ *A. junquillea*, 296
18b Colour different: **19**

19a Cap ochraceous bistre to brownish or milky coffee colour bearing regular pure white strongly contrasting scales ≫ *A. pantherina*, 296
19b Cap pale pinkish ochraceous, sometimes whitish, scales irregular, volva sunk in the ground, somewhat friable and discoloured ≫ *A. eliae*, 296

20a Volva as rings of scales on the stipe, those on the cap thick or pyramidal: **21**
20b Volva virtually absent or reduced to fine scales. Veil in broad patches or flakes on the cap: **23**

21a Big fleshy fungus with creamy ring. Under broadleaved trees on calcareous soils *A. strobiliformis*, 298
21b Medium size or less fleshy, with membranous ring and pyramidal scales: **22**

22a Gills dingy ochraceous cream to glaucous; stipe ± equal or bulbous, colours soon becoming dull ≫ *A. echinocephala*, 298
22b Gills creamy or milk-white; stipe spindle-shaped, very scaly ≫ *A. vittadinii*, 298

23a Flesh reddening, scales ochraceous to vinaceous ≫ *A. rubescens*, 296
23b Flesh not changing colour or tinged brownish: **24**

24a Scales on cap dingy white to greyish on a brown ground ≫ *A. excelsa*, 296
24b A more regular yellow veil, visible also on ring and stipe ≫ *A. franchetii*, 296

Veil opening upwards. Only a basal volva, no remains on cap.

A. phalloides

type 1

Veil opening in the middle. A 'half' volva and remains on cap.

A. citrina

type 2

Veil splitting up regularly. Remains arranged regularly both on base of stipe and top of cap.

A. muscaria

type 3

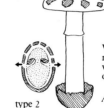

Veil opening from the base. Remains almost entirely carried by cap, basal remains insignificant or powdery.

A. spissa

type 4

Family *Amanitaceae*. General veil taking the form of a basal volva or ± evanescent patches on the cap. Gills free, trama bilateral.

Limacella lenticularis (Lasch.) Earle [*L. guttata*]
Cap 10-15cm, convex, creamy ochre to pale fawnish, slimy. Gills crowded, white, broadest at the middle. Stipe 10×2cm, bulbous, whitish; ring membranous, often bearing droplets or spotted brownish yellow, as sometimes is the stipe apex. Flesh white; smell and taste somewhat mealy. Spores rounded, 5-6μm, smooth. Under beech, conifers etc, especially on chalk or limestone, throughout Britain. Uncommon. Edible. E2.

L. glioderma (Fr.) Earle is smaller, with very slimy orange-brown cap and russet base to the stipe and has a strong smell of meal or cucumber. Mainly under conifers. Not common though widespread in Britain. E1.

Genus *Amanita*. Universal veil membranous, pulverulent or with variable patches.

Subgenus *Amanitopsis*. Ring absent, cap margin striate or furrowed, stipe hollow, often conical. Spores nonamyloid.

Amanita vaginata (Bull.) Vitt.   GRISETTE
Cap 6-12cm, umbonate, varying from brownish grey or white (var.*alba*) to dull ochraceous, smooth except for the deeply striate margin. Gills white with downy edges. Stipe 12×1cm, conical, white, rarely with dingy ochraceous zones, soon becoming hollow or tubular, with a membranous white volva. Flesh white, inodorous. Spores globose, 10-12μm; gill edge with balloon-shaped cells. Mainly under broad-leaved trees, beech, birch and especially oak on heavy soils throughout Britain. Common. Edible and good. E3. var. **alba** (E2) has a whitish cap, not to be confused with the white **A. oreina** (Favre) Bon [*A. nivalis* auct.] with more friable volva, which grows with montane willows in Scotland (Em2).

Amanita fulva (Sch.) Seyot   TAWNY GRISETTE
Cap 5-10cm, umbonate, a beautiful bright fawn, sometimes reddish brown or chestnut at the centre, fading to milky coffee, margin closely striate. Gills cream, edges sometimes finely toothed. Stipe 10×1cm, thickened at the base, white, slightly zoned fawnish, with membranous white volva spotted with fawn or orange. Flesh whitish, phenol reaction chocolate brown. Spores globose, about 12μm; cells of gill edge rather broadly clavate. Under broadleaved trees, especially on acid soils, commoner than *A. vaginata*, especially in the north. Edible with a distinctive flavour. E4.

A. crocea (Quél.) Sing., often stouter, with a yellow-orange or saffron cap with no trace of fawn; gives a bright vinaceous reaction with phenol. Uncommon. E2.

Amanita battarae (Boud.) Bon [*A. umbrinolutea* p.p.]
Resembling *A. fulva* in size, or more slender. Cap soon expanded or even depressed around the disc, olivaceous grey-brown with a yellowish margin, often with a dark ring at the end of the striation. Gills dingy white. Stipe 8×0.8cm, almost equal or slightly thickened below, dingy whitish or somewhat zoned brownish grey on an ochraceous ground; volva membranous, ochraceous. Flesh pale. Spores ± globose, 12-14μm; cells of gill edge not distinctive. Under various conifers. Uncommon. E2.

Amanita lividopallescens (Gilb.) Gilb. & Kühn.
Cap 10-15cm, rather fleshy, only slightly striate, pale greyish ochre. Gills white or cream with somewhat denticulate margin, sometimes browning. Stipe 15×2cm, conical, smooth or sometimes concolorously pruinose, with zones in var. *tigrina*; volva russet. Flesh creamy white. Spores 12μm; more elliptical, 14×12μm, in var. *tigrina*. Under broadleaved trees, especially poplar. Very rare in Britain. Edible. E2.

Amanita ceciliae (Bk. & Br.) Bas [*A. inaurata, A. strangulata*]
Cap 12-18cm conical or umbonate, yellowish brown to brownish grey, with numerous grey powdery scales on the surface. Gills dingy cream or edged brownish. Stipe 18×3cm, ± bulbous; volva friable, blackish grey, disintegrating as a series of bands round the stipe from the base upwards or simulating a ring. Flesh dingy whitish. Spores globose, 11-13μm; cells of gill edge broadly balloon-shaped. In copses on heavy soils. Rare. E2. **A. submembranacea** (Bon) Gröger has a rather more coherent, paler veil and occurs among bilberries under conifers or beech; occasional. E(m)3.

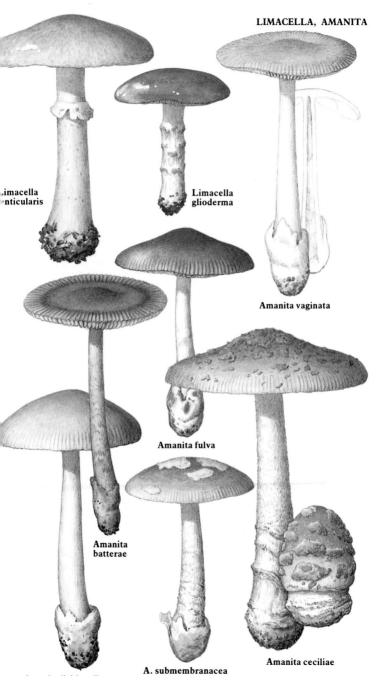

Limacella
nticularis

Limacella
glioderma

Amanita vaginata

Amanita fulva

Amanita
batterae

Amanita lividopallescens

A. submembranacea

Amanita ceciliae

295

Subgenus *Amanita*. Ring membranous, cap margin striate. Spores nonamyloid.

Amanita caesarea (Scop.) Pers.
Cap 10-20cm, convex or fleshy smooth to greasy, a striking bright orange, rarely bearing a few membranous fragments of the veil. Gills yellow. Stipe 12×2cm, slightly club-shaped, yellow, with a white sack-like volva. Flesh yellow near the surface, taste pleasant. Spores 10×6.5μm, ± ovoid. A southern species, roughly as far north as vines but not in Britain. The most highly prized edible mushroom of ancient Rome. Edible and excellent. sE2

Amanita muscaria (L.) Hook.   FLY AGARIC
Cap similar or more quickly expanded, slightly umbonate, bright vermilion red, fading to orange or mottled with yellow, as when washed out by heavy rain. At first covered with small, regular, floccose, white scales, yellow in f. *formosa*, arranged concentrically but fugaceous. Margin distinctly striate, incurved. Gills white. Stipe 15×2cm, white, somewhat bulbous, whitish to yellowish, with a basal ring of scales as a volva; ring white or edged yellow. Flesh white, taste somewhat nutty. Spores broadly elliptical 10×8μm. Under birch or pine, occasionally spruce. Very common. **Poisonous**. nE4. **A. regalis** (Fr.) Michael has an ochraceous brown or somewhat reddish brown cap, under spruce and may be better regarded as only a variety. Very uncommon in Britain. **Poisonous**. nE2.

Amanita pantherina (DC.) Krombh.
Cap 6-10cm, soon expanded, russet brown or milky coffee colour to fawnish ochre, veil forming regular floccose pure white unchanging scales, not changing colour. Gills milk white. Stipe 8×1cm, pure white, with a basal bulb ornamented by 1-2(3) rather spirally arranged bracelets of the volva, pure white like the ring. Flesh permanently white. Spores 11×7μm. Under broadleaved trees. Rather uncommon in Britain. **Very poisonous**. E2.

Amanita junquillea Quél. [*A. gemmata*]
Cap 5-10cm, convex, soon expanded, margin with short striae, surface smooth, yellow ochre or lemon to somewhat orange, with a few scattered fragments of a whitish veil. Gills white. Stipe 6×1cm, almost equal, white or lemon, ring fugaceous, volva a fragile fringe to the top of the basal bulb. Flesh white, inodorous, taste pleasant. Spores 11×7μm, elliptical. Under broadleaved trees. Uncommon. Not edible. E3.

A. eliae Quél. has pale pinkish ochre cap on a slender stipe with volva commonly sunk in the soil; spores 13×8μm. Uncommon. E2.

Subgenus *Lepidella*. Margin not striate, unless when very old; spores amyloid. Section *Validae*. [Subgenus *Amplariella*]. Volva friable, present almost only on the cap; type 4.

Amanita spissa (Fr.) Kumm.
Cap 10-18cm, fleshy, dark brown to greyish ochre, veil dingy white to greyish, as irregularly disposed scales. Gills and stipe white; ring membranous, persistent. Stipe 12×2cm, base slightly club-shaped and somewhat rooting, with volva virtually absent or powdery. Flesh white, only slightly tinged russet; smell slightly radishy. Spores 10×8μm. Under broadleaved trees. Very common throughout Britain. Edible but not of high quality: better avoided for fear of confusion with the highly poisonous *A. pantherina*. E4. **A. excelsa** (Fr.) Bertill. More slender, unchanging and with a pleasant smell, is often considered as a synonym or variety of *A. spissa*. E2.

Amanita rubescens Pers.   THE BLUSHER
Similar in stature to *A. spissa*. Cap more pinkish brown, irregularly covered with small dingy yellowish scales from the veil, or tinged reddish brown. Gills white, somewhat speckled pink. Stipe 10×1.5cm, white to vinaceous pink, especially in maggot holes; ring hanging and striate, white (but sulphur-yellow in var. *annulo-sulphurea*); volva floccose on the base (2cm across) or almost absent. Flesh white, flushing pink. Spores 8×6μm. Under trees of all kinds from early summer to late autumn. Very common throughout Britain. Edible and usually excellent. E4.

A. franchetii (Boud.) Fayod [*A. aspera*] is similar but not or scarcely becoming reddish, and the scales of the veil on the cap are yellow – as is the ring margin and stipe base. Rare. E2.

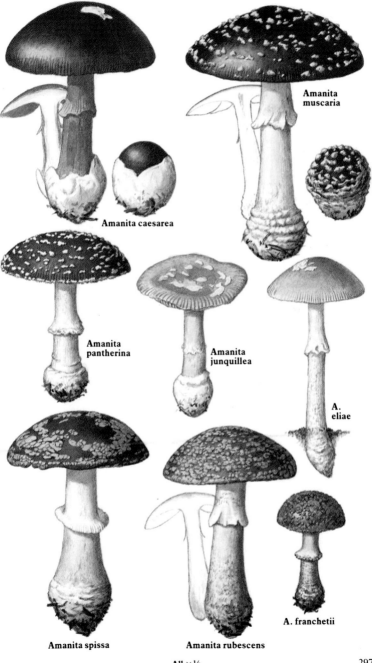

Amanita muscaria

Amanita caesarea

Amanita
pantherina

Amanita
junquillea

A.
eliae

Amanita spissa

Amanita rubescens

A. franchetii

All × ⅓

Section *Lepidella* [*Strobiliformes*]. Volva friable and rather scaly; type 3.

Amanita strobiliformis (Vitt.) Bertill. [*A. solitaria* p.p.]
Cap 15-25cm, very fleshy, with large thick but flat scales, whitish on a pale beige ground, sometimes eventually ochraceous. Gills white, broadest at the middle. Stipe massive, 15×5cm thick, with a ring like clotted cream and a slightly club-shaped or rooting base bearing fugaceous patches of volva. Flesh white. Spores 12×8μm, rather cylindrical. Fairly common in or near beech woods on chalk and Jurassic limestone in S. England, rare northwards. Edible E2.

Amanita echinocephala (Vitt.) Quél. [*A. solitaria* p.p.]
Cap 6-12cm, soon expanded, bearing white pyramidal scales on an ivory or dingy cream ground. Gills with a glaucous tint. Stipe ×1.5cm, slightly bulbous and rooting with membranous ring and bands of scales round the base. Flesh dingy white; smell and taste unpleasant. Spores 10×7μm, ± elliptical. Beechwoods on chalk and limestone in southern England. Uncommon. Not edible. E2. **A. vittadinii** (Moretti) Vitt. has a spindle-shaped stipe scaly up to the ring. S. England, very rare. sE2.

Section *Amidella*. Rather robust whitish fungi, sometimes reddening, with sack-like volva (type 1) and fragile ring. Spores rather elongated.

Amanita ovoidea (Bull.) Link.
Cap 12-25cm, fleshy, thick, smooth, white then dingy ochraceous. Gills well spaced, broad, creamy white. Stipe 20×5cm, cylindrical, white, with a tattered ring that becomes mealy or cream-like. Volva tough, membranous, slightly ochraceous. Flesh white; smell slight then fishy. Spores 12×7μm, ± cylindrical. In sunny copses on calcareous soils. S. England, very rare. Edible but poor. sE2.

Section *Phalloideae* [Subgenus *Amanitina*]. Medium sized fungi, not changing colour, with persistent volva (type 1-2) and membranous ring. Spores globose or short-elliptical, amyloid.

Amanita citrina (Sch.) Pers.
Cap 6-10cm, soon expanded, lemon yellow (white in var. *alba*), bearing irregular somewhat ochraceous patches of the veil. Gills white to yellowish. Stipe 7×1cm, white or yellowish with a bulbous base the upper edge of which is fringed by a whitish rim of volva. Flesh white; smell of raw potato or radish; taste unpleasant. Spores 10×8μm, broadly elliptical. Common throughout Britain, mainly under broadleaved trees (white form especially under beech) but also pine and on heaths. Not poisonous but best avoided. E4. **A. porphyria** A.-S. is similar in stature and smell but with cap purplish brown and more fragile ring tinted grey-violet. Uncommon, more frequent northwards. E2.

Amanita virosa Lamk.   DESTROYING ANGEL
Cap 5-8cm, obtusely conical, often lopsided or lobed, milk-white, slightly greasy, free from scales. Gills somewhat ascending, white. Stipe 12×1cm, white, typically floccose; volva a white sack, often bilobed; ring oblique or imperfect. Flesh white; smell becoming unpleasant with age. Spores globose, about 9μm. Under broadleaved trees on acid soil, beech, oak and especially birch in the Highlands. Uncommon. **Deadly poisonous**. E2.

Amanita phalloides (Fr.) Link   DEATH CAP
Cap 6-12cm, soon expanded, surface smooth, generally without remnants of the veil, a distinctive shade of yellow with greenish or bronze tinge, often radially streaked greyish. Gills white with short truncate ones interspersed. Stipe 7×1cm, with faint greenish zones; ring membranous, white; volva sack-like, pure white. Flesh white or glaucous; smell faint, then a little unpleasant, like roses when drying. Spores ± globose, 9×8μm. Under broadleaved trees and sometimes conifers. Widespread, especially in southern England and locally common. **Deadly poisonous**. E4.

Var. **alba** (E1) is white throughout. Also whitish is **A. verna** (Bull.) Lamk. but with a tinge of pale greenish ochre at the centre and a fragile ring and volva. These are equally lethal and particularly dangerous as being more likely to be mistaken for some edible white species. Care should always be taken to check the presence of a membranous volva in fungi of this kind. **Deadly poisonous**. sE3 (n1).

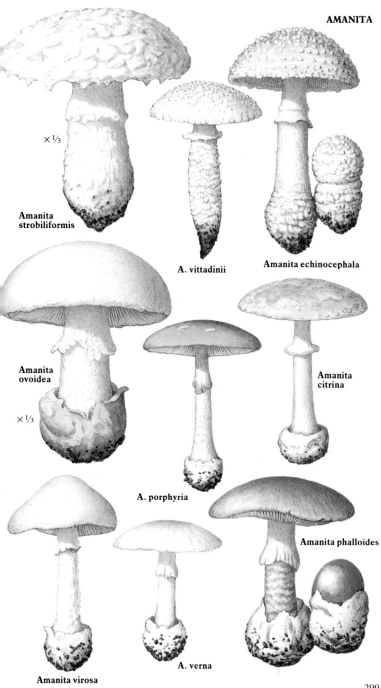

$\times \frac{1}{3}$

**Amanita
strobiliformis**

A. vittadinii

Amanita echinocephala

**Amanita
ovoidea**

$\times \frac{1}{3}$

**Amanita
citrina**

A. porphyria

Amanita phalloides

Amanita virosa

A. verna

Subclass *Gasteromycetidae*. Hymenium inside fruit-bodies or late free.

Family *Phallaceae*. Mature hymenium (gleba) gelatinous, on outer face of a receptacle emerging from a volva-like base, unexpanded juvenile state like a bird's egg.

Phallus impudicus L.   STINKHORN
So distinctive that description seems superflous; the stinking greenish gleba eventually disappears, eaten by flies, exposing a morel-like cap. In the egg state the species can be recognised when cut in half longitudinally to disclose an edible white central portion with a flavour of radish, surrounded by a highly gelatinous ochraceous russet tissue which persists as the basal volva after the centre has expanded. Spores 4-5×2μm. In woods of all kinds, very common throughout Britain. E4. **P. hadrianii** Vent. is more slender, with pinkish volva and confined to maritime sand-dunes. nE2.

Mutinus caninus (Huds.) Fr.
Structurally similar to *Phallus* but without the separate membranous cap, the gleba covers the apex of a column 10×0.8cm, reddish beneath the greenish, less foetid gleba. Spores 4×1.5μm. Beech woods on acid soil. Less common than *P. impudicus*. E3.

Family *Clathraceae*. Gleba on inner surface of a hollow or branched receptacle.

Clathrus ruber Pers. [*C. cancellatus*]
Fruit-body ovoid, a coral red lattice emerging from a cream to greyish fawn volva, texture spongy and very brittle, with foetid gleba on the inner surface of the lattice. Spores 6×2μm. In gardens with *Hebe* in the Scilly Is. Probably introduced but naturalised in several stations scattered across S. England and the Isle of Wight. E1.

Clathrus archeri (Berk.) Dring [*Anthurus aseroiformis*]
Fruit-body with a short stalk divided above into 4-8 divergent arms, blood red on their inner surface and tips paler pink elsewhere, bearing olive gleba on their inner surface; ± foetid smell of radish. Volva whitish to buff. Spores 7×2μm. Native of Australasia but naturalised in western and central Europe during the present century as well as in a few stations in Cornwall, Sussex, Surrey and Kent. E1.

Family *Nidulariaceae*. Spores embedded in small hard seed-like peridioles, themselves enclosed in a peridium which opens irregularly (*Nidularia*) or so as to resemble a vase or nest.

Cyathus striatus (Huds.) Willd.   BIRDS NEST FUNGUS
Peridium urn-shaped, 1-1.5cm, ovoid then conico-cylindrical, at first closed by a whitish operculum; outer face shaggy, grey-russet, inner face fluted, shining. Peridiolea greyish, ovoid, somewhat flattened, attached individually to the wall by a thread. Spores 17×8μm. On fallen branches and rotten wood. Fairly common. E2. **C. olla** (Batsch) Pers. Similar in stature to *C. striatus* but more conical and wide open, externally more silky and with smooth inner surface. In gardens and arable land, sand-dunes etc, usually attached to woody or herbaceous debris, throughout Britain. More common than *C. striatus*. E2.

Crucibulum laeve (Bull.) Kambly
Fruit-bodies globose, then drum-shaped, 0.5-1cm, wall thin, externally fibrillose, orange-yellow, opening to expose a pale smooth inner surface; operculum paler orange then paler. Peridioles lens-shaped, pale creamy yellow. Spores 10×5μm, ± elliptical. On fallen branches and rotting wood. Common. E3.

Family *Tulostomataceae*. Fruit-body globose, with dry powdery gleba at apex of a tall cylindrical stipe.

Tulostoma brumale Pers.
Head about 1cm, ± globose or slightly flattened, greyish white, with an apical pore surrounded by a brownish zone. Stipe 3×0.3cm, whitish to ochraceous, smooth or flaking on drying. Spores 4μm, slightly warted. Sandy pastures and maritime dunes. Locally common. E3.

Battarea phalloides (Dicks.) Pers. has a rather similar outline but much larger, 15-25cm high, reddish brown, with shaggy stem emerging from a basal volva. Very rare in southeast England. E1.

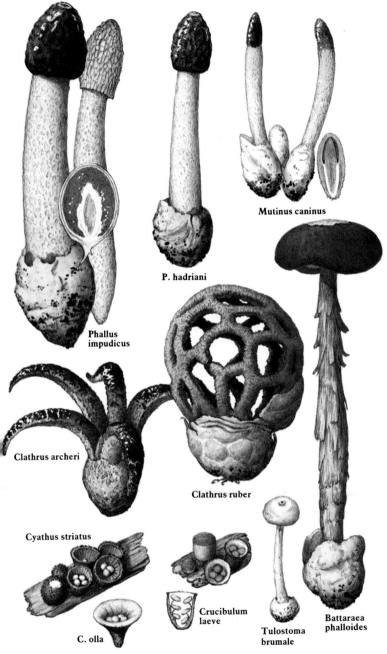

Mutinus caninus

P. hadriani

Phallus
impudicus

Clathrus archeri

Clathrus ruber

Cyathus striatus

Crucibulum
laeve

C. olla

Tulostoma
brumale

Battaraea
phalloides

Family *Hymenogastraceae*. Leathery, ± subterranean and hence seldom collected.

Rhizopogon obtextus (Spreng.) Rauschert. [*R. luteolus*]
Half-buried, like a small potato, surface almost smooth, yellowish ochre or slightly olivaceous, covered with numerous brownish thread-like rhizoids forming a net towards the base. Flesh (gleba) white, then dingy olive-yellow, with many rounded chambers, at first empty then filled with spores. Smell faint, then unpleasant. Spores 7×3μm, narrowly elliptical, pale olive, smooth. Under pine. Common. E3.

Family *Sclerodermataceae*. Terrestrial, ± globose, with simple or leathery envelope.

Pisolithus tinctorius (Pers.) Desv. [*P. arenarius, P. arhizus*]
6-15(25)×5-7cm, sometimes club-shaped on a stout base, blackish brown, smooth, tearing open above and then dusted reddish brown by the spores. Gleba consisting of numerous closely packed, ± spherical false peridioles, like small peas, whitish, then russet, eventually powdery. Base sterile and more or less prolonged into a stipe attached to yellowish mycelium. Spores globose, 10μm, with spines or slightly crested. On sandy soils, often under birch or pine. Very rare and sporadic in the S. and W. of England; also recently collected in S. Ireland. E1.

Genus *Scleroderma*. Gleba mottled but no "peridioles," envelope leathery, scaly.

Scleroderma citrinum Pers. [*S. aurantium, S. vulgare*]
± globose, 6-12cm, sessile, with thick, leathery, coarsely scaly wall, lemon yellow at first, then ochraceous beige, sometimes pale or with contrasting scales. Gleba greyish then purplish-black, long remaining firm and traversed by whitish veins, then powdery. Smell distinctive, rubbery. Mycelium of root-like cords, yellow. Spores globose, 11μm, with a small-meshed network beneath short crowded spines. Under oak and other broadleaved trees and on mossy heaths. Very common. E4.

S. bovista Fr. has a smoother, thinner wall, a somewhat earthbound pitted stipe and distinctly reticulate spores. E2.

Scleroderma areolatum Ehrenb.
3-5cm, wall rather thinner than in *S. citrinum*, more finely scaly or bearing polygonal areolate warts, reddish brown on a yellowish ground, bruising vinaceous; base short-stalked. Smell faint. Spores 10μm, finely spiny. Under various broadleaved trees. Common. E3. **S. verrucosum** (Bull.) Pers. is very similar but more finely warted with a well developed pitted stipe. Very common everywhere. E2.

Family *Geastraceae*. Peridium with a 3-layered wall, the outermost a thin mycelial layer adhering to a thicker fleshy layer; when mature these strip away from the third innermost layer, a papery wall enclosing the powdery gleba.

Genus *Geastrum*. Outer layers of the peridium splitting, curving back to expose the inner wall with the gleba, which opens by an apical pore.

Geastrum sessile (Sow.) Pouz. [*G. fimbriatum*]   EARTH STAR
4-6cm, with 5-7 rays, rather yellowish ochraceous grey-brown, apical pore with fringed margin, not surrounded by a defined halo. Gleba pale greyish brown. Spores globose, 3.5μm, indistinctly warted. Copses and coniferous woods, fairly common. E3. **G. triplex** Jungh. is usually larger, 8-12cm, with thicker flesh to the rays, often cracking away from a shallow saucer enclosing the gleba-sack, which shows a distinct halo around the apical pore. Widespread in woods, stinging nettles etc., probably more common than *G. sessile* in Britain. E3.

Geastrum quadrifidum Pers. [*G. coronatum*]
Fruit-body 2-4cm, brownish ochraceous, opening by 4 rays which become strongly recurved with their tips still adhering to the detached basal mycelial layer, whitish. Inner sack elongate, 2×1cm on a short stalk, pore surrounded by a marginate halo. Spores 5μm, warted. Under conifers. Uncommon. E3.

Astraeus hygrometricus (Pers.) Morg. (Family *Astraeaceae*)
3-5cm, opening as a 6-8-rayed star, the rays reacting strongly to moisture – expanding when damp, rolling tightly inwards when dry. Gleba dark greyish, at first enclosed by a thin inner wall which tears open at the apex. Smell faint. Spores globose, 10μm, finely warted. Sandy soil, rare though widespread in S. England. E1.

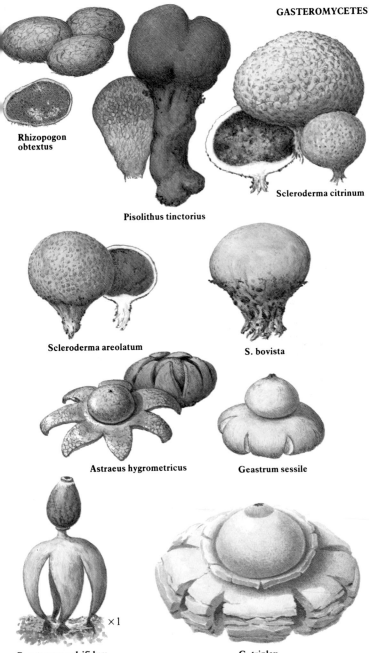

Rhizopogon obtextus

Pisolithus tinctorius

Scleroderma citrinum

Scleroderma areolatum

S. bovista

Astraeus hygrometricus

Geastrum sessile

×1

Geastrum quadrifidum

G. triplex

Family *Lycoperdaceae*. Fruit-bodies ± spherical to pear-shaped, with two-layered peridium, the outer layer breaking up into scales. PUFFBALLS

Genus *Lycoperdon*. With a pitted sterile base and a defined apical pore.

Lycoperdon pyriforme Sch.
Fruit-bodies produced in clusters, ± pear-shaped or scarcely stiped, 4×2cm, surface finely warted, like coarse sandpaper, greyish beige or yellowish, apex pointed or umbonate. Gleba white, then ochraceous. Spores 4μm, smooth. On fallen trunks, stumps, rotting half-buried wood etc. Very common. E4. **L. lividum** Pers. [*L. spadiceum*] is more globose and occurs singly in pastures and lawns. E4.

Lycoperdon perlatum Pers. [*L. gemmatum*]
Fruit-body 4-6cm, club-shaped and rather capitate with ± globose head slightly pointed above, white at first then brownish, peridium typically covered with short pyramidal spines each surrounded by a ring of tiny warts, leaving the surface covered with a finely dotted network with polygonal meshes after the spines have fallen off. Gleba white, then yellow, creamy textured and finally olivaceous and dusty. Smell slight, then ± unpleasant. Spores 3.5μm, warted. On ground in woods and pastures, very common. Edible while the gleba is white. E4. **L. mammiforme** Pers. is less spiny, with the exoperidium tending to form irregular floccose scales. Rare. E2.

Lycoperdon echinatum Pers.
Fruit-body 3-5cm, globose, scarcely stiped surface shaggy with russet brown spines 4-7mm long, without surrounding warts. Gleba brownish then chocolate. Spores 4.5μm, coarsely warted, dark. Under broadleaved trees, especially beech. Occasional in Britain. E2. **L. foetidum** Bonord. is like a small *L. perlatum* with dark-brown to blackish spines cohering at their tips in groups of 4-6. Very common everywhere on moors and heaths, especially in Highland districts. E2.

Vascellum pratense (Pers.) Kreisel [*Lycoperdon depressum*]
Fruit-body 3-6cm, stipe often lacking, entirely white or cream, surface mealy or with minute floccose spines soon shed, tearing open at the apex, often eventually down to the base. Gleba long remaining white, then yellowing and finally powdery ochraceous. Sterile base separated from the gleba by a diaphragm. Spores 4×3.5μm slightly ovoid, punctate. In lawns, pastures and sand-dunes. Edible when young. Very common throughout Britain. E4.

Calvatia excipuliformis (Sch.) Perdeck [*Lycoperdon saccatum*]
Fruit-body 10-15×7-10cm, with rounded head on a well developed cylindrical stipe. Surface covered with granules or short fine scales which are soon shed, creamy-ochraceous then brownish. Gleba beige, then olivaceous brown; sterile base spongy, persisting for a long time in situ after the upper fertile portion has disintegrated. Spores 5μm, warted, rather dark. In woods, often with pine or spruce, also in pastures and grassy places. Common. E3. **C. utriformis** (Bull.) Jaap [*Lycoperdon caelatum*] is more massive and fleshy, remains white for a long time rather like an enormous *Vascellum pratense*; common in pasture and on dunes. E2.

Langermannia gigantea (Batsch) Rostk. GIANT PUFFBALL
Fruit-body often very large, ± globose, up to 40cm and weighing several kilos. Peridium smooth or with fleeting white scales, long remaining white, then discolouring brownish and flaking away, without a defined apical opening. Gleba white, then yellowish and finally rusty brown. Spores 5-6μm, ± elliptical, scarcely punctate. Parks, gardens, hedges, improved grassland. Quite common in England, extending to Shetland. A good edible fungus as long as the gleba is white and firm. E2.

Bovista plumbea Pers.
Fruit-body globose, 2-3cm, with neither stipe nor sterile base, outer layer whitish, flaking off in patches to expose the inner silvery then bluish grey wall, eventually bistre. Gleba white, then yellow and finally powdery olive brown. Spores 5.5×4.5μm, ± elliptical, scarcely warted but with a slender pedicel 7-10μm long. In lawns, pastures and dunes. Common throughout Britain. E3. **B. nigrescens** Pers. is larger, 4-7cm, with a floccose surface shed to expose an inner wall which soon becomes blackish and shining, with gleba finally dark purple-brown. Similar situations but more prevalent on moors and in the north, where it is very common. E2.

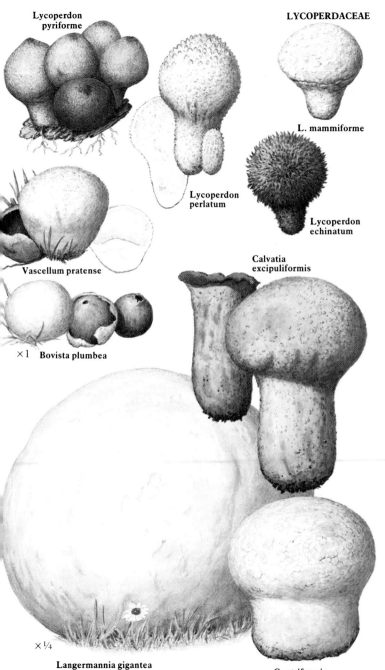

Lycoperdon
pyriforme

LYCOPERDACEAE

L. mammiforme

Lycoperdon
perlatum

Lycoperdon
echinatum

Vascellum pratense

×1 Bovista plumbea

Calvatia
excipuliformis

×¼ Langermannia gigantea

C. utriformis

305

Subclass *Aphyllophoromycetidae* [Order *Aphyllophorales*]. Hymenial surface smooth, corrugated, like pores, spines or veins but not covering true gills or tubes.

Order *Cantharellales*. Erect with smooth or veined hymenium. Family *Cantharellaceae*. Funnel-shaped or bearing a ± expanded cap. Hymenial surface on the outside, smooth or corrugated.

Craterellus cornucopioides (L.) Pers. HORN OF PLENTY
Cap 5-15cm, shaped like a narrow trumpet with flared margin, thin-fleshed and wavy, blackish brown or dark bistre throughout, inner surface slightly scaly or velvety. Outer surface (hymenium) smooth or with vague longitudinal veins, concolorous (yellow in var. *flavicans*). Stipe short, hollow. Flesh greyish, elastic, thin. Spores 15×9μm, pale ochraceous, elliptical; basidia 2-spored, clamp connections absent. Under broadleaved trees, especially beech and oak. Common throughout Britain. Edible and good. E4. **Cantharellus cinereus** Pers. is a similar colour but has thick longitudinal ridges like rudimentary gills. Rare in Britain. E2.

Pseudocraterellus sinuosus (Fr.) Corner ex Heinem.
Cap 3-5cm, deeply depressed, with undulating, crisped or crimped margin, pale ash-grey or brownish, smooth or floccose. Hymenial surface smooth, then irregularly radially rugose, grey then somewhat yellowish or tinged pinkish cream. Stipe concolorous, solid. Flesh pale; smell faintly fruity. Spores 10×8μm, ochraceous, smooth; basidia 4-spored, clamp connections absent. Under broadleaved trees and conifers, throughout Britain. Uncommon now. Edible. E3.

Cantharellus lutescens (Pers.) Fr. [*C. xanthopus*]
Fruit-body trumpet-shaped, brownish orange or sometimes bright yellowish, rather scaly at the centre. Outer (hymenial) surface marked by distant, decurrent but not gill-like veins, bright salmon-orange or reddish. Stipe hollow, yellow-orange. Flesh yellowish; smell fruity. Spores 10×7μm, whitish, smooth. Virtually restricted to the Highlands, where it is not uncommon in native pine woods. Edible. E2.

Cantharellus tubaeformis (Bull.) Fr.
Cap 3-6cm, flat, then umbilicate with expanded margin; surface fibrillosely floccose, yellowish brown, or entirely yellow in var. *lutescens*. Hymenial surface with distant well-developed, branching gill-like ridges, yellowish to greyish orange. Stipe hollow, concolorous. Flesh thin, rather yellow, smell faint. Spores 11×9μm, pale ochraceous, smooth. In troops, especially under conifers. Fairly common. Edible and good. E4. **C. melanoxeros** Desm. [*C. ianthinoxanthus* auct.] is more expanded, with reticulately ridged lilaceous hymenial surface and rather pinkish yellow cap; outer surface and stipe easily blackening. Under beech and oak. Not British. E2.

Cantharellus cibarius Fr. CHANTARELLE
Cap 5-12cm, fleshy, convex, then irregularly depressed, margin obtuse and ± lobed; surface smooth or scaly at the centre, egg yellow or fading. Hymenial surface covered with thick, low, decurrent, gill-like ridges, forking and anastomosing. Stipe tapered below, solid, concolorous or brownish orange. Flesh pale; smell fruity, like apricots. Several named varieties, e.g. var. *bicolor*, cap and stipe white; var. *amethysteus*, cap covered with lilac down. Spores 10×6μm, orange-yellow, elliptical. Under various broadleaved trees and conifers, especially on mossy ground. Very common throughout Britain. Edible and delicious. E4. **C. friesii** Quél. is more slender, tinged with orange or orange-brown, with narrower more gill-like ridges. Uncommon. E1.

Family *Gomphaceae*. Spores brownish, warted; cap fleshy, hymenial surface somewhat reticulate.

Gomphus clavatus (Pers.) S.F. Gray
Cap 6-12cm, top-shaped or an inverted cone, irregular with truncate or lumpy summit and undulating margin; ochraceous to lilac-violet or purplish pink, velvety. Hymenial surface with anastomosing veins, purplish violet, tinged brownish ochre by the spores. Stipe short, attenuated at the base, pale lilac. Flesh whitish; smell faint, taste sweetish. Spores 15×6μm, ochraceous, warted; clamp connections present. Often in dense clusters or deformed; under broadleaved trees and conifers in mountainous districts. Very rare in Britain. Edible. E3 (m).

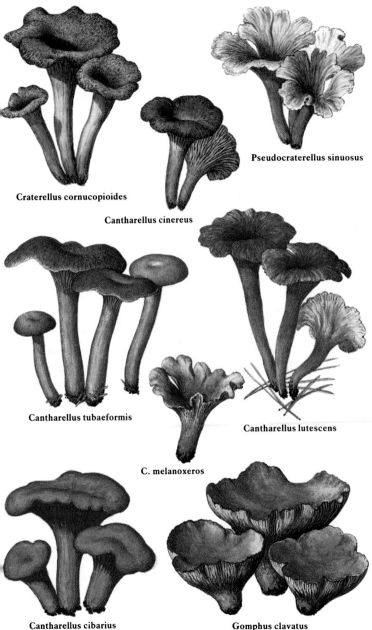

Craterellus cornucopioides

Pseudocraterellus sinuosus

Cantharellus cinereus

Cantharellus tubaeformis

C. melanoxeros

Cantharellus lutescens

Cantharellus cibarius

Gomphus clavatus

Family *Clavariaceae* [including *Clavulinaceae* and *Ramariaceae*].　FAIRY CLUBS

Clavaria fragilis Holmsk. [*C. vermicularis*]
Fruit-body unbranched but often densely clustered, 8-15×0.2-0.5cm, spindle-shaped, pure white, apex pointed or obtuse and apt to turn yellowish brown with age, hollow and very brittle. Spores 6×3.5μm, somewhat tear-shaped. Among grass. Occasional throughout Britain in pastures and lawns. E2.

Clavulinopsis fusiformis (Sow.) Corner has rather tall bright yellow spindle-shaped fruit-bodies in dense clusters. Common among grass on heaths and moors. E3.

Clavulinopsis corniculata (Sch.) Corner
Fruit-body repeatedly branched from the base, 3-7cm tall, branches slender (0.2cm), apices crescent-shaped with incurved tips, bright yellow throughout. Stipe virtually absent, flesh yellowish. Spores ± globose, hyaline, 6μm, smooth. In lawns, pastures and copses. Extremely abundant throughout Britain. E3.

Clavariadelphus pistillaris (L.) Donk
Fruit-body solitary, a simple club, 25×2-5cm, surface slightly longitudinally rugose, apex obtusely rounded, yellowish brown to vinaceous ochre. Stipe ill-defined, downy. Flesh white, slightly spongy, rather bitter or peppery. Spores 15×9μm, yellowish. In broadleaved woods, especially beech, but with birch and pine in the Highlands. Not uncommon. Edible and used as a condiment. E3. **C. truncatus** (Quél.) Donk has a truncate sterile apex, under conifers. Exceedingly rare. E2.

Clavulina cristata (Holmsk.) Schroet.
Fruit-body 3-10cm, much branched, tips expanded, somewhat toothed and crested, white throughout. Flesh white. Spores 10×9μm, white, smooth. Under broadleaved trees and conifers. Very common throughout Britain. Edible. E4. **C. cinerea** (Bull.) Schroet. is grey to ash-brown but tends to intergrade with *C. cristata*. Equally common. E4.

Ramaria botrytis (Pers.) Ricken
8-15cm, with thick trunk, whitish, branches very numerous, crowded, forking repeatedly, apical portions rather yellowish with pink to purplish tips. Flesh white; smell pleasant. Spores 15×5μm, ochraceous, longitudinally striate. In copses of broadleaved trees. Uncommon. Edible but care is needed to avoid confusion with *R. formosa* and *R. pallida*. E3. **R. aurea** (Sch.) Quél. is structurally similar but entirely golden yellow. E2. **R. flava** (Sch.) Quél. has more elongated paler yellow branches. Both edible but uncommon. E3.

Ramaria formosa (Fr.) Quél.
Similar in stature, branches often more elongated, a pretty orange salmon pink with yellow tips. Flesh pinkish white to rather vinaceous when cut, bitter. Spores variable, about 12×5μm ochraceous, surface rugose. Under broadleaved trees, especially beech. Uncommon. Purgative but not dangerous. E3.

R. pallida (Sch.) Ricken [*R. mairei*] is pale yellowish, the branches tinged lilac or pale purple towards the tips; easily confused with old specimens of *R. botrytis* and *R. flava*. Very indigestible or even toxic. Uncommon. E2.

Ramaria stricta (Pers.) Quél.
5-10cm tall, very much branched, branches stiff, vertical, yellowish ochre to cinnamon brown with pale creamy yellowish tips. Stipe thin, whitish, attached to white mycelium. Flesh white, browning, elastic, acrid or bitter. Spores 9×4.5μm, ochraceous brown, nearly smooth. On dead wood, stumps, logs and fallen branches of broadleaved trees and conifers. Common, just edible but not good. E4. **R. ochraceo-virens** (Jungh.) Donk [*Clavaria abietina* p.p.] has more entangled branches, ochraceous ochre, staining greenish, and occurs in litter under conifers. Common. E3.

Family *Sparassidaceae*. Branches flattened.

Sparassis crispa (Wulf.) Fr.
Fruit-body globose, cauliflower-like, 15-30cm, branches fleshy, brittle, flattened and ribbon-like, wavy or curled, creamy white, tinged brown at the edges with age. Flesh pale. Stem short, thick, whitish, often rooting. Spores 7×5μm, hyaline, smooth. On or near stumps of pine or at foot of pine trunks. Fairly common throughout Britain. Edible and good. E2.

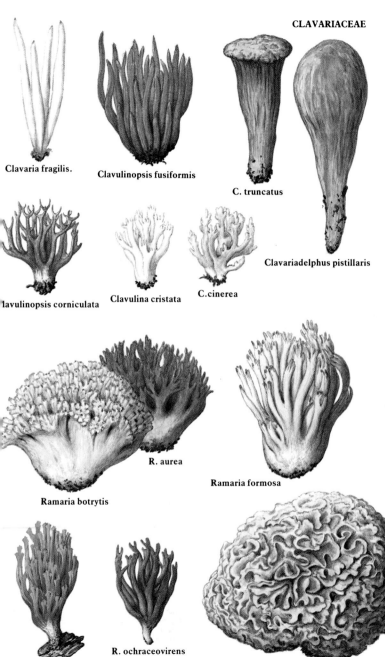

CLAVARIACEAE

Clavaria fragilis.

Clavulinopsis fusiformis

C. truncatus

Clavariadelphus pistillaris

lavulinopsis corniculata

Clavulina cristata

C.cinerea

R. aurea

Ramaria botrytis

Ramaria formosa

Ramaria stricta

R. ochraceovirens

Sparassis crispa × ⅓

309

Order *Stereales*. Only one Family (*Stereaceae*). Encrusting then reflexed species. Smooth hymenium, often with cystidia; spores smooth.

Chondrostereum purpureum (Pers.) Pouz. [*Stereum purpureum*]
Encrusting wood or with an upturned margin or forming tiers of small brackets on vertical surfaces, then with cap thin, leathery, undulating, whitish to greyish, woolly or hairy. Hymenial surface lilac to purplish when fresh but soon discolouring to chocolate with age. Spores ± cylindrical, 8×3μm, non-amyloid; cystidia vesicular, embedded. On dead branches, logs, stumps of any broadleaved tree. Very common. Causes the disease "Silver-leaf" of woody plants. E4.

Stereum hirsutum (Willd.) S.F. Gray
Encrusting wood, disk-like, often running together, upper edge reflexed to form sessile caps, often imbricate, velvety or hairy on upper surface, with fawn zones on yellowish to orange, margin sometimes brighter yellow. Hymenial surface bright ochre to orange-yellow, fading greyish with age. Flesh concolorous, leathery or elastic. Spores 7×3.5μm, amyloid; cystidia tubular or enlarged at the tip. On stumps, logs, fallen branches, occasionally on living wood near a wound. Abundant at all seasons. E4.

Haematostereum rugosum (Pers.) Pouz.
Encrusting bark, often running together, becoming detached at the margin but rarely narrowly reflexed, hard, surface uneven, buff to pinkish buff, bleeding red if scratched or bruised while fresh; greys with age. Flesh thick, whitish to yellowish, leathery,sometimes becoming stratified. Spores 11×4μm, amyloid; cystidia immersed, with brownish contents. On dead and living branches of broadleaved trees. Very common. E3.

Hymenochaete rubiginosa (Dicks.) Lév. (belongs to Family Hymenochaetaceae, p. 320). Encrusting, margin reflexed to form small, imbricate, leathery caps with velvety dark russet brown furrowed upper surface and bright orange fawn margin. Hymenial surface rusty to chestnut, speckled with fawn setae under a hand lens. Spores 5×3μm. elliptical; hymenial setae thick-walled, awl-shaped, brown. On dead stumps and branches. Fairly common in S. England. E3. **H. cruenta** (Pers.) Donk. [*H. mougeotii*] is entirely encrusting, adhering to bark, bright carmine red to purplish, finely cracked in a network, with brown setae visible under a hand lens. Widespread but not common, on hazel, less so on other broadleaved trees. E2.

Order *Thelephorales*. Encrusting, reflexed or stiped species. Spores spiny or knobbly. Family *Thelephoraceae*. Hymenium smooth.

Thelephora terrestris Ehrenb.
Fruit-body erect and fan-shaped or sometimes encrusting with only a small upturned margin, tough and fibrous; upper surface chocolate brown to blackish, scaly, with radiating fibrils, margin paler and fringed. Hymenial surface pale cocoa colour, wrinkled or slightly granulose. Flesh thin, brown. Spores 9×7μm, dark brown, warted, angular. On the ground and attached to fallen twigs in pine woods and heaths. Common. E3. **T. anthocephala** (Bull.) Pers. is more erect and branched, strap-like, clustered, leathery, rusty brown to grey-violet with whitish margin. Uncommon. E3.

Family *Bankeraceae*. Fungi with cap, stipe and a spiny hymenial surface.

Hydnellum caeruleum (Horn.) Karst. [*Calodon c.*]
Cap 5cm, leathery, top-shaped, upper surface rugose, tomentose, bluish, fading or spotted with reddish fawn. Under surface covered with slender decurrent spines, bluish, then white and finally purplish brown. Stipe 2×1.5cm, central, short, irregularly bulbous, 2cm across, ochraceous orange. Flesh leathery, blue-grey in the cap, zoned; orange-brown in the stipe; smell slightly mealy. Spores 6×4μm, pale brown, knobbly. In groups under conifers. Rare except in central Highlands. E2.

Sarcodon imbricatum (L.) Karst.
Cap 10-30cm, convex, fleshy, soon expanded or depressed, covered with coarse scales with raised tips, concentrically arranged, grey-brown on a pale russet ground. Spines decurrent, whitish then concolorous. Stipe 8×2cm, slightly excentric, almost equal or attenuated below, fibrillose, whitish to similar colour. Flesh not very leathery, whitish. Spores 7-8×μm, ± globose, brownish, pimply and spiny – as in Family *Telephoraceae*. Under conifers. Widespread in Highlands, a few stations in SE. England. E3.

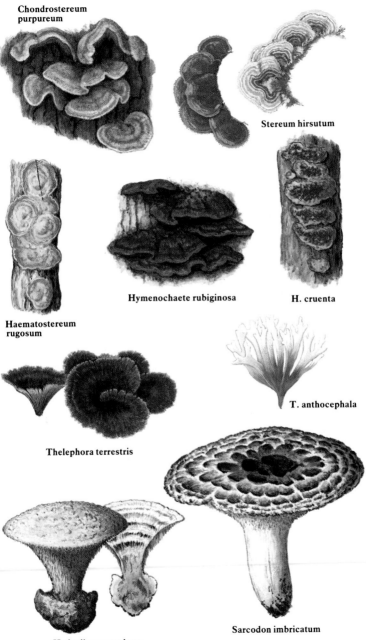

Chondrostereum
purpureum

Stereum hirsutum

Hymenochaete rubiginosa

H. cruenta

Haematostereum
rugosum

T. anthocephala

Thelephora terrestris

Hydnellum caeruleum

Sarcodon imbricatum

Bankera fuligineoalba (Schmidt) Pouz. [*Aarcodon f.*]
Cap 5cm, convex or depressed, whitish then pinkish or pale brown, smooth. Spines white or lilac. Stipe 6×1cm, similar colour. Fleshy slightly pinkish, not leathery. Spores 5×4μm, finely spined hyaline. Under conifers, mainly pine. Not uncommon in the central Highlands. E2.

B. violascens (A.-S.) Pouz. is more violaceous brown, with short greyish white spines, flesh grey-violet, smell weak. Not British. E2.

Phellodon niger (Fr.) Karst. [*Calodon nigrum*]
Cap 6cm, conical, bumpy, downy or coarsely scaly, dark bluish grey with blackish zones. Spines slender, greyish white then ashen. Stipe 2×0.8cm, club-shaped, tomentose, black. Flesh leathery black. Spores 4×3μm, ± globose, finely asperulate. Strong smell of tobacco when dry. Under conifers, often in troops with connate caps. Widespread in the Highlands, in scattered stations elsewhere. E3. **P. confluens** (Pers.) Pouz. is yellow-brown to dark brown and occurs mainly under beech and oak. Uncommon. E2.

Phellodon tomentosus (L.) Banker [*Calodon cyathiforme*]
Cap 3cm, flat, then depressed, russet brown with somewhat darker zones, paler at the margin. Spines short, white, eventually grey. Stipe 3×0.5cm, slender, grey-brown. Flesh leathery similar colour. Spores 3.5×3μm, ± globose, finely spiny. In troops, often running together, under broadleaved trees, on acid soil, and on heaths. Widespread in Britain but not common. E2.

Family *Hydnaceae*. Pileate, flesh soft and not zoned; spores white, smooth, non-amyloid.

Hydnum repandum L.   HEDGEHOG FUNGUS
Cap 8-15cm, convex then irregularly expanded, lobed, fleshy, margin flexuous, incurved; upper surface matt or rather rugulose, pale ochre to yellow or orange (rusty fawn in var. *rufescens*). Spines decurrent, crowded, brittle, ochraceous cream to russet. Stipe 6×2cm, whitish, pruinose, then similar colour, often misshapen. Flesh compact, or concolorous; smell faint, of orange flower water, taste becoming acrid. Spores 8×6.5μm, smooth. Under broadleaved trees and conifers. Common throughout Britain. Edible and good, with a good texture and nutty taste. E4.

Family *Hericiaceae*. Fruit-body often coral-like, hymenium on spines, spores amyloid.

Hericium clathroides (Pal.) Pers. [*Hydnum coralloides*, *H. ramosum* auct. p.p.]
Fruit-body 20-40cm, made up of numerous brittle coral-like branches, their upper surface pubescent and the lower covered with ± long pendant spines, cream or ivory white throughout, sometimes pink to reddish with age. Flesh white. Spores 6×5.5μm, ± globose, smooth. On stumps, logs and inside hollow trunks mainly beech, occasionally elm. In England, uncommon. Edible. E2.

H. erinaceum (Bull.) Pers. has an unbranched fleshy pileus with very long spines, 2-4cm. Widespread on beech and oak in southern England. E1.

Creolophus cirrhatus (Pers.) Karst.
Fruit-body 12-20cm, a collection of twisted imbricate caps arising from a thick common base, upper surface whitish, rough with conical outgrowths; lower surface covered with slender crowded creamy yellowish spines. Flesh thick, soft, whitish to somewhat orange. Taste and smell commonplace. Spores 4×3μm, smooth. Widespread in southern England, mainly on beech but also ash and elm. Edible but poor. E2.

Auriscalpium vulgare S.F. Gray
Cap 1-2cm, slightly convex, circular to kidney-shaped, greyish brown to vinaceous brown. Spines short, adnate, ± distant, similar colour becoming paler with the spores. Stipe vertical, slender, 5×0.2cm, smooth, concolorous, attached to the side of the cap. Flesh tough, similar colour, taste becoming acrid. Spores 5×3μm, finely warted. On fallen pine cones, often buried in the ground, less often on rotting branches. Throughout Britain, not uncommon. E3.

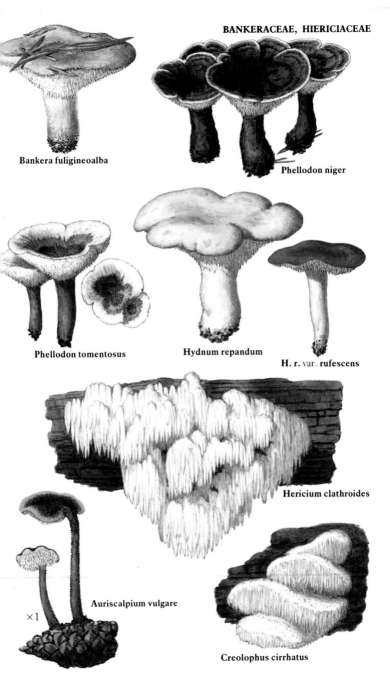

BANKERACEAE, HIERICIACEAE

Bankera fuligineoalba

Phellodon niger

Phellodon tomentosus

Hydnum repandum

H. r. var. **rufescens**

Hericium clathroides

Auriscalpium vulgare

×1

Creolophus cirrhatus

Order *Polyporales*. Hymenium with pores.

Family *Polyporaceae*. Flesh light coloured, somewhat soft; spores white; distinctive cystidia absent.

Genus *Polyporus*. Stipe well developed, central to lateral.

Polyporus brumalis (Pers.) Fr.
Cap 4-8cm, slightly convex with margin incurved and ± fringed; surface smooth, greyish bistre to yellowish brown. Pores round, white, slightly toothed. Stipe 4×0.3cm, pale. Flesh whitish, elastic. Spores 7×2μm, cylindrical. On wood of many broadleaved trees, especially in winter. Common throughout Britain. E3.

P. ciliatus (Fr.) Fr. [*P. lepideus* p.p.] has a zoned stipe, smaller pores, and is more of a springtime species. E2.

Polyporus varius (Pers.) Fr.
Cap 2-12cm, soon umbilicate, undulate, more leathery; surface shining, slightly radially veined or streaky, chamois to reddish cinnamon or ochraceous. Pores minute, white or cream, appearing fringed under a hand lens. Stipe excentric, 3×0.8cm, ochraceous with blackish bistre base. Flesh whitish, hard. A number of varieties have been recognised, e.g. var. *nummularius*, cap small, circular, pale ochre. Spores 9×3.5μm, cylindrical-fusiform. On dead wood of many broadleaved trees, especially willow. Long-lived. Very common throughout Britain. E3. **P. durus** Tim. [*P. badius, P. picipes*] is more fleshy and a beautiful warm fawnish chestnut. Uncommon. E2.

Polyporus squamosus (Huds.) Fr.
Cap 15-30cm, soon flattened or depressed, creamy ochraceous or pale golden with concentric bright rusty fawn then brown contrasting scales. Pores broad, angular, whitish to creamy-ochraceous. Stipe lateral or highly excentric, 6×3cm, blackish bistre at the base. Flesh rather soft; smell slightly of honey. Spores 13×5μm, cylindrical. On trunks, stumps and logs of many broadleaved trees, especially ash, beech, elm, horse chestnut, sycamore. Very common throughout Britain, often in early summer. Edible when quite young. E3. **P. tuberaster** (Pers.) Fr. [*P. lentus, P. forquignoni, P. floccipes*] is much smaller, 3-6cm, with circular cap, more central stipe and less contrasting ochraceous scales. Especially on gorse. Common. E2.

Dendropolyporus umbellatus (Pers.) Jülich [*Polypilus umbellatus*]
Caps numerous, 4-6cm, flat to umbilicate, russet ochre, smooth or slightly streaky. Pores white, angular, toothed, decurrent. Stipes white, branched, springing from a thick common base. Flesh white, smell strong, fungoid. Spores 10×3.5μm. On stumps, especially oak. Edible. Rare, in SE England. E2.

Grifola frondosa (Dicks.) S.F. Gray [*Polyporus intybaceus*]
Caps numerous, imbricate, horizontal, thin, rugulose to streaky, yellowish grey to chamois, in a cluster 20-30cm across. Pores decurrent, rather elongated towards the base, white. Stipes lateral or almost absent, connate below in a massive base. Flesh white, not very leathery, smelling of mice, hops and cold mashed potato. Spores 6×4μm, elliptical. On stumps of broadleaved trees and at the base of living trunks. Edible when young. Fairly common in southern England, less so northwards. E3.

Meripilus giganteus (Pers.) Karst. has much larger broader caps, up to 1 metre in diameter, with minute white pores which blacken on bruising. Very common, especially from dead roots of beech. E3.

Albatrellus pescaprae (Pers.) Pouz.
Cap 8-10cm, convex or fleshy, with dark chestnut brown scales. Pores angular, creamy yellowish, slightly decurrent. Stipe somewhat excentric, 7×1cm, white or yellowish, with reticulate summit. Flesh pale, yellowish at the surface; smell slight. Spores 10×6μm. On the ground under broadleaved trees. Not British. E2.

A. ovinus (Sch.) Kotl. & Pouz. is entirely creamy white and rather like a *Hydnum repandum* (p. 310) with pores instead of spines. Not British. E2 (m).

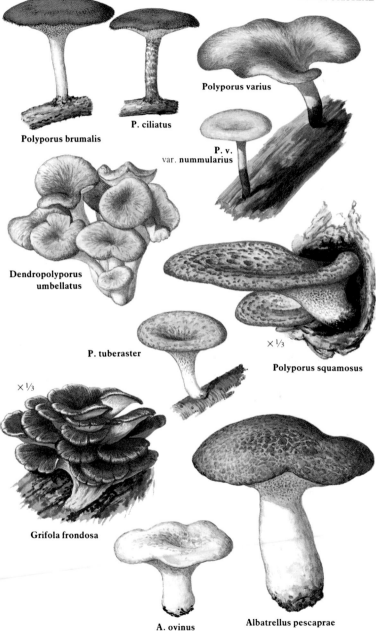

Polyporus brumalis

P. ciliatus

Polyporus varius

P. v. var. nummularius

Dendropolyporus umbellatus

P. tuberaster

× ⅓

Polyporus squamosus

× ⅓

Grifola frondosa

A. ovinus

Albatrellus pescaprae

Family *Bjerkanderaceae*. Stipe lacking, flesh soft or brittle.

Laetiporus sulphureus (Bull.) Murr.
30-50cm with numerous imbricate caps, each somewhat elongate, flattened, tongue-shaped, wavy, at first bright orange, sometimes tinged salmon, fading to cream-ochraceous. Pores minute, same colour. Flesh white, soft, cheesy, hardening and friable when dried. Smell of damp wood. Spores 6×4μm, yellowish. On trunks of living trees, causing heart rot, especially oak, sweet chestnut, willow and yew, also *Robinia* and occasionally fruit trees. Common in England and Wales, less so in Scotland. E3.

Skeletocutis nivea (Jungh.) Kell. [*Tyromyces semipileatus*, *T. chioneus*]
Cap thin, 2-4cm, somewhat imbricate or encrusting and narrowly reflexed; upper surface smooth or velvety, ochraceous fawn, more or less zoned bistre. Pores minute, even invisible without a hand lens, snow white. Flesh rather elastic, whitish. Spores narrow, curved, 3.5×0.5μm. On dead branches of broadleaved trees of all kinds. Very common throughout Britain. E2.

Postia caesia (Schr.) Karst. [*Tyromyces c.*, *Spongiporus c.*]
Cap dimidiate, 3-6cm, sometimes 1-2cm thick, upper surface rugulose or scurfy, greyish white, then tinged with blue. Pores small, whitish then tinged blue in places. Flesh soft, white, then bluish. Spores 4×1μm, cylindrical, curved. On rotting wood of all kinds. Very common throughout Britain. E3. **P. styptica** (Pers.) Jülich [*T. albidus*] is entirely white, without blue patches, and has an unpleasant harsh flavour; common on wood of conifers. E2.

Bjerkandera adusta (Willd.) Karst.
Cap 4-10cm, ± imbricate or encrusting with reflexed margin, thin, pubescent to rugulose above, ochraceous or greyish fawn with a few bistre zones, margin pale, blackening, obtuse. Pores rounded, light grey to somewhat ashen, bruising brownish. Flesh pale, greying; smell of damp wood. Spores 5×3μm, elliptical, slightly depressed. On branches and logs, occasionally living trunks, especially common on beech but also on other broadleaved trees and occasionally conifers. Causes an active white rot. Very common throughout Britain. E3.

Climacocystis borealis (Fr.) Kotl. & Pouz. [*Spongipellis b.*]
Cap 8-15cm, dimidiate, rather thick, 2-4cm, upper surface spongy and shaggy, whitish to creamy ochraceous. Pores rather large, angular, slightly toothed, white then ochraceous. Stipe absent or a short extension of the cap base, similar colour. Flesh white, spongy, zoned towards the base. Spores 6×4μm, ovoid. On stumps and trunks of conifers in Europe. Not British, E2.

Abortiporus biennis (Bull.) Sing. is ± stiped, irregularly dimidiate, pinkish, even vinaceous, with concolorous, elongated or unequal, irregular and labyrinthine pores; flesh hard when dry. Spores 6×4μm. Common in England, less so northwards; often seemingly terrestrial, arising from roots and woody debris in the soil. E3.

Hapalopilus rutilans (Pers.) Karst. [*Phaeolus nidulans*]
Cap 6-12cm, dimidiate, rather thick, sometimes expanded; upper surface velvety or pitted, a distinctive ochraceous fawn. Pores rather small, concolorous, round or polygonal. Flesh soft and compressible, similar colour. Reaction with ammonia a spectacular purplish violet. Spores 4×2μm, cylindrical, yellowish. On dead branches of broadleaved trees of all kinds. Common throughout Britain. E3. **Phaeolus schweinitzii** (Fr.) Pat. is larger, more massive and fleshy, brighter coloured, often saffron-fawn towards the margin, contrasting with the large, labyrinthine, olivaceous yellow pores. Spores 5-6×4μm. Common at the base of living conifer trunks, on which it is a dangerous parasite. E2.

Piptoporus betulinus (Bull.) Karst,
Cap 10-15cm, convex, fleshy, smooth, grey-brown to milky coffee colour, with thick obtuse sterile margin. Pores minute, tubes short, white, Stipe absent or merely a concolorous cushion, Flesh soft, white, hardening when dried. Spores 5×1μm, curved. On birch, parasitic. Very common throughout Britain. E4.

BJERKANDERACEAE

Skeletocutis nivea

Laetiporus sulphureus

Bjerkandera adusta

Postia caesia

P. styptica

Climacocystis borealis $\times \frac{1}{3}$

Abortiporus biennis

= NH₃ reaction
Hapalopilus rutilans

Piptoporus betulinus $\times \frac{1}{4}$

Family *Coriolaceae*. Flesh leathery, thin or whitish; spores white or pale.

Trametes versicolor (L.) Pil. [*Coriolus v.*]
Caps imbricate,3-6cm, thin, soon flattened, upper surface satiny, conspicuously zoned in various iridescent shades of grey, green, brown, violaceous and even black, Pores small, angular, whitish. Flesh white, leathery, elastic, Spores cylindrical, slightly curved, 6×2µm. On dead wood of every description, extremely common everywhere. E4. **T. pubescens** (Schum.) Pil. is softer-fleshed, cream-ochraceous, brittle when dry, occasional and chiefly in the North, on birch. E3.

Trametes gibbosa (Pers.) Fr.
Cap 10-20cm, dimidiate, flat, upper surface velvety at first, rather lumpy, white or with pale ochraceous but commonly green with epiphytic microscopic algae. Pores slot-like, radially elongated, white. Flesh white, compact, tough and drying very hard. Spores 5×2µm, cylindrical. On wood of broadleaved trees causing an active white rot; usually on beech stumps in Britain but also on many other trees. Common throughout the country. E4.

Pycnoporus cinnabarinus (Jacq.) Karst., also often referred to *Trametes*, is brick red to orange throughout, on wood of birch, rowan etc. Very rare; only a few records from Britain. E1.

Trichaptum abietinum (Dicks.) Ryv. [*Hirschioporus a.*]
Caps 1-3cm, encrusting-reflexed then imbricate, very thin, elastic; upper surface greyish, velvety, tinged with purple towards the margin. Pores small, round to labyrinthine, pale, violet when fresh, fading to light brown. Flesh thin, with a dark line above the short tubes, leathery. Spores 8×3µm, cylindrical; cystidia small, thickwalled with encrusted tips. Almost exclusively on coniferous wood. Very common throughout Britain. E3. **T. hollii** (Schmidt) Kreisel [*T. fuscoviolaceum*] differs in having a spiny to shredded hymenial layer. E2.

Daedaleopsis confragosa (Bolt.) Schroet. [*Trametes rubescens*] Cap 8-15cm, dimidiate, flat, ochraceous flesh colour to pale russet, concentrically zoned and furrowed and also often radially striate, downy becoming smooth. Pores somewhat radially elongate, sometime sinuous or labyrinthine, whitish, then pinkish ochre and bruising vinaceous. Flesh leathery or corky, tough, similar colours. In var. *tricolor*, darker reddish brown to purplish, the pores are replaced by gill-like plates. Spores 9×3µm cylindrical, curved. On dead or living wood of various broadleaved trees, especially alder, birch, and willow. Very common in England, less so in the north. E4.

Daedalea quercina (L.) Fr.
Cap 10-20cm, dimidiate, flat, thick, upper surface rugulose, slightly zoned, dull ochre to greyish. Pores elongated, broad and deep, ± labyrinthine. Flesh pale, corky. Spores 7×3µm, ± cylindrical; cystidia absent but skeletal hyphae may protrude from the hymenial surface. On stumps of broadleaved trees, mainly oak and sweet chestnut in Britain. Common. E3.

Lenzites betulina (L.) Fr.
Cap 5-10cm, rather thin, flat, sometimes imbricate, upper surface tomentose, concentrical furrowed, with alternating grey and light brown zones, Pores very elongated, separating ± anastomosing gill-like plates, whitish. Flesh pale, elastic or corky, Spores 5×2µm, cylindrical. On dead wood of various broadleaved trees, especially birch, Quite common. E2.

Gloeophyllum sepiarium (Wulf.) Karst. Like a *Lenzites* but dark brown flesh and a yellowish-brown, blackening, outer surface. On coniferous logs, more common northwards. E2.

Heterobasidion annosum (Fr.) Bref.
Cap 10-20cm, sometimes entirely encrusting more often reflexed with a thin flat cap, rigid surface rather wrinkled or lumpy, chocolate brown to dark bay with an obtuse, white, lobed or crinkled margin. Pores small, angular, white with a beautiful apricot tinge in age. Flesh pale, woody. Spores 5×4µm, broadly ovoid, minutely ornamented. Usually at the base of conifer trunks, a dangerous parasite in plantations, but also on broadleaved trees. Very common. E3.

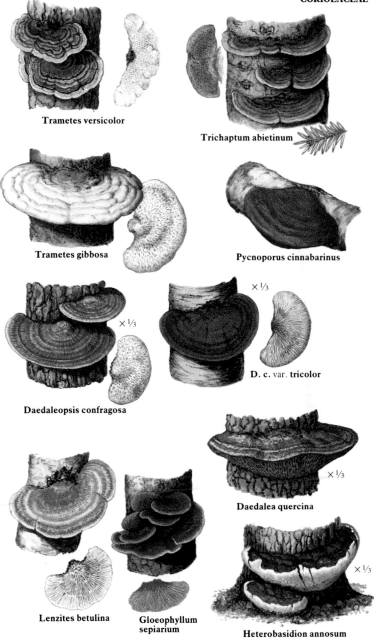

Trametes versicolor

Trichaptum abietinum

Trametes gibbosa

Pycnoporus cinnabarinus

× 1/3

× 1/3

D. c. var. tricolor

Daedaleopsis confragosa

× 1/3

Daedalea quercina

× 1/3

Lenzites betulina

Gloeophyllum sepiarium

Heterobasidion annosum

319

Family *Hymenochaetaceae*. Flesh reddish brown, spores coloured, hymenium often with distinctive cystidia or setae. Produces white rots. For the type genus *Hymenochaete* (hymenium not with pores) see p. 310.

Phellinus igniarius (L.) Quél. [*Ochroporus i.*]
Cap 15-25cm, dimidiate, 8-12cm thick, with concentric furrows, grey at first but blackening in the older part, margin velvety, thick, cushion-like, soon becoming smooth. Pores minute, fulvous to deep brown, greying. Flesh bright fawn, satiny, zoned, woody; tubes deep rusty brown, indistinctly stratified. Spores ± globose 6×5µm; hymenial setae thick-walled, reddish brown, up to 20×9µm. On trunks of broadleaved trees, mainly willow in Britain. Not common. E3.

Inonotus radiatus (Sow.) Karst.
Cap 5-10cm, dimidiate, imbricate, upper surface radially wrinkled, velvety, rusty brown, blackening, margin yellowish brown. Pores small, irregular, bright fawn beneath a greyish pruina. Flesh bright fawn-orange, finely fibrillose, concentrically zoned. Spores 6×4µm, yellowish, setae abundant, up to 35×15µm. Very common on alder, occasional on birch, hazel, willow etc. throughout Britain. E3.

Coltricia perennis (L.) Murr.
Cap 4-7cm, disk-shaped, soon flat or depressed, thin, rather velvety, with rusty zones on an ochraceous fawn ground. Pores rather angular, yellowish russet. Stipe velvety, rusty yellow. Spores ± elliptical, 8×5µm, golden brown; setae absent. On the ground usually under pines but also birch and on burnt soil. Very common. E2.

Fomitopsis pinicola (Sow.) Kickx [*Ungulina marginata*] (Family Fomitopsidaceae) is superficially similar to *Phellinus igniarius*, hard, hoof-shaped, but less black, without hymenial setae, with colourless spores 15-20×4.5-7µm. Only 3 collections from Britain in the last 50 years, on both birch and pine. E2.

Family *Ganodermataceae*. Woody bracket or stalked fungi with hard or resinous crust and distinctive spores with germ-pore and thick ornamented wall.

Ganoderma applanatum (Pers.) Pat.
Cap 15-50cm, flat, often imbricate, concentrically furrowed, crust smooth, whitish, soon ochraceous beige and often covered with a dusty layer of rust coloured spores; margin white, thin or ± acute. Pores minute, white. Flesh dark reddish brown, fibrous, hard, finely zoned, sometimes with white specks. Tubes concolorous, stratified, bitter. Spores 8×6µm, with truncate base, finely warty. On trunks of living broadleaved trees, especially beech and lime. Not common in Britain. E3.

Ganoderma lucidum (Leyss) Karst.
Cap 6-12cm, often kidney-shaped, crust strikingly varnished purplish red, somewhat uneven or depressed. Pores minute, whitish becoming ochraceous. Stipe commonly lateral and vertical, nodulose, glossy, concolorous or darker. Flesh fawn. Spores 11×7µm, warty, with truncate base. On wood of broadleaved trees, mainly in the south. Uncommon. E2.

Family *Fistulinaceae*. Tubes close packed but separate on under side of fruit-body.

Fistulina hepatica (Sch.) Fr.   BEEFSTEAK FUNGUS
Cap 15-40cm, dimidiate or tongue-shaped, fleshy, thick, 3-6cm towards the base, margin thin; upper surface papillate, gelatinous, garnet red-brown. Pores small, round, creamy pink. Flesh fibrous, juicy, red and veined. Tubes pale, reddish. Taste rather acid. Spores 5×3.5µm, ovoid. Stumps and old trunks of oak and sweet chestnut. Common. Edible. E2 .

Family *Schizophyllaceae*. "Gills" split lengthwise, curling apart when dry.

Schizophyllum commune (L.) Fr.
Cap fan-shaped or shell-shaped, 2-5cm, upper surface strigose or fleecy, greyish white to dull ochraceous beige, margin splitting or lobed. Hymenium covering radial false gills longitudinally split, pinkish beige to vinaceous reddish. Flesh pale, tough. Spores 4×1µm, cylindrical. On dead wood, mainly beech in south-east England, rare elsewhere in Britain. E2.

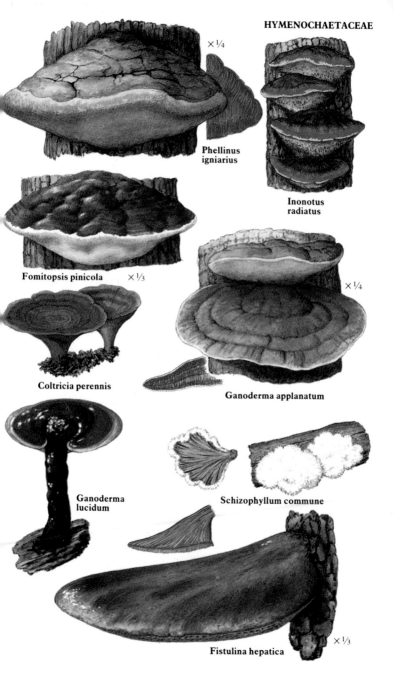

× ¼

Phellinus
igniarius

Inonotus
radiatus

Fomitopsis pinicola   × ⅓

Coltricia perennis

× ¼

Ganoderma applanatum

Ganoderma
lucidum

Schizophyllum commune

Fistulina hepatica   × ⅓

Order *Corticiales*. Hymenium smooth or viscid. Family *Corticiaceae*. Resupinate and encrusting, usually on bark or wood, rarely with reflexed margin or forming a narrow cap; hymenial surface smooth, veined or wrinkled. Spores whitish or pinkish. Numerous species in many genera, almost all defined by microscopic characters and impossible to recognise otherwise. Below are a few unusually distinctive representatives.

Terrana caerulea (Lam.) Kuntze [*Pulcherricium caeruleum*]
Disk-shaped, ± running together, extended, margin well defined and sometimes eventually reflexed, surface smooth to velvety, wholly bright sea blue, sometimes zoned. Spores 9×6µm, cystidia diverticulate. On dead wood of broad-leaved trees of all kinds. Widespread in Britain but not common. E1.

Lyomyces sambuci (Pers.) Karst. [*Rogersella sambuci*]
Effused, without defined margin, smooth or slightly granulate, snow-white. Spores 6x4.5mu; clamp connections present; also small, hyaline, capitate cystidioles. On dead wood of broadleaved trees of all kinds but especially old trunks of elder. Abundant everywhere. E3.

Vuilleminia comedens (Nees) R. Mre.
Recognised by developing beneath the bark of small dead branches which is then split and rolled back to expose the waxy, soapy hymenium, translucent when fresh, drying pinkish. Spores 20×7µm, cylindrical-curved; cystidioles branched. On any broad-leaved tree. Very common everywhere. E2-3.

Peniophora quercina (Pers.) Cooke
At first thin and spreading, then thickening towards the edges and becoming reflexed with age; surface smooth, then knobbly, pinkish brown then dark violaceous grey or chocolate with blackish margin. Spores 11×4µm, slightly curved; cystidia short, apex conical and encrusted. Dead branches of broadleaved trees, mainly beech and oak. Common. E4.

Phlebia radiata Fr.
Disk-shaped, spreading and running togther, rarely somewhat reflexed, margin fibrillose, surface radially veined or knobbed at the centre, bright orange to dingy red or violet. Spores 4.5×2µm, slightly curved; cystidia sunk in the trama. On bark of dead branches of all kinds. Very common everywhere. E3.

Merulius tremellosus Schrad.
Effused to somewhat reflexed or forming soft, narrow, imbricate caps; upper surface rather hairy, whitish, hymenial surface honeycombed or reticulate from shallow pores, pinkish ochre to reddish. Spores 4×1µm, sausage-shaped; cystidioles narrow, somewhat encrusted. On rotten wood. Common. E3.

Family *Coniophoraceae*. Indefinitely spreading fruit-bodies, thin and arid to fleshy; hymenial surface smooth, veined or knobbly; spores ochre-brown to russet.

Coniophora puteana (Schum.) Karst.
Widely spreading, thin-fleshed, knobbly, ± zoned with a broad whitish or yellow margin, centre floccose, creamy ochraceous to olivaceous fawn, then bistre, finally powdery. Spores 12×7µm; basidia elongate. On rotting wood. Common. E2.

Serpula lacrymans (Wulf.) Schroet.   DRY ROT
At first an abundance of cottony dingy white or greyish mycelium; fruit-body an indefinite reddish orange area with coarsely honeycombed or warted surface, weeping copious droplets of watery fluid, with smooth yellow border. Spores 9×5.5µm, elliptical, rust-coloured. On timber in cellars and damp cold houses, beneath ill-ventilated wooden floors, panelling etc. Very destructive and hard to eradicate. E2-3.

Plicaturopsis crispa (Pers.) Reid [*Plicatura faginea*]
This is of uncertain systematic position, narrowly spreading, soon reflexed to form a small fan-shaped cap; upper surface somewhat zoned fawn on a yellowish ground, velvety; hymenial surface whitish, with radiating narrow gill-like folds which tend to break up and anastomose. Spores 5×1µm, cylindrical. On dead branches of broadleaved trees, especially beech but also alder, birch and hazel. Rare, chiefly in the Highlands, occasionally in N. England. E2.

Terrana caerulea

Lyomyces sambuci

Vuilleminia comedens

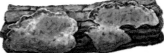

Peniophora quercina

Phlebia radiata

Merulius tremellosus

Coniophora puteana

Serpula lacrymans

×1

Plicaturopsis crispa

Class *Phragmobasidiomycetes*. Fungi of very diverse external form from indefinitely spreading to cap-like, but usually with gelatinous or waxy texture; basidia transversely or longitudinally septate.

Family *Auriculariaceae*. Basidia transversely septate.

Auricularia auricula-judae (L.) Schroet. [*Hirneola auricula-judea*] JEW'S EAR
5-12cm, at first irregularly cup-shaped, becoming ear-shaped; outer surface velvety, reddish bistre or vinaceous ochraceous to blackish purple, rendered whitish hoary when dry; inner surface concave, veined with distant branching ridges, smooth or slightly pruinose, similar colour. Flesh gelatinous, firm, translucent, similar colour. Spores 18×6μm, cylindrical. On dead branches, abundant everywhere on elder but also found on many other broadleved trees and larger shrubs. Edible. E2.

Auricularia mesenterica (Dicks.) Pers.
Effused, reflexed with imbricate caps, narrow and lobed; upper surface shaggy with whitish hairs, somewhat zoned, ochraceous towards the margin. Hymenial surface veined, vinaceous ochre to purple. Spores 15×5μm, cylindrical. On logs and stumps, especially of elm. Not edible. Common in England. E3-4.

Family *Tremellaceae*. Basidia longitudinally septate, ± globose with long sterigmata.

Tremella mesenterica Retz.
3-10cm, contorted, with brain-like or flattened folds and lobes, attached by a small base and wobbly, entirely lemon yellow then egg yellow, drying orange. Flesh completely gelatinous, watery, translucent. Spores 9×8μm, broadly ovoid. On dead branches, especially abundant on ash and gorse, throughout Britain. E4.

T. foliacea Pers. is more robust, more distinctly lobed, reddish brown throughout. On dead branches. Common throughout Britain. E2.

Exidia truncata Fr. [*E. glandulosa*]
± globe- or top-shaped, flat above, entirely blackish bistre, the upper fertile surface undulate, dotted with tiny black papillae; under surface slightly downy. Flesh rather firmer than in a *Tremella*. Spores variable, cylindrical-curved, 10-16×4-5μm. On dead branches, especially of oak, often in clusters. Very common in Britain. E3.

E. thuretiana (Lev.) Fr. [*E. albida*] is spreading, highly gelatinous, whitish opalescent. On dead twigs and branches of every broadleaved tree, and on ivy. Very common everywhere in Britain, less so in Europe. E2.

Tremiscus helvelloides (DC.) Donk [*Guepinia helvelloides*]
7-12cm tall, trumpet-shaped or spatulate, lobed or channelled, pruinose, pinkish russet to reddish brown with a vinaceous tint; inner fertile surface rugulose and slightly pinker. Flesh soft, translucent. Spores 10×5μm, ± cylindrical. On ground under conifers. Rare in England and Wales, apparently spreading N. E2(m).

Pseudohydnum gelatinosum (Scop.) Karst.
Has a fleshy horizontal fruit-body, pallid, with the lower, hymenial surface covered with soft whitish spines. Spores ± globose, 7×6μm. On rotting stumps and logs of conifers. Fairly common throughout Britain. E2.

Family *Dacrymycetaceae*. Gelatinous, with long narrow horn-like 2-spored basidia.

Calocera viscosa (Pers.) Fr.
Clavaria-like, 3-6×0.2-0.5cm, branched a few times, bright orange, waxy, slimy. Flesh concolorous. Spores 10×4μm, cylindrical. Rotten stumps of conifers, especially pine. Very common everywhere. E4.

C. cornea (Batsch) Fr. is shorter and unbranched, on wood of broadleaved trees. Common. E3.

Dacrymyces stillatus Nees [*D. deliquescens*]
Rather regular tubercles, 0.2-0.5cm, viscid to waxy, deliquescent, yellow-orange to somewhat russet. Spores 13x5mu, cylindrical, slightly curved, becoming 3-septate. In clusters on wood stripped of bark and decaying timber of all kinds. Common. E4.

Auricularia auricula-judae

Auricularia mesenterica

Tremella mesenterica

×⅓

T. foliacea

Exidia truncata

Tremiscus helvelloides

Pseudohydnum gelatinosum

Calocera viscosa

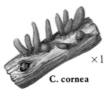

×1

C. cornea

×1

Dacrymyces stillatus

Class *Ascomycetes*. Spores developed within tubular cells called asci, usually 8 to an ascus, interspersed with parallel sterile hyphae, paraphyses.

Subclass *Pezizomycetidae* [*Discomycetes*]. Hymenium covering the upper surface of a cup-, disk- or club-shaped fruit-body.

Order *Pezizales*. Asci somewhat cylindrical, thin-walled, with rather flat apex opening by a lid, the operculum. Mostly rather fleshy fungi, often bright coloured.

Family *Morchellaceae*. Spores large, smooth, without guttules but with small rounded external granules at the poles. Genus *Morchella*. Fertile portion strongly ribbed and pitted on a large scale, conical to spherical, seated on a well developed cylindrical stalk. MORELS

Morchella rotunda (Pers.) Boud.
Fertile portion 10-20cm, ± globose, pitted like a honeycomb, fawn ochraceous, rather darker yellow brown in the bottom of the pits. Stipe 8×5cm, rather stocky or club-shaped, whitish, soon hollow, clearly separated from the cap by an apical furrow. Flesh pallid, smell fungoid. Spores 20×12μm, elliptical. In copses on medium heavy soil, rather late in spring, even to June. Edible and very good. E3.

Morchella esculenta (L.) Pers.
Cap 5-8×4-6cm, elliptical, obtuse, pits irregular with sinuous whitish walls contrasting with the ash grey-brown centres. Stipe 4×1.5cm, somewhat deformed, whitish, slightly furrowed, hollow, not clearly delimited from the cap by a depression. Flesh greyish smell faint. Spores as in *M. rotunda*. Sandy copses and rubbish heaps in early spring. Edible and good. E2.

M. vulgaris (Pers.) Boud. has more sinuous, often compound pits with concolorous edges. E2.

Morchella costata (Vent.) Pers.
Cap 6-10×3-4cm, conical to pear-shaped, with pits often broader than high, in vertical series between ± parallel nearly straight ribs, general colour fawnish brown, sometimes olivaceous, with browner edges to the ribs. Stipe 5×2cm, almost equal, white, hollow, furrowed, with ill-defined depression between it and the cap. Flesh whitish, smell of truffles. Spores 25×10μm. Among debris, on rubbish heaps, in gardens. Edible. E2.

M. conica Pers. is rather similar but with more elongated pits ranked between more undulating ribs. E2.

Mitrophora semilibera (DC.) Lév. [*Morchella hybrida*)
Cap 2-4cm, conico-campanulate, pitted, with rather regular vertical ribs, brownish on a sometimes olivaceous ochraceous ground. Stipe 12×1.5cm, cylindrical, upper part sheathed by the cap, creamy white, scurfy, hollow, brittle. Flesh thin, greyish; smell fungoid. Spores 25×15μm; paraphyses enlarged. In damp copses on heavy soil. Edible. Common in Spring. E3.

Verpa conica (Müll.) Swartz [*V. digitaliformis*)
Cap 1-2cm, a truncate cone or thimble-shaped, nearly smooth or veined, olive-brown to fawn, suspended from the summit of a cylindrical whitish stipe, 6×1cm, ± zoned with brownish granules. Flesh pallid, brittle. Spores 22×13μm. In grassy places in Spring. Edible. Uncommon. E3.

Ptychoverpa bohemica (Krombh.) Boud. has a more campanulate cap, with rather honeycombed folds and enormous spores 70×20μm. Not British. E1.

Disciotis venosa (Pers.) Boud.
Fruit-body 12-18cm, cup-shaped, somewhat lobed, brownish, hymenial surface usually irregularly veined or brain-like at the centre, fawnish ochre. Outer surface slightly scurfy, ochraceous cream. Stipe almost absent or slightly rooting in soil. Flesh thick, 0.5cm, pallid, very brittle, even falling apart in situ; smell distinctive, of hypochlorite solution, driven off during cooking. Spores 23×14μm; paraphyses brownish. Grassy places in Spring. Not uncommon. Edible. E3.

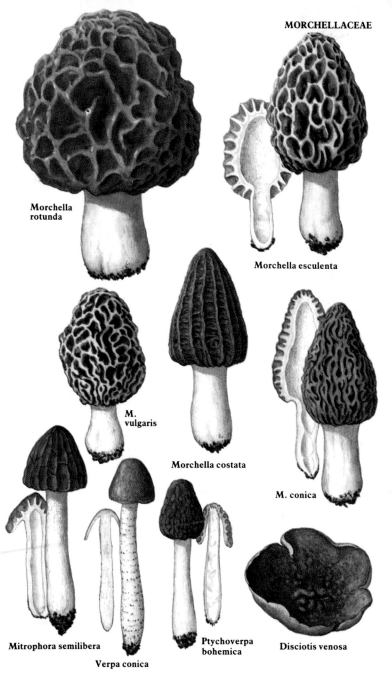

Morchella
rotunda

Morchella esculenta

M.
vulgaris

Morchella costata

M. conica

Mitrophora semilibera

Verpa conica

Ptychoverpa
bohemica

Disciotis venosa

327

Family *Helvellaceae*. Fruit-body with a ± developed stalk, cup-shaped, saddle-shaped or with a lobed cup; spores smooth, with large internal guttules. The species of *Helvella* and allies are **toxic** in the raw state, and although considered edible after thorough cooking are best avoided.

Helvella crispa (Scop.) Fr.
Cap 3-5cm, saddle-shaped with 2 or 3 lobes, pale creamy ochraceous or whitish above with only slightly more ochraceous under surface. Stipe 7×2cm, ± cylindrical or club-shaped, whitish, hollow, glabrous but longitudinally furrowed. Flesh thin, white. Spores 18×13μm. In damp woods of broadleaved trees, especially in autumn. Common throughout Britain. E4.

Helvella lacunosa Afz.
Rather similar in outline to *H. crispa* but with more undulating lobes to the cap, dark grey, sometimes tinged lilaceous, under surface only slightly paler. Stipe 6×1.5cm, cylindrical, hollow, deeply furrowed, greyish. Spores 20×14μm. In woods, often on burnt soil. Forms in which the cap has one lobe directed upwards were formerly distinguished as *H. sulcata* but it is not possible to draw a clear distinction between them and more typical *H. lacunosa*. Common. E3.

Leptopodia elastica (Bull.) Boud.
Cap saddle-shaped with 2-3 irregular lobes, yellowish ochraceous to pale grey-brown, under surface paler. Stipe 8×0.7cm, hollow, smooth, sometimes compressed but not furrowed, whitish. Flesh thin, concolorous. Spores 20×12μm. Under broadleaved trees on heavy soils. Fairly common. E3. **L. atra** (König) Boud. is blackish throughout, like a small *H. lacunosa* with smooth slender stipe. E2.

Macroscyphus macropus (Pers.) S.F. Gray
Cap shallow cup-shaped, 3-5cm, greyish, exterior downy. Stipe 4×0.5cm, narrowed upwards, solid, whitish to ochraceous grey, smooth to rather floccose. Flesh pale, smell faint. Spores 25×11μm, tapered at the ends and typically with 3 guttules. Under broadleaved trees and conifers. Common. Edible. E2.

Gyromitra infula (Sch.) Quél.
Cap 6-10cm, irregularly saddle-shaped with 3(5) flexuous lobes, dark reddish brown to rusty brown. Stipe 8×2cm, almost equal, slightly furrowed, whitish to russet brown. Flesh thin, brittle, pallid; smell fungoid. Spores 20×8μm. Under broadleaved trees and conifers in summer and autumn. Edible only after thorough cooking, best avoided. Rare in Britain. E3.

Gyromitra esculenta (Pers.) Fr.
Cap 5-10cm, ± globose or broader than tall, with rather close-set brain-like lobes, russet-bistre to dark rusty brown. Stipe short, 4×3cm, often misshapen, slightly furrowed, whitish with a tinge of pink or lilac. Flesh pale, brittle; smell strong, aromatic. Spores 20×10μm. Under pine, especially on sandy soil, or near sites of bonfires, in spring. Common only in the central Highlands. In spite of its name the fungus is highly **poisonous** when raw but the toxin, gyromitrin, is destroyed by heat. It is eaten, especially in the Nordic and hilly countries, after thorough boiling, especially if cooked twice with the water of the first cooking discarded. E2.

Rhizina undulata Fr. is a curious, spread-out, convex, ± lobed mass, with the same colour and under surface bearing many root-like rhizoids. Common in coniferous woods. E2.

Paxina acetabulum (L.) Kuntze [*P. vulgaris*]
Cup 4×6cm across, shallow, inner surface dark brown, exterior pale creamy ochraceous, rather velvety, with forking ribs continuing from the stipe towards the margin. Stipe short, longitudinally ribbed, pale creamy clay colour. Flesh pale greyish. Spores 20×13μm. Calcareous pastures, woodland glades and copses in spring. Rare in Britain, possibly more frequent northwards. E2. **P. leucomelas** (Pers.) Kuntze is much darker grey, with very short or rudimentary stalk from which the ribs do not spread on to the cup. Fairly common in gardens and conifer plantations. E2.

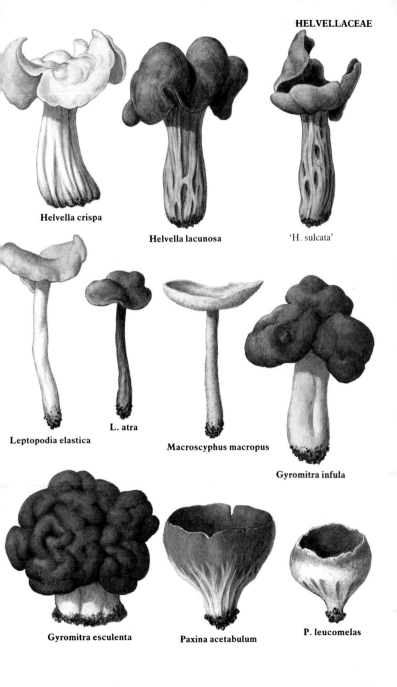

Helvella crispa

Helvella lacunosa

'H. sulcata'

Leptopodia elastica

L. atra

Macroscyphus macropus

Gyromitra infula

Gyromitra esculenta

Paxina acetabulum

P. leucomelas

329

Family *Pezizaceae*. Cup-shaped at first, sometimes expanded-reflexed with age.

Peziza vesiculosa Bull.
Cups 6-8cm, margin at first incurved, hymenium greyish ochraceous, outer surface pale fawn, distinctly scurfy or granular. Flesh relatively thick, brittle, whitish, without coloured juice. Spores $22 \times 13 \mu m$, smooth, without oil drops. On manure heaps, manured soil and rotting straw-bales. Rather uncommon but often confused with smaller species on soil in woods, gardens etc. **Toxic** when raw, sometimes eaten cooked. E3. **P. succosa** Berk., smaller, with slight olivaceous tint, coarsely ornamented spores with large guttules, bright yellow juice (press the broken surface against a white handkerchief. Common in woods, especially beech. E4.

Peziza badia Pers.
Cups 6-8cm, soon expanded and flattened, hymenium very dark olive brown, outer surface rather scurfy, reddish brown with a vinaceous tinge. Flesh pallid to nearly concolorous, watery. Spores $18 \times 12 \mu m$, ornamented with fine network of low ridges, mostly biguttulate. On damp soil, especially of heaths and moors and in the North. Very common. Said to be edible when thoroughly cooked. E3.

Sarcosphaera crassa (Santi) Pouz. [*S. coronata, S. eximia*]
At first a hollow sphere, 10-18cm, below the soil surface, then breaking through, cup-shaped, splitting from the margin star-wise, expanding to 10-15cm, hymenium purplish violet, outer surface whitish, rugulose. Flesh pale, brittle. Spores $14 \times 7 \mu m$, smooth, with 2 guttules. In beech woods on chalk and limestone, locally common in S. England, in spring. **Highly poisonous** when raw. E2.

Family *Pyronemataceae*. Cup-shaped or asymmetrical to ear-shaped, sessile or stalked, smooth or hairy; asci not blued by iodine, spores smooth or ornamented.

Otidea onotica (Pers.) Fuck.
Fruit-body 6-10×3-5cm, like a trumpet slit down one side or elongated like a rabbit's ear, ochraceous yellow with tinge of orange inside, more dingy yellow or tinged pinkish outside. Flesh pale, brittle. Spores $12 \times 5 \mu m$. Under broadleaved trees, fairly common. Edible. E4. **O. alutacea** (Pers.) Mass. Cup-shaped slit down one side and asymmetrical, ochraceous. E3.

Aleuria aurantia (Pers.) Fuck. ORANGE-PEEL FUNGUS
Cup 6-12cm, cup-shaped, often slit down one side like an *Otidea*, lobed, or expanded and flattened, bright orange-red colour, outer surface paler, pruinose. Flesh thin, brittle, similar colour. Spores $20 \times 10 \mu m$, ornamented with a coarse-meshed network of ridges, often projecting as an apiculus at each end; biguttulate. On soil. Very common. Edible. E4.

Sarcoscypha coccinea (Jacq.) Lamb. (Family Sarcoscyphaceae – tough and fibrous). Cup up to 4cm, hymenium bright red, exterior whitish, on a white stipe. Spores smooth, $30 \times 13 \mu m$, cylindro-elliptical. Occurs on woody debris, especially of hazel and elm. Winter to early spring. Apparently now rare, more likely to be found in the West. E2.

Tarzetta catinus (Holmsk.) Korf & Rogers
2-4cm, cup-shaped with an irregularly scalloped margin, hymenium pale creamy ochraceous, exterior covered with whitish downy hairs. Stalk short or sunk in the soil. Flesh thin, pale, brittle. Spores $22 \times 12 \mu m$. Under broadleaved trees on heavy soils. Fairly common. E3. **Geopyxis carbonaria** (A.-S.) Sacc. is similar but smaller, 1-2cm, pinkish ochre, on burnt ground or charred wood. Spores smooth, 13-16×6-8μm, without guttules. Common. E2.

Scutellinia scutellata (L.) Lamb.
About 1cm, disk-like, sessile, disc bright red, fringed with radiating blackish thick-walled hairs; outer surface brownish, velvety; flesh thin, reddish. Spores $18 \times 12 \mu m$, minutely warted; paraphyses with orange contents turned green by iodine. On damp logs, moist soil etc. Very common but there is a complex of allied species only separable on microscopic features. E3.

Humaria hemisphaerica (Wigg.) Fuck. Cup 2-3cm, sessile, hymenium pearly white, exterior clothed completely with short stiff reddish-brown hairs. Flesh pale, firm. Spores $22 \times 11 \mu m$, warted, biguttulate. Soil of damp woods and on woody debris. Common. E2.

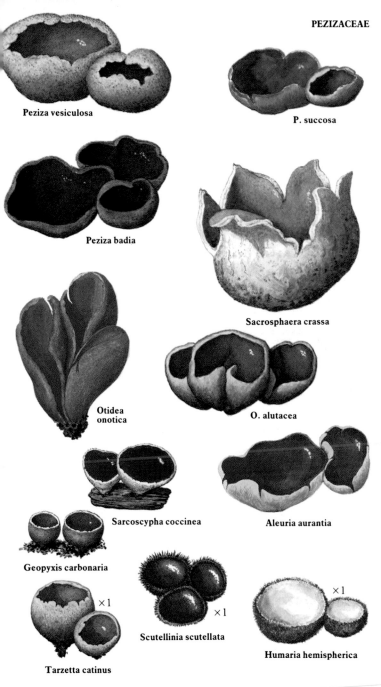

Peziza vesiculosa

P. succosa

Peziza badia

Sacrosphaera crassa

Otidea onotica

O. alutacea

Sarcoscypha coccinea

Aleuria aurantia

Geopyxis carbonaria

×1

×1

Scutellinia scutellata

×1

×1

Humaria hemispherica

Tarzetta catinus

Order *Helotiales*. Asci without an apical lid but opening by a pore in a usually rather tapered tip; spores commonly ± narrowed towards the base or very long and often septate. Family *Geoglossaceae*. Erect, simple, stalked, sometimes resembling a *Clavaria*.

← **Trichoglossum hirsutum** (Pers.) Boud.
Cylindrical, often compressed. Blackish and clothed with stiff black hairs. Flesh bistre. Spores 100-150×6-7μm, cylindrical-clavate, brown, 15-septate; paraphyses enlarged at the tip, dark brown, curved or coiled. Pastures and moors, sometimes in *Sphagnum*. Common. E3. The genus **Geoglossum** differs in lacking the black pointed hymenial hairs. Many very common species, but only distinguishable microscopically. **G. cookeianum** Nannf. is the commonest on sandy lawns.

Spathularia flavida Pers.
Racket-shaped, 2-4×1-2cm, upper part flattened with undulating margin, bright yellow ochre on a whitish stipe. Flesh pale. Spores 350-400μm, hyaline, thread-like, multiseptate. Under conifers. Uncommon. E3 (m).

Mitrula paludosa Fr.
Club-shaped, 2-4cm, fertile portion bright orange yellow, shining and viscid. Stipe cylindrical, white. Flesh watery, soft, yellowish. Spores 12×3μm, nonseptate. On fallen leaves of broadleaved trees in wet ditches, sometimes on moors in rotting leaves or *Sphagnum*. Common especially in the W and N, much less so in SE England. E2.

Family *Leotiaceae*. Club-shaped or cup-shaped to saucer-shaped, stalked or sessile, hairy or not; spores hyaline or brown, septate or not.

Leotia lubrica (Scop.) Pers.
4-6cm, fertile head convex, lobed, margin recurved, somewhat viscid, yellow ochre to olivaceous brown. Stipe cylindrical, light yellowish, often dotted with greenish specks. Flesh yellowish, elastic. Spores 22-25×5μm, hyaline, becoming 5-7 septate. In damp woods under broadleaved trees and bracken. Very common. E4.

Cudonia confusa Bres. is creamy-ochraceous throughout, not viscid, even downy on the stipe; under conifers. Rare. E3(m).

Family *Helotiaceae* and allies. Peziza-like fruit-bodies.

Bisporella citrina (Batsch) Korf & Carp.
Cups 1-3cm, ± sessile, slightly concave bright yellow to orange-yellow hymenium, margin obtuse, naked, exterior paler or cream, smooth. Spores 10×4μm, almost fusiform, hyaline, sometimes 1-septate. In clusters on dead wood of broadleaved trees, especially beech. Common everywhere. E4.

Chlorociboria aeruginascens (Nyl.) Kan. et al. [*Chlorosplenium a.*]
Cups 0.5-1cm, somewhat stalked, flexuous, sometimes deformed or compressed, bright blue-green at first, fading yellowish. Flesh very thin, concolorous. Spores 8-2mu, rod-shaped. On rotting broadleaved wood, stained blue-green by the fungus. Very common everywhere. The green-stained wood was formerly used in marquetry, associated with Tunbridge Wells. E3.

Rutstroemia firma (Pers.) Karst.
Cups about 1cm, yellowish brown, stipe short. Flesh firm, similar colour. Spores 15×5μm, becoming 3-5-septate and budding small round secondary spores in the ascus. On blackened wood of fallen twigs and branches, mainly oak. Common. E2.

R. echinophila (Bull.) v. Höhn. Similar and confined to old husks of Sweet Chestnut. E2.

Neobulgaria pura (Fr.) Petr.
Fruit-body 2-4cm, top-shaped, often closely crowded or deformed by mutual pressure, soft pale translucent pink with browner margin. Flesh gelatinous like a *Tremella*. Spores 8×4μm, with 2 small guttules. On dead logs, esp. beech. Very common. E2.

Ascocoryne sarcoides (Jacq.) Grov. & Wils. is smaller, deep violet, common on dead wood of all kinds. E3.

Bulgaria inquinans (Pers.) Fr. forms fruit-bodies similar in shape to *Neobulgaria* or more flat, black above, with scurfy bistre outer surface. On dead trunks of broadleaved trees. Could be confused with *Exidia glandulosa* but spores brown, variable, 11-14×6-7μm. E4.

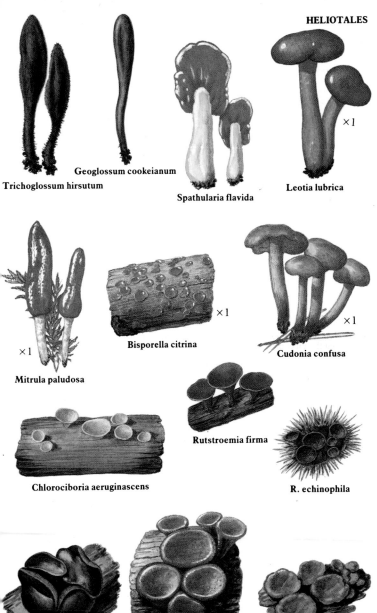

Trichoglossum hirsutum

Geoglossum cookeianum

Spathularia flavida

Leotia lubrica ×1

Mitrula paludosa ×1

Bisporella citrina ×1

Cudonia confusa ×1

Chlorociboria aeruginascens

Rutstroemia firma

R. echinophila

Bulgaria inquinans

Neobulgaria pura

Asocoryne sarcoides ×1

Order *Tuberales*. Subterranean ascomycetes.

Tuber melanosporum Vitt.   TRUFFLE
Fruit-body 6-12cm, ± globose, covered with quite regular obtuse warts, shining coal black. Flesh with numerous whitish veins in an ochraceous to brown ground tissue; smell strong, pleasant but oppressive if shut up for a long period. Spores 40×25m, covered with short spines, asci ± globose and 4- (sometimes 6-)spored. Under oak in southern France, Italy etc. Not British, (where it has been confused with *T. blotii*). Edible and valuable. sE2.

T. blotii Desl. [*T. aestivum*] (WHITE TRUFFLE) is lighter coloured, more brown. Spores with a very coarse-meshed reticulum. Common in soil of beech woods on chalk and limestone in England and formerly collected for market. There are 11 other British species, mostly with much smaller fruit-bodies and of no culinary interest. sE2.

Choiromyces meandraeformis Vitt.
Fruit-bodies irregularly globose or knobbly, 6-12cm, ochraceous with a pinkish tinge, like a potato. Flesh white, veined, drying yellowish; smell strong, fruity or spirituous. Spores globose, covered with stout obtuse spiny warts, 20μm; asci clavate, 8-spored. Semisubterranean in woods of broadleaved trees. Widespread in England but not common. Edible as a substitute for genuine truffle but of poor quality. E2.

Subclass *Pyrenomycetidae*. Asci produced within a closed receptacle (perithecium), which may be solitary or embedded in a fleshy fruit-body (stroma).

Xylaria hypoxylon (L.) Grev.
Stroma erect, simple or forked above, commonly either small, ± cylindrical and pointed on a more slender downy stalk, black throughout or more strap-shaped, forked and flattened above; powdery white tips covered with conidia. Flesh white. Spores 11-14×5-6μm, blackish, strongly curved on one side. On stumps and dead branches of all kinds. Very abundant. E4. **X. polymorpha** (Pers.) Grev. is much stouter, cylindrical to club-shaped, 1cm or more thick, rounded above, black all over with solid white flesh. Spores 25×7μm. Common on beech stumps in England. E4.

Hypoxylon fragiforme (Pers.) Kickx
Fruit-bodies almost spherical, 1cm, pink ochre then brick red or rusty, hard, rugulous, papillate from the apices of perithecia. Flesh brown, hard. Spores 13×6cm brown, slightly fusiform. On dead branches, chiefly beech. E4.

Nectria cinnabarina (Tode) Fr.   CORAL SPOT
Perithecia ± spherical, 0.5mm, in clusters 2-3mm across, deep cinnabar red, surface minutely warty under a hand lens. Perithecia are preceded by or mingled with coral pink cushions of the conidial state (*Tubercularia vulgaris* Tode); hence the English name. Spores cylindrical with rounded ends and a median septum, variable, 12-20×4-9μm. Ubiquitous on dead twigs of broadleaved trees of every kind, occasionally parasitic, but not actively so. E4.

← **Cordyceps ophioglossoides** (Ehrh.) Link
Perithecia immersed in the upper part of a yellowish then reddish-brown to blackish, club-shaped fruit-body, with slender yellow stalk, springing from yellow cords of mycelium wrapped round a fruit-body of *Elaphomyces* (p. 334). Spores thread-like, multiseptate, 150-200×2μm. Fairly common. E2. [For *C. militaris*, see p. 334].

Class *Myxomycetidae*. Organisms whose vegetative state is a mass of naked protoplasm (plasmodium) usually on dead wood, maturing as minute dry fruit-bodies enclosing powdery spores, like tiny puff-balls. Three representative species are shown here.

Lycogala epidendrum L. ± globose, 1cm, bright pink then whitish to light grey-brown, breaking open to expose the powdery pinkish spore mass. On dead wood. Ubiquitous. E3. **Enteridium lycoperdon** (Bull.) Far. [*Reticularia l.*] is much larger, white then silvery grey, often quite high on bark of living trees. Spores globose, 6×7μm, ± reticulate. Common everywhere. E2. **Arcyria nutans** (Bull.) Grev. Cylindrical 3×0.4cm, erect, stalked, bending over, pale buff; interior cottony yellow, Spores globose, 7μm, yellowish, almost smooth; capillitium a loose network of threads with finely spined walls. On dead wood. E2.

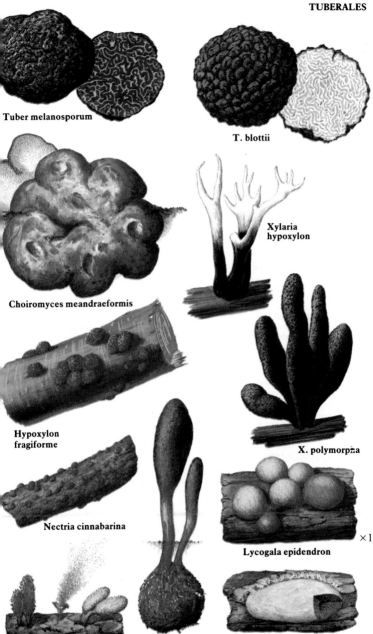

Tuber melanosporum

T. blottii

Choiromyces meandraeformis

Xylaria
hypoxylon

Hypoxylon
fragiforme

X. polymorpha

Nectria cinnabarina

Lycogala epidendron

×1

Arcyria nutans ×1

Cordyceps
ophioglossoides

Enteridium lycoperdon

335

Some further Ascomycetes

Microglossum viride (Pers.) Gill. is similar to *Geoglossum cookeianum* (p. 332), with a green colour. On debris and mosses. Spores elongated, 23×4.5μm. Common in Britain but E1.

Elaphomyces granulatus Fr. resembles *Choiromyces meandraeformis* (p. 334) but is smaller, 2-4cm, and reddish brown covered with small warts. Flesh purplish at maturity. Spores round, 25-30μm, blackish brown and warted. E3.

Daldinia concentrica (Boet.) de Not.
Fruit-body 2-5cm, hemisperical, not stiped, dark brown then blackish, surface rugulose, punctate and shiny. Flesh dark slaty with concentric silvery zones, and small perithecia beneath the external crust. Asci 150-200×10-12μm; spores 15×8μm, blackish. On branches of broadleaved trees, especially ash; often after fires. Common. E2.

Ustulina deusta (Fr.) Petr. has a similar texture to *Daldinia* but is only a thin flat crust (×2-5mm), ± greyish when young, then black and brittle. On rotten stumps. Spores fusiform, blackish, 25×6μm. Common. E3.

Cordyceps militaris (L.) Link resembles *Cordyceps ophioglossoides* (p. 334) but has bright red to orange narrowly club-shaped stromata up to 5cm tall. Spores long cylindrical, 90×4μm, dividing into *c.* 10, each 8×4μm. Common in pastures, springing from dead larvae or pupae of Lepidoptera buried in the ground. E1.

C. capitata is capitate, not club-shaped, and is parasitic on *Elaphomyces*. E2.

Claviceps purpurea (Fr.) Tul. produces the Ergot of grasses and cereals, especially rye; the fertile stromata are produced on fallen overwintered ergots in summer, as small pinkish drum-stick-like fruiting bodies. E2.

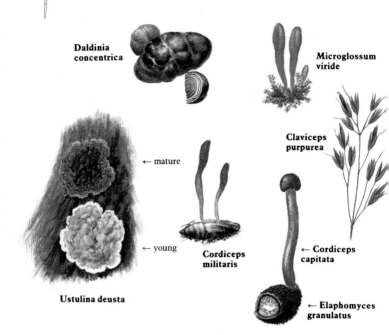

Daldinia
concentrica

Microglossum
viride

Claviceps
purpurea

← mature

← young

Cordiceps
militaris

← Cordiceps
capitata

← Elaphomyces
granulatus

Ustulina deusta

Key to *Lactarius* (pages 80-99) – principal groups

1a	Milk red or orange ≫	section *Dapetes*, 80
1b	Milk remaining white or merely yellowing: **2**	
1c	Milk white, turning pink or reddish brown, cap cuticle matt to downy or finely wrinkled (structure palisadic): **6**	
1d	Milk white, turning vinaceous or lilaceous violet on exposure to air ≫	
		section *Uvidi*, 86
1e	Milk scanty or watery: **7**	

2a	Cap scarcely viscid, colours pale or gay, often zoned: **3**	
2b	Very viscid species or with dark or dull colours: **4**	
2c	Cap surface dry to somewhat felted, tomentose or woolly ≫	section *Colorati*, 88
	(If a robust white fungus see *L. vellereus* group, 94)	
2d	Cap surface smooth, neither distinctly matt nor markedly viscid, colours some shade of reddish brown to pink or orange: **5**	
2e	Cap surface matt to rugose, velvety or finely cracked; very robust fungi with milk often abundant and cap colours whitish or zoned with pink ≫	
		section *Albati*, 94

3a	Cap glabrous and zoned ≫	section *Zonarii*, 82
3b	Cap margin bearded or woolly ≫	section *Tricholomoidei*, 82

4a	Milk remaining white or not staining gills when dried ≫	section *Pyrogali*, 84
4b	Milk turning grey or brownish on drying ≫	section *Vieti*, 86

5a	Colour of milk remaining the same, even on a handkerchief ≫	
		section *Subdulces*, 90
	(If the same but colours more orange see *L. aurantiacus*, 90)	
5b	Milk quickly turning yellow, at least on a handkerchief ≫	section *Tabidi*, 92

6a	Large fungi with orange or brownish colours; smell like cooked Jerusalem artichokes, milk staining the flesh brownish ≫	section *Volemi*, 94
6b	Medium to fairly large, colours whitish or milky coffee to almost blackish bistre; milk or flesh turning pink or carrot colour; smell weak or none ≫	
		section *Fuliginosi*, 96

7a	Small or thin-fleshed fungi with finely wrinkled or lumpy cap; (structure subcellular): **8**	
7b	More robust fungi and/or surface ± downy ≫	section *Colorati*, 88

8a	Milk watery, smell strong ≫	section *Olentes*, 88
8b	Milk scanty, smell faint, margin striate ≫	section *Obscurati*, 98

Key to *Mycena* and allies (pages 180-7)

1a	Brittle or slender fungi with cap 1-2cm: **2**	
1b	Rather fleshier fungi or with cap soon expanded 3-5(7)cm: **11**	

2a	Yielding white or coloured milk when broken ≫	section *Lactipedes*, 180
2b	Gill edge a different colour ≫	section *Calodontes*, 180
2c	No milk and gill edge concolorous with gill surface: **3**	

3a	Viscid ≫	section *Hygrocyboideae* and allies, 182
3b	Cap and stipe dry: **4**	

4a	White fungi: **5**	
4b	Coloured, at least on the cap: **6**	

5a	Gills normal, ascending or slightly decurrent ≫	*Hemimycena*, 186
5b	Gills extensively forked and anastomosing ≫	*Delicatula integrella*, 186

6a	Colour bright pinkish red or yellow ≫	section *Adonidae*, 182
6b	Colours dull yellowish brown to greyish or blackish: **7**	

7a	Smell alkaline or of poppy petals >>	section *Fragilipedes*, 184
7b	Smell rather faint of iodoform on drying >>	section *Filipedes*, 182
7c	Smell none or not as above: **8**	

8a	Among grass, cap blackish brown >>	*M. aetites*, 184
8b	On moss, cap brownish grey >>	*Mycenella bryophila*, 186
8c	On dead and fallen leaves, stipe very slender >>	*M. capillaris*, 186
8d	On soil, humus etc: **9**	
8e	On bark of living or dead trees (section *Supinae* etc): **10**	

9a	Stipe slender but tough, greasy, solitary under broadleaved trees >>	
		M. vitilis, 184
9b	Stipe short, spotted rusty like the cap; in troops under conifers >>	
		M. zephyra, 184

10a	Grey-brownish with adnate or sinuate gills >>	*M. hiemalis*, 186
10b	Similar in colour but decurrent gills >>	*M. speirea*, 186
10c	Pinkish-purple brown to steel blue, on living bark >>	*M. pseudocorticola*, 186
10d	White with yellow centre, smell rancid >>	*M. olida*, 186

| 11a | Strong smell of turnip or radish >> | *M. pura*, 180 |
| 11b | Smell none or different; fruit-bodies often in tufts >> | section *Mycena*, 184 |

Key to *Agaricus* (pages 274-9)

| 1a | Flesh reddening when cut: **2** | |
| 1b | Flesh yellowing: **10** | |

2a	Turning blood-red, ring simple >>	section *Sanguinolenti*, 276
2b	Only weakly reddening or somewhat orange (section *Agaricus*): **3**	
2c	Flesh reddening dull or slightly vinaceous, madeira: **7**	
2d	Flesh reddening mingled with yellow staining; massive fungi: **9**	

| 3a | Gills remaining bright pink for a while; ring shaggy, fragile; stipe slightly spindle-shaped >> | group of *A. campestris*, 274 |
| 3b | Gills pale pink then dingy bistre: **4** | |

| 4a | Ring cottony, complex >> | *A. bisporus*, 274 |
| 4b | Ring membranous, like a skirt: **5** | |

5a	Big fungus with much cracked cap surface; in saline pastures >>	
		A. bernardii, 274
5b	Less fleshy and ± scaly caps: **6**	

6a	Scales in a star-shape over the disk; stipe with white mycelial cords >>	
		A. romagnesii, 274
6b	Scales concentrically arranged; no such rhizomorphic strands; smell like *Lepiota cristata* >>	*A. variegans*, 276

| 7a | Ring double, membranous >> | *A. bitorquis*, 274 |
| 7b | Ring shaggy, accompanied by a somewhat garlanded sheathing ring or rings: **8** | |

8a	Cap scaly, brownish yellow; basal sheathing ring broken into bracelets >>	
		A. subperonatus, 274
8b	Cap and stipe somewhat felted-fleecy >>	*A. lanipes*, 276

| 9a | Cap smooth or scales whitish >> | *A. macrosporus*, 278 |
| 9b | Cap ± scaly, brown >> | *A. augustus*, 278 |

| 10a | Yellowing rapid and bright then fading, especially marked in stipe base and towards cap margin; smell of phenolic or iodine >> | section *Xanthodermatei*, 278 |
| 10b | Yellowing slower but persisting; smell of aniseed or cherry laurel, bitter almond etc: **11** | |

| 11a | Small fungi with thin flesh, ring simple >> | section *Minores*, 276 |
| 11b | Medium size to massive and fleshy, ring double with a cog-wheel on its underside >> | section *Arvenses*, 278 |

Index of Scientific Names

Entries in *italics* to synonyms.

340

351

Index of English Names

There are relatively few genuine English common names for fungi, and some are rather vaguely applied. Where none exists, it is better – certainly more precise – to use the scientific name rather than an invented English one.

Acknowledgments

Any book like this is a growth – saprophytic, symbiotic – on the great mycelium of Other People's Work, and more mycologists have helped the author in 50 years of fungus-hunting than it would be possible to name. But in the production of this guide we must especially acknowledge the kindness, most generous help and invaluable criticism of both text and pictures, of four leading British mycologists, Dr R.W.G. Dennis, Dr. Derek Reid, Dr Brian Spooner and Dr Roy Watling. They also provided all the information on British frequency and distribution.

We are also grateful to colleagues in several countries who commented on the original species-list, and particularly to Drs. Gro Gulden and K. Mohnjenssen in Oslo and several friends in France, for corrections to the colour plates.